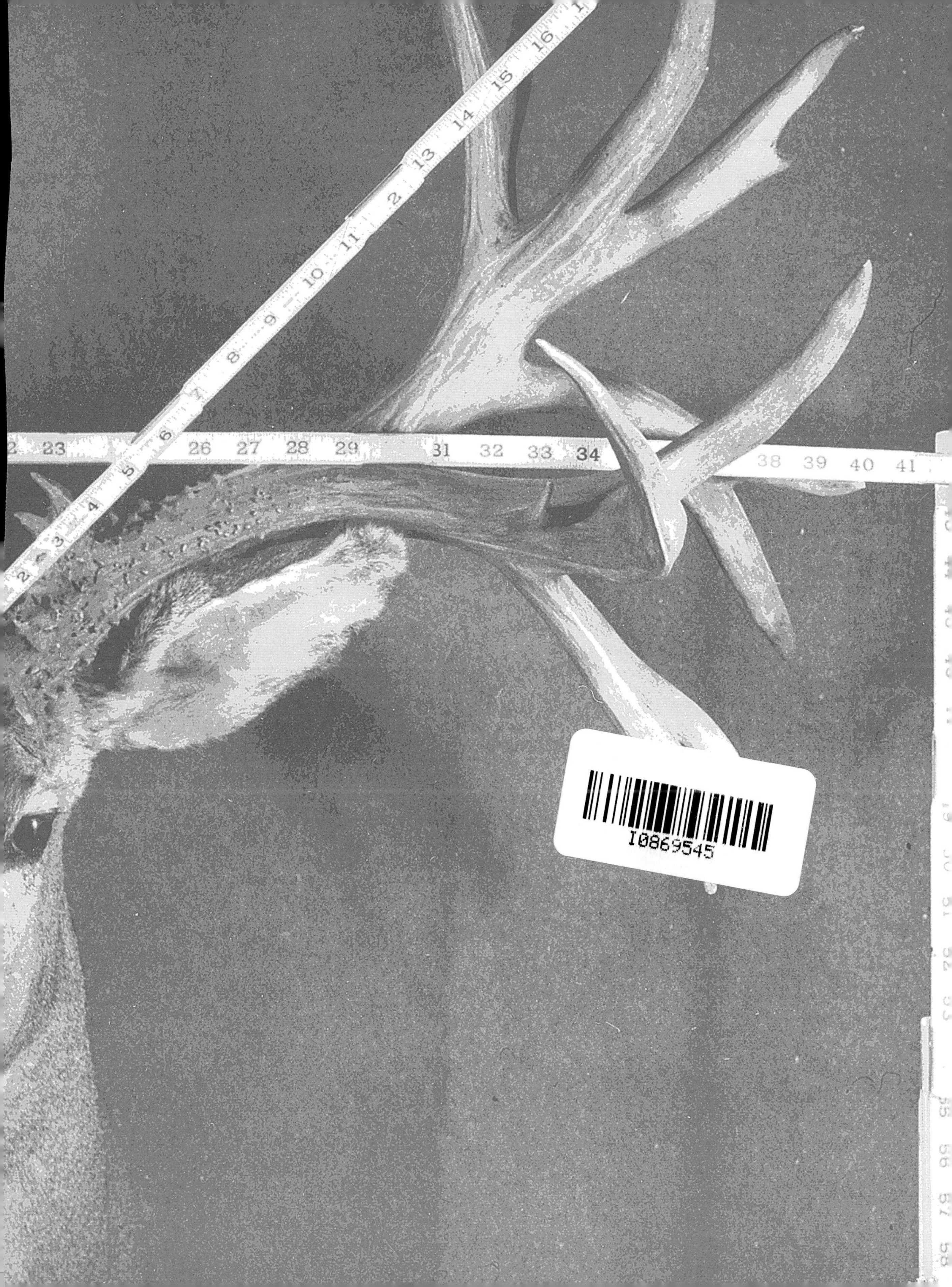

A MULE DEER RETROSPECTIVE:

Vintage Photos and Memorabilia from the Boone and Crockett Club Archives

Good Hunting!

Theodore Roosevelt

A NOTE ON THE BACK OF THIS PHOTOGRAPH FROM BOONE AND CROCKETT CLUB'S ARCHIVES STATES IT IS A MULE DEER TAKEN IN SEPTEMBER 1884 BY THEODORE ROOSEVELT. ENGRAVED IMAGE ON THE FOLLOWING PAGE CLOSELY RESEMBLES THE ANTLERS, MINUS THE DROP TINE.

A MULE DEER RETROSPECTIVE:

Vintage Photos and Memorabilia from the Boone and Crockett Club Archives

Edited by Julie Tripp

Foreword by Hanspeter Giger

Contributing Authors:
Guy Eastman
Ryan Hatfield
Jim Heffelfinger
Miles Moretti
Wayne van Zwoll

BOONE AND CROCKETT CLUB | MISSOULA, MONTANA
2013

A MULE DEER RETROSPECTIVE:

Vintage Photos and Memorabilia from the Boone and Crockett Club Archives

First Printing – September 2013
Second Printing – March 2014

Library of Congress Catalog Card Number: 2013913996
ISBN Number: 978-0-940864-95-5
Published September 2013

Published in the United States of America
by the Boone and Crockett Club
250 Station Drive, Missoula, MT 59801
406/542-1888
www.boone-crockett.org

Head of Black-Tail Buck
(Shot by TR on September 14, 1884)
DRAWN BY F.C. BEARS. ENGRAVED BY S.P. DAVIS.

To my mind there is a peculiar fascination in hunting the mule-deer. By the time the hunting season has arrived the buck is no longer the slinking beast of the thicket, but a bold and yet wary dweller in the uplands.

Theodore Roosevelt
Outdoor Pastimes of an American Hunter
1905

I have your 19

Record Heads of North

heard your next Edi

next year. Glad to

We are intere

a the best head we hav

of 162 4/8 according

we lost a difference of 6

hunt, the deer had

on the other side. That

that six inches.

I am sendin

newspaper of a fr

killed. He killed

November

in Arizona's Kaib

in your 1952

edition you have freak heads pictured; so if

you would like a picture of this animal

let me know. Hoping to hear from

you.

Arthur John Mozetti

16—San Francisco News —Wed., Dec. 5, 1956

THIS FREAK deer head was bagged in Arizona's Kaibab Forest by Charles V. Mozzetti, 61 Waterville-st, San Francisco. Note that instead of conventional four points on left side, the buck has a pair of forked horns, each with its own branch. He made hunt with O. M. Corbett and Ed Shapiro, both local sportsmen.

OLYMPIC RESULTS

WRESTLING, GRECO-ROMAN

FLYWEIGHT

THIRD ROUND: Dorivoje Vukov, Yugoslavia, defeated Maurice Mewis, Belgium. Ignazio Rabra, Italy, defeated Istvan Baranya, Hungary. Dumitru Pirvulescu, Romania, defeated Bengt Johansson, Sweden. Dursun Egribas, Turkey, threw John Wilson, United States. (6:00). Nikolai Soloviev, Russia, bye. (Vukov, Mewis, Baranya, Johansson, Wilson eliminated.)

BANTAMWEIGHT

THIRD ROUND: Francisc Horvat, Romania, defeated Reijo Nykanen, Finland. Konstantin Vyroupaev, Russia, threw Dinko Stoykov, Bulgaria. (11:30). Imre Hodos, Hungary, threw Adolfo Anselme Diaz, Argentina. (3:30). F... Kammerer, Germany, defeated ... Townley, United States. Edvin ... by, Sweden, defeated Yashar ... Turkey. (Nykanen, Stoyk... Towneley, Y... eliminat...

THIR... gary...

Morgan, Australia; Eva Szekely, Hungary; and Heda Frost, France.

WOMEN'S 100-METER BACKSTROKE FINAL

1. Judy Grinham, Britain, 1:12.9 (new Olympic record); 2. Carin Cone, United States, 1:12.9; 3. Margaret Edwards, Britain, 1:13.1; 4. Helga Schmidt, Germany, 1:13.4; 5. Maureen Murphy, United States, 1:14.1; 6. Julie Hoyle, Britain, 1:14.3; 7. Sara Barber, Canada, 1:14.3; 8. Gerganyia Beckitt ... 1:14.7. (Old record ... Edwards in 1956.)

WOMEN'S ...

1. ...

Rus... Leac...

By United Pr...

MELBOU... point ... mi...

FOREWORD

A timeless human dilemma: preparing one's life for *something*, but not having the slightest idea of what it might be. (Maybe it's just me…)

Among other things related and unrelated, I possess a lifelong love of the outdoors and the natural world. In addition, I have a perpetual fascination with deer, the magnificent animals that grow and shed deciduous bone annually. I've been mesmerized since childhood by deer and deer antlers. In them, I see great beauty, proof of life, and a call to wild places.

Even more narrowly, I hold a great interest in mule deer. They live in California, where I was born and raised, as well as throughout most of the West and Midwest, many parts of western and central Canada, and in the deserts of northern Mexico. Though most frequently noted as the "Deer of the West," the mule deer shares its range with two other, albeit smaller-bodied, but nevertheless great deer—the Columbia blacktail of the Pacific Northwest, and the Coues' whitetail of the Desert Southwest.

Although I have now spent nearly half my life in the Carolinas and white-tailed deer country, I am perpetually drawn back to the mule deer. I've had the pleasure of reading about, studying, hunting, photographing, and occasionally and unapologetically dining on these magnificent animals. I have also enjoyed countless hours viewing thousands of photographs of deer, deer antlers and taxidermy, and discussing mule deer habits, habitat, observations, and hunting with friends, outfitters, game wardens, field biologists, writers, artists, taxidermists, and other hunter-conservationists with similar, oddly magnified attachments to this deer. These folks, and many other people concerned with wildlife and wild places, share a deep desire to know and see to it that these deer and their habitats maintain a place in this world alongside us.

Along with thousands of trophy entry files from over a century of records-keeping, the Boone and Crockett Club archives also include numerous letters and newspaper clippings like this one from Arthur J. Mozzetti that shows a "freak" deer his brother shot in the Kaibab in 1956.

When the Boone and Crockett Club began its *Retrospective* books series, I knew it was just a matter of time before the mule deer would have one of its own. Earlier this year, I had the distinct privilege of spending a week at the Club's headquarters in Missoula, Montana. There, I was able to dive into the vast records files specific to mule deer and Columbia black-tailed deer. Official records book entry materials and score charts, fascinating photographs, inspiring and sometimes odd stories, and many peculiar notes and annotations—in several cases, tracing back to the late 1800s; far more material than even I could have imagined. Luckier still, I was able to sequester and immerse myself in these materials in one of the towers of the historic train station that houses the Boone and Crockett Club's library, fantastic museum, storyboards, archives, and incredibly dedicated and hard-working staff. It just doesn't get any better than that—the best 60-hour "work" week/vacation I could ever imagine! My heartfelt thanks to Director of Publications Julie Tripp and the folks at Boone

OFFICIAL SCORING SYSTEM FOR NORTH AMERICAN BIG GAME TROPHIES

Records of North American Big Game Committee

BOONE AND CROCKETT CLUB

Address Correspondence to:
Mrs. Grancel Fitz, Secretary
5 Tudor City Place, NYC 17, NY.

NON-TYPICAL MULE DEER

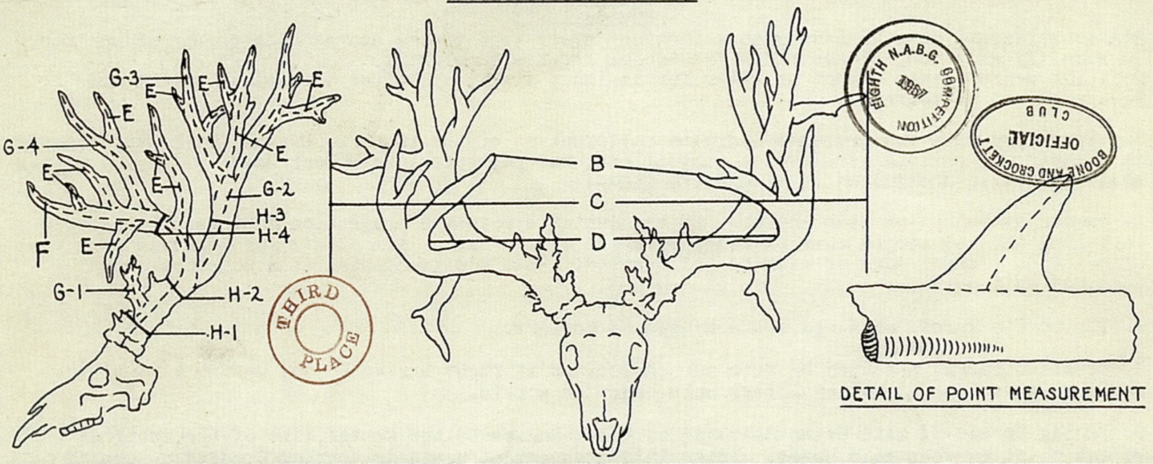

SEE OTHER SIDE FOR INSTRUCTIONS	Supplementary Data R.	Supplementary Data L.	Column 1 Spread Credit	Column 2 Right Antler	Column 3 Left Antler	Column 4 Difference
A. Number of Points on Each Antler	20	13				
B. Tip to Tip Spread	24 4/8					
C. Greatest Spread	42					
D. Inside Spread of MAIN BEAMS 26 4/8 — Spread credit may equal but not exceed length of longer antler			26 4/8			
IF Inside Spread of Main Beams exceeds longer antler length, enter difference						
E. Total of Lengths of all Abnormal Points	73 1/8					
F. Length of Main Beam				27 4/8	26 1/8	1 3/8
G-1. Length of First Point, if present				2 4/8	2 2/8	2/8
G-2. Length of Second Point				14 2/8	15 1/8	7/8
G-3. Length of Third Point, if present				9 2/8	10 1/8	7/8
G-4. Length of Fourth Point, if present				7 4/8	12 4/8	5.
H-1. Circumference at Smallest Place Between Burr and First Point				6 2/8	6 1/8	1/8
H-2. Circumference at Smallest Place Between First and Second Points				5 4/8	5 4/8	—
H-3. Circumference at Samllest Place Between Main Beam and Third Point				5 6/8	6 6/8	1.
H-4. Circumference at Smallest Place Between Second and Fourth Points				5 7/8	5	7/8
TOTALS (personal RH interview 8-13-04) BLAINE Co., ID	73.1		26.4 4/8	84.3	89.4	10 3/8

ADD	Column 1	26.4	Exact locality where killed NORTH FORK BIGWOOD RIV. IDAHO
	Column 2	84.3	Date killed 10/9/56 By whom killed ROBT. C. YOUNG
	Column 3	89.4	Present owner ROBERT C. YOUNG
	Total	200.3	Address
SUBTRACT	Column 4	10.3	Guide's Name and Address
	Result	190.0	Remarks: (Mention any abnormalities)
	Add Line E Total	73.1	
	FINAL SCORE	263 1/8	

355

and Crockett Club for the opportunity—and to my dear wife Kimberly and daughter Alexis for their incredible support in this adventure!

Whether through divine intervention or serendipity, I was able to do what I love—research and participate in the discussion of broad ideas for inclusion in this book. As with many such mysteries, this all came together at a time when a new purpose and focus was sorely needed in my humble existence. Being asked to write this foreword was truly icing on the cake.

As many readers already know, there are many challenges facing mule deer today. The mule deer is a current underdog in the great success story that is the North American Model of Wildlife Conservation. I have long had a tendency to root for the underdog in my professional and personal life. It is my sincerest hope—actually, my promise—that readers of all backgrounds and interests will find something inspiring in the following pages about the mule deer and what it represents in our nation's history.

This book is full of great photos and stories, giving us all an additional glimpse into elements of hunting history, and of exceptional mule deer bucks not only pursued and consumed as food, but also recognized, admired, cherished, and preserved. In no small part, it is also a book about the hunters (guys, you'll be envious of the ladies) and their families and friends who shared in the deer's previous abundance as the West was settled and developed. Their collective spirit during these times, often revealing struggle, success, and humility, are presented here as well.

As the pursuit of mankind's knowledge and greater wisdom continues, I personally hope that the mule deer remains with us and once again thrives as a symbol of the health and wealth of our North American wild places.

Hanspeter "HP" Giger, CFA®, CFP®
B&C Official Measurer (G083)
B&C Lifetime Associate (No. 11)

Robert C. Young shot this amazing non-typical on the north fork of Bigwood River in Idaho on October 9, 1956. The buck (score chart shown opposite) was shipped to the American Museum for the Club's eighth competition, where it received a third prize with a score of 263-1/8 points.

COURTESY RYAN HATFIELD | IDAHO'S GREATEST MULE DEER

TABLE OF CONTENTS

A MULE DEER RETROSPECTIVE

OFFICIAL.

LADY NIMROD—Alice O'Brien, 5515 Cottage, used just one bullet from a .32 Winche[illegible] to drop this big buck 20 miles south of Bly midway in the now-past season. The horn spread measured 39½ inches, with 13 points on one side, 11 on the other.

As someone who has spent a large amount of time researching mule deer hunting history for both work and hobby, author Ryan Hatfield's passion goes far beyond just big antlers and vintage photos. He has interviewed literally thousands of hunters from the early era of mule deer hunting. They had a real charm to them. He says that almost without exception, they were/are a genuinely happy lot, with great charisma and social skills. Mostly unassuming and always with a welcoming smile, they were truly a special bunch.

Ryan Hatfield

Adventure has drawn women to the wilderness since covered wagons crossed deer trails. Augusta Higgins Farnham—perhaps one of the most famous early day female hunters—arrived in Denver with her husband during the summer of 1860 atop a wagonload of whisky barrels behind six oxen. More than a century later, women remain a small subset of big game hunters worldwide, but they're an important part of that group; more so, in fact, than the numbers suggest. Both their participation and success in hunting mule deer have grown recently.

Wayne van Zwoll

The Kaibab Plateau is known to most serious mule deer hunters as home to the most famous deer herd of all time. This chapter covers the history of the plateau, including the true history of eruption of deer in the 1920s. It also reveals various techniques used over the decades to manage deer populations with translocations, a failed deer drive, fawn factories, and hunting. Recent surveys and direction of the current deer management program indicate—by comparison—we are experiencing the Good Ol' Days now.

Jim Heffelfinger

6-3762

Is This a Record-breaking Deer Spread

The yardstick is too short to measure the spread of this mule-deer rack from Arizona. It's 47⅞ inches, no less!

A MULE-DEER BUCK with a 47⅞-in. spread was killed not long ago in the Kaibab National Forest, Arizona. This figure exceeds by ⅜ in. the greatest spread of any muley head whose measurements appear in North American Game, the record book of big-game trophies; so the newcomer—with 11 points on one antler and 9 on the other—probably rates well toward the top of the list, which is graded according to length of outside curve.

However, the expert hunter that bagged this deer will never see his name in the records for he himself was shot dead within a mile of where he brought down his deer. That sudden end was justified, for this was no ordinary hunter, but a four-footed killer in the form of a 150-lb. mountain lion.

To go back a bit: Jack Butler, Jack Rice, and Ralph Steinhoff were hunting the north rim of the Grand Canyon with a pack of five dogs. The hounds picked up the big cat's trail and jumped him right after he had made his record kill, treeing him about a mile farther on. A shot from a .30/30 carbine finished the lion's career, and his tawny hide now hangs on the wall of Steinhoff's den, along with the mounted head of the giant buck.

The trio who caught up with the deer-slayer are well known to sportsmen throughout the West. Rice is a seasoned hunter. Butler, one of the greatest mountain-lion trackers living today, has more than 500 of the felines to his credit. And many marines and ex-marines will remember Capt. Ralph Steinhoff as range officer at Camp Mathews, Calif., and later at Parris Island, S. C., where he helped train thousands of "boots" in the use of the Garand M-1 rifle.

Mountain lions are the Western stockmen's No. 1 public enemy, for they have an insatiable appetite for calves and colts. However, they also prey on deer—concentrating in early spring on does that are heavy with fawn, then switching to the fawns themselves as soon as they are dropped by does that haven't been molested. From late spring until early fall the cats kill whatever they can catch, but after the deer's rutting season the lions' diet consists almost exclusively of old bucks.

In short, the predators follow the path of least resistance and feed on whatever is the easiest to catch at the time. Thus even whopping-big grandpas, like this near-record buck, are not safe from the fangs and claws of the stealthy stalkers.—*Stan de Treville.*

Buck Luck — and How!

(Continued from page 25)

standing behind a fallen pine tree 100 feet away, watching me closely as I balanced on the pile of down stuff.

I was puzzled. According to my figuring he should be nearing the end of the count by this time. But there he stood, coolly looking me over. I didn't waste much time speculating about it. I had no wish to trail him any farther in that place. Better give him another slug while I had the chance. I raised the gun slowly and carefully, knowing any sudden movement would send him crashing into the thicket behind him.

Only his head was in the clear. I held the sight on his eye and was about to squeeze off when another rifle blasted, off to my left. The deer dropped like a ton of bricks.

Who in thunder was trying to horn in on me? That was my first indignant reaction as I heard the shot and saw the animal collapse. On second thought, I realized that the other hunter—not knowing that the buck was already wounded—may have been quite innocent in shooting as he did. In that case, how his face would fall when he learned that "his" deer belonged to me!

Or did it? That was a poser, and it brought me up short. Maybe the stranger would have the last laugh after all. For I'd heard tales of more than one squabble over a game carcass, in which two claimants were involved, and to the best of my recollection the outcome was hardly ever twice the same. There was the chap, for instance, who had the right on his side, but lost out to a gang of plug-uglies who turned their weapons on him. . . . By the way, what *was* the right of it?

In one case, I remembered, the dispute was settled peaceably; the hunter who drew first blood got the head and hide, while the man who downed and killed the buck got the meat. (Hey! Did that mean no meat at all for me?) On the other hand, surely I'd heard that no matter who shoots first, or where the

INTRODUCTION

It's been seven years since my colleague Ryan Hatfield, who at the time was our assistant director of Big Game Records, worked with me to develop a new series of books that were a retrospective look at the vast collection of records-keeping files we house here at B&C Headquarters. The first book off the presses, released in the fall of 2006, featured the ever-popular whitetail deer. That book was followed by another, this time focusing the American elk.

When it came time to think about the third installment of our *Retrospective* series, the mule deer was top on the list. There were plenty of materials in the archives, not to mention the fact that mule deer are a true icon of the West. The choice was made even easier when Hanspeter (HP) Giger, a long-time supporter of B&C—Lifetime Associate No. 11, as well as one of our Official Measurers—called me to discuss lending a hand with the research. He told me he'd be willing to fly out west and spend countless hours of volunteer time on the project—an offer I couldn't refuse. When you have a book idea that gets people so excited they'll spend their own time and money to help, you know it's got potential. HP arrived in April 2013 and immediately got down to work. He spent hours and hours going through the archives and pulling the necessary files that made the book a reality. His help was invaluable and greatly appreciated.

Once HP's work was completed, it was my turn to take over and pull everything together. I quickly made two observations when reviewing all of the files—one, there were lots of photos with yardsticks nestled in the antlers, and secondly, there were far more non-typical mule deer than the classic typical-framed bucks. As a matter of fact, between 1931 and 1960 most states recorded at least double the non-typical entries than typical in our records program. During that time frame, out of the top-10 mule deer states, only Colorado and New Mexico had more typical entries. The chart below shows the breakdown of typical versus non-typical entries

The greatest-spread measurement does not calculate into the final score for mule deer—or for any big-game animals recognized by the Club for that matter—but that doesn't mean it's not an important feature, especially for mule deer.

TOP STATES FROM 1931 THROUGH 1960

LOCATION	TYPICAL ENTRIES	NON-TYP ENTRIES	TOTAL ENTRIES
1. Colorado	70	42	112
2. Utah	29	43	72
3. Idaho	17	47	64
4. Oregon	10	30	40
4. Arizona	11	29	40
6. Montana	10	19	29
7. Wyoming	9	16	25
8. Washington	4	13	17
9. Nevada	4	9	13
10. New Mexico	6	5	11

in the Club's records program. I know a few of you will disagree, but a set of non-typical mule deer antlers seem far more fascinating than their classically structured 5x5 brethren. Maybe it's this uniqueness that pushed these old-time hunters to enter their "freak" heads and not the typical forked racks. I'm sure other factors play into these numbers, but whatever the case, I hope you enjoy seeing these truly awesome bucks.

Aside from the large number of non-typical mule deer shown throughout this book, readers will also notice several images with yardsticks prominently displayed within antlers. Almost all historic references—modern-day too—mention the spread of a mule deer rack. With today's scoring system, Official Measurers take three separate spread measurements—tip-to-tip spread, greatest spread, and inside spread. Of those, only the inside spread is calculated into the final B&C score. Even though greatest spread measurement is not included, it's still something worth noting. See the newspaper article on the previous page from 1947.

A quick search in the Club's database shows that the greatest spread on record for a typical mule deer is 43-4/8 inches and for a non-typical, it's 49-2/8 inches. Those crazy abnormal points definitely factor into this measurement. When we switch gears to the inside spread—the one that actually contributes to the score—the largest on record for typical and non-typical mule deer are 36-1/8 inches and 36-5/8 inches, respectively. Pretty close if you ask me. I'm guessing this is one of the reasons our scoring system's founders chose the inside spread measurement as opposed to the greatest spread. At the end of the day, the spread measurement on a mule deer is just one small part of many that make up the final score, but it's pretty cool to see all those vintage photos with the yardsticks.

There's more to *A Mule Deer Retrospective* than yardsticks and non-typicals. We've pulled together a serious team of mule deer aficionados to contribute as well. Spend some time with Guy Eastman of *Eastman's Hunting* and Ryan Hatfield, now with *Western Hunter Magazine*. Both of these gentlemen sport a keen sense for the history of mule deer hunting in the West, and they sweeten the pot with vintage family photos—longstanding records of hunting in the West.

We also called upon Miles Moretti, CEO and president of the Mule Deer Foundation, one of the many wildlife organizations the Club is proud to partner with on many levels. Miles has provided an overview of the historical status of mule deer, dating back to 1804 when Lewis and Clark observed the curious deer on their travels. He also includes a current map detailing the numerous and varying mule deer habitats in North America. Wildlife biologists from each of the western states and two Canadian provinces participated in collecting the data. Funding for this project was provided by the National Fish and Wildlife Foundation.

A special chapter dedicated to women and western deer includes an introduction by outdoor writer Wayne van Zwoll. One of my favorite "characters" I've come across over the last twenty years at B&C is Gusty Wallihan. She was the quintessential outdoors woman and is rightfully shown on the opening pages of this chapter. Wayne's introduction is followed by dozens of pages showing collages of photos, score charts, and newspaper articles of women who've shot some impressive mule deer from 1911 to 1971.

Lastly, Jim Heffelfinger—noted wildlife biologist and current director of the Mule Deer Working Group (part of the Western Association of Fish & Wildlife Agencies)—provided an in depth history of mule deer populations on the Kaibab Plateau including observations about their mismanagement, a crazy deer drive, fawn capture, and how the herd is being properly managed today. We've supplemented his chapter with a nearly complete collection of mule deer trophy entries from the 1930s through the 1950s.

A Mule Deer Retrospective provides a glimpse into hunting in the West during the early 20th century. I hope you enjoy looking through the hundreds of photographic collages featuring score charts, mule deer hunters in the field with their game, and other memorabilia, as much as I enjoyed sorting through our vast collection and putting it all together. The mule deer is truly an icon of the West.

Julie Tripp
Director of Publications
Professional Member
Boone and Crockett Club

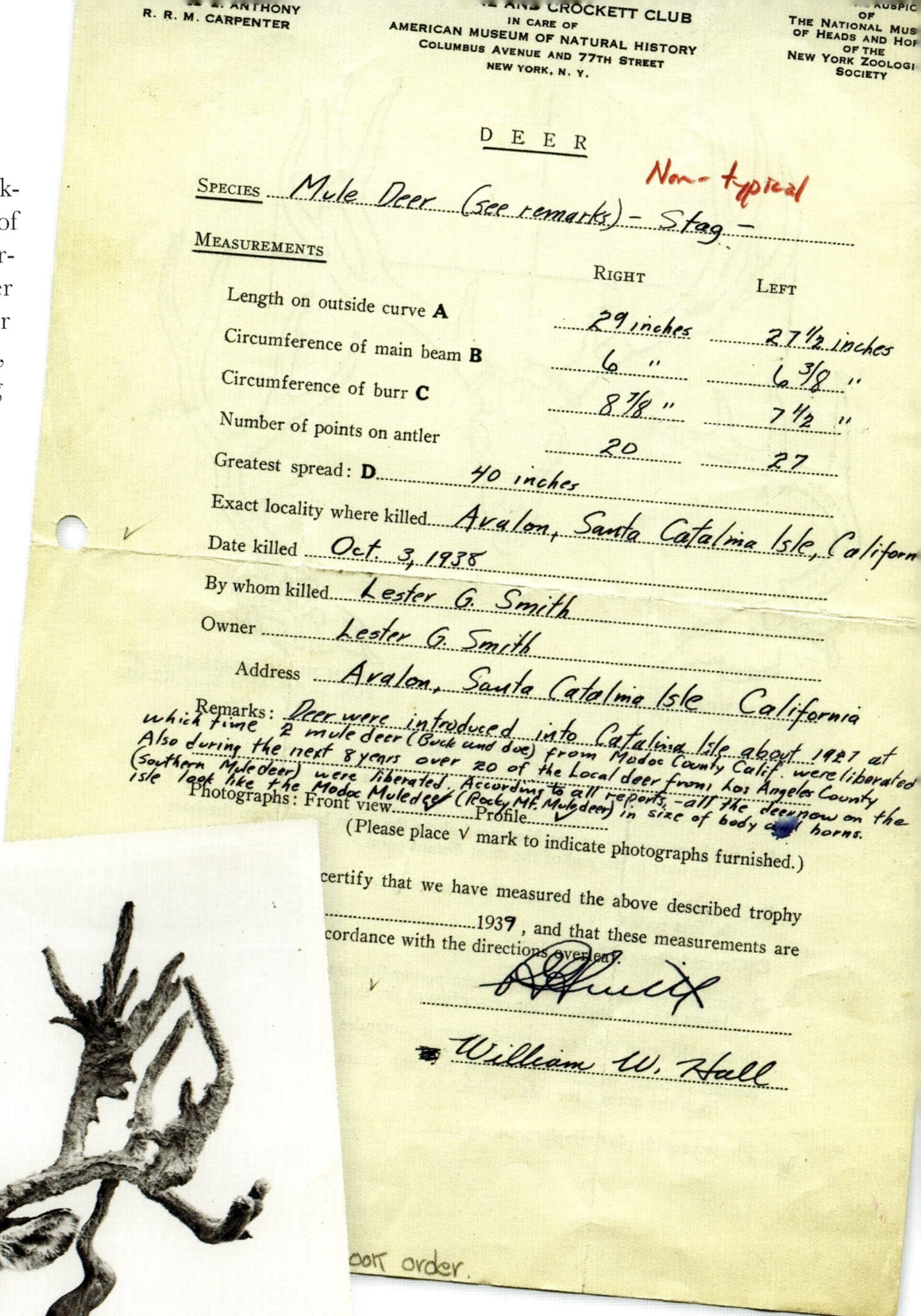

E. ANTHONY
R. R. M. CARPENTER

AND CROCKETT CLUB
IN CARE OF
AMERICAN MUSEUM OF NATURAL HISTORY
COLUMBUS AVENUE AND 77TH STREET
NEW YORK, N. Y.

AUSPIC
OF
THE NATIONAL MUS
OF HEADS AND HO
OF THE
NEW YORK ZOOLOGI
SOCIETY

DEER

Species: Mule Deer (see remarks) – Stag – Non-typical

Measurements

	Right	Left
Length on outside curve A	29 inches	27½ inches
Circumference of main beam B	6 "	6 3/8 "
Circumference of burr C	8 7/8 "	7½ "
Number of points on antler	20	27

Greatest spread: D 40 inches

Exact locality where killed: Avalon, Santa Catalina Isle, Californ

Date killed: Oct. 3, 1938

By whom killed: Lester G. Smith

Owner: Lester G. Smith

Address: Avalon, Santa Catalina Isle California

Remarks: Deer were introduced into Catalina Isle about 1927 at which time 2 mule deer (Buck and doe) from Modoc County Calif. were liberated. Also during the next 8 years over 20 of the Local deer from Los Angeles County (Southern Muledeer) were liberated. According to all reports, – all the deer now on the isle look like the Modoc Muledeer (Rocky Mt. Muledeer) in size of body and horns.

Photographs: Front view ✓ Profile ✓

(Please place ✓ mark to indicate photographs furnished.)

certify that we have measured the above described trophy ... 1939, and that these measurements are ... cordance with the directions overleaf.

William W. Hall

oor order.

The photograph and chart for this incredible mule deer were sent to the Club along with an order for one of our records books in 1939—obviously a stag buck and therefore not eligible for entry in the Club's records program, but interesting nonetheless. Remarks on the chart indicate it was part of a translocation from Modoc County, California, to Catalina Island in the 1920s.

OFFICIAL.

A MULE DEER RETROSPECTIVE:

Vintage Photos and Memorabilia from the Boone and Crockett Club Archives

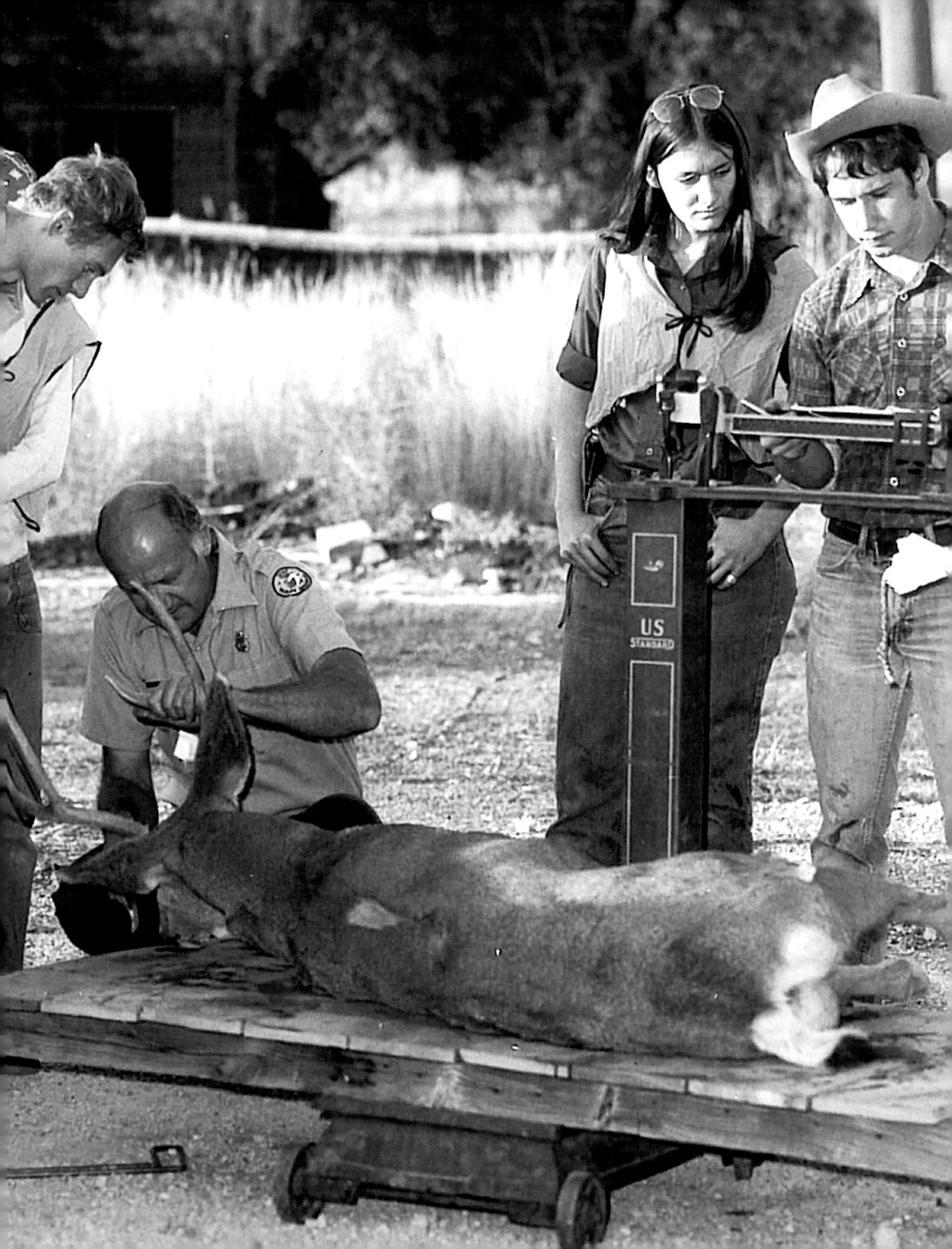
US
STANDARD

STATUS OF MULE DEER IN N.A.

MILES MORETTI | MULE DEER FOUNDATION

I was fortunate to grow up in the golden age of mule deer—born and raised in southwest Wyoming when mule deer numbers were at their peak in the West. When I was young, mule deer in southwest Wyoming were more numerous than pronghorn. My earliest memories of hunting were with my family, hunting for mule deer. I would get so excited, I could not sleep the night before we headed out to hunt. It seemed like an eternity before the alarm would go off and we would all gather around the breakfast table—everyone talking at once about the day's hunt. I thought I would never be able to carry a gun and was forever destined to dog the brush on a drive of an aspen grove or patch of juniper or serviceberry.

In the late 50s and 60s, we chained up our two-wheel drive trucks, loaded our .30-30s or .30-06s with a single 4x scope in the truck, and off we went. It sure was different then—no other hunters, no four-wheelers, no high-powered spotting scopes or long-range rifles, trail cams, GPS units, handheld radios. Yes, it truly was the good ol' days!

To take a retrospective look at where mule deer populations are today, first we must look back to where we came from.

Why have mule deer declined, while other big game species have increased throughout North America? Let's look back.

Early explorers gave conflicting reports of the abundance of mule deer. Lewis and Clark made note of mule deer in their journals. Lewis was also the first to describe the black-tailed deer.

The author as a college student (cowboy hat) working a deer-checking station.

In Johnsgard's book titled, *The Journals of the Lewis & Clark Expedition*, he quotes,

"The mule deer was first recognized and accurately described by Lewis and Clark but not formally described until 1817. It was first mentioned on September 5, in the vicinity of the Niobrara River, when the descriptive term 'black-tailed deer' was applied to several deer seen by one of the crew members. The first specimen of this species was shot near the mouth of the White River, South Dakota, on September 17, 1804. Captain Clark immediately recognized it to be different from the white-tailed deer, especially in its large and long ears, its more rounded and black-tipped tail, and in its distinctive bounding behavior when frightened. Four more were shot near the Big Bend of the Missouri on September 19, when the equally characteristic symmetrical forking pattern of the species' antlers was also noted by Captain Clark. A much more detailed anatomical description was provided by Captain Lewis on May 10, 1805, when he initially referred to it as a 'mule deer,' as distinct from the white-tailed or 'common deer.' Relatively few mule deer were mentioned during the North Dakota phase of the trip. During the return trip, mule deer were last noted in the vicinity of the White River, South Dakota."

In his book, *The Mule Deer of Wyoming*, Neal Blair wrote from studying the diaries of Wyoming's early trappers and explorers that mule deer were an infrequent sight in the 1800s, and the men subsisted mainly on pronghorn, bison and bear, with deer a rare camp meat entry.

In his book, *The Oregon Trail*, Parkman described shooting what he thought was an elk in 1846 but realizing it was a deer—yet not exactly like the mule deer or whitetails he had encountered on his westward trek. He wrote about shooting a black-tailed deer within a two-day ride of Fort Laramie, which scientists say puts blacktails as far east as Wyoming.

Rawley (1985) wrote that early explorers and trappers described an abundance of wildlife in Utah, but rarely mentioned mule deer. In 1846 John C. Fremont wrote about what is now central Utah where they had encountered more mule deer and sheep than any other part of their journey. This is not surprising, due to the migration patterns of mule deer in Utah. Most of the early trappers and explorers followed the valleys and river bottoms. If they traveled through the area in the summer, the deer were probably in the high country. Fremont probably traveled through central Utah when deer and sheep had migrated to the valleys to winter.

Historically, several factors contributed to the low numbers of mule deer. We know that the West had more grass than today. Buffalo, elk and sheep flourished under these conditions. Habitat conditions didn't favor mule deer. Another major factor, based on the numerous reports by the early trappers and explorers, was the abundance of wolves, coyotes, grizzly bears, black bears and cougars. Mule deer were easy prey for these large and abundant predators.

What conditions changed that favored a dramatic increase in mule deer? Look at a map that shows the distribution of mule deer in the West. Mule deer inhabit a variety of habitats. One would think they could survive most anywhere. The problem is, they have a selective diet and are susceptible to severe winter conditions. Deer feed primarily on forbs, shrubs and some young aspen shoots during the summer months. Shrubs dominate their diet from fall to early spring. In stressed winter conditions, they will eat juniper.

A perfect storm began in the late 1800s that resulted in the dramatic rise in mule deer numbers throughout the West. With the coming of the settlers, cattle barons, timber barons and market hunters, the landscape in the West began to change. Large herds of cattle and later, sheep began to graze the abundant grasses from Montana to the Southwest. A dramatic shift occurred in the vegetation throughout the West. Early reports of settlers in the Great Basin reported grass up to a horse's belly. The grazing of the abundant grasses by cattle gave way to a more palatable diet of forbs and shrubs. The cutting of conifers for fuel and building supplies allowed aspen groves to expand. In the late 1960s, in those same valleys, one could look out over a sea of sagebrush, which allowed mule deer to survive the harsh western winters.

This change in vegetation, which was beneficial to mule deer coincided with the elimination of predators from the landscape.

First to be eliminated were the large carnivores like grizzly bears and wolves. These large predators were trapped, hunted and poisoned by early settlers. By the 1920s wolves and grizzlies were either eliminated or at extremely low population levels. In 1931 the Animal Damage

Excerpts from the journals of Lewis and Clark describing their first sighting of mule deer and a later, more-detailed description.

[Lewis]

Friday May 10th 1805.

Set out at sunrise and proceeded but a short distance ere the wind became so violent that we were obliged to come too, [1] which we did on the Lard. side in a suddon or short bend of the river where we were in a great measure sheltered from the effects of the wind. the wind continued violent all day, the clouds were thick and black, had a slight sprinkle of rain several times in the course of the day. we sent out several hunters to scower the country, to this we were induced not so much from the want of provision as to discover the Indians whome we had reasons to believe were in the neighbourhood, from the circumstance of one of their dogs comeing to us this morning shortly after we landed; we still beleive ourselves in the country usually hunted by the Assinniboins, and as they are a vicious illy disposed nation we think it best to be on our guard, accordingly we inspected the arms and accoutrements the party and found them all in good order. The hunters returned this evening having seen no tents or Indians nor any fresh sign of them; they killed two Mule deer, one common fallow or longtailed deer, 2 Buffaloe and 5 beaver, and saw several deer of the Mule kind of immence size, and also three of the Bighorned anamals. from the appearance of the Mule deer and the bighorned anamals we beleive ourselves fast approaching a hilly or mountainous country; we have rarely found the mule deer in any except a rough country; they prefer the open grounds and are seldom found in the woodlands near the river; when they are met with in the woodlands or river bottoms and are pursued, the[y] invariably run to the hills or open country as the Elk do. the contrary happens with the common deer ther are several esscential differences between the Mule and common deer as well in form as in habits. they are fully a third larger in general, and the male is particularly large; I think there is somewhat greater disparity of size between the male and female of this speceis than there is between the male and female fallow deer; I am convinced I have seen a buck of this species twice the volume of a buck of any other species. the ears are peculiarly large; I measured those of a large buck which I found to be eleven inches long and 3½ in width at the widest part; they are not so delicately formed, their hair in winter is thicker longer and of a much darker grey, in summer the hair is still coarser longer and of a paleer red, more like that of the Elk; in winter they also have a considerable quantity of a very fine wool intermixed with the hair and lying next to the skin as the Antelope has. the long hair which grows on the outer sides of the 1st joint of the hinder legs, and which in the common deer do not usually occupy more than 2 inches in them occupys from 6 to eight; their horns also differ, these in the common deer consist of two main beams from which one or more points project the beam graduly deminishing as the points procede from it. with the mule deer the horns consist of two beams which at the distance of 4 or … om the head divide themselves each into two equal branches … into two other equal branches or terminate in a sm… aving either 2 4 or 6 points on a … ommon deer and are invariably … of all, is the white rump and tale. … pot perfectly white, of abot 3 … emitys of the buttocks and joins … y from 8 to 9 inches long, ⟨is … ity is covered with sho[r]t … ; from hence for about one … ger, the tail then terminates … black hair of the tail they … the black taled deer, but … much the larger portion of … ompared with those of the … compared with the horse, … he mule deer which I thi…

September 17, 1804
William Clark

Colter Killed a Goat like the one I killed and a curious kind of Deer (Mule Deer) of a Dark gray Colr. more so than common, ... this Spec[i]es of Deer jumps like a goat or Sheep

September 17, 1804
Meriwether Lewis

Having for many days past confined myself to the boat, I determined to devote this day to amuse myself on shore with my gun and view the interior of the country lying between the river and the Corvus Creek. ... the shortness and virdu[r]e of grass gave the plain the appearance throughout it's whole extent of beatifull bowling-green in fine order. ... this senery already rich pleasing and beatiful was still farther hightened by immence herds of Buffaloe, deer Elk and Antelopes which we saw in every direction feeding on … plains. I do not think I exagerate when I estimate the … behandled at one view to

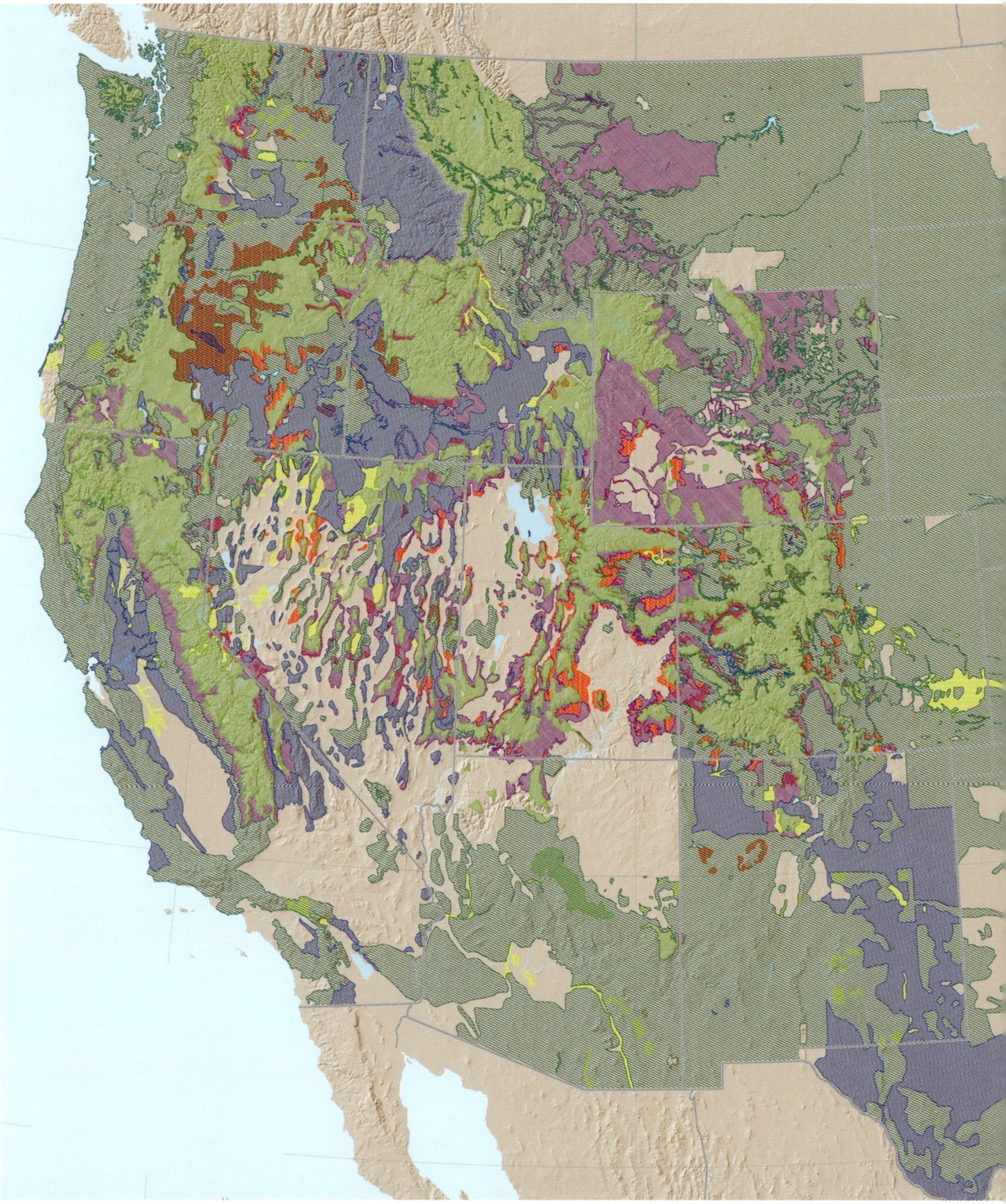

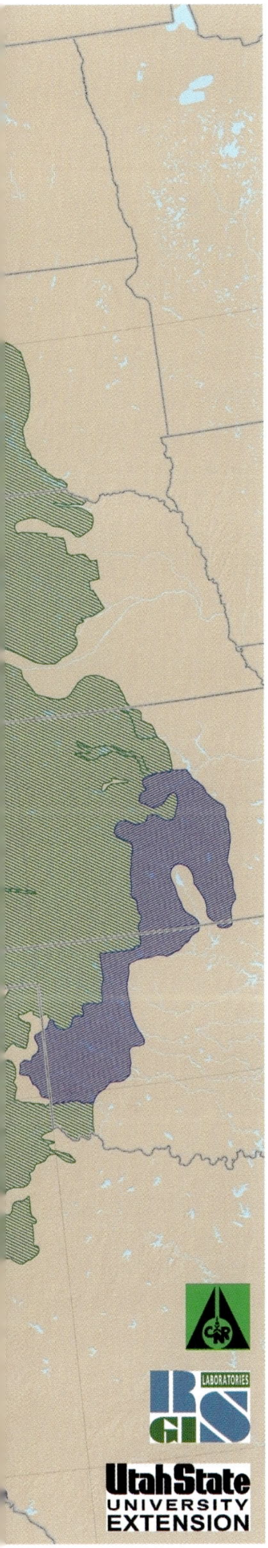

Limited Range: Includes habitat which are occasionally inhabited and/or contain small populations of scattered mule deer.

Year-Round Population: An area that provides year-round range for a population of mule deer. The resident mule deer use all of the area all year; it cannot be subdivided into seasonal ranges although it may be included within the overall range of the larger population.

Summer Range: That part of the overall range where 90% of the individuals are located between spring green-up and the first heavy snowfall.

Winter Range: That part of the overall range where 90 percent of the individuals are located during the average five winters out of ten from the first heavy snowfall to spring green-up, or during a site-specific period of winter. A subset of this definition would include a "severe winter range" definition to include areas within the winter range where 90% of the individuals are located when annual snow pack is at its maximum and/or temperatures are at a minimum in the two worst winters out of ten.

Other Important Habitat: Areas that are part of the overall range where higher quality habitat supports significantly higher densities than surrounding areas. These areas are typically occupied year round and not necessarily associated with a specific season. Examples include: rough break country, riparian areas, small drainages and large areas of irrigated cropland, migration corridors, highway crossings, fawning areas, etc.

Winter Concentration: That part of the winter range where densities are at least 200% greater than the surrounding winter range density during the same period used to define winter range in the average five winters out of ten.

ABOUT THIS MAP: The GIS data for this map were created as part of a collaborative effort to delineate mule deer habitat throughout North America. Wildlife biologists from each of the western states and two Canadian provinces participated in a Delhi process to delineate six habitat types shown in this map. Separate workshops were conducted in each state wherein state experts delineated known mule deer habitat on 1:250,000 scale topographic maps. In addition to habitat types, wildlife experts attributed each polygon with numeric codes identifying factors limiting habitat viability (e.g. domestic livestock forage competition, habitat succession/maturation, urban expansion, etc.). Limiting factors are not shown on this map. Definitions for habitat types and limiting factors were those adopted by the Mule Deer Working Group of the Western Association of Fish and Wildlife Agencies (WAFWA). Funding for this project was provided by the National Fish and Wildlife Foundation. Utah State University Extension and the Remote Sensing/GIS Laboratory at Utah State University were responsible for project coordination and implementation. The mule deer habitat data for this project are available for free on CD-ROM or via internet download.

For more information please contact: RS/GIS Laboratory, College of Natural Resources, Utah State University (phone: 435-797-2385, web: http://www.gis.usu.edu/)

New York 24, New York

KIND OF DEER — MULE

Greatest spread
373 : 25 = x : 1
(units)
x = 14.91
1" = 14.91 (units)
Smallest H-2 diameter on rt. antler from photo measure is 23 units or 1.542 inches diam. giving 4.85 circum when multiplied by 3.1416. Large photograph, not press photo, was used. This compares with 5 1/8 claimed, and 1 1/4 in. dia. mentioned in press story. Press story too low probably due to measure inside horn bumps.
G-4 rt. seems to check OK.
G-2 doesn't but angle may be great.

MEASUREMENTS

			Column 3	Column 4 Difference
Num...				
Tip...				
Grea...				
Insi... of M...				
IF I... antl...				
Total...				0
Lengt...				0
Len...		2/1/8"	23/1/4"	1/1/8
Len...		4/1/2	4/3/4	1/4
Length of Third Point, if present		15/1/4	14/3/4	1/2
Length of Fourth Point, if present		8/1/2	7/1/8	1/3/8
Circumference at Smallest Place Between Burr and First Point		8/7/8"	8/3/8	1/2
Circumference at Smallest Place Between First and Second Points		5/1/4"	5/1/4"	0
Circumference at Smallest Place Between Main Beam and Third Point.		5/1/8"	5"	1/8
Circumference at Smallest Place Between Second and Fourth Points		4/3/4"	6"	1/1/4
		4/5/8	4/5/8	0
TOTALS	22/3/4	~~77~~ 81	79/1/8	5/1/8

6/8 Column 1	22/3/4	Exact locality where killed Little Yamsey Mt. Kl/Co. Oregon Klamath County
8 Column 2	77	Date killed 10/21/1951 By whom killed CARL T. NELSON
7/8 Column 3	79/1/8	Present owner CARL T. NELSON
TOTAL	178/7/8	Address
...ACT Column 4 7/8	5/1/8"	Oregon Ph. 5-9068
		Guide's Name and Address Ray Shunterman.
...NAL SCORE 177 6/8	173/3/4	Remarks: (Mention any abnormalities) There is one point 1" long between the burr and G-1 on left Antler as per picture.

Control (ADC) Act authorized the U.S. Fish and Wildlife Service (USFWS) to initiate programs to remove predators for livestock protection. ADC agents were extremely aggressive at predator control. Coyotes, black bears and cougars were the target species. When the government really became aggressive with the use of poisons such as 1080, predator populations like coyotes, black bears and cougars were dramatically reduced. The byproduct was wildlife species like mule deer, sage grouse and pronghorn flourished.

As a result, wildlife managers in the late 40s and 50s saw dramatic increases in the survival of adult deer and a sharp increase in the number of fawns surviving each year. It was not unusual in those days to see a mule deer doe with triplets. Mule deer numbers increased so dramatically in some states that wildlife agencies began implementing unlimited license sales, multiple deer tags, either-sex deer tags and long hunting seasons (reminding us of whitetail management today in some eastern states). This practice continued into the late 60s for some states.

Mule deer hunts became the most popular big game hunting in the West. Mule deer became the icon of the West for most hunters and wildlife management agencies. Rural communities had school holidays on the opening week of deer season. Rural communities welcomed mule deer hunters with special dinners held the night before opening day. Rural businesses flourished catering to hunters.

Mule deer numbers increased dramatically in the 1940s and 1950s in the West, and many states saw seasons with multiple deer tags or unlimited license sales. This buck was taken by Carl T. Nelson in Klamath County, Oregon, during the 1951 season and unofficially taped at 177-6/8 points. A newspaper clipping that accompanied the trophy entry notes the buck weighed 298 pounds and was shot on the west slope of Yamsey Mountain. Nelson shot the deer from about 100 yards.

Elk numbers during this time were at low levels in most states. Managing deer herds in the 40s, 50s and 60s was easy. Biologists' jobs focused on reducing deer numbers to prevent overgrazing their winter ranges (which were their limiting habitat). Between livestock grazing and high numbers of mule deer, transition ranges and winter ranges began to decline in productivity.

What happened to change this dramatic increase in mule deer populations to a downward decline throughout their range? As a perfect storm of events happened to increase mule deer numbers, a series of factors combined to impact mule deer populations differently, depending on the circumstances in each state. Not all mule deer herds declined as dramatically as others, and no one factor contributed to the decline.

First, habitat experienced a change. Too many mouths on the landscape favored different vegetation types. Sagebrush plants, which flourished in the 40s and 50s, became decadent and lost their nutritional value for mule deer. Sagebrush was sprayed, plowed and burned to make way for livestock forage. The former U.S. Soil Conservation Service encouraged ranchers to plant crested wheatgrass, and thousands of acres of sagebrush were converted to monocultures of crested wheatgrass. While good for spring grazing by cattle, crested wheatgrass was a desert to mule deer. As the West became more and more settled, vast areas of mule deer habitat were converted to alfalfa, winter wheat, corn etc.

Juniper and other invasive plant species like cheatgrass, medusa head, whitetop, etc., began dominating the landscape.

When settlers first arrived in Oregon, western juniper occupied only around a million acres. Today it is estimated that 3 to 4 million acres of western juniper occupy the Oregon landscape. Western juniper as well as its cousin, Utah juniper and pinyon pine have choked out millions of acres of western mule deer habitat, especially in the Great Basin, which includes Utah, Nevada and southern Idaho. While some

Four impressive mule deer bucks taken in the 1940s in Nevada. The buck featured top-center was entered in the Club's records program with a score of 248-2/8 points, which includes over 57 inches of abnormal points. A clipping with the entry notes that "although these are exceptional spreads, Elko county hunters agreed that there are many more where they came from."

juniper is needed for thermal cover in the winter, it has little or no nutritional value for mule deer. Juniper has displaced sagebrush, bitterbrush and other shrubs and forbs essential to mule deer. Most juniper trees in the West are less than 100 years old.

The West began to experience tremendous population growth in the 50s and 60s. Since the West was primarily public land—United States Forest Service (USFS) or Bureau of Land Management (BLM)—city and towns did not plan for open space but allowed development to occur on critical mule deer winter ranges and eliminated migration corridors. In the West, growth occurred in the valleys, where deer migrated in the winter.

While some states like Montana and Wyoming escaped the dramatic population increases, other states were not spared the rush to develop. In Colorado, Utah, Arizona, California, Oregon and Washington, the human populations exploded, and development occurred at unprecedented levels. Historic mule deer wintering habitat is where much of the development in the West occurred. Foothills and valley benches where mule deer wintered were covered with housing developments. Each winter when mule deer arrived on their winter ranges they found more and more development encroaching on the landscape. Carrying capacities of winter ranges plummeted.

With urbanization came an increase in highway building. Two-lane roads became freeways and major highways crisscrossing the landscape. The improvement of highways led to higher speeds and higher volumes of traffic. As more cars traveled the highways, more deer were killed in auto/deer collisions. Critical winter ranges were cut off by freeways. Migrating deer herds were subjected to highway mortality at least twice a year—in the fall, as they moved down from the mountains to the valleys and again in the spring, as they followed the greening vegetation back up the mountain. Highway deer kills began to outnumber deer harvested by hunters in some management units.

Biologists estimated in the late 1960s that overall mule deer numbers were less than 50 percent of what they were at their peak. Some states were able to remain above that level, but most were not.

Wildlife agencies adjusted the number of licenses issued. Limited-quota hunting and antler-point restrictions began to become part of hunting recommendations. Hunters began to demand reductions in tag numbers and reduced-season lengths.

The central theme from wildlife agencies regarding the biggest threat to mule deer was loss of habitat and habitat fragmentation.

Despite the fact that very few predators were present, mule deer numbers were on a slow decline range-wide.

Factors contributing to mule deer population declines were:

- Loss of habitat and habitat fragmentation
- Urban development
- Highway mortality and migration barriers
- Overgrazing
- Energy development
- Invasive species
- Predators
- Lack of rangeland fires

Habitat management on our national forests and BLM lands led to a decline in healthy habitat for mule deer and other wildlife. These lands were primarily managed for livestock grazing, not for wildlife. Overgrazing on many allotments contributed to a change in plant composition that was replaced by plants not part of the mule deer's diet. It was also during this time that the Forest Service and BLM started aggressively fighting wild fires. The lack of naturally occurring fires contributed to the loss of aspen—critical for mule deer fawning—and a dramatic increase in the invasion of pinyon juniper.

According to the USFS and BLM fire records from the 1920s to the 1960s, the chart above shows the number of acres burned.

DECADE	NUMBER OF ACRES BURNED
1920s	26 million acres
1930s	39 million acres
1940s	23 million acres
1950s	9 million acres
1960s	4 million acres

Farming practices in the eastern portion of the mule deer's range resulted in thousands of acres of native prairie being plowed under and planted with corn, wheat and other crops. Conditions in these areas began to favor white-tailed deer over mule deer.

The number of mule deer didn't change overnight. The reversal of the highs of the 1950s to the declines in the 1960s and beyond was subtle in nature and not as dramatic as the increase. As vegetation changed or was lost and development occurred, mule deer became more susceptible to severe winters and disease. Winter mortality became a major problem in areas that had lost or had their critical ranges greatly reduced. When weather conditions favored mule deer, the recovery of local populations occurred. The problem was exacerbated when population declines became more dramatic and the recovery slower or not at all.

At the end of the 60s, mule deer numbers had declined so significantly that wildlife managers began to assemble at conferences to discuss the decline. Research studies were initiated to find out why mule deer populations were in decline.

Mule deer, the icon of the West, were becoming fewer and fewer in relation to the glory days of the 40s, 50s and early 60s. Still today, mule deer hold a special place in the hearts and minds of hunters. The term "buck fever" was derived from hunters getting so excited at seeing a magnificent trophy mule deer that they often missed their target. Many a hunter has experienced missing a trophy buck and watched him bound out of sight over the ridge.

MOUNTAIN CARIBOU
Bradford O'Connor
1st. PRIZE
WHITETAIL DEER
Matthew Lahti
Wolfeboro, N.H
3rd. PRIZE
OODLAND CARIBOU
G.H. Lesser
Johnstown, N.Y.
1st. PRIZE
WHITETAIL DEER
Mrs. Thelma Martens
Upton, Wyo.
1st. PRIZE
WHITETAIL DEER
Ralph Morrill
New Haven, Conn.
2nd. PRIZE
MULE DEER
Win Coultas
Spokane, Wash.
1st. PRIZE
DEER
Wash.
2nd. PRIZE
MULE DEER
B.E. George
Berkeley, Calif.
3rd. PRIZE
MULE DEER
Cleo Brown
Baggs, Wyo.
HONORABLE MENTION

AWARD-WINNING MULE DEER

JULIE TRIPP | B&C DIRECTOR OF PUBLICATIONS

The Club held its first big game competition in New York City at the American Museum of Natural History in 1947. There were 37 trophies shipped to the museum to be verified by a panel of judges, which included Samuel B. Webb, William C. Chanler, E. Roland Harriman, Greville Haslman and Carl Rungius. In those days, trophies were ranked by one measurement, and for mule deer, that was the longest main beam. However, the competition was judged more by the looks of the deer than anything concrete like antler measurements. Only first, second, and third prizes were awarded; the balance received honorable mention.

This same format for judging continued for the 1948 and 1949 competitions. But the Club soon realized this type of judging wasn't the best way to recognize the finest trophies taken in North America, so a more precise and scientific method was developed. By the time the fourth competition was held in 1950, a new system had been put in place and quickly became the universally accepted standard for measuring native North American big game.

This new system ushered in a completely different—and highly objective—method for ranking big game trophies. It also established a non-typical category for mule deer entries. Five mule deer were recognized at the 1950 competition—three typical and two non-typical bucks.

Four non-typical mule deer were on display at the Club's fifth competition at the American Museum of Natural History in 1951.

The next six competitions also took place at the American Museum of Natural History. Beginning with the eleventh competition in 1964, the location changed to the Carnegie Museum in Pittsburgh, Pennsylvania, where it remained until 1973 when the Club's records-keeping activities merged with the National Rifle Association. In 1974 the venue and name changed: the Club hosted the 15th Awards Program in Atlanta, Georgia. This marked a change from a competition to an awards program, which was more fitting of the Club's objectives—a title that remains in effect today.

Throughout the history of the Club's records program, minimum scores for entries have fluctuated, and minor changes have been made to the calculation of scores for mule deer as well as other categories. When the new scoring system debuted in 1950, the minimum score for typical mule deer was 165 points; and 195 points

Alton Huntsaker, right, and his son Grand with deer taken during the 1943 season in Utah. Huntsaker's non-typical mule deer wasn't entered until the twelfth competition in 1966 where it received a Certificate of Merit. With an official score of 330-1/8 points, the buck still ranks as the number three non-typical mule deer of all-time.

for non-typical bucks. Those minimum entry scores continually rose over the next 18 years. By 1968, the minimum entry scores for typical and non-typical mule deer were 195 and 240, respectively. Beginning with the 19th Awards Period (1983-1985), the Club instituted two different minimum scores for most categories. The lower of the two minimums granted entry into the Awards Period; the higher minimum granted entry into the Club's All-time records book. It was also during the 19th Awards Period that mule deer minimum scores were lowered to 185 for typical and 225 for non-typical mule deer. The non-typical minimum score remains at 225 today. In 1993 the typical mule deer score was lowered one more time to the current minimum of 180 points.

Unfortunately, the Club did not have the manpower or, in some cases, the necessary entry materials to reinstate the mule deer entries that were dropped when the minimum score was raised. These trophies are eligible again with the new lower minimum score. The good news: all efforts are being made to get as many of these entries from the 1960s back into our records database. These reinstated trophy entries will improve the scientific viability of our records data going forward by providing a more complete data set.

Another key change for mule deer scoring occurred in the early 1990s. The Club realized some deductions were actually double-penalizing a trophy—specifically when it came to deducting points for the inside spread when it exceeded the longer main beam. The Club changed the deduction rule to allow the recording of an inside spread up to the length of the longer main beam with no deduction taken if it measures greater. Numerous mule deer entries were affected by this change, and their new scores were updated in our trophy database.

This chapter focuses on some of the finest mule deer entered in the Club's first competition in 1947 up through 1966 with the twelfth competition. Enjoy studying their historic score charts, photographs, and all manner of correspondence. You'll be amazed at the amount of history you'll be able to uncover!

AWARD-WINNING MULE DEER

FIRST COMPETITION THROUGH TWELFTH COMPETITION

Following is a complete list of the award-winning mule deer from the first through twelfth competitions. Details for several of these deer can be found on the following pages or in other chapters of this book.

THIS CHAPTER | WOMEN AND DEER HUNTING CHAPTER | VINTAGE PHOTOS CHAPTER | KAIBAB CHAPTER

1947 - FIRST COMPETITION

FIRST PRIZE
Main Beam Length: (R) 28-1/2 (L) 31-1/8
Hunter: August W. Bogenhagen

SECOND PRIZE
Main Beam Length: (R) 30-7/8 (L) 29-7/8
Hunter: Robert D. Rogers

THIRD PRIZE
Main Beam Length: (R) 30-1/2 (L) 30-1/4
Hunter: George Coolures

HONORABLE MENTION
Main Beam Length: (R) 31 (L) 30-5/8
Hunter: Kelly Agee

HONORABLE MENTION
Main Beam Length: (R) 27-7/8 (L) 29-1/2
Hunter: C.E. Walker

1948 - SECOND COMPETITION

FIRST PRIZE
Main Beam Length: (R) 31 (L) 27-1/4
Hunter: Walter Gardner

SECOND PRIZE
Main Beam Length: (R) 30-1/2 (L) 29-1/2
Hunter: A.B. Jackson Jr.

THIRD PRIZE
Main Beam Length: (R) 28-1/2 (L) 30
Hunter: John L. Kemmerer

HONORABLE MENTION
Main Beam Length: (R) 30 (L) 29-1/2
Hunter: Bob Mitchell

AWARD-WINNING MULE DEER

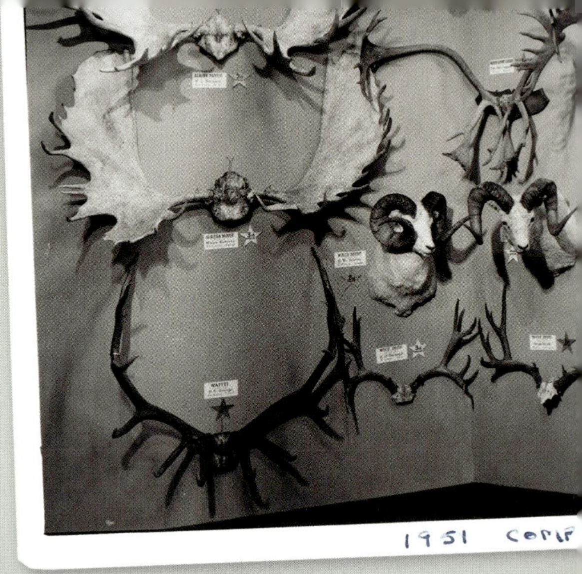

1949 – THIRD COMPETITION

FIRST PRIZE
Main Beam Length: (R) 30-1/4 (L) 31-3/4
Hunter: George D. Ballard

1950 – FOURTH COMPETITION

FIRST PRIZE – TYPICAL
Score: 188-7/8 | Hunter: Lyle K. Leedle

SECOND PRIZE – TYPICAL
Score: 169-3/8 | Hunter: Laurel Graham

THIRD PRIZE – TYPICAL
Score: 168-1/8 | Hunter: Clarence Schmidt

HONORABLE MENTION – TYPICAL
Score: 165-1/8 | Hunter: Tony Ganci

FIRST PRIZE – NON-TYPICAL
Score: 241-3/8 | Hunter: Manuel Mingoia

HONORABLE MENTION – NON-TYPICAL
Score: 233-1/8 | Hunter: C.B. Welch

1951 – FIFTH COMPETITION

FIRST PRIZE – TYPICAL
Score: 197-1/8 | Hunter: Lucille Gooch

SECOND PRIZE – TYPICAL
Score: 188-3/8 | Hunter: R.I. Jerner

THIRD PRIZE – TYPICAL
Score: 183 | Hunter: Ollie O. Barney, Jr.

FIRST PRIZE – NON-TYPICAL
Score: 261-2/8 | Hunter: Win Coultas

SECOND PRIZE – NON-TYPICAL
Score: 246-6/8 | Hunter: Fred C. Heuer

THIRD PRIZE – NON-TYPICAL
Score: 240-5/8 | Hunter: Bert Ellis George

1953 – SIXTH COMPETITION

FIRST PRIZE – TYPICAL
Score: 203-7/8 | Hunter: Edison A. Pillmore
Sagamore Hill Award Winner and
New World's Record

SECOND PRIZE – TYPICAL
Score: 197-6/8 | Hunter: Ralph E. Platt, Jr.

THIRD PRIZE – TYPICAL
Score: 194-3/8 | Hunter: W.C. Condict

FOURTH PRIZE – TYPICAL
Score: 189 | Hunter: Win Condict

HONORABLE MENTION – TYPICAL
Score: 188-2/8 | Hunter: W.C. Condict

HONORABLE MENTION – TYPICAL
Score: 186-6/8 | Hunter: L. Jack Lyon

HONORABLE MENTION – TYPICAL
Score: 184-2/8 | Hunter: Win Condict

HONORABLE MENTION – TYPICAL
Score: 184-1/8 | Hunter: James F. Smith

FIRST PRIZE – NON-TYPICAL
Score: 253-3/8 | Hunter: A.H. Henkel

SECOND PRIZE – NON-TYPICAL
Score: 230-1/8 | Hunter: Joan Powell

1954-1955 – SEVENTH COMPETITION

FIRST PRIZE - TYPICAL
Score: 208-6/8 | Hunter: Horace T. Fowler
New World's Record

SECOND PRIZE - TYPICAL
Score: 203-4/8 | Hunter: Herb Graham

THIRD PRIZE - TYPICAL
Score: 201 | Hunter: Ernest Mancuso

FOURTH PRIZE - TYPICAL
Score: 200-3/8 | Hunter: E.R. Crooks

HONORABLE MENTION - TYPICAL
Score: 198-2/8 | Hunter: Clifford Le Neve

HONORABLE MENTION - TYPICAL
Score: 197-2/8 | Hunter: Peter Perrin

CERTIFICATE OF MERIT - TYPICAL
Score: 199-7/8 | Hunter: G.B. Berger, Jr.

CERTIFICATE OF MERIT - TYPICAL
Score: 198 | Hunter: Unknown
Owner: Lund's Wildlife Exhibit

FIRST PRIZE - NON-TYPICAL
Score: 287-5/8 | Hunter: Joseph W. Dooley

SECOND PRIZE - NON-TYPICAL
Score: 282-2/8 | Hunter: Herman Cox

THIRD PRIZE - NON-TYPICAL
Score: 278-2/8 | Hunters: Milroy Powell and Dan Auld, Jr.

HONORABLE MENTION - NON-TYPICAL
Score: 273-6/8 | Hunter: J.J. McDaniels

1956-1957 – EIGHTH COMPETITION

FIRST PRIZE - TYPICAL
Score: 195-1/8 | Hunter: Donald G. Heidtman

SECOND PRIZE - TYPICAL
Score: 194-5/8 | Hunter: David Prager

THIRD PRIZE - TYPICAL
Score: 194-3/8 | Hunter: Paul Gamble

FOURTH PRIZE - TYPICAL
Score: 194-2/8 | Hunter: Daniel Moore

HONORABLE MENTION - TYPICAL
Score: 192-4/8 | Hunter: M.A. Gamblin

HONORABLE MENTION - TYPICAL
Score: 192-1/8 | Hunter: Pasco Scarpella

HONORABLE MENTION - TYPICAL
Score: 191-1/8 | Hunter: Bob James

HONORABLE MENTION - TYPICAL
Score: 190-4/8 | Hunter: Wm. A. McTyre, Jr.

HONORABLE MENTION - TYPICAL
Score: 190-4/8 | Hunter: George Northman

CERTIFICATE OF MERIT - TYPICAL
Score: 200-5/8 | Hunter: Carl F. Worden

CERTIFICATE OF MERIT - TYPICAL
Score: 200-1/8 | Hunter: John F. Schurle

FIRST PRIZE - NON-TYPICAL
Score: 278-3/8 | Hunter: Jack White

SECOND PRIZE - NON-TYPICAL
Score: 273-2/8 | Hunter: Mrs. Jack Keen

THIRD PRIZE - NON-TYPICAL
Score: 263-1/8 | Hunter: Robert C. Young (see page ix)

HONORABLE MENTION - NON-TYPICAL
Score: 241-7/8 | Hunter: Spencer L. Darrar

CERTIFICATE OF MERIT - NON-TYPICAL
Score: 279-4/8 | Hunter: Unknown
Owner: W.G. Scholz

CERTIFICATE OF MERIT - NON-TYPICAL
Score: 243-6/8 | Hunter: Ben Crandell

AWARD-WINNING MULE DEER

1958-1959 - NINTH COMPETITION

FIRST PRIZE - TYPICAL
Score: 199 | Hunter: Wilford Zaugg

SECOND PRIZE - TYPICAL
Score: 194-6/8 | Hunter: John Zuffa, Jr.

THIRD PRIZE - TYPICAL
Score: 193-1/8 | Hunter: Edward E. Hall, Jr.

HONORABLE MENTION - TYPICAL
Score: 192-1/8 | Hunter: Bob McCollum

CERTIFICATE OF MERIT - TYPICAL
Score: 217 | Hunter: Unknown
Owner: W.C. Lawrence
New World's Record

CERTIFICATE OF MERIT - TYPICAL
Score: 198-4/8 | Hunter: Picked Up
Owner: Rollo S. Robinson

CERTIFICATE OF MERIT - TYPICAL
Score: 196-6/8 | Hunter: Nels H. Pehrson

CERTIFICATE OF MERIT - TYPICAL
Score: 196-5/8 | Hunter: Earl Frantzen

FIRST PRIZE - NON-TYPICAL
Score: 240-2/8 | Hunter: Roger A. Crowder

SECOND PRIZE - NON-TYPICAL
Score: 239-7/8 | Hunter: Roy Vail

CERTIFICATE OF MERIT - NON-TYPICAL
Score: 272 | Hunter: Picked up
Owner: Newell Gilbert

CERTIFICATE OF MERIT - NON-TYPICAL
Score: 268-5/8 | Hunter: Cocks Brothers

1961 - TENTH COMPETITION

FIRST AWARD (TIE) - TYPICAL
Score: 214-2/8 | Hunter: Ray Talbot

FIRST AWARD (TIE) - TYPICAL
Score: 214-2/8 | Hunter: Gary L. Albertson

THIRD AWARD - TYPICAL
Score: 208-4/8 | Hunter: Robert L. Zaina

FOURTH AWARD - TYPICAL
Score: 204-1/8 | Hunter: Juan Monarco

FIRST AWARD - NON-TYPICAL
Score: 275-1/8 | Hunter: Peter Zemljak

SECOND AWARD - NON-TYPICAL
Score: 270-5/8 | Hunters: Roger Turnsback and John Van Elsen

CERTIFICATE OF MERIT - NON-TYPICAL
Score: 355-2/8 | Hunter: Ed Broder
New World's Record

CERTIFICATE OF MERIT - NON-TYPICAL
Score: 268-5/8 | Hunter: Richard Jensen

CERTIFICATE OF MERIT - NON-TYPICAL
Score: 264-5/8 | Hunter: Buster Dodson

CERTIFICATE OF MERIT - NON-TYPICAL
Score: 255-7/8 | Hunter: Unknown

1964-1965 Judging - 12th Competition - Carnegie Museum

Left to right:
Emily S.Toerge, Edd McGuire, Dr. J. Kenneth Doutt, John Andrews, George L. Norris, John H. Batten, Dr. John Hammett, Frank Cook and George Church.

1963 - ELEVENTH COMPETITION

FIRST AWARD - TYPICAL
Score: 210-2/8 | Hunter: Jack D. Johnston

SECOND AWARD - TYPICAL
Score: 209-2/8 | Hunter: Herbert Graham

THIRD AWARD - TYPICAL
Score: 207-4/8 | Hunter: Richard Cobb

FOURTH AWARD - TYPICAL
Score: 204 | Hunter: Dr. Richard V. Price

CERTIFICATE OF MERIT - TYPICAL
Score: 206-2/8 | Hunter: Harley Hinds

CERTIFICATE OF MERIT - TYPICAL
Score: 203-4/8 | Hunter: William P. Burger

CERTIFICATE OF MERIT - TYPICAL
Score: 203-2/8 | Hunter: Ron Vance

FIRST AWARD - NON-TYPICAL
Score: 306-2/8 | Hunter: Joseph A. Garcia*

FIRST AWARD - NON-TYPICAL
Score: 303-6/8 | Hunter: James Austill

SECOND AWARD - NON-TYPICAL
Score: 300 | Hunter: George Blackmon, Jr.

HONORABLE MENTION - NON-TYPICAL
Score: 270-6/8 | Hunter: Peter Zemljak, Sr.

CERTIFICATE OF MERIT - NON-TYPICAL
Score: 288-6/8 | Hunter: Frank B. Maestas

CERTIFICATE OF MERIT - NON-TYPICAL
Score: 275-6/8 | Hunter: Jim Hewitt

CERTIFICATE OF MERIT - NON-TYPICAL
Score: 275-3/8 | Hunter: Unknown
Owner: Cliff Cox

**A clarifying remeasurement moved Joseph A. Garcia's non-typical mule deer to the top spot for the eleventh competition after the medals had been awarded to the other participants. He was subsequently given a first award, as well.*

1966 - TWELFTH COMPETITION

FIRST AWARD - TYPICAL
Score: 202-5/8 | Hunter: Louis V. Schlosser

SECOND AWARD - TYPICAL
Score: 200 | Hunter: Tom Corey

THIRD AWARD - TYPICAL
Score: 199-7/8 | Hunter: H.E. Gerhart

CERTIFICATE OF MERIT - TYPICAL
Score: 209-4/8 | Hunter: Dr. John Calvin Evans

CERTIFICATE OF MERIT - TYPICAL
Score: 204 | Hunter: Jens O. Solberg

FIRST AWARD - NON-TYPICAL
Score: 269-3/8 | Hunter: Shirley Smith

SECOND AWARD - NON-TYPICAL
Score: 264 | Hunter: Jimmy Stichter

THIRD AWARD - NON-TYPICAL
Score: 243-7/8 | Hunter: Robert Rambo

CERTIFICATE OF MERIT - NON-TYPICAL
Score: 330-1/8 | Hunter: Alton T. Huntsaker

CERTIFICATE OF MERIT - NON-TYPICAL
Score: 306-2/8 | Hunter: Steve H. Herndon
Owners: Dr. Vernon D. and Dan F. Holleman

...IDE FOR INSTRUCTIONS

	Supplementary Data R.	Supplementary Data L.	Column 1 Spread Credit	Column 2 Right Antler	Column 3 Left Antler	Column 4 Difference
Number of Points on Each Antler	6	6				
Tip to Tip Spread	25 5/8					
Greatest Spread	43 7/8					
Inside Spread of MAIN BEAMS 30 1/8 — Spread credit may equal but not exceed length of longer antler			30 1/8			
IF Inside Spread of Main Beams exceeds longer antler length, enter difference						
Total of Lengths of all Abnormal Points R 8, L 6 7/8						~~8~~ 14 7/8
Length of Main Beam				25½	27	1½
Length of First Point, if present				2½	3 7/8	1 3/8
Length of Second Point				17 3/8	16 1/8	1¼
Length of Third Point, if present				7 5/8	6 3/4	7/8
Length of Fourth Point, if present				10¼	9 7/8	3/8
Circumference at Smallest Place Between Burr and First Poi...				5 3/4	6	1/4
Circumference at S... Between F...				5¼	5 1/8	1/8
				4 3/4	4 5/8	1/8
				5½	6¼	3/4
			84½		85 5/8	~~7 3/4~~ 21 4/8

...Creek Elko County Nevada

...led R. D. Rogers

...eld, Calif

...ort - Cloverdale, Calif

2nd Prize 1947 (1st)

OFFICIAL

Boone and Crockett Club

RECORDS OF NORTH AMERICAN BIG GAME AND NORTH AMERICAN BIG GAME COMPETITION

IN CARE OF AMERICAN MUSEUM OF NATURAL HISTORY CENTRAL PARK WEST AT 79TH STREET NEW YORK 24, N. Y.

UNDER THE AUSPICES OF THE NATIONAL MUSEUM OF HEADS AND HORNS OF THE NEW YORK ZOOLOGICAL SOCIETY

DEER

MULE

	RIGHT	L...
...tside curve A	30-7/8	
...ead B	43-7/8	
...ce of main beam C	5	
...points on antler	6	
...nce of burr D	7-1/4	

...lity where killed .... Mill Creek, Elko, ...

...d .... October 21, 1943

... killed ..... Robert D. Rogers

.... Robert D. Rogers

...ss .... Box H, Fairfield, California

ROBERT D. ROGERS

FIRST COMPETITION | SECOND PRIZE

Californian Robert D. Rogers shot this buck while hunting near Jack Creek in Elko County, Nevada, in the afternoon of October 21, 1943. The mule deer was scored for the first competition in 1947. With a longest main beam of 30-7/8 inches, it received a second prize. The deer was rescored using the new measuring system in 1952, resulting in a final score of 178-6/8 points. The buck has two non-typical points totaling 14-7/8 inches.

...FRED ELY, CHAIRMAN
...AROLD E. ANTHONY
...R. M. CARPENTER

Record of North American Big Game

IN CARE OF
AMERICAN MUSEUM OF NATURAL HIS...
COLUMBUS AVENUE AND 77TH STREE...
NEW YORK, N. Y.

UNDER THE AUSPICES OF ...

DEER

SPECIES... MULE

MEASUREMENTS

	RIGHT
Length of outside curve A	30 3/4
Greatest spread B ... 40 1/2"	
Circumference of main beam C	5 1/4"
Number of points on antler	8"
Circumference of burr D	7 1/2

Exact locality where killed Ruby Mtn. West of Ruby Valley, Nevad...

Date killed Oct. 19, 1946

By whom killed Walter Gardner

Owner Walter Gardner

Address Ruby Valley, Nev.

Present location of ...

OFFICIAL SCORING SYSTEM FOR NORTH AMER...

Records of North American Big Game and North American Big Game Competition

BOONE AND CROCKETT C...

MULE and BLACKTAIL ...

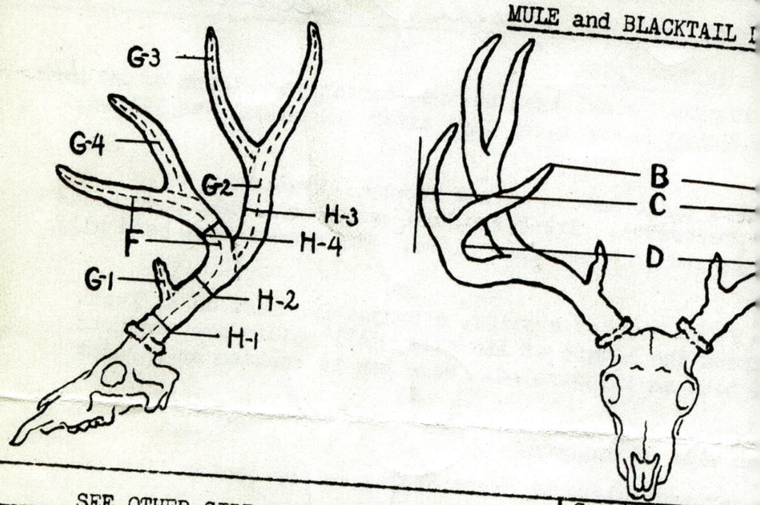

SEE OTHER SIDE FOR INSTRUCTIONS		Supplementary Data R.	Supplementary Data L.	Co...
A. Number of Points on Each Antler		8	9	Sp... Cr...
B. Tip to Tip Spread		26 1/8		
C. Greatest Spread		42		
D. Inside Spread of MAIN BEAMS	27 1/2	Spread credit may equal but not exceed length of longer antler		2...
IF Inside Spread of Main Beams exceeds longer antler length, enter difference				
E. Total of Lengths of all Abnormal Points				
F. Length of Main Beam		16 3/8		
G-1. Length of First Point				

Breadth Palm—(R) ...
Circumference—(R) 7-5/8 (L) 7-5/8

Owner—Frank Singleton

(L) 15
L) 8-3/4

Spread—23-1/8
Circumference—(R) 5 (L) 5-1/4
Points—(R) 6 (L) 8
Hunter—French Canadian Farmer
Owner—Academy of Natural Sciences, Philadelphia, Pa.

1947 JUDGES
Samuel B. Webb, Chairman
William C. Chanler
E. Roland Harriman
Greville Haslam
Carl Rungius

1948 JUDGES
Samuel B. Webb, Chairman
James L. Clark
E. Hubert Litchfield
F. Carrington Weems

MULE DEER—1st Prize - 1948
Length—(R) 31 (L) 27-1/4
Spread—42
Circumference—(R) 5 (L) 5-1/4
Points—(R) 8 (L) 9
Hunter—Walter Gardner
Owner—Walter Gardner

COUES DEER (World Record)
1st Prize - 1947
Length—(R) 19-3/4 (L) 22
Spread—16-7/8
Circumference—(R) 3-7/8 (L) 3-7/8
Points—(R) 4 (L) 4
Hunter—Rene Stallings
Owner—Rene Stallings

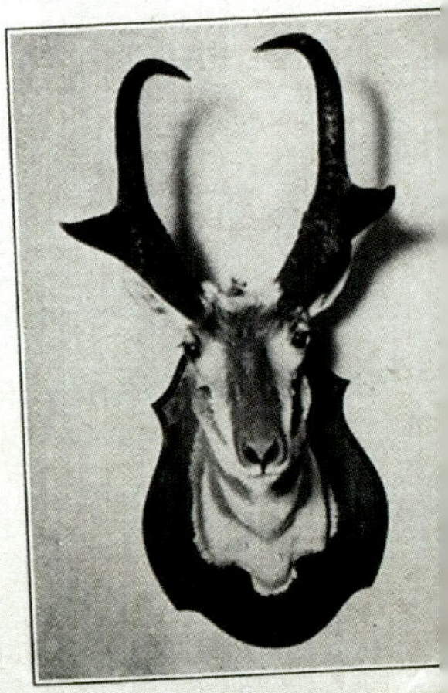

PRONGHORN
1st Prize - 1947
Length—(R) 17-3/4 (L) 17-1/2
Circumference—(R) 6-1/2 (L) 6...
Spread—11
Tip to Tip—3-1/4
Length Prong—(R) 5 (L) 5
Hunter—William G. Davis, Jr.
Owner—William G. Davis, Jr.

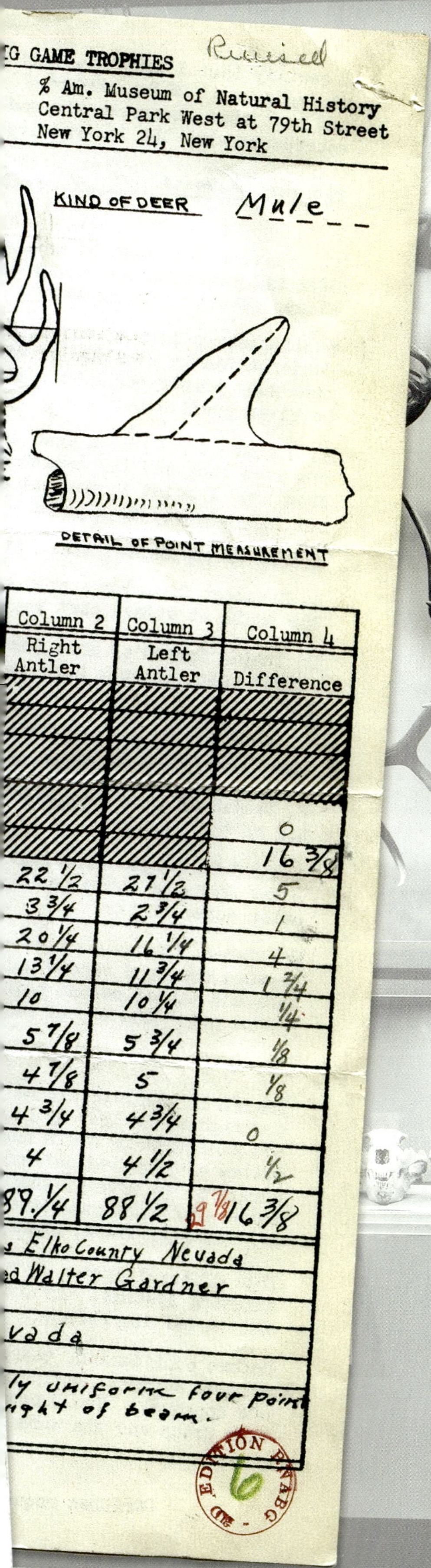

G GAME TROPHIES

% Am. Museum of Natural History
Central Park West at 79th Street
New York 24, New York

KIND OF DEER Mule

DETAIL OF POINT MEASUREMENT

Column 2 Right Antler	Column 3 Left Antler	Column 4 Difference
		0
		16 3/8
22 1/2	27 1/2	5
3 3/4	2 3/4	1
20 1/4	16 1/4	4
13 1/4	11 3/4	1 3/4
10	10 1/4	1/4
5 7/8	5 3/4	1/8
4 7/8	5	1/8
4 3/4	4 3/4	0
4	4 1/2	1/2
89 1/4	88 1/2	29 7/8 16 3/8

s Elko County Nevada
ed Walter Gardner
vada
ly uniform four point
ight of beam.

WALTER GARDNER

SECOND COMPETITION | FIRST PRIZE

Walter Gardner's prize-winning mule deer was shot in Nevada's Ruby Valley in Elko County during the 1946 season. Walter entered it in the 1948 competition where it received a first prize with a main beam measurement of 31 inches. In 1950, Gardner received a letter from the Boone and Crockett Club with a score chart for the Club's new system. Ralph L. Druehl, owner of Western Sportsman Sporting Goods in Elko, took the necessary measurements to complete the final scoring. He notes in a letter to B&C headquarters, *There is one part of your new system that appears to penalize a head for having abnormal points, in that you deduct these measurements from a head...*

Walter's tremendous buck was never officially scored as a non-typical even though the non-typical category debuted with the fourth competition. A rough estimate, based on the measurements available, indicate the buck would score just over 209 points in today's non-typical category.

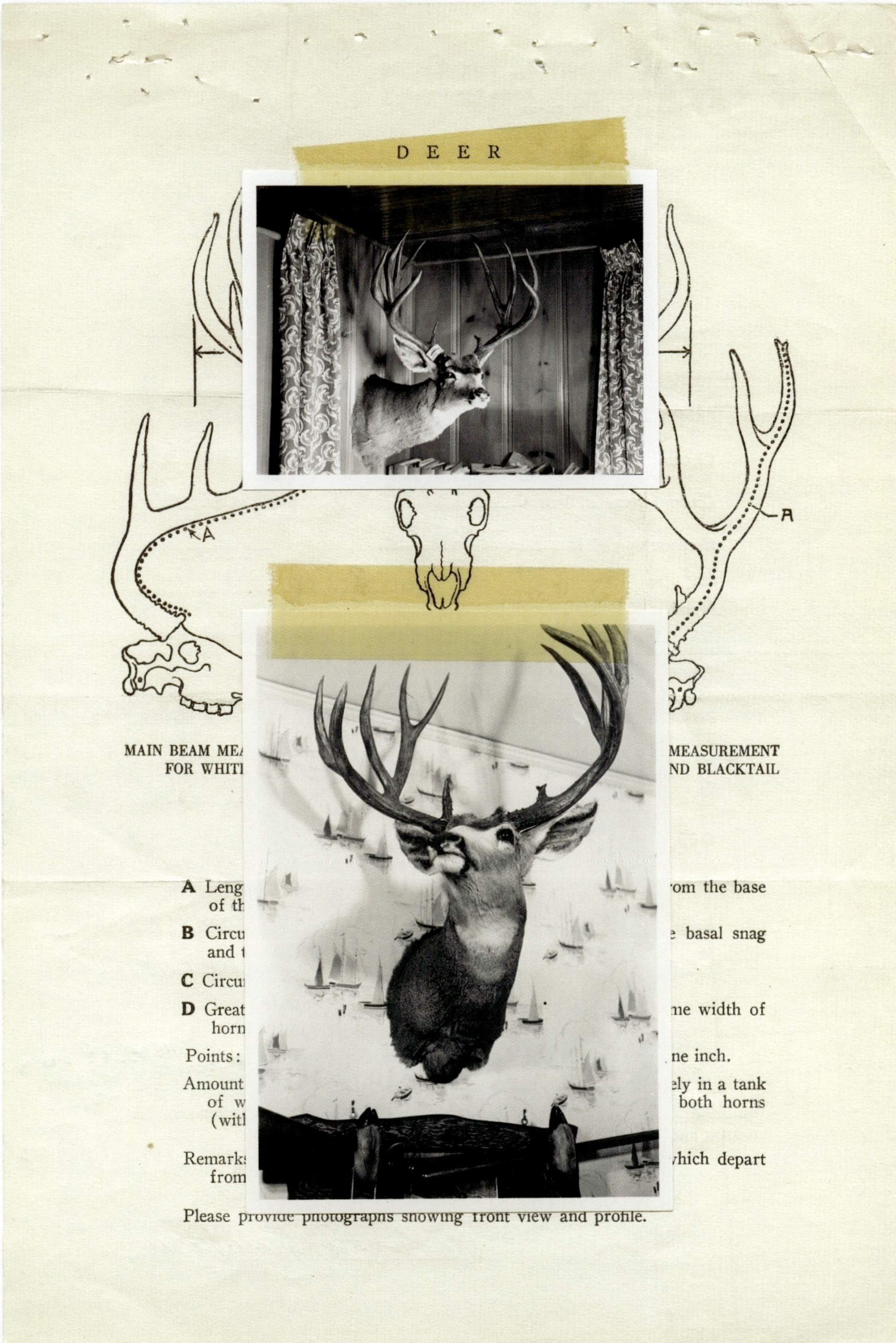
DEER
A
A
MAIN BEAM MEA
FOR WHIT
MEASUREMENT
ND BLACKTAIL
A Leng
of th
rom the base
B Circu
and t
e basal snag
C Circu
D Great
horn
me width of
Points:
ne inch.
Amount
of w
(with
ely in a tank
both horns
Remarks
from
which depart
Please provide photographs showing front view and profile.

A.B. [BUD] JACKSON, JR.
SECOND COMPETITION | SECOND PRIZE

Correspondence from Bud Jackson indicates he traveled from his home state of Missouri to the West to go hunting on a fairly regular basis. Bud shot this mule deer on October 15, 1946. He was shooting a .300 Savage Model 99 lever-action rifle. The buck was awarded a second prize at the Club's second competition with a main beam length of 30-1/2 inches. You'll get a sense of his excitement and pride in this buck by reading the correspondence on the following pages.

The file on this deer contains a plethora of correspondence between Bud and the Club's records department regarding the complexity of the new system and the effort it took to have it officially measured. In one letter, Samuel B. Webb (chair of the Club's Records Committee from 1951-1958), states,

> *You are certainly entitled to your own opinions of the present official scoring system and its series of measurements. However, at the time the official scoring system was decided on, the committee and many other interested sportsmen, scientists, game officials and guides couldn't see how it could be simplified and still accurately grade heads. We had to make fruit cake because the former plain cake method of grading by a single measurement was unsatisfactory to 95% of those interested.*

In 1951, the buck was remeasured by the hunter using the new scoring system with a final score of 194-1/2 inches. Efforts to have an Official Measurer verify the measurements were not successful, and unfortunately, the trophy was dropped from the books.

Bud Jackson.

October 13, 1948

Mr. Harold E. Anthony, Chairman
Boone & Crockett Records Committee,
American Museum of Natural History,
Central Park West at 79th Street,
New York City 24, New York

Dear Mr. Anthony:

This will acknowledge your letter of October 11, in which you request photographs of my large male mule deer, examined and reported upon by Dr. Colin C. Sanborn. I am delighted to comply to the extent of my abilities. Your communication arrived this morning, a few hours in advance of my takeoff for a scheduled Wyoming hunt and I am not sure my pictures will entirely fill the bill; since I plan to return here early in November, however, there may still be time to get you what pix you want before the deadline. I shall appreciate hearing from you in this regard.

Because five pix tell the story better than two (as a matter of fact, I believe I will add a sixth), I'm sending you that many. These are snapshots from my own or other snapshot cameras and may not come within the classification of "photographs" but of that, I will have to wait until you inform me. I have numbered these (six) and the explanation follows:

1 - Showing a half-turn view of the head as displayed on the wall of my Tulsa, Okla. home. Twelve points, visible, six to each antler.
2 - Another half-turn view same location but from the other side. Again 12 points visible but this time, only 5 on the left antler, 7 on the right. The seventh may be observed growing just above the right antler burr and below the tag. It may be seen more clearly in a subsequent picture.
3 - The buck shortly after being despatched. The rifle is a .300-Savage standard length Model 99 lever action and may give necessary comparisons.
4 - Closeup view taken at same time, again showing rifle. The 7th point (referred to in No. 2 above) is clearly visible here. The 8th point on this antler still is invisible and I do not believe I have any pictures showing it; as best I recall (this is being written hastily from my office, the head is mounted on the wall of my Evanston home and there is insufficient time to have someone check), the eighth point is buried in the hair behind the seventh point. While it is inappropriate to this particular discussion, an interesting fact may be seen in this picture. Note the buck's left foreleg. Although he ran without any noticeable fault, we discovered this leg to have been broken some years previously and removed from the joint the jacket of a small-calibre bullet with which he apparently had been shot. The joint was swollen but the injury apparently was acquired some several years previously.
5 - No photographic value to this but I enclose it to show two things - (a) the small 7th point on the right antler referred to above, and (b) an "almost" point on the rear of the left main beam. As I recall, this protuberance measured about 7/8ths of an inch.
6 - This shot of the head as displayed on the wall of my home in Evanston has little value to you although, again, the 7th point on the right antler is clearly displayed. Note that I removed the tag for this shot. Note also the greater length of the brow-tine (I believe that is the proper designation) on the right antler as compared to the left. Note also the branching of the latter (insufficient

to be counted as two points) and the swelling of the outside of the second (from the front) main point on the right antler. There is another such swelling on the outside of the third main point, same antler, but it is not visible here.

I have a feeling that there are freakish aspects to this head (I am far from being an authority on the subject !) but I doubt seriously that the head itself could be classified as a freak.

In reference to the fourth paragraph of your letter, may I say that I have never as yet been able to jar my Kansas City taxidermist into measuring it and sending me the information; however, I wrote him last week and again made the request. I have his reply that he will do it "soon". I shall write him today, insisting that he do so today or have someone else do so. I scarcely believe this second trophy is the equal of the one upon which you have information but it is an excellent head nonetheless.

I am most regretful that I do not have pictures of it but I shall have them made as quickly as I have received information on the measurements. We will certainly attempt to get them in before the deadline.

Incidentally, I also must apologize for lacking pictures which show the entire full spread of 14 points on the deer which you are now considering. If it is your pleasure that I should do so, I will attempt to have one made and, in any event, will be delighted to have you (or anyone designated by you) examine it to confirm Dr. Sanborn's and my own measurements and count. I doubt that the point-count is highly important - right?

Again many thanks for your kindness and courtesy. I prize this mule deer trophy most highly and that it "measures up" with other great mule deer heads will be a never-ending source of enjoyment and pleasure.

With all good wishes, I am

Cordially yours,

Bud Jackson

Bud Jackson

k

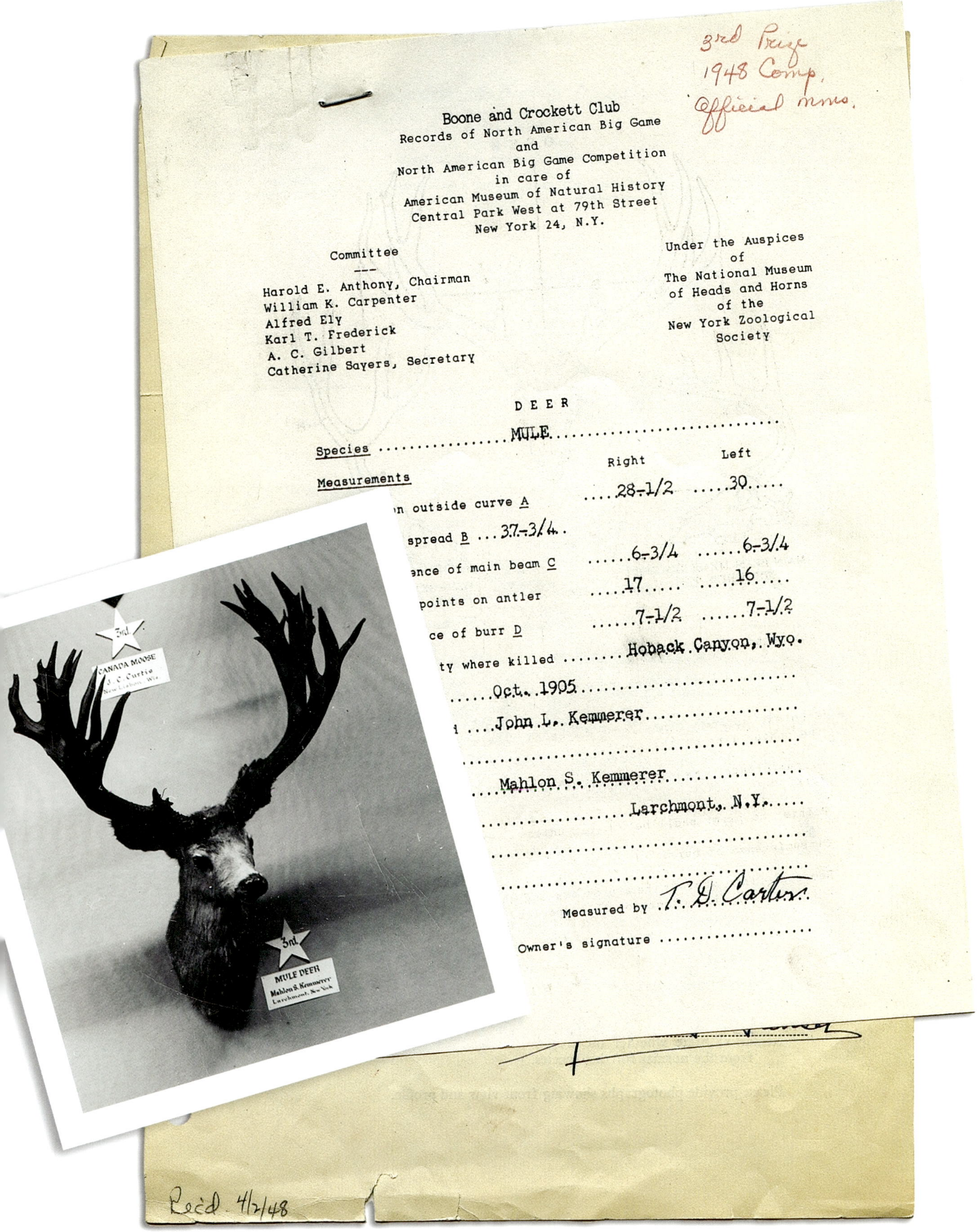

3rd Prize
1948 Comp.
Official mms.

Boone and Crockett Club
Records of North American Big Game
and
North American Big Game Competition
in care of
American Museum of Natural History
Central Park West at 79th Street
New York 24, N.Y.

Committee

Harold E. Anthony, Chairman
William K. Carpenter
Alfred Ely
Karl T. Frederick
A. C. Gilbert
Catherine Sayers, Secretary

Under the Auspices
of
The National Museum
of Heads and Horns
of the
New York Zoological
Society

DEER

Species .... MULE ....

Measurements — Right — Left

...n outside curve A .... 28-1/2 .... 30 ....

... spread B ... 37-3/4 ..

...ence of main beam C ..... 6-3/4 ..... 6-3/4

... points on antler ..... 17 ..... 16 ....

...ce of burr D ..... 7-1/2 ..... 7-1/2

...ty where killed .... Hoback Canyon, Wyo.

...... Oct. 1905 ....

...i .... John L. Kemmerer ....

....

.... Mahlon S. Kemmerer ....

.... Larchmont, N.Y. .....

Measured by T. D. Carter

Owner's signature ....

Recd. 4/2/48

J.L. KEMMERER

SECOND COMPETITION | THIRD PRIZE

John L. Kemmerer shot this buck in October 1905 in Hoback Canyon, Wyoming—the same location the current Wyoming state record typical mule deer would be harvested 20 years later. John's buck received a third prize at the Club's second competition with a main beam length of 30 inches. It was later remeasured with the modern scoring system by Grancel Fitz and Samuel B. Webb, who calculated a final B&C score of 266-7/8 points and a greatest spread of 33 inches. The buck still ranks as the seventh-largest non-typical from Wyoming. The American Museum of Natural History in New York City is listed as the owner of the trophy. However, there is no record of when they took ownership from the Kemmerer family.

DETAIL OF POINT MEASUREMENT

SEE OTHER SIDE FOR INSTRUCTIONS	Supplementary Data R.	Supplementary Data L.	Column 1 Spread Credit	Column 2 Right Antler	Column 3 Left Antler	Column 4 Difference
Number of Points on Each Antler 7-8	13	15				
Tip to Tip Spread	16 1/8					
Greatest Spread	33					
Inside Spread of MAIN BEAMS 22 4/8 — Spread credit may equal but not exceed length of longer antler			22 4/8			
IF Inside Spread of Main Beams exceeds longer antler length, enter difference						
Total of Lengths of all Abnormal Points 73 3/8						- ~~73 3/8~~
Length of Main Beam 2-3				26	25 1/8	7/8
Length of First Point, if present				2 4/8	2	4/8
Length of Second Point				16 4/8	18 7/8	2 3/8
Length of Third Point, if present				10 4/8	12	1 4/8
Length of Fourth Point, if present				6 7/8	8	1 1/8
Circumference at Smallest Place Between Burr and First Point 5-6				6 4/8	6 1/8	3/8
Circumference at Smallest Place Between First and Second Points				6 5/8	6 4/8	1/8
Circumference at Smallest Place Between Main Beam and Third Point				6 3/8	6	3/8
Circumference at Smallest Place Between Second and Fourth Points				5 7/8	6 2/8	3/8
TOTALS 73 3/8			22 4/8	87 6/8	90 7/8	~~81~~ 7 5/8

Column 1	22 4/8	Exact locality where killed Wyoming 9
Column 2	87 6/8	Date killed 1905 10 By whom killed J. L. Kemmerer 11
Column 3	90 7/8	Present owner American Museum of Natural History 12
TOTAL	201 1/8	Address
ACT Column 4	~~81~~ 7 5/8	Guide's Name and Address
INAL SCORE	~~201 1/8-81 - 282 1/8~~ 193 4/8	Remarks: (Mention any abnormalities) Large Nontypical head

Catalogue No. 147567

3d Prize - 1948 Comp

193 4/8 : 73 3/8

AWARD-WINNING MULE DEER

FOURTH COMPETITION

FOURTH COMPETITION – 1950

The Club's fourth competition was the first to use the new and improved scoring system. Six mule deer trophies were on display including four typical entries and two bucks in the newly established non-typical category.

MULE DEER (typical) — 1st Prize
Score — 188-7/8
Length—(R) 26 (L) 25
Greatest Spread—35-4/8
Basal Circumference—(R) 5-2/8 (L) 5-2/8
Points—(R) 6 (L) 5
Locality—Okanogan Co., Wash. - 1940
Hunter—Lyle K. Leedle
Guide—None
Owner—Lyle K. Leedle

MULE DEER (nontypical) — 1st Prize
Score — 213-3/8 : 28
Length (R) 26-2/8 (L) 25-4/8
Greatest Spread—40-1/8
Basal Circumference—(R) 6-2/8 (L) 6-1/8
Points—(R) 12 (L) 9
Locality—Elko Co., Nev. - 1948
Hunter—Manuel Mingoia
Guide—None

PRIZE WINNING TROPHIES
Submitted for the
1950 NORTH AMERICAN
BIG GAME COMPETITION
of the
BOONE AND CROCKETT CLUB

e Competition

EXHIBITED

DEER MULE

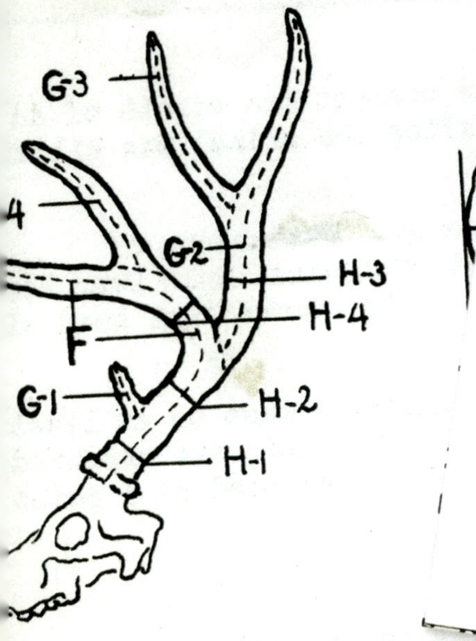

SEE OTHER SIDE FOR INSTRUCTIONS

	R.	L.	Spread Credit			
mber of Points on Each Antler	7	8				
p to Tip Spread	25-5/8					
eatest Spread	30-7/8					
nside Spread of MAIN BEAMS 28-3/4	Spread credit may equal but not exceed length of longer antler		26			
F Inside Spread of Main Beams exceeds longer antler length, enter difference						2-6
otal of Lengths of all Abnormal Points						7
ength of Main Beam				24-1/8	26	1-
Length of First Point, if present				3-3/8	3-4/8	
Length of Second Point				12-2/8	12	
Length of Third Point, if present				7	8-7/8	1-
Length of Fourth Point, if present				9-7/8	9-2/8	
Circumference at Smallest Place Between Burr and First Point				6-4/8	6-4/8	0
Circumference at Smallest Place Between First and Second Points				5-3/8	5-2/8	
Circumference at Smallest Place Between Main Beam and Third Point				4-1/8	4	
Circumference at Smallest Place Between Second and Fourth Points				5-2/8	5-2/8	0
TOTALS			26	77-7/8	80-5/8	14

Column 1	26	Exact locality where killed Chama, N.M.
Column 2	77-7/8	Date killed 11/12/50 By whom killed Laurel Graham
Column 3	80-5/8	Present owner Laurel Graham
TOTAL	184-4/8	Address
BTRACT Column 4	14-6/8	Guide's Name and Address None
		Remarks: (Mention any abnormalities)
FINAL SCORE	169-6/8	

EDITION 29

Guide–Charles Easton
Owner–Harry Olcott

MULE DEER–
(typical)
2nd Prize
Score -- 169-6/8

Length–(R) 24-1/8	(L) 26
Greatest Spread–30-7/8	
Basal Circumference–(R) 6-4/8	(L) 6-4/8
Points–(R) 7	(L) 8
Locality–Chama, N. M. - 1950	
Hunter–Laurel Graham	
Guide–None	
Owner–Laurel Graham	

LAUREL GRAHAM

FOURTH COMPETITION | SECOND PRIZE

The Club's fourth competition heralded in the revised scoring system and a separate category for non-typical deer. Four typical and two non-typical mule deer received recognition at the competition. Laurel Graham's typical—with a final B&C score of 169-6/8 points—received the second prize. He was hunting near Chama, New Mexico, when he shot the buck on November 12, 1950.

AWARD-WINNING MULE DEER

FIFTH COMPETITION - OLLIE O. BARNEY, JR.

OLLIE O. BARNEY, JR.

FIFTH COMPETITION | THIRD PRIZE

The fifth competition included three typical mule deer, including Ollie O. Barney's buck scoring 183 points, which earned him a third prize. Ollie was hunting the famed Kaibab Forest in Arizona when he shot the buck in 1948. It's a classic 5x5 with no abnormal points and a greatest spread of 30-2/8 inches.

BOONE AND CROCKETT CLUB

% Am. Museum of Natu[ral History]
Central Park West at
New York 24, New York

MULE and BLACKTAIL DEER

OFFICIAL

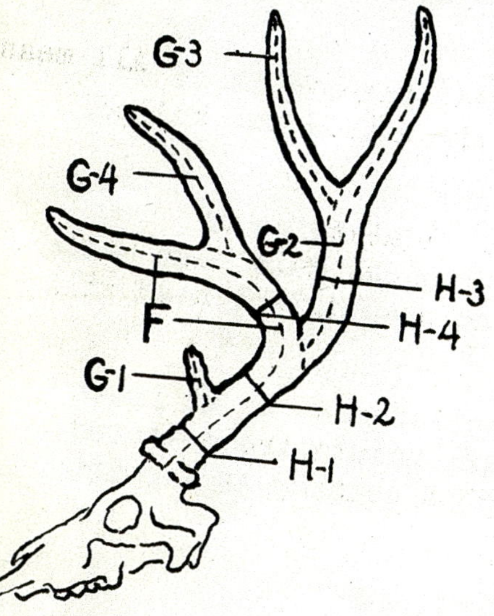

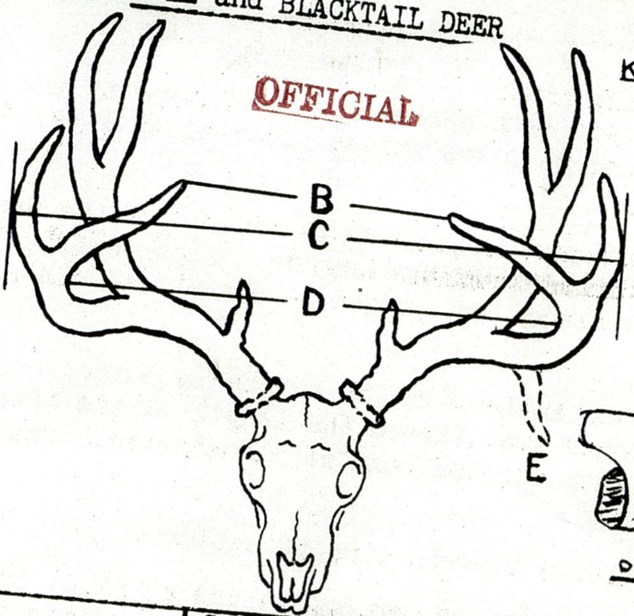

KIND OF DEER M[ule]

MULE D[EER]
(ty[pical])

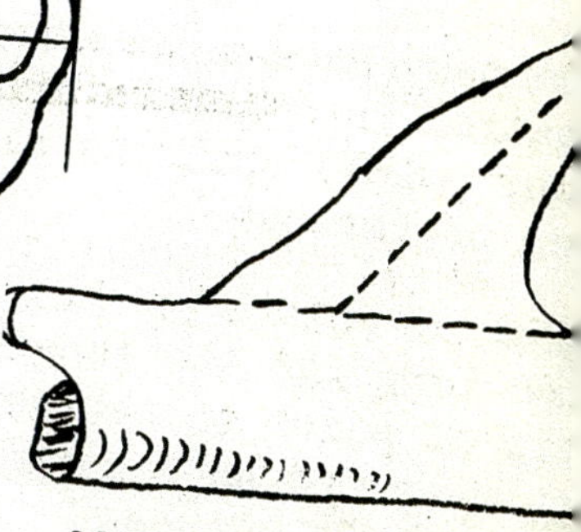

DETAIL OF POINT MEASUR[EMENT]

SEE OTHER SIDE FOR INSTRUCTIONS

	Supplementary Data R.	Supplementary Data L.	Column 1 Spread Credit	Column 2 Right Antler	Column 3 Left Antler	Col[umn 4] Dif[ference]
Number of Points on Each Antler	5	5				
Tip to Tip Spread	24 4/8					
Greatest Spread	30 2/8					
Inside Spread of MAIN BEAMS 24 4/8 — Spread credit may equal but not exceed length of longer antler			24 4/8			
IF Inside Spread of Main Beams exceeds longer antler length, enter difference						
Total of Lengths of all Abnormal Points						
Length of Main Beam				25	22 3/8	[illegible]
Length of First Point, if present				1 6/8	2 4/8	
Length of Second Point				18 2/8	19 4/8	[illegible]
Length of Third Point, if present				9 6/8	10 6/8	[illegible]
Length of Fourth Point, if present				11	10 5/8	[illegible]
Circumference at Smallest Place Between Burr and First Point				5	4 6/8	[illegible]
Circumference at Smallest Place Between First and Second Points				4 3/8	4 4/8	[illegible]
Circumference at Smallest Place Between Main Beam and Third Point.				3 7/8	3 6/8	[illegible]
Circumference at Smallest Place Between Second and Fourth Points				4 2/8	4 1/8	[illegible]
TOTALS			24 4/8	83 2/8	82 3/8	7 1/8

Column 1	24 4/8
Column 2	83 2/8
Column 3	82 3/8
TOTAL	190 1/8
Column 4	7 1/8
FINAL SCORE	183

Exact locality where killed North Kaibab Forrest, Arizona

Date killed Oct. 1948 By whom killed Ollie O. Barney, J[r.]

Present owner Ollie O Barney

Address

Guide's Name and Address none

Remarks: (Mention any abnormalities) [illegible]

WIN COULTAS

FIFTH COMPETITION | FIRST PRIZE

This impressive non-typical buck was shot by Win Coultas on November 4, 1924, near Iron Creek just north of Keller, Washington. This mule deer received the first prize at the fifth competition with a score of 261-2/8 points. Key measurements include 32 scorable points totaling 90-3/8 inches in abnormal points, plus a greatest spread of 35 inches.

...North American Big Game Competition

BOONE AND CROCKETT CLUB

...TROPHIES
% Am. Museum of Natural ...
Central Park ... 79 ...
...York

AWARD-WINNING MULE DEER

FIFTH COMPETITION - WIN COULTAS

...and BLACKTAIL DEER

KIND OF DEER Mule de...

Non-ty...

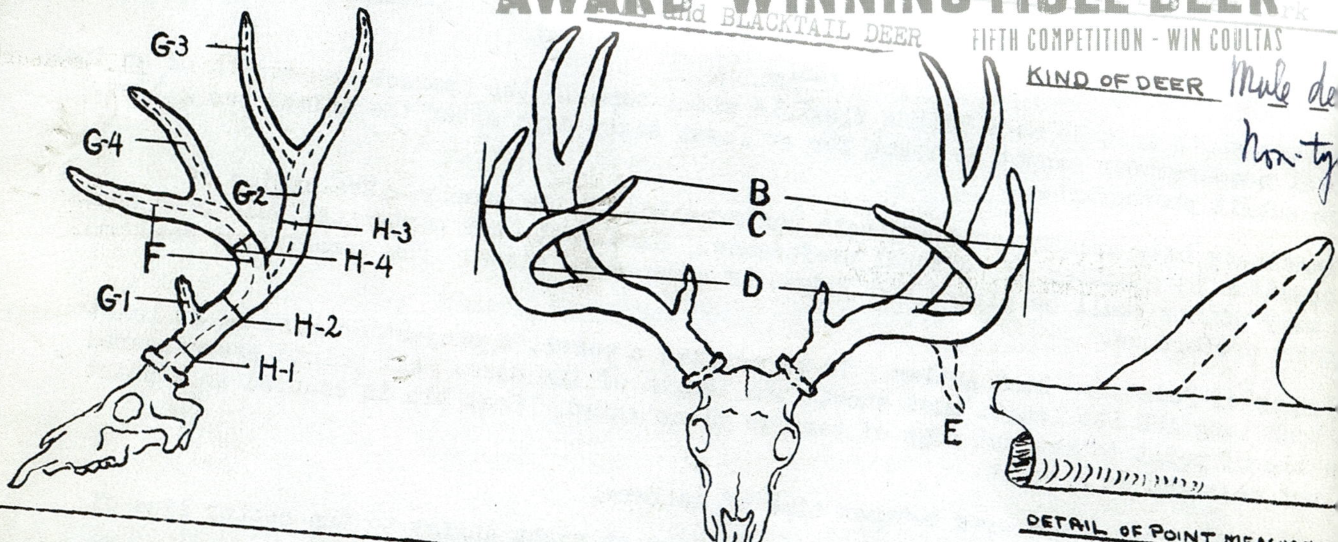

SEE OTHER SIDE FOR INSTRUCTIONS	Supplementary Data R.	Supplementary Data L.	Column 1 Spread Credit	Column 2 Right Antler	Column 3 Left Antler	Column 4 Differ...
A. Number of Points on Each Antler	13	19				
B. Tip to Tip Spread	24 1/8					
C. Greatest Spread	35					
D. Inside Spread of MAIN BEAMS 24 3/8 — Spread credit may equal but not exceed length of longer antler			24 3/8			
IF Inside Spread of Main Beams exceeds longer antler length, enter difference						
E. Total of Lengths of all Abnormal Points						90
F. Length of Main Beam				25 3/8	26 2/8	1
G-1. Length of First Point, if present				4 2/8	4 3/8	
G-2. Length of Second Point				10 2/8	14 5/8	4
G-3. Length of Third Point, if present				10 4/8	5 5/8	4
G-4. Length of Fourth Point, if present				10 7/8	10	
Circumference at Smallest Place H-1. Between Burr and First Point				4 6/8	5 1/8	
Circumference at Smallest Place H-2. Between First and Second Points				4 7/8	5 3/8	
Circumference at Smallest Place H-3. Between Main Beam and Third Point,				3 7/8	3 7/8	—
Circumference at Smallest Place H-4. Between Second and Fourth Points				4 3/8	4 5/8	
TOTALS			24 3/8	79	79 7/8	12 3/8

90 3/8

ADD	Column 1	24 3/8
	Column 2	79
	Column 3	79 7/8
	TOTAL	183 2/8
SUBTRACT Column 4		12 3/8
FINAL SCORE		170 7/8
		90 3/8

Exact locality where killed Iron Creek, N. of Keller, Wash.

Date killed Nov. 4, 1924 By whom killed Win Coultas

Present owner Win Coultas Win Coultas

Address

Guide's Name and Address None

Remarks: (Mention any abnormalities)

~~183 2/8~~ 170 7/8 + 90 3/8 = 261 2/8

OK 261 2/8

3D EDITION RNABG 7

FRED C. HEUER

FIFTH COMPETITION | SECOND PRIZE

Fred C. Heuer's non-typical mule deer received a second prize at the Club's fifth competition. He shot the buck—scoring 248-6/8 points—in October 1940 in Washington's Okanogan County. This unique set of antlers has 9 points on the right side and 14 points on the left side for a total of 62 inches of abnormal points. The file includes correspondence detailing the measuring technique for the abnormal points. The Club's Records Committee Chair Harold E. Anthony responded, *I hope I have made myself clear but it would be a whole lot easier if these animals grew their horns without such abnormalities.*

OFFICIAL

OFFICIAL SCORING SYSTEM FOR NORTH AMERICAN BIG GAME TROPHIES — 2d prize 1951

Records of North American Big Game and North American Big Game Competition — BOONE AND CROCKETT CLUB — % Am. Museum of Natural History, Central Park West at 79th Street, New York 24, New York

MULE and BLACKTAIL DEER

KIND OF DEER Mule deer
Non-typical

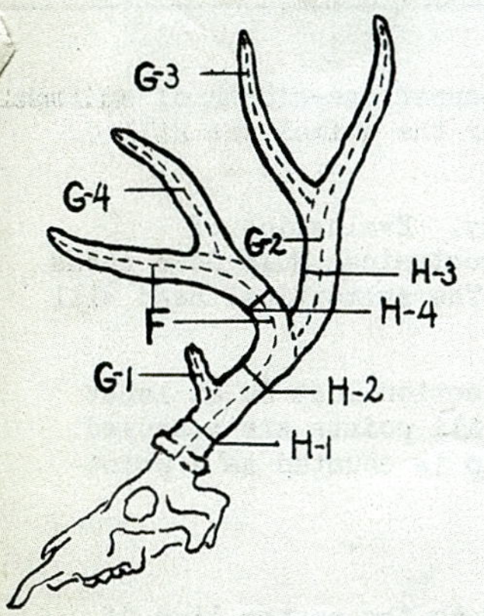

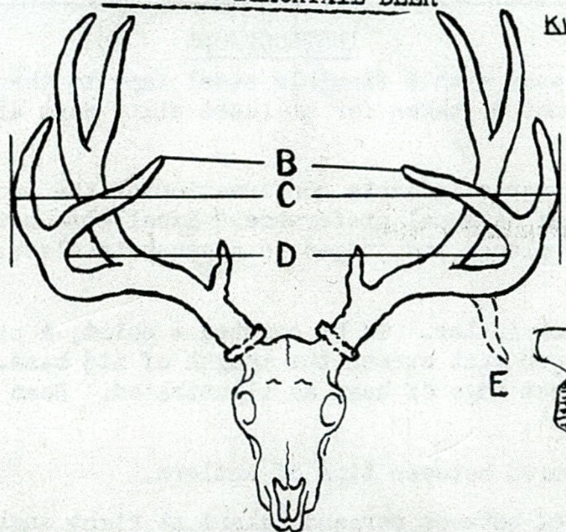

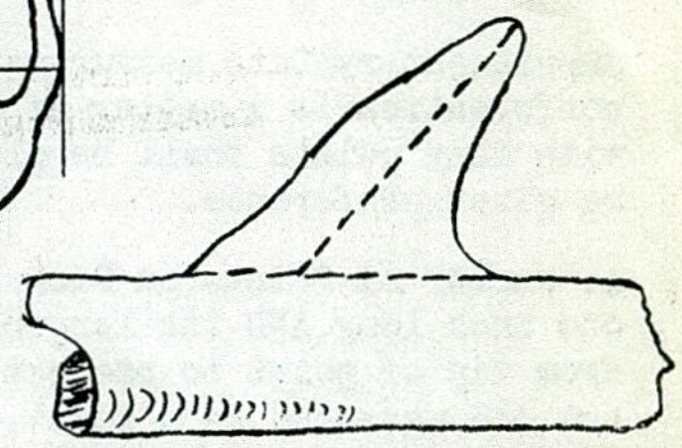

DETAIL OF POINT MEASUREMENT

SEE OTHER SIDE FOR INSTRUCTIONS	Supplementary Data R.	Supplementary Data L.	Column 1 Spread Credit	Column 2 Right Antler	Column 3 Left Antler	Column 4 Difference
A. Number of Points on Each Antler 7-8	9	14				
B. Tip to Tip Spread	22 7/8					
C. Greatest Spread	39 3/8					
D. Inside Spread of MAIN BEAMS 28 4 — Spread credit may equal but not exceed length of longer antler			27			
IF Inside Spread of Main Beams exceeds longer antler length, enter difference						—
E. Total of Lengths of all Abnormal Points						62
F. Length of Main Beam 2-3				27	25 4/8	1 4/8
G-1. Length of First Point, if present				2	2 5/8	5/8
G-2. Length of Second Point				15 2/8	14	~~2 2/8~~ 1 2/8
G-3. Length of Third Point, if present				10 4/8	10 5/8	1/8
G-4. Length of Fourth Point, if present				11 2/8	8 1/8	3 1/8
H-1. Circumference at Smallest Place Between Burr and First Point 5-6				5 5/8	5 6/8	1/8
H-2. Circumference at Smallest Place Between First and Second Points				4 6/8	5	2/8
H-3. Circumference at Smallest Place Between Main Beam and Third Point				4 5/8	4 4/8	1/8
H-4. Circumference at Smallest Place Between Second and Fourth Points				4 7/8	5 3/8	4/8
TOTALS Okanogan Co., Wash			27	85 7/8	81 4/8	6 3/8 ~~9 5/8~~ 15/8

ADD			
Column 1	27	Exact locality where killed	8 miles reserve Okanogan Co. Wash
Column 2	85 7/8	Date killed Oct. 1940	By whom killed Fred C. Heuer
Column 3	81 4/8	Present owner	~~Heuer~~ ~~Fred C. Heuer~~ Raymond R. Cross
6 3/8 TOTAL	194 3/8	Address	Washington
SUBTRACT Column 4	~~8~~ 9 5/8	Guide's Name and Address	None
FINAL SCORE	~~185 6/8~~ 184 6/8 62	Remarks: (Mention any abnormalities)	Payette ID See attached; 184 6/8 : 62 = 246 6/8; 83661

OK ~~246 6/8~~ ~~247 6/8~~ 248 6/8

3D EDITION RNABG 8

5th

328

BISON
BISON
BISON
STONE SHEEP
STONE SHEEP
STONE SHEEP
STONE SHEEP
WAPITI

SIXTH COMPETITION - 1953

The Club's sixth competition had an unprecedented number of mule deer trophies with eight typical and two non-typicals on display. Included in this impressive group was Edison Pillmore's Sagamore Hill Award-winning buck, scoring 203-7/8 points.

OFFICIAL SCORING SYSTEM FOR NORTH AMERICAN BIG GAME TROPHIES

North American
...e Committee

BOONE AND CROCKETT CLUB

Address Correspondence to:
Mrs. Grancel Fitz, Secretary
5 Tudor City Place, NYC 17, NY.

MULE and BLACKTAIL DEER

KIND OF DEER Mule deer

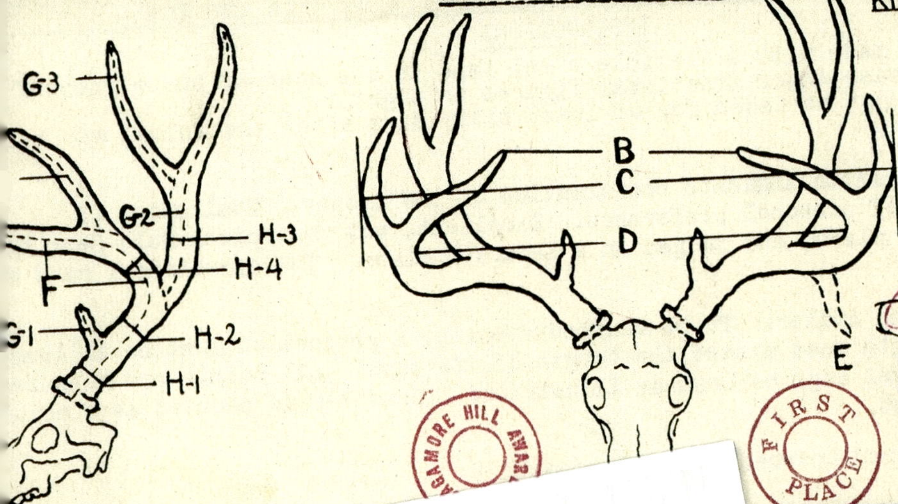

SIXTH N.A.B.G. COMPETITION 1953

BOONE AND CROCKETT OFFICIAL CLUB

medal
Sagamore Hill Award 1953
To Edison A. Pillmore

SAGAMORE HILL AWARD

FIRST PLACE

DETAIL OF POINT MEASUREMENT

	Column 1 Spread Credit	Column 2 Right Antler	Column 3 Left Antler	Column 4 Difference
	4/8			
				3 3/8
		24 5/8	26	1 3/8
		3	3	-
		18 3/8	18 2/8	1/8
		12 4/8	14 1/8	1 5/8
		12 7/8	14 4/8	1 5/8
		5 7/8	5 6/8	1/8
		5	5 2/8	2/8
... and Third Point,		4 5/8	4 1/8	4/8
Circumference at Smallest Place Between Second and Fourth Points		5 2/8	5 4/8	2/8
TOTALS	24 4/8	92 1/8	96 4/8	9 2/8

Column 1	24 4/8	Exact locality where killed	N. of Cowdrey, Colo., North Park, Col
Column 2	92 1/8	Date killed Oct. 1949	By whom killed Edison A. Pillmore
Column 3	96 4/8	Present owner	Mrs. E. A. Pillmore
TOTAL	213 1/8	Address	
SUBTRACT Column 4	9 2/8	Guide's Name and Address	
FINAL SCORE	203 7/8	Remarks: (Mention any abnormalities)	World Record 1953

North American Big Game Competition

sponsored by

BOONE AND CROCKETT

EDISON A. PILLMORE

SIXTH COMPETITION | FIRST PRIZE - SAGAMORE HILL AWARD

Edison A. Pillmore's typical mule deer scoring 203-7/8 inches was the highlight of the mule deer section during the Club's sixth competition at American Museum of Natural History. That score secured the buck as the new World's Record at the time and also garnered the Sagamore Hill Award—the first mule deer to receive that distinction. Edison was hunting north of Cowdrey, Colorado, near North Park when he harvested the buck during the 1949 season. The 6x6 buck has a 28-4/8 inch greatest spread and just two abnormal points deducting 3-3/8 from the final score.

At that time, the Sagamore Hill Medal was awarded for the best trophy entered in the contest, and was given by the Roosevelt family in memory of Theodore Roosevelt, Theodore Roosevelt Jr., and Kermit Roosevelt.

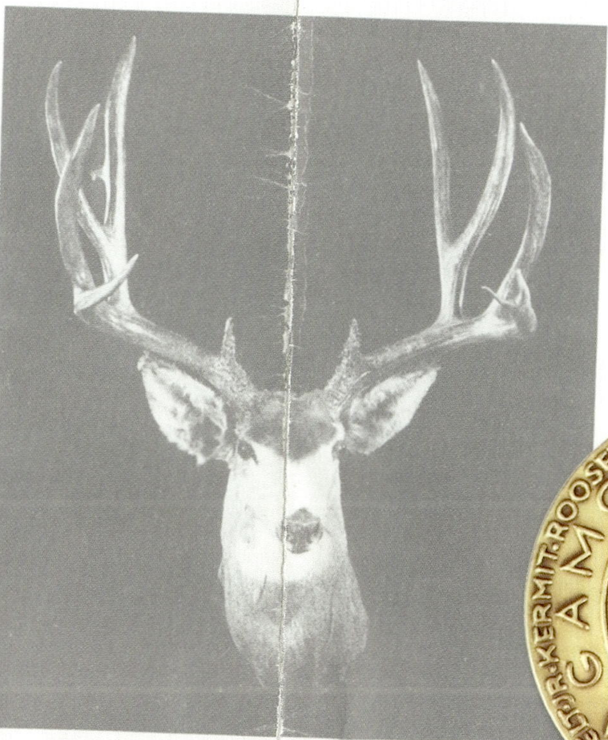

EER — (typical) — 1st Prize — NEW WORLD'S RECORD — SAGAMORE HILL AWARD
Score—203-7/8
Locality—Jackson County, Colo.—1949
Guide—None
Owner—Mrs. Edison A. Pillmore

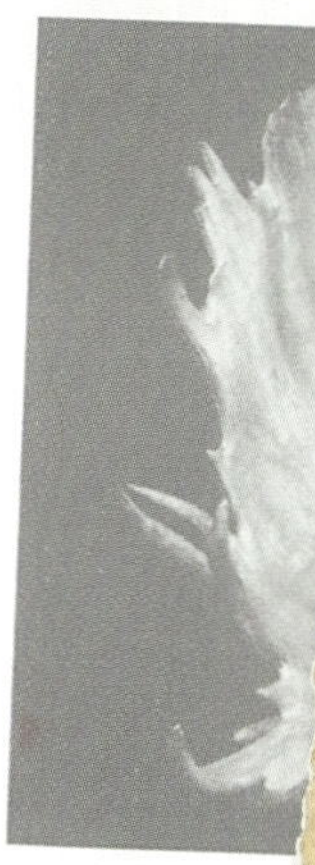

ULE DEER (non-typical) — 1st Prize

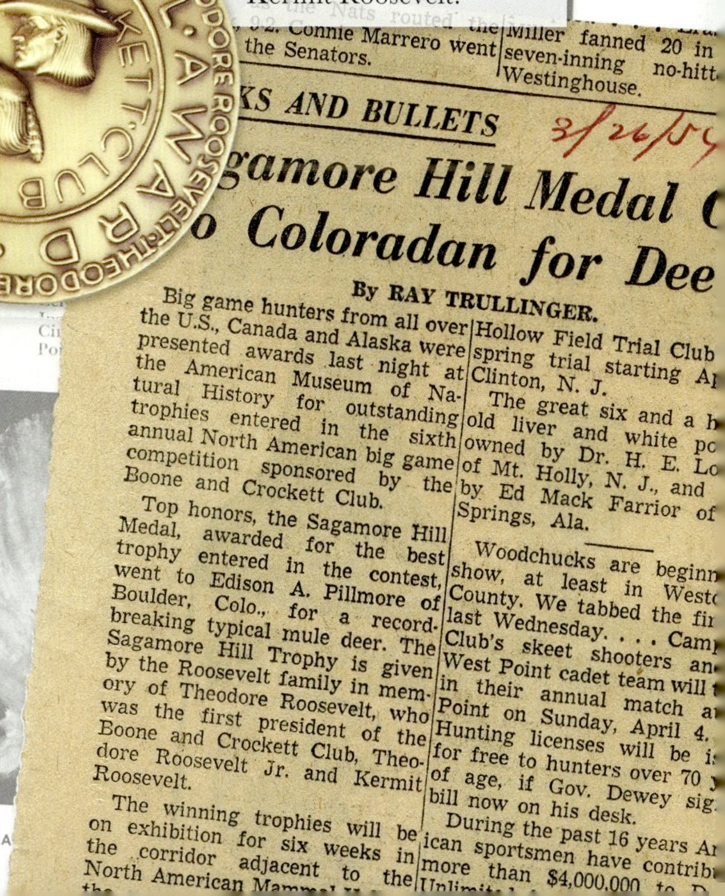

as the Nats routed the 9-2. Connie Marrero went the Senators.

Miller fanned 20 in seven-inning no-hitt Westinghouse.

KS AND BULLETS

3/26/54

gamore Hill Medal o Coloradan for Dee

By RAY TRULLINGER.

Big game hunters from all over the U.S., Canada and Alaska were presented awards last night at the American Museum of Natural History for outstanding trophies entered in the sixth annual North American big game competition sponsored by the Boone and Crockett Club.

Top honors, the Sagamore Hill Medal, awarded for the best trophy entered in the contest, went to Edison A. Pillmore of Boulder, Colo., for a record-breaking typical mule deer. The Sagamore Hill Trophy is given by the Roosevelt family in memory of Theodore Roosevelt, who was the first president of the Boone and Crockett Club, Theodore Roosevelt Jr. and Kermit Roosevelt.

The winning trophies will be on exhibition for six weeks in the corridor adjacent to the North American Mammal ...

Hollow Field Trial Club spring trial starting A Clinton, N. J.

The great six and a h old liver and white p owned by Dr. H. E. Lo of Mt. Holly, N. J., and by Ed Mack Farrior of Springs, Ala.

Woodchucks are beginn show, at least in West County. We tabbed the fi last Wednesday. . . . Cam Club's skeet shooters an West Point cadet team will in their annual match a Point on Sunday, April 4. Hunting licenses will be i for free to hunters over 70 of age, if Gov. Dewey sig bill now on his desk.

During the past 16 years A ican sportsmen have contrib more than $4,000,000 to ...

A.H. HENKEL

SIXTH COMPETITION | FIRST PRIZE

A.H. Henkel's non-typical mule deer has 22 scorable points, 11 per side, with a total of 52-7/8 inches of abnormal points adding into the final score of 253-3/8 points. A.H. shot the buck near his home in Rawlins, Wyoming, on September 15, 1952. The trophy was sent to the American Museum of Natural History in New York City for the sixth competition where the score was verified by B&C official measurers Ed McGuire and Grancel Fitz.

SEE OTHER SIDE FOR INSTRUCTIONS

	Supplementary Data R.	Supplementary Data L.					
ber of Points on Each Antler	11	11					
to Tip Spread	17	3/8					
atest Spread	34	3/8					
de Spread / AIN BEAMS 20 4/8 — Spread credit may equal but not exceed length of longer antler							
nside Spread of Main Beams exceeds longer er length, enter difference							
of Lengths of all Abnormal Points	52 7/8						
h of Main Beam					24 4/8	24 3/8	
gth of First Point, if present					2 4/8	4	
gth of Second Point					14 6/8	16	1
th of Third Point, if present					13 1/8	13 3/8	1
th of Fourth Point, if present					13 6/8	15 7/8	2
umference at Smallest Place een Burr and First Point					5 3/8	5 3/8	
umference at Smallest Place een First and Second Points					5 2/8	5 2/8	
umference at Samllest Place een Main Beam and Third Point					4 6/8	4 6/8	
mference at Smallest Place en Second and Fourth Points					6 2/8	6 1/8	
s	52 7/8		20 4/8		90 2/8	95 1/8	5

lumn 1	20 4/8	Exact locality where killed Rawlins, Wyoming
lumn 2	90 2/8	Date killed 9/15/52 By whom killed A. H. Henkel
lumn 3	95 1/8	Present owner A. H. Henkel
al	205 7/8	Address Rawlins, Wyoming
umn 4	5 3/8	Guide's Name and Address none
ult	200 4/8	Remarks:

Address Correspondence ... OFFICIAL
Mrs. Grancel Fitz, Secretary
5 Tudor City Place, NYC 17, NY.

KIND OF DEER Mule

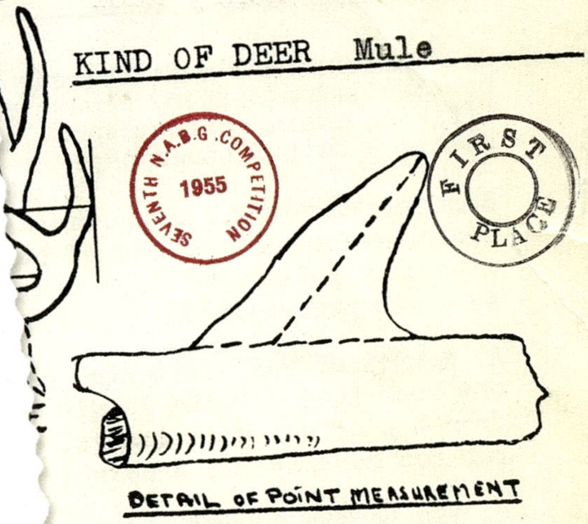

		Column 2 Right Antler	Column 3 Left Antler	Column 4 Difference
may equal but not ... of longer antler	26 2/8			
...eds longer				-
				3 4/8
...oints		27 6/8	26 7/8	7/8
		2 6/8	2 6/8	-
...nt		16 2/8	17 6/8	1 4/8
		12 4/8	13	4/8
...ent		15 5/8	15 1/8	4/8
...sent		5 1/8	5	1/8
...e		5 2/8		
...ce ...ts		4 3/8		
...ace ...Point.		5		
-3. Between ... Circumference at ... ace				
-4. Between Second and Fourth Points				
	26 2/8	94 5/8		

new World Record

TOTALS

...DD	Column 1	26 2/8	Exact locality where killed North Kaibab, A...
	Column 2	94 5/8	Date killed 1938 — By whom killed Ho...
	Column 3	95 1/8	Present owner ~~Horace T. Fowler~~ ALY M. Bo...
	TOTAL	216	Address
...UBTRACT	Column 4	7 2/8	Guide's Name and Address none
FINAL SCORE		208 6/8	Remarks: (Mention any abnormalities) card Trophy at ...

44

HORACE T. FOWLER
SEVENTH COMPETITION | FIRST PRIZE

The first prize at the seventh competition was given to Horace T. Fowler's typical mule deer scoring 208-6/8 points. It was declared the new World's Record, pushing out Edison Pillmore's buck that had set the mark at the previous competition. Horace was hunting in Arizona's north Kaibab in 1938 when he harvested the buck, which has a 30-inch greatest spread and G-2s measuring 16-2/8 and 17-6/8 inches.

Horace's buck has been surpassed by numerous deer and fallen down considerably in the overall ranking where it currently sits at 44. However, it still holds the No. 3 spot in Arizona.

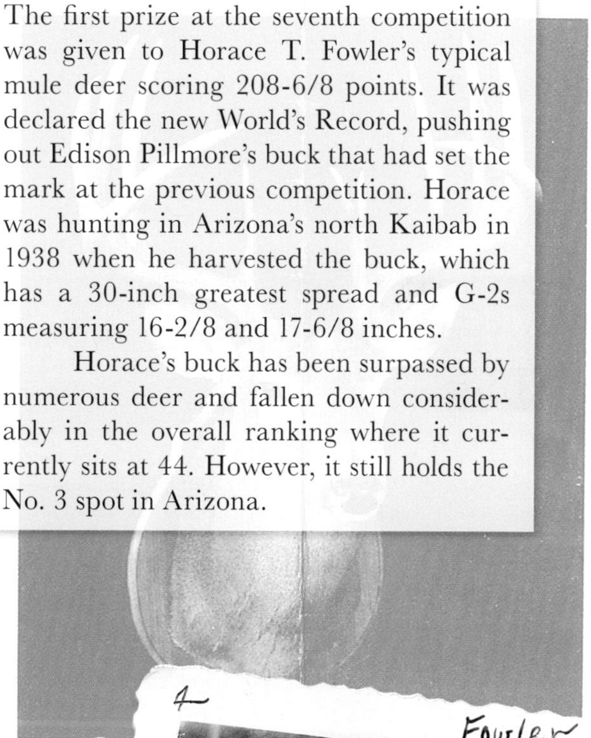

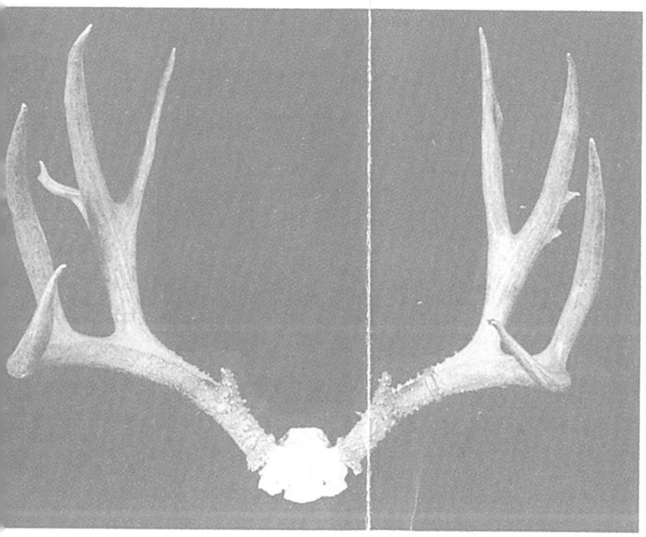

MULE DEER — (typical) — 1st Prize — NEW WORLD'S RECORD
Score—208-6/8

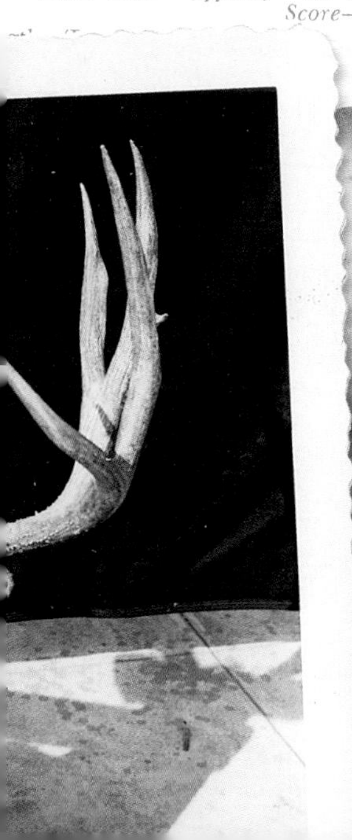

CLUB

Mrs. Grancel Fitz, Secr...
5 Tudor City Place, NYC 17

DEER

KIND OF DEER Mule De...

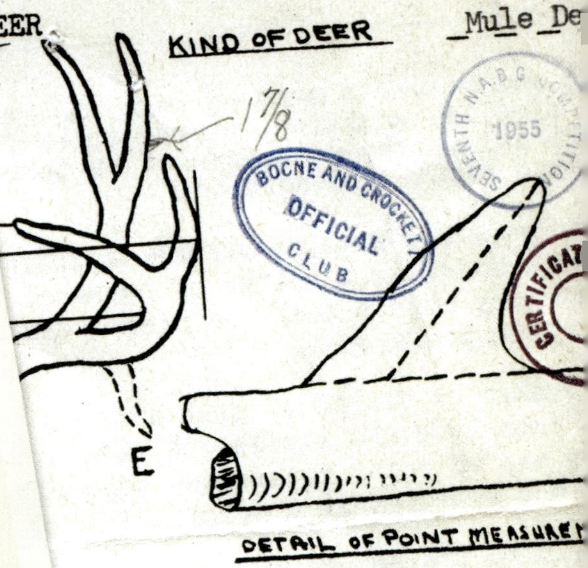

SEE ...

		Column 1 Spread Credit	Column 2 Right Antler	Column 3 Left Antler	Col... Dif...
...umber of ...	18 1/4				
...ip to Ti...	30 1/4				
...reatest Spread					
Inside Spread of MAIN BEAMS 22 3/4	Spread credit may equal but not exceed length of longer antler	22 3/4 ?			
IF Inside Spread of Main Beams exceeds longer antler length, enter difference					
Total of Lengths of all Abnormal Points					
Length of Main Beam			22 3/4	23 1/4	
... Length of First Point, if present			2 3/8	2	
... Length of Second Point			18 1/2	18	
...3. Length of Third Point, if present			14 7/8	14 3/4	
...4. Length of Fourth Point, if present			15 1/2	15 3/4	
Circumference at Smallest Place ...1. Between Burr and First Point			5 1/8	5 1/8	
Circumference at Smallest Place ...2. Between First and Second Points			4 5/8	4 3/4	
Circumference at Smallest Place ...3. Between Main Beam and Third Point,			4 1/4	4 1/4	
Circumference at Smallest Place ...4. Between Second and Fourth Points			4	4 1/4	
TOTALS		22 6/8	92	92 1/8	

...DD	Column 1	22 6/8	Exact locality where killed About 20 mi. NW of Walden, Jac...
	Column 2	92	Date killed 10/15/34 By whom killed G. B. Berger, ...
	Column 3	92 1/8	Present owner Denver Museum of Natural History
	...	206 7/8	Address City Park, Denver, Colorado
			None

G.B. BERGER, JR.

SEVENTH COMPETITION | CERTIFICATE OF MERIT

George B. Berger, Jr., shot this impressive typical mule deer on October 15, 1934, about 20 miles northwest of Walden in Jackson County, Colorado. The deer has a final B&C score of 199-7/8 points and received a Certificate of Merit at the Club's seventh competition. It was entered by the Denver Museum of Natural History (DMNH), which had received the trophy mule deer as a gift from George. The DMNH had it remounted as a full-body deer and placed it in a habitat group depicting mule deer in their winter phase (see photo, bottom left). The buck has three abnormal points, which deducted 4-7/8 inches from its final score.

COLORADO NATIONAL BANK

DENVER, COLO.

GEORGE B. BERGER
VICE PRESIDENT

Septe

Mrs. Grancel Fitz, Secret
Boone and Crockett Club
5 Tudor City Place,
New York 17, New York

Dear Mrs. Fitz:

Enclosed herewith are three photographs of the antlers of a mule deer which I killed about twenty miles northwest of Walden in Jackson County, Colorado, October 15, 1934.

I am also enclosing the Boone and Crockett Club official scoring chart showing the measurements. The antlers were measured by Mr. Albert C. Rogers, Curator of Mammals at the Denver Museum of Natural History. Both Mr. Rogers and I are a little uncertain as to the use of the two lines indicated D and accordingly ve not been totaled.

s to me that this mule deer head com- y with the one stated to be the new world's of which appears in your 1953 Big Game n.

s ago I presented this trophy to the tural History where it has now been mule deer buck in the Museum's new ting mule deer in their winter phase.

uld like further information as to this se me.

Yours very truly,

G. B. Berger

JOSEPH W. DOOLEY

SEVENTH COMPETITION | FIRST PRIZE

Joseph W. Dooley shot this award-winning non-typical mule deer in October 1954. Its entry score was 286-1/8 points with 25 scorable points. Decades later the buck was remeasured to verify discrepancies with the non-typical points and a new final score was established at 297-1/8 with 26 scorable points. This deer is the largest non-typical taken in Elko County, and still ranks as the No. 3 buck from Nevada.

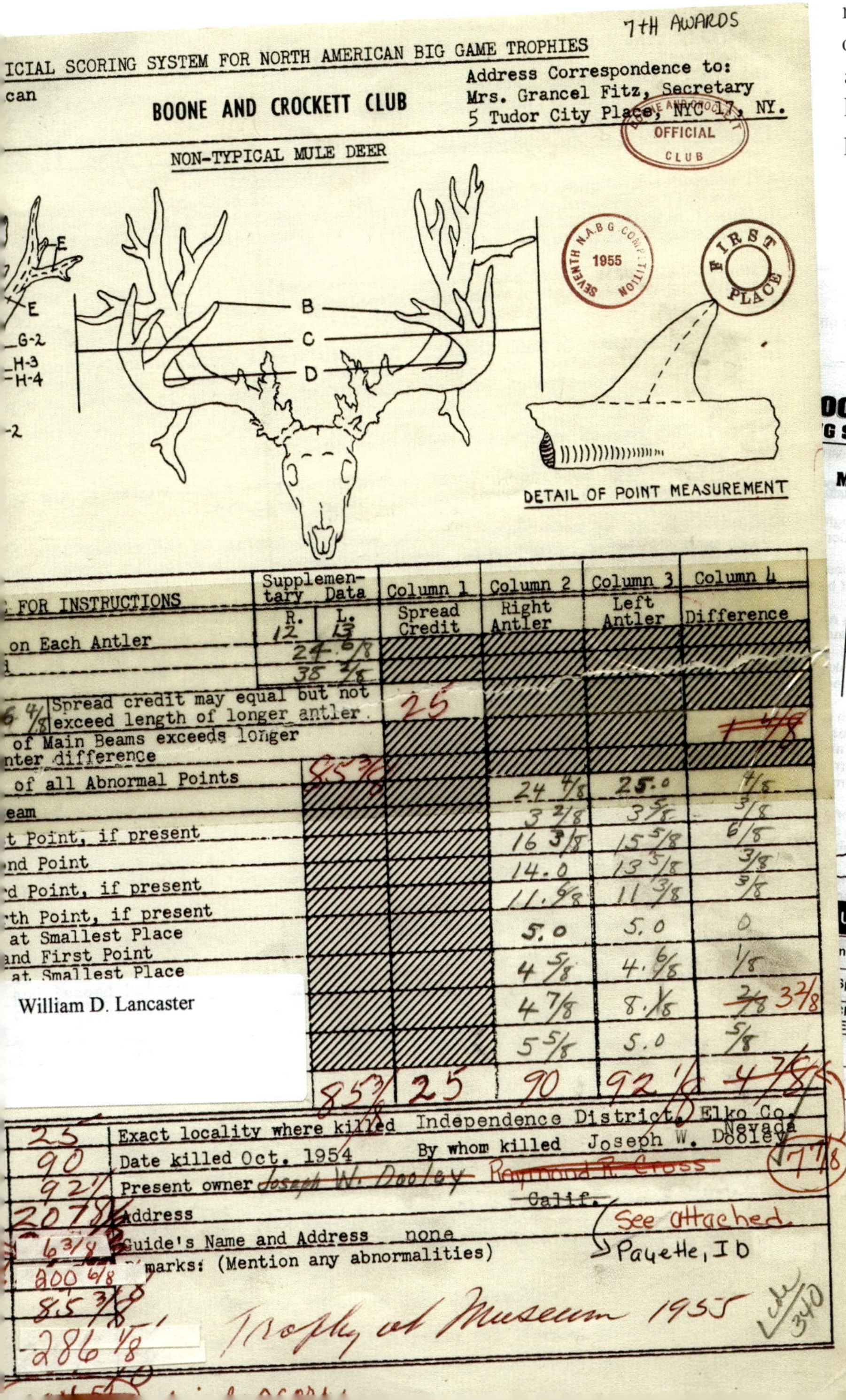

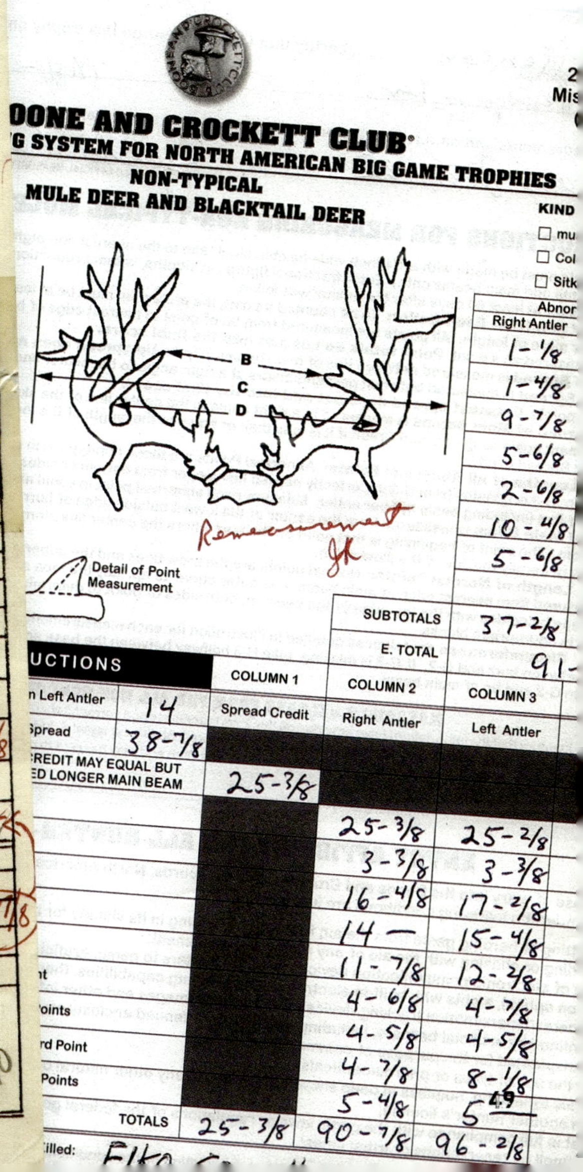

AWARD-WINNING MULE DEER

EIGHTH COMPETITION - PASCO SCARPELLA

PASCO SCARPELLA

EIGHTH COMPETITION | HONORABLE MENTION

The eighth competition featured 11 typical mule deer in the public display including Pasco Scarpella's unique buck. He was hunting six miles above Lyons, Colorado, on October 31, 1955, when he shot the deer. It has a final score of 192-1/8 points. The impressive G-2 points measure 21-2/8 and 21 inches. In a letter to the Club dated November 2, 1956, Pasco states, ...*There is very little we can add to the picture and statistics, other than the circumferences are unusually large and the height of points are beyond belief.... Incidentally, I practice taxidermy and have this head in my trophy room.*

BOONE AND CROCKETT CLUB

Address Corr
Mrs. Grancel
Tudor City

KIND OF D

DETAIL OF POIN

	Column 1	...n 2 ...t ...r	Column ... Left Antle...
...Point, if present		24 4/8	24 1/8
G-2. Length of Second Point		2 2/8	1 6/8
G-3. Length of Third Point, if present		21 2/8	20 6/8
G-4. Length of Fourth Point, if present		15 4/8	13
Circumference at Smallest Place H-1. Between Burr and First Point		7 7/8	11
Circumference at Smallest Place H-2. Between First and Second Points		5 2/8	5 3/8
Circumference at Smallest Place H-3. Between Main Beam and Third Point.		5	5 2/8
Circumference at Smallest Place H-4. Between Second and Fourth Points		6	5 1/8
		4 2/8	4 6/8
TOTALS	20.3	91.7	91.1

ADD OK	Column 1	20.3
	Column 2	91.7
	Column 3	91.1
	TOTAL	203.3
SUBTRACT Column 4		11 2
FINAL SCORE		192 1/8

Exact locality where killed South of [illegible] Co.

Date killed 10/31/55 By whom killed PASCO SCARPELL

Present owner Pasco Scarpella

Address Lafayette

Guide's Name and Address none

Remarks: (Mention any abnormalities)

at Museum

AWARD-WINNING MULE DEER

EIGHTH COMPETITION - JOHN F. SCHURLE

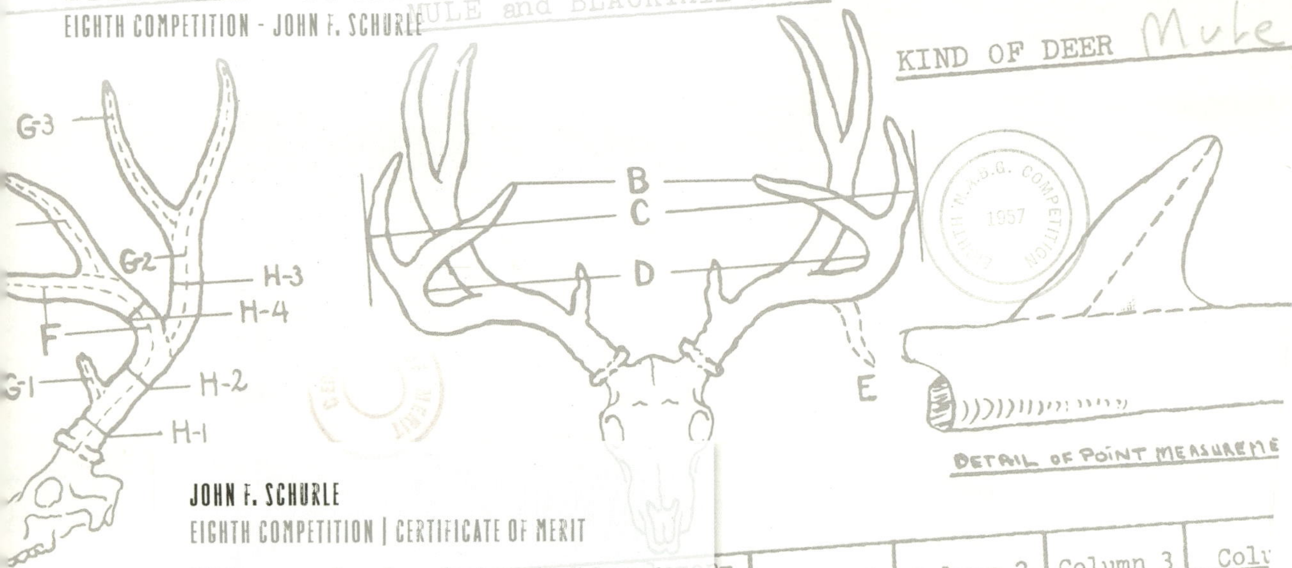

JOHN F. SCHURLE

EIGHTH COMPETITION | CERTIFICATE OF MERIT

This exceptional typical mule deer taken near Cashmere, Washington, was shot in 1913 by John F. Schurle. Forty-five years later, it was entered in the Club's eighth competition by William H. Schott. The buck has a final score of 200-1/8 points with no abnormal points and a greatest spread of 32-2/8 points. Included with the entry was a photo of another mule deer owned by William that was also shot by John. No scoring information was enclosed, just the photo and this noted in the letter, *"We are also enclosing picture of another of our collection—a Mule Deer Freak head of many points. A beautiful head of 31 points."* Inscription on the back indicates the bird is a stuffed magpie.

Mule Deer head. As this trophy
we are sending two 8x10 Photograp
exhibited.

Should the trophy win an award,
Certificate made out to William H. Schott ,as
~~xxxx~~ died in 1930.

We are also enclosing picture of another of our
collection a Mule Deer Freak head of many points
A beautiful head of 31 points.

We also have another Mule Deer . Montana White Tail
A Mountain Sheep Head very large horns but not the largest
Large Elk Head . small Bear Head . You see the Market with
these trophies hanging on the walls
of our own

OFFICIAL SCORING SYSTEM FOR NORTH AMERICAN BIG GA[illegible]

Spencer L. Darrar 241 7/8
Madras, OR ID: 40743
non-typical mule deer 8th
Date of Kill:
Kill Location:

Records of North American
Big Game Committee

BOONE AND CROCKETT CLUB

NON-TYPICAL MULE DEER

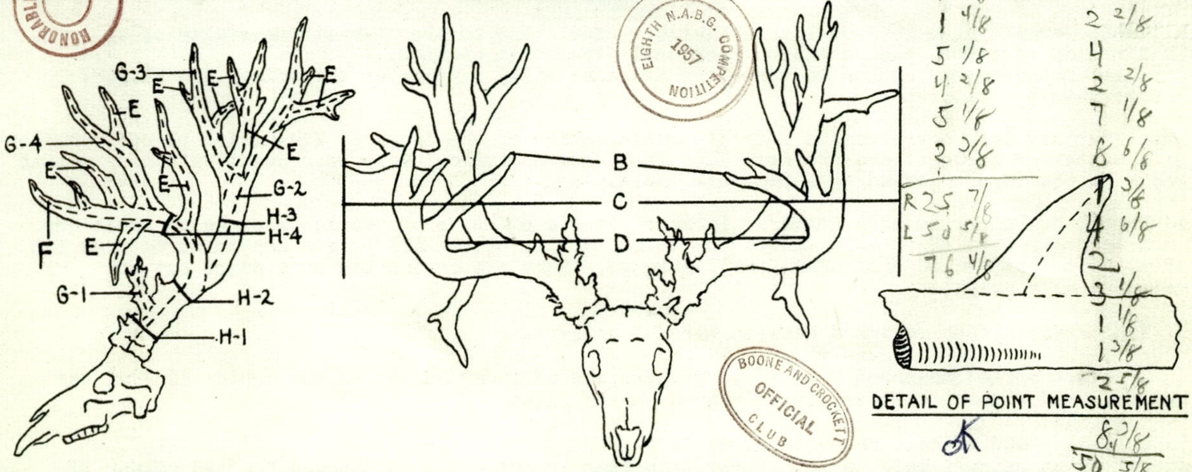

SEE OTHER SIDE FOR INSTRUCTIONS	Supplementary Data R.	Supplementary Data L.	Column 1	Column 2	Column 3	Column 4
A. Number of Points on Each Antler	11	19	Spread Credit	Right Antler	Left Antler	Difference
B. Tip to Tip Spread	17					
C. Greatest Spread	37 6/8					
D. Inside Spread of MAIN BEAMS 25 — Spread credit may equal but not exceed length of longer antler			24 5/8			
IF Inside Spread of Main Beams exceeds longer antler length, enter difference						3/8
E. Total of Lengths of all Abnormal Points	76 4/8					
F. Length of Main Beam				24 5/8	24 2/8	3/8
G-1. Length of First Point, if present				2 2/8	2 1/8	1/8
G-2. Length of Second Point				13 6/8	10 1/8	3 5/8
G-3. Length of Third Point, if present				8 5/8	7	1 5/8
G-4. Length of Fourth Point, if present				10 1/8	7 4/8	2.5
H-1. Circumference at Smallest Place Between Burr and First Point				5 2/8	5 2/8	—
H-2. Circumference at Smallest Place Between First and Second Points				4 6/8	4 7/8	.1
H-3. Circumference at Samllest Place Between Main Beam and Third Point				4 2/8	4 7/8	.5
H-4. Circumference at Smallest Place Between Second and Fourth Points				4 7/8	5 2/8	.3
TOTALS	76 4/8		24 5/8	78.4	71.2	9.4 9 4/8

ADD	Column 1	24.5	Exact locality where killed Jefferson Co. Oregon
	Column 2	78.4	Date killed 10/17/53 By whom killed Spencer L Darrar
	Column 3	71.2	Present owner SPENCER L DARRAR
	Total	175.2	Address STAR ROUTE
SUBTRACT	Column 4	9.4	Guide's Name and Address MADRAS, OREGON
	Result	165.3	Remarks: (Mention any abnormalities) none
	Add Line E Total	76.4	
	FINAL SCORE	[illegible] 241 3/8	At Museum

SPENCER L. DARRAR

EIGHTH COMPETITION | HONORABLE MENTION

This 30-point non-typical mule deer was shot on October 17, 1953, by Spencer Darrar near Hay Creek in Jefferson County, Oregon. Spencer sent the buck to the Club's eighth competition where it received an honorable mention. For unspecified reasons, the deer was dropped from the Club's records database. Fortunately, the hunter contacted the Club in 2012 and his trophy was reinstated, taking its rightful place in the archives. The buck has an impressive 37-6/8-inch greatest spread. Over 76 inches of abnormal points contribute to the final B&C score of 241-3/8 points.

COLUMBIAN BLACKTAIL DEER—1st Prize
Score—*151-4/8*

Length—(R) 20-3/8 (L) 19-1/8
Circumference—(R) 4-5/8 (L) 4-7/8
Points—(R) 5 (L) 5
Inside Spread—16-4/8
Locality—Marion Co., Oregon—1958
Hunter—John Davenport

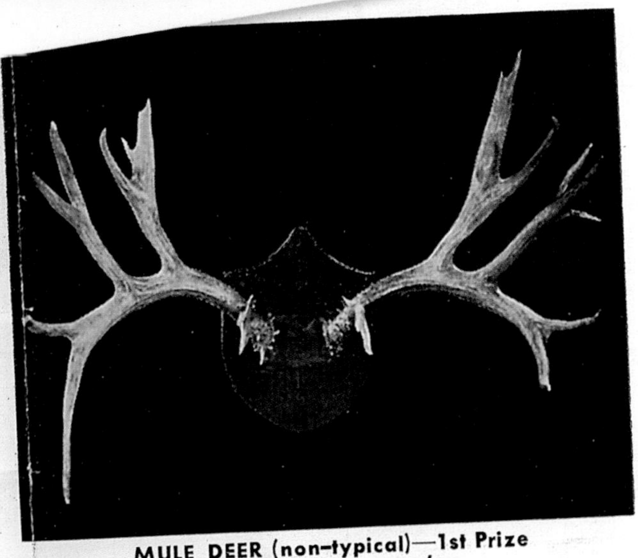

MULE DEER (non-typical)—1st Prize
Score—*178-2/8 : 62 = 240-2/8*

Length—(R) 27-2/8 (L) 25-3/8
Circumference—(R) 5 (L) 5
Points—(R) 10 (L) 11
Inside Spread—29-4/8
Locality—Blaine Co., Idaho—1957
Hunter—Roger A. Crowder

ROGER A. CROWDER

NINTH COMPETITION | FIRST PRIZE

The Club's ninth competition featured 12 impressive mule deer entries, eight typical deer, and four non-typical deer. Roger A. Crowder's non-typical, scoring 240-2/8 points, was the top prize winner. The buck—killed on November 9, 1957, in Blaine County, Idaho—has 21 scorable points with a total of 62 inches of abnormal points adding into the final score. The final score changed to 242-4/8 after the double penalty for excessive spread was eliminated in 1990.

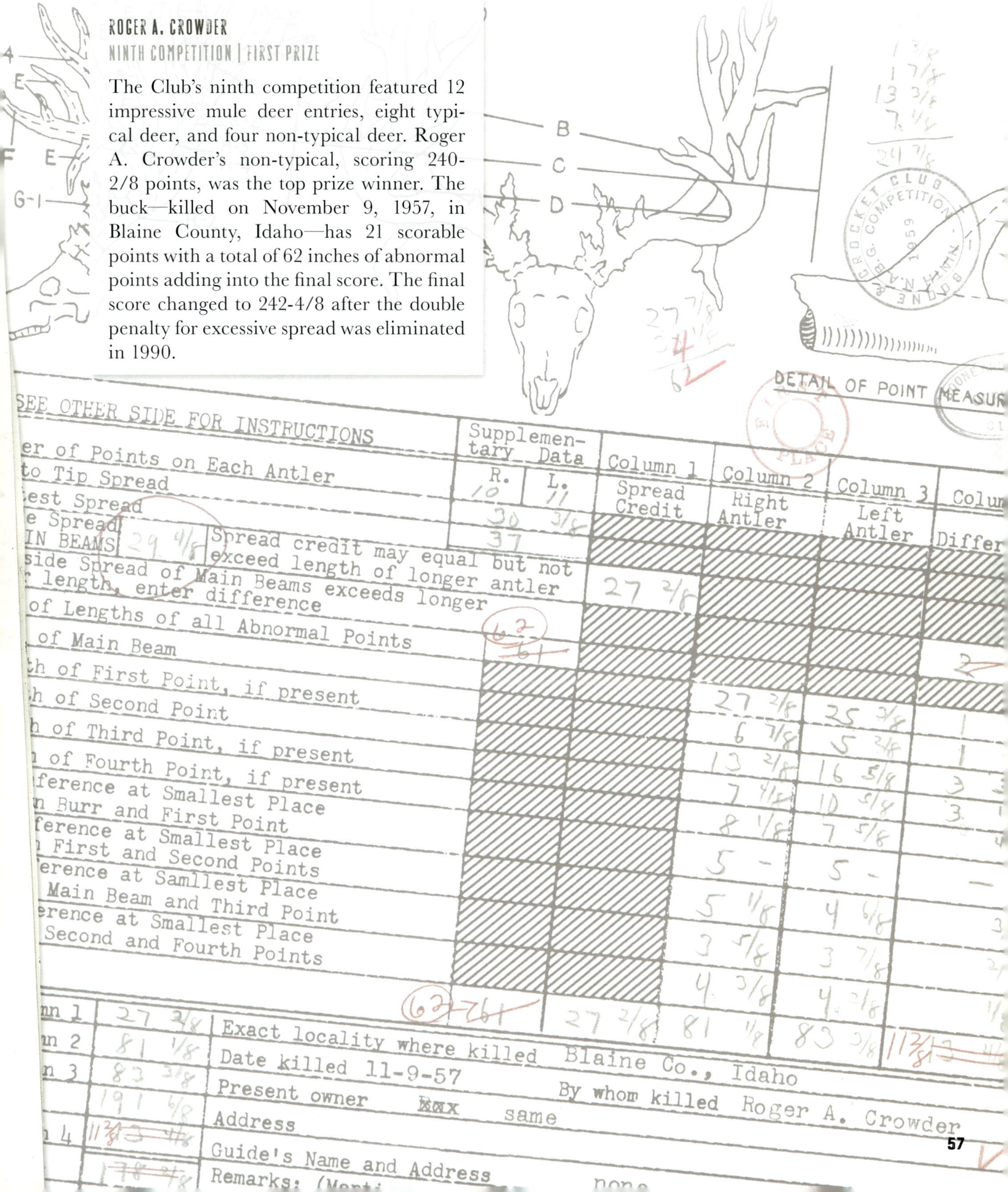

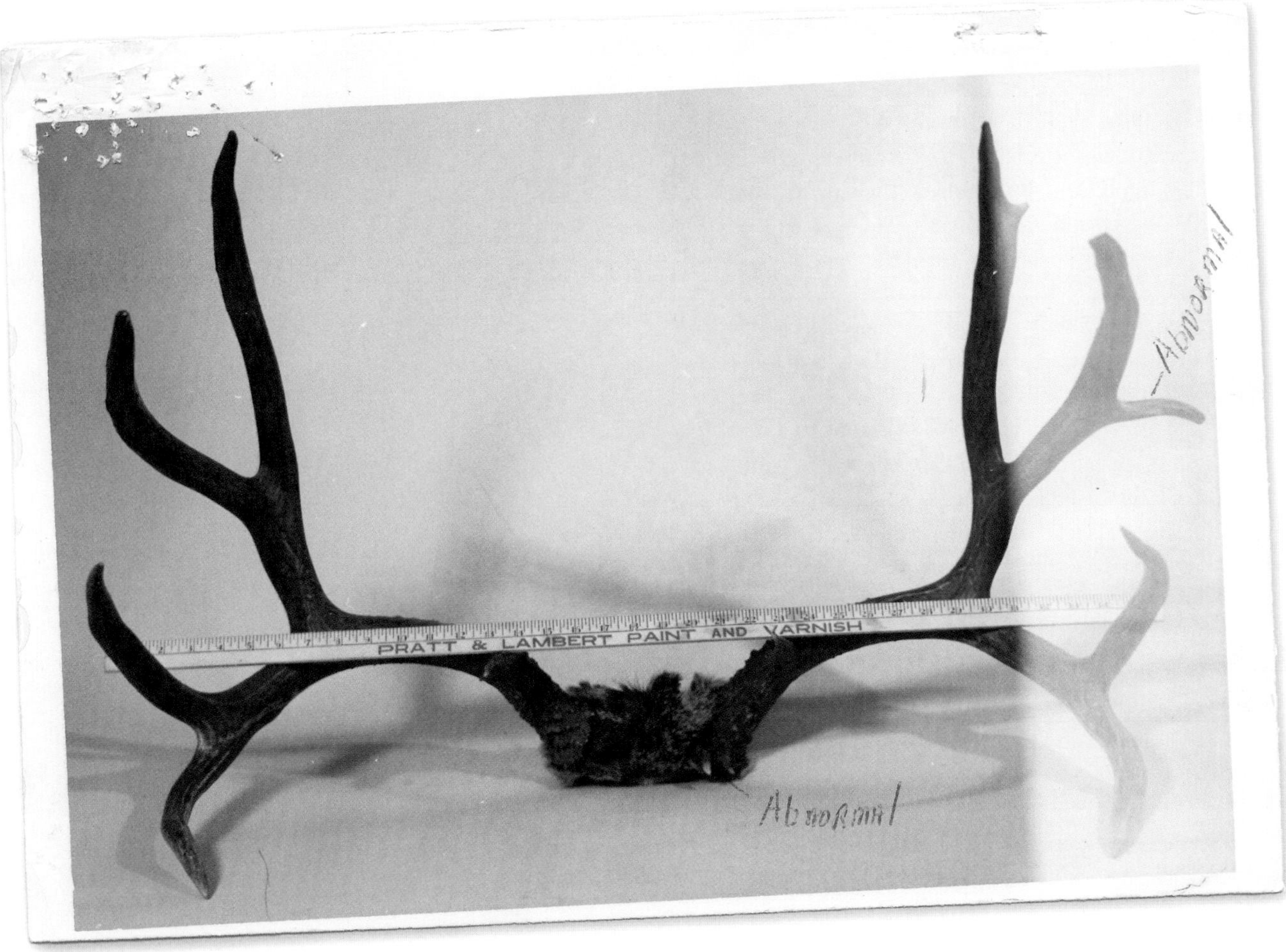

GARY L. ALBERTSON

TENTH COMPETITION | FIRST PRIZE

Gary L. Albertson was hunting near Uinta County, Wyoming, on October 30, 1960, when he harvested this impressive typical buck scoring 214-2/8 points. It has two small abnormal points as indicated in the photographs resulting in a total deduction of 5-2/8 inches. The buck's score was adjusted in 1990 when the Club removed the excessive spread penalty from the scoring system. This change increased the score on Gary's deer to 215-5/8 points once the 1-3/8-inch penalty was discarded. The buck currently ranks as a tie for the fifth-largest typical mule deer ever entered. It also ranks as the second-largest buck from Wyoming, listed only behind the famed Hoback Buck.

OFFICIAL SCORING S

Records of North American
Big Game Committee

NY.

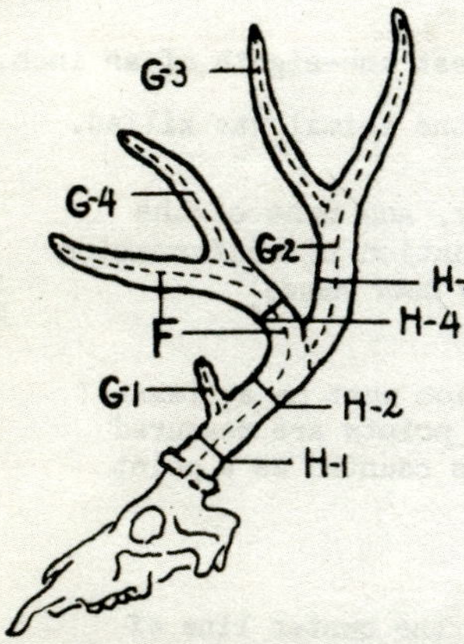

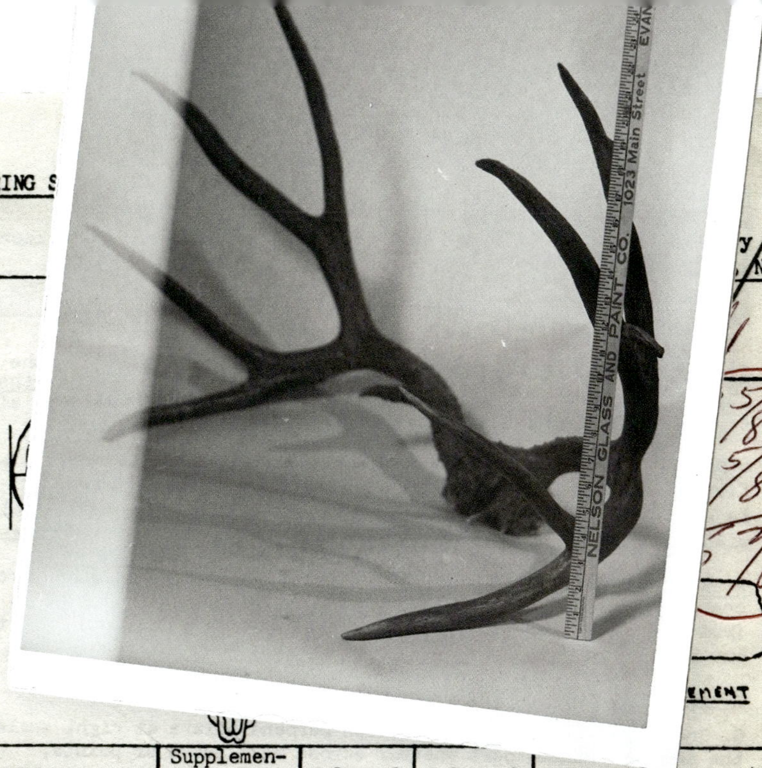

FIRST PLACE

SEE OTHER SIDE FOR INSTRUCTIONS	Supplementary Data R.	Supplementary Data L.	Column 1 Spread Credit	Column 2 Right Antler	Column 3 Left Antler	Column 4 Difference
A. Number of Points on Each Antler	5	7				
B. Tip to Tip Spread	27.5					
C. Greatest Spread	36.3					
D. Inside Spread of MAIN BEAMS 29.4 — Spread credit may equal but not exceed length of longer antler			28 1/8			
IF Inside Spread of Main Beams exceeds longer antler length, enter difference						~~1.3~~
E. Total of Lengths of all Abnormal Points						5.2
F. Length of Main Beam				26.7	28.1	1.2
G-1. Length of First Point, if present				3.7	4.3	.4
G-2. Length of Second Point				20.	19.	1.
G-3. Length of Third Point, if present				14.5	16.	1.3
G-4. Length of Fourth Point, if present				13.4	12.5	.7
H-1. Circumference at Smallest Place Between Burr and First Point				5.3	5.3	—
H-2. Circumference at Smallest Place Between First and Second Points				4.6	4.6	—
H-3. Circumference at Smallest Place Between Main Beam and Third Point.				4.4	4.4	—
H-4. Circumference at Smallest Place Between Second and Fourth Points				4.6	4.6	—
TOTALS			28 1/8	98.2	99.4	~~11.5~~ 10 3/8

ADD	Column 1	28.1	Exact locality where killed Uinta Co. Wyo.
	Column 2	98.2	Date killed 10/30/60 By whom killed Sara L. Albertson
	Column 3	99.4	Present owner Cabela's, Inc. One Cabela Drive Sydney, NE 69160 ~~Don Schaufler~~
	TOTAL	225.7	Address Evanston Wyo.
SUBTRACT Column 4		10 3/8 11.5	Guide's Name and Address
FINAL SCORE		~~214.2~~ OK	Remarks: (Mention any abnormalities) Ennis MT 59729

215 5/8 ~~owner: Spanky Greenville~~

see attached

OFFICIAL SCORING SYSTEM FOR NORTH AMERICAN BIG GAME TROPHIES

Records of North American Big Game Committee

BOONE AND CROCKETT CLUB

Address Correspondence to: Mrs. Grancel Fitz, Secretary 5 Tudor City Place, NYC 17, NY.

NON-TYPICAL MULE DEER

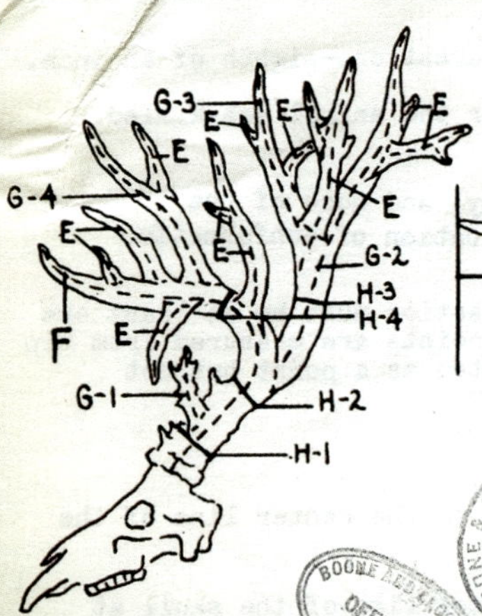

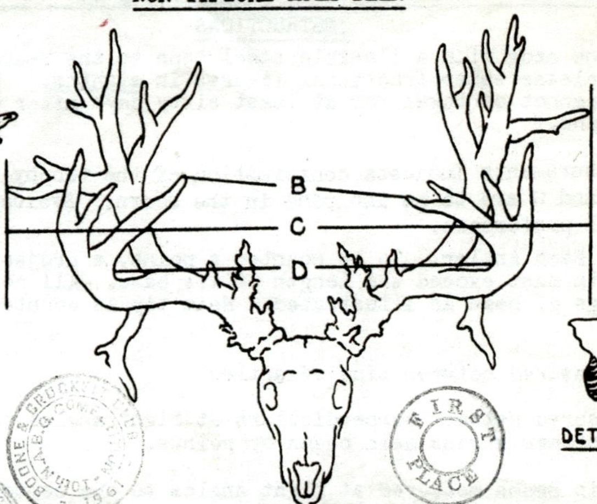

R	L
8.1	2.1
3.3	10.3
7.4	3.5
2.7	5.3
2.4	3.0
1.5	3.7
3.1	7.1
3.1	4.7
4.7	2.6
38.1	1.0
	44.1

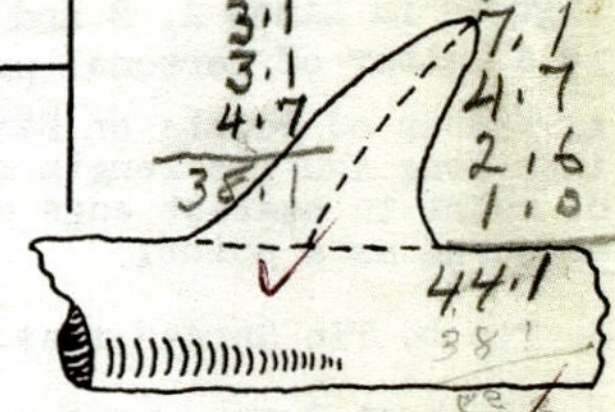

DETAIL OF POINT MEASUREMENT

SEE OTHER SIDE FOR INSTRUCTIONS	Supplementary Data R.	Supplementary Data L.	Column 1 Spread Credit	Column 2 Right Antler	Column 3 Left Antler	Column 4 Difference
A. Number of Points on Each Antler	14	13				
B. Tip to Tip Spread	20					
C. Greatest Spread	43 4/8					
D. Inside Spread of MAIN BEAMS 20 5/8 — Spread credit may equal but not exceed length of longer antler			20 5/8			
IF Inside Spread of Main Beams exceeds longer antler length, enter difference						—
E. Total of Lengths of all Abnormal Points	82 2/8					
F. Length of Main Beam				23 6/8	22 4/8	1 2/8
G-1. Length of First Point, if present				5 2/8	5 6/8	4/8
G-2. Length of Second Point				19 4/8	19 7/8	3/8
G-3. Length of Third Point, if present				12 6/8	11 4/8	1 2/8
G-4. Length of Fourth Point, if present				7 3/8	6 5/8	6/8
H-1. Circumference at Smallest Place Between Burr and First Point				5 7/8	6 —	1/8
H-2. Circumference at Smallest Place Between First and Second Points				5 1/8	5 1/8	—
H-3. Circumference at Samllest Place Between Main Beam and Third Point				5 3/8	5 2/8	1/8
H-4. Circumference at Smallest Place Between Second and Fourth Points				4 4/8	4 6/8	2/8
TOTALS	82 2/8		20 5/8	89 4/8	87 3/8	4 5/8

ADD	Column 1	20 5/8	Exact locality where killed Ruby Mts. Mont
	Column 2	89 4/8	Date killed 10/30/60 By whom killed Peter Zemljak
	Column 3	87 3/8	Present owner Peter Zemljak
	Total	197 4/8	Address
SUBTRACT	Column 4	4 5/8	Guide's Name and Address None
	Result	192 7/8	Remarks: (Mention any abnormalities)
Add Line E Total		82 2/8	
FINAL SCORE		275 1/8	368

PETER ZEMLJAK
TENTH COMPETITION | FIRST PLACE AWARD

Peter Zemljak's non-typical mule deer received a first place award at the Club's tenth competition with a score of 275-1/8 points. This buck has 29 scorable points with the total length of abnormal points recorded at 82-2/8 inches. Peter shot the deer in Montana's Ruby Mountains. In a note from Betty Fitz in the B&C office to Jack Atcheson, who was handling the taxidermy and measuring for Peter's buck, she states, "*Thank you very much for the non-typical mule deer photograph. This is a beautiful trophy, and my only regret is that I did not shoot it!*"

The buck remains the second-largest non-typical taken in Montana. It's topped only by Peter's father, who shot a non-typical scoring 275-6/8, just two years after his son harvested this deer. Peter is pictured at right with both bucks.

Non-typical Mule Deer Shot by Mr. [illegible] on Nov. 26, 1926. Killed 20 miles [illegible] of Chip lake, Alberta. Holding same is my charming secre[illegible] Mrs. Pare' (Photographed by W. H. McDonald, [illegible] Officer).

ED BRODER

TENTH COMPETITION | CERTIFICATE OF MERIT

The highlight of the tenth competition was Ed Broder's new World's Record non-typical mule deer, which scores 355-2/8 points. It has held this top spot ever since it was declared the World's Record in 1961. The buck has an incredible 43 scorable points, with a total of 147-7/8 non-typical inches. Ed sent the Club his account of the hunt for use in the 1964 edition of *Records of North American Big Game*. The buck was taken on November 26, 1926, near Chip Lake in Alberta.

Ed died in 1968, and a court battle over the ownership of the deer would split his family apart for decades. Son Don Broder claimed the deer was given to him, but no official document existed. The family claimed it should be returned to the estate. After losing a civil suit against his siblings, Don spent more than 10 days in jail for failing to turn over the antlers. He was 74 years old at the time. Don finally admitted he couldn't surrender the rack because he had sold it to Don Schaufler, an antler collector in Montana, for $325,000 (according to an article in the *Calgary Herald)*. The impressive deer mount remains with Schaufler to this day.

Circumference at Smallest Place Between First and Second Points
Circumference at Samllest Place Between Main Beam and Third Point
Circumference at Smallest Place Between Second and Fourth Points

TOTALS

Column 1	22 1/8
Column 2	96 1/8
Column 3	95 5/8
Total	213 7/8
SUBTRACT Column 4	6 4/8
Result	207 3/8
Line E Total	147 7/8

Exact locality where killed: Chip Lake, Alta., Can.
Date killed 11/26/26 By whom killed: Ed Broder
Present owner: Ed Broder DON SCHAUFIER
Address:
Guide's Name and Address: none
Remarks: (Mention any abnormalities)

AWARD-WINNING MULE DEER

TENTH COMPETITION - ED BRODER

1961 North Amer

MULE DEER (Non-Typical)—Certificate of NEW WORLD'S RECORD
Score—207-3/8 + 147-7/8 = 355-2/8
Length—(R) 26-2/8 (L) 26-1/8
Circumference—(R) 5 (L) 4-7/8
Points—(R) 22 (L) 21
Inside Spread—22-1/8
Locality—Chip Lake, Alta.—1926
Hunter—Ed Broder

Apr 9th

#1

I with 2 friends

On november 25, 1926, Robert Bailey
Philip Mohor and myself (Edmund Broder)
left Edmonton for our regular
autumn hunting trip. I drove a
1914 modle T Ford touring Car, Robert
Bailey drove his 1924 McLaughlin
touring car, over the old Grand
Trunk railway grade west from
Edmonton to Chip Lake, a distance
of approximaly one hundred miles.
The weather was approximately twenty
degrees wirh one foot of soft snow.
We Stayed the night in a saw mill
camp, which was five miles south
of Chip Lake. We made arrangments
to hire a team of horses and Sleigh
to haul our gear + equipment approx-
imatly ten miles south of here, to
an abondon lumber mill. There was
a very good cabin there so we decided
to stay there rather than set up
our tent. After having a lunch
we decided to go out for a short
afternoon hunt. It was approximately
~~one~~ 1 PM when I left camp.

#2

I set out through some heavy timber, and witch in about a quarter mile I come across a deer track. Tracking this deer for a half a mile I found where he had bedded down. I knew that the deer could not be too far off. I track him down off the timber ridge, through a jackpine swamp. There I came across where two moose had crossed the deer track. Looking at the moose tracks, I had to make a decission whether to go after the moose or the deer. Through post experience I knew moose would travel farther and faster than deer, and with only a short time before dark, I decided to carry on with the deer. Following these tracks through the swamp I came up onto higher land with a clearing not to far off. In this clearing I Spotted the Dear. The deer was approximelly 200 yard away, standing and feeding facing away from me.

#3.

So immidiatly I had to make a decission when and how to shoot. The distance was right, but his position was wrong. I knew I had to select a rear shot. The shot would have to be placed high in the spine so I pulled up my 32 Windchester special to a firing positeon, waited for his head to rise so as to back up a high spine shot. I fired and the animal dropped, I had broken its spine. "What a rack that one's got!" was the first thing I thought of. I hurried and dressed out the animal and set out for camp. I arrived back to camp as darkness closed in. In the next four days my other two partners had bag their deer, we left for home, completeing the most emportant trip of my life time. I first started hunting in the year 1909 and never missed a assasion yet. I am 72 and in fair health now,

Ed Broder

(Take out the best of this letter to make the storie)

Emilie and Fritz A. Toepperwein
Boerne, Texas

September 18, 1961

Mrs. Grancel Fitz, Secretary
Records of North American Big Game
Boone and Crockett Club
5 Tudor City Place
New York 17, New York

Dear Mrs. Fitz:

Your note was handed to me two days ago. I have since made a photo of our non typical mule deer, - which is herewith attached.

We note you have the record measurements ... Mr. Nowotny of San Antonio.

..., this head has been ... it is one of the prize ...n Collection. I took ... wall in the old Buckhor... ...resent location. I have ...ord size.

...over we are sending you ...TES OF THE BUCKHORN." ...our compliments.

... could come down and see ...

...y other information, plea... ...ll send it right along. ... here in Boerne. It is a ...doesn't get lost around th...

... personal regards.

Sincerely yours

ecords of North American
Big Game Committee

AWARD-WINNING MULE DEER

TENTH COMPETITION - LONE STAR BREWING COMPANY

NON-TYPICAL MULE DEER

UNKNOWN HUNTER - LONE STAR BREWING COMPANY

TENTH COMPETITION | CERTIFICATE OF MERIT

This interesting buck was entered in the Club's tenth competition by the Lone Star Brewing Company in 1962. The hunter and location of kill are listed as unknown, but an approximate kill date of 1901 was later determined. This non-typical mule deer, scoring 255-7/8, was later transferred to the Buckhorn Saloon & Museum. The deer has 30 scorable points. The total length of abnormal points is 88-3/8 inches.

SEE OTHER SIDE FOR INSTRUCTIONS	Supplementary Data R.	L.	Column 1 Spread Credit	Column 2 Right Antler	Column 3 Left Antler	Column 4 Difference
...mber of Points on Each Antler	18	12				
...p to Tip Spread	20	2/8				
...eatest Spread	31	6/8				
...side Spread MAIN BEAMS 22 6/8 — Spread credit may equal but not exceed length of longer antler			22 6/8			
...Inside Spread of Main Beams exceeds longer ...ler length, enter difference						
...al of Lengths of all Abnormal Points		88.3				
...th of Main Beam				23 —	24 1/8	1 1/8
...ngth of First Point, if present				5 2/8	6 —	6/8
...ngth of Second Point				12 6/8	13 5/8	7/8
...gth of Third Point, if present				6 7/8	9 5/8	2 6/8
...gth of Fourth Point, if present				5 1/8	5	1/8
...cumference at Smallest Place ...ween Burr and First Point				5 1/8	5 —	1/8
...umference at Smallest Place ...een First and Second Points				5 2/8	5 —	2/8
...umference at Samllest Place ...een Main Beam and Third Point				3 5/8	4 —	3/8
...umference at Smallest Place ...een Second and Fourth Points				5 6/8	6 1/8	3/8
...S		88.3	22 6/8	72.6	79	7.

...olumn 1	22.6
...olumn 2	72.6
...lumn 3	79.
...tal	174.4
...lumn 4	7.
...ult	167.4
...otal	88.3

Exact locality where killed: Unknown

Date killed: unknown By whom killed: unknown

Present owner: Lone Star Brewing Co

Address: 542 Simpson St, San Anto...

Guide's Name and Address

Remarks: (Mention any abnormalities)

Detached and added points disregarded

1963 North American Big Game Competition

sponsored by BOONE AND CROCKETT CLUB

WHITETAIL DEER (Non-Typical)—1st Award
Score—185-7/8+91-4/8=277-3/8
Length—(R) 28-1/8 (L) 28-3/8
Circumference—(R) 6-5/8 (L) 6-7/8
Points—(R) 19 (L) 18
Inside Spread—21-1/8
Locality—Hall County, Nebr.—1962
Hunter—Del Austin
Guide—Al Dawson

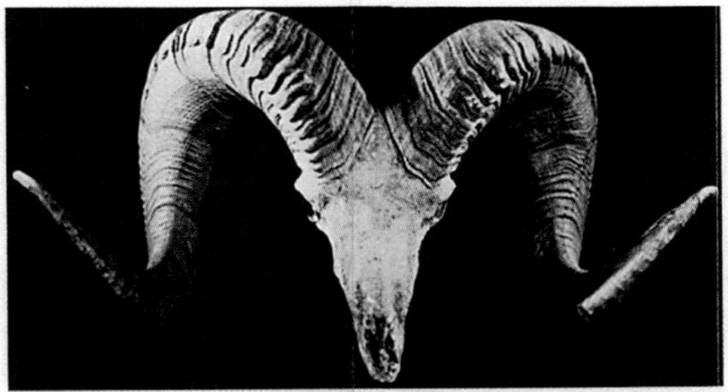

SAGAMORE HILL AWARD
STONE SHEEP—1st Award
Score—190
Length—(R) 46-6/8 (L) 46-6/8
Basal Circumference—(R) 15-2/8 (L) 15-1/8
Locality—Sikanni River, B. C.—1962
Hunter—Norman Blank
Guide—R. Lynn Ross

MULE DEER (Non-Typical)—1st Award
Score—217-7/8+85-7/8=303-6/8
Length—(R) 26-4/8 (L) 26-7/8
Circumference—(R) 5-2/8 (L) 5
Points—(R) 13 (L) 11
Inside Spread—24-3/8
Locality—Minturn, Colo.—1962
Hunter—James Austill

WHITE SHEEP—1st Award
Score—183-7/8
Length—(R) 46-5/8 (L) 47-4/8
Basal Circumference—(R) 13-6/8 (L) 13-6/8
Locality—Wrangell Mts., Alaska—1963
Hunter—Dr. Tony Oney

WYOMING MOOSE—1st Award
Score—167-7/8
Greatest Spread—43-5/8
Length of Palm—(R) 39-4/8 (L) 33-2/8
Width of Palm—(R) 10-5/8 (L) 11
Normal Points—(R) 13 (L) 12
Locality—Gros Ventre, Wyo.—1960
Hunter—Bonita Young
Guide—Bill Isaacs

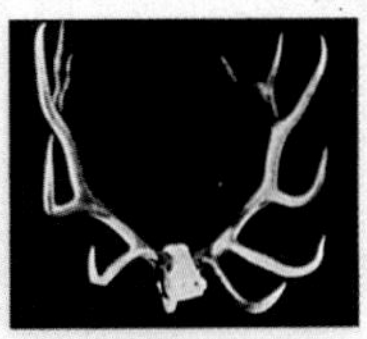

WAPITI—1st Award
Score—391-6/8
Length—(R) 52-6/8 (L) 53-6/8
Circumference—(R) 7-7/8 (L) 7-7/8
Points—(R) 6 (L) 6
Inside Spread—35-6/8
Locality—Slater, Colo.—1963
Hunter—W. J. Bracken

DESERT SHEEP—1st Award
Score—181-5/8
Length—(R) 39-2/8 (L) 41-3/8
Basal Circumference—(R) 15-2/8 (L) 15-1/8
Locality—Sheep Mt. Range, Nev.—1962
Hunter—David Ingram

MULE DEER (Typical)—1st Award
Score—210-2/8
Length—(R) 29-1/8 (L) 29-2/8
Circumference—(R) 5-2/8 (L) 5-2/8
Points—(R) 6 (L) 5
Inside Spread—27
Locality—Southern Ute Reservation, Colo.—1963
Hunter—Jack D. Johnston

PRONGHORN—1st Award
Score—89-6/8
Length—(R) 17-5/8 (L) 17-6/8
Basal Circumference—(R) 7-3/8 (L) 7-3/8
Length of Prong—(R) 6-1/8 (L) 6-2/8
Locality—Rawlins, Wyo.—1961
Hunter—Mary Carol Kircher

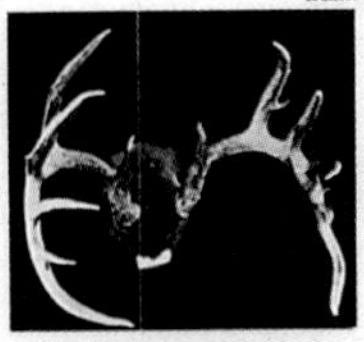

WHITETAIL DEER (Typical)—1st Award
Score—191-5/8
Length—(R) 26-5/8 (L) 26-2/8
Circumference—(R) 5-1/8 (L) 5
Points—(R) 6 (L) 7
Inside Spread—19
Locality—Flathead Co., Mont.—1963
Hunter—Earl McMaster

ROCKY MOUNTAIN GOAT—1st Award
Score—52
Length—(R) 10-3/8 (L) 10-2/8
Basal Circumference—(R) 5-7/8 (L) 5-7/8
Locality—Coquihalla, B. C.—1962
Hunter—Fred D. Fouty

COUES DEER—1st Award
Score—120-6/8
Length—(R) 19-4/8 (L) 18-2/8
Circumference—(R) 4 (L) 4
Points—(R) 5 (L) 5
Inside Spread—14-4/8
Locality—Los Adobes, Sonora, Mex.—1960
Hunter—Manuel Alcaraz Caravantez

COLUMBIAN BLACKTAIL DEER—1st Award
Score—155-2/8
Length—(R) 21-7/8 (L) 20-2/8
Circumference—(R) 4-2/8 (L) 4-2/8
Points—(R) 5 (L) 5
Inside Spread—17-6/8
Locality—King County, Wash.—1960
Hunter—Horst Vierthaler

BISON—1st Award
Score—114-4/8
Length—(R) 17-2/8 (L) 17-2/8
Basal Circumference—(R) 14-2/8 (L) 14-4/8
Locality—Gillette, Wyo.—1963
Hunter—Julian B. Hatton

PACIFIC WALRUS—1st Award
Score—124-6/8
Length of Tusk—(R) 30-7/8 (L) 32
Basal Circumference—(R) 9-1/8 (L) 9-4/8
Locality—St. Lawrence Is., Alaska—1962
Hunter—Bert Klineburger
Guide—Eldon Brandt

BIGHORN SHEEP—1st Award
Score—191-1/8
Length—(R) 40-1/8 (L) 42
Basal Circumference—(R) 15-2/8 (L) 15-3/8
Locality—Cadomin, Alta.—1962
Hunter—Frank Nuspel

MOUNTAIN CARIBOU—1st Award
Score—423-7/8
Length—(R) 46-2/8 (L) 45-3/8
Width of Brow Palms—(R) 10-3/8 (L) 4-3/8
Points—(R) 19 (L) 16
Inside Spread—34-6/8
Locality—Cold Fish Lake, B. C.—1963
Hunter—Edward E. Wilson
Guide—T. A. Walker

ALASKA-YUKON MOOSE—1st Award
Score—242-1/8
Greatest Spread—78-7/8
Length of Palm—(R) 44-4/8 (L) 44
Width of Palm—(R) 21-7/8 (L) 19-4/8
Normal Points—(R) 11 (L) 11
Locality—Alaska Peninsula—1963
Hunter—H. S. Kamil
Guide—Ray Loesche

CANADA MOOSE—1st Award
Score—201-4/8
Greatest Spread—56
Length of Palm—(R) 36-6/8 (L) 34-5/8
Width of Palm—(R) 18 (L) 19-2/8
Normal Points—(R) 17 (L) 13
Locality—Island Lake, Quebec—1962
Hunter—Silvene Braculente
Guide—Geo. A. Krikory

BARREN GROUND CARIBOU—1st Award
Score—443-7/8
Length—(R) 51-6/8 (L) 50-3/8
Width of Brow Palms—(R) 3-1/8 (L) 15-7/8
Points—(R) 19 (L) 21
Inside Spread—45-1/8
Locality—Wrangell Mts., Alaska—1962
Hunter—A. E. Bruggeman
Guide—Lee Holen

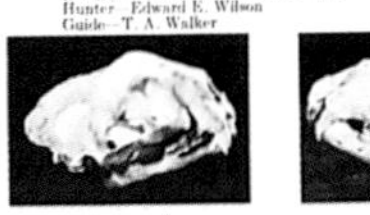

COUGAR—1st Award
Score—15-11/16
Skull Length—9-3/16
Skull Width—6-8/16
Locality—Valley County, Idaho—1961
Hunter—Louis Reballet

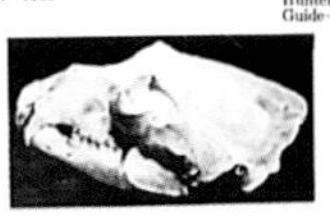

GRIZZLY BEAR—1st Award
Score—26-1/16
Skull Length—16-1/16
Skull Width—10
Locality—Smiths Inlet, B. C.—1963
Hunter—Donald M. Swarthout

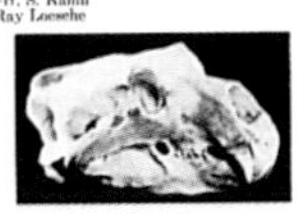

POLAR BEAR—1st Award
NEW WORLD'S RECORD
Score—29-15/16
Skull Length—18-8/16
Skull Width—11-7/16
Locality—Kotezbue, Alaska—1963
Hunter—Shelby Longoria
Guides—John Swiss and Nelson Walker

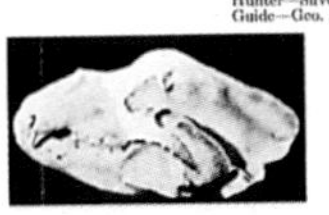

ALASKA BROWN BEAR—1st Award
Score—29-13/16
Skull Length—18-5/16
Skull Width—11-8/16
Locality—Alaska Peninsula—1962
Hunter—Don Johnson

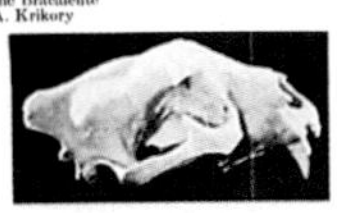

JAGUAR—1st Award
Score—17-8/16
Skull Length—10-8/16
Skull Width—7
Locality—Pital, Campeche, Mex.—1962
Hunter—Alex Hudson, III
Guide—Ramundo Calvador

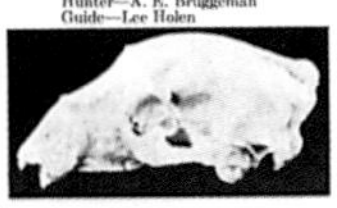

BLACK BEAR—1st Award
Score—21-7/16
Skull Length—13-3/16
Skull Width—8-4/16
Locality—Megal Mt., Nfld.—1963
Hunter—Ben Hillicoss
Guide—Don McKeen

Photographs by Leo Sarnaki

SEE REVERSE SIDE FOR OTHER AWARDS & HONORABLE MENTIONS

JACK D. JOHNSTON

ELEVENTH COMPETITION | FIRST PLACE AWARD

Jack D. Johnston's Colorado mule deer was the top scoring typical buck at the Club's eleventh competition—the first held at the Carnegie Museum in Pittsburgh, Pennsylvania. Jack's deer had one abnormal point resulting in a 3-inch deduction making the final score 210-2/8 points. He shot the buck on November 23, 1963, on the Southern Ute Reservation.

SEE OTHER SIDE FOR INSTRUCTIONS

ber of Points on Each Antler (4)				
to Tip Spread				
test Spread (5)				
de Spread AIN BEAMS — 27 — Spread credit may exceed length of longer antler				
nside Spread of Main Beams exceeds longer er length, enter difference				
of Lengths of all Abnormal Points				3
h of Main Beam (2)		29 1/8	29 2/8	1/8
gth of First Point, if present		5 5/8	3 7/8	1 6/8
gth of Second Point		18 7/8	17 1/8	~~1 6/8~~
gth of Third Point, if present		12	11 7/8	1/8
gth of Fourth Point, if present		13 2/8	13 3/8	1/8
cumference at Smallest Place veen Burr and First Point (3)		5 2/8	5 2/8	—
cumference at Smallest Place veen First and Second Points		4 6/8	4 4/8	2/8
cumference at Smallest Place veen Main Beam and Third Point		3 7/8	3 7/8	—
umference at Smallest Place een Second and Fourth Points		4 2/8	4 2/8	—
LS	27.000 27	97.000 97	93.250 93 2/8	6.375 ~~6 3/8~~

Column 1	27	Exact locality where killed Southern Ute Reservation, Colorado
Column 2	97	Date killed 11-23-63 By whom killed Jack D. Johnston
Column 3	93 3/8	Present owner Jack D. Johnston
TOTAL	217 3/8	Address
Column 4	7 1/8 ~~6 4/8~~	Guide's Name and Address None
SCORE	210 2/8	Remarks: (Mention any abnormalities) OK

POPHAM, THOM…

11TH FLOOR SCARRITT BUILDING

KANSAS CITY, MISSOURI

OFFICIAL SCORING SYSTEM FOR NORTH AMERICAN BIG GAME TROPHIES

RECORDS OF NORTH AMERICAN BIG GAME COMMITTEE

BOONE AND CROCKETT CLUB

Address Correspondence to:
Mrs. Grancel Fitz, Secretary
5 Tudor City Place, NYC 17, NY.

NON-TYPICAL MULE DEER

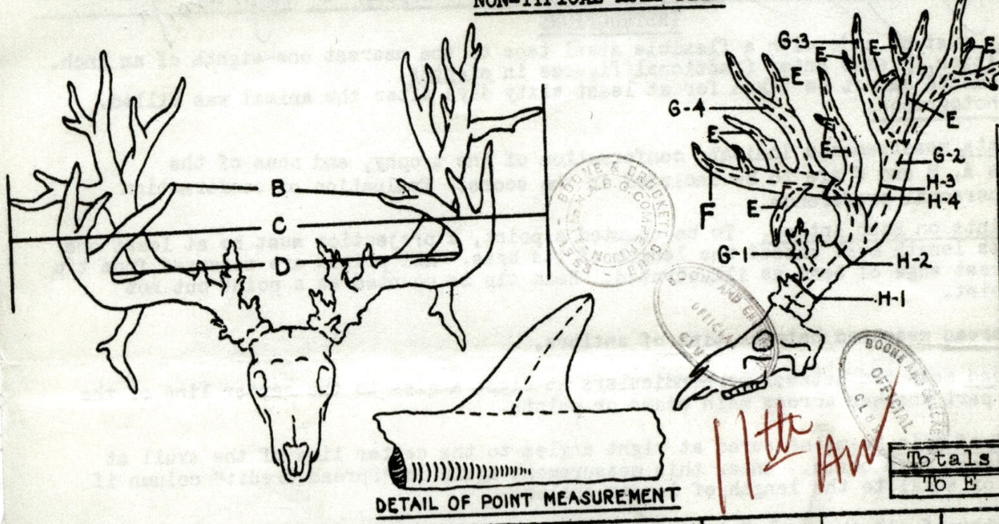

Popham

ABNORMAL

Points Line E	
1 R 3	3 L 7
6 - 7	1 - 2
2 - 1	10 - -
12 - -	1 - 3
2 - 3	1 - 4
9 - -	5 - 2
1 - 5	5 - -
3 - 6	2 - 3
1 - 2	1 - 4
3 - 2	4 - -
4 - 3	10 - 4
2 - 2	1 - 4
Totals 2 - 7	2 - 4
To E 53 - 1	50 - 2

SEE OTHER SIDE FOR INSTRUCTIONS	Supplementary Data R. 18	Supplementary Data L. 18	Column 1 Spread Credit	Column 2 Right Antler	Column 3 Left Antler	Column 4 Difference
A. Number of Points on Each Antler	28-1/8					
B. Tip to Tip Spread	40-6/8					
C. Greatest Spread						
D. Inside Spread of MAIN BEAMS 28 7/8 — Spread credit may equal but not exceed length of longer antler			28-7/8			
IF Inside Spread of Main Beams exceeds longer antler length, enter difference						—
E. Total of Lengths of all Abnormal Points	103-3/8					
F. Length of Main Beam				29 —	28-5/	-3/
G-1. Length of First Point, if present				2-2/	2-4/	-2/
G-2. Length of Second Point				15-1/	15--	-1/
G-3. Length of Third Point, if present				11-1/	10-4/	-5/
G-4. Length of Fourth Point, if present				9-3/	10-4/	1+1/
H-1. Circumference at Smallest Place Between Burr and First Point				5-4/	5-5/	-1/
H-2. Circumference at Smallest Place Between First and Second Points				5-4/	5-4/	~~-1~~ (ok)
H-3. Circumference at Samllest Place Between Main Beam and Third Point				5-4/	5--	-4/
H-4. Circumference at Smallest Place Between Second and Fourth Points				5-3/	5-2/	-1/
TOTALS	103 3/8		28-7/8	88-6/8	88-4/8	3-2/8

ADD	Column 1	28 7/8	Exact locality where killed Mundy Ranch, Chama, New Mex.
	Column 2	88 6/8	Date killed 10-26-63 By whom killed Joseph A. Garcia
	Column 3	88 4/8	Present owner ~~Same~~ ~~Homer Saye~~ ~~Don Schaufler~~
	Total	206-1/8	Address
SUBTRACT Column 4		3-2/8	Guide's Name and Address Emmitt Mundy, Chama, New Mex.
	Result	202-7/8	Remarks: (Mention any abnormalities) owner: Cabela's, Inc. One Cabela Drive Sydney, NE 69160
Add Line E Total		103 3/8	
FINAL SCORE		306 2/8	

California and Nevada to verify the …
for it.

Because of this factor, and as he pointed out, the status of the Club … rankings accorded by it were considerably involved, and I … important that this matter be resolv… measurers whi…

JOSEPH A. GARCIA

ELEVENTH COMPETITION | FIRST PLACE AWARD

Joseph A. Garcia holds his award-winning non-typical mule deer alongside his wife Celia, whose typical deer is also in the records books (see the chapter about "Women and Deer Hunting" for more information about her deer – page 176). The Garcias were hunting on the Mundy Ranch in Chama, New Mexico, when they shot these two impressive deer in October 1963. According to correspondence in the files, great debate centered around Joseph's deer due to the complicated configuration of the non-typical antlers. The official score for the buck is 306-2/8 points, which was determined by long-time B&C member and Official Measurer, Arthur C. Popham of Kansas City. He traveled to California to make the final and official ruling on the measurements. Joseph received a first place award once the new score was finalized. The buck remains the No. 1 non-typical in New Mexico, and currently ranks 13th overall in a tie with a mule deer entered by Dr. Vernon D. Holleman in the twelfth competition.

Mr. Walter B. McClurkan
Official Measurer Boone and Crockett Club
812 West Oak Street
Denton, Texas

Re; Non-typical mu
Score 308 6/8

Dear Mr. McClurkan:

Recently I returned from an early season mule de in the Rawah Wilderness area in Colorado. While I Colorado I went to Norwood to try to find Steve H. the rancher who killed the non-typical mule deer you measured for me in July. I was informed that Mr. Steve H. Herndon died about three years ago. I was also informed that he had a son who still lived near Norwood and I was able to locate his place of residence. The son was away from home at the time but I was able to talk to the daughter-in-law of Steve H. Herndon. She told me that the late Steve H. Herndon had taken the large mule deer in fair chase during the 1954 hunting season though she did not know the exact date. She showed me a snap-shot she had taken of the deer after it had been field dressed. It was hangin on a pole alongside an elk and another deer. The daughter-in-la said that Mr. Herndon was a good friend of the owner of the liqu store in Norwood and that is how the antlers came to be displaye in the liquor store window. This is where the antlers were firs discovered by Mr. Paschal who purchased them. The daughter-in-l knew that Mr. Herndon sold the antlers but she did not know who had bought them nor where they were at this time.

She told me that the Late Mr. Herndon liked to hunt and that he was a good sportsman however he apparently was not particular interested in trophies. She says that she was surprised however that he did not just give the antlers away rather than sell them as he was a man of substantial means and did not need the money. She said that Mr. Herndon had commented that the antlers were no particularly large but that they were unusual in that they had s many points.

After talking to the daughter-in-law of the Late Mr. Herndon I am of the belief that the deer was taken fairly and I believe that his name should be listed in the Records as the hunter who was fortunate enough to take this fine specimen.

I am enclosing a duplicate of this letter so that you may for this information to the Boone and Crockett Club.

Sincerely:

Vernon D. Holleman

Dr. Vernon D. Holleman

AWARD-WINNING MULE DEER

V.D. & D.F. HOLLEMAN

TWELFTH COMPETITION | CERTIFICATE OF MERIT

Taxidermist, W.D. Paschall found these impressive non-typical antlers in a Colorado saloon while on a hunting trip in 1955. A secondhand account of the hunt and purchase follows:

> *...up early one morning before sunrise. As it became light enough for him to see he saw the mule deer eating on a stack of al-fal-fa hay nearby. He got his thirty-thirty from behind the kitchen door and shot the animal. He dragged the animal to the barn where he dressed it out. Mr. Paschall said the head was cut off at the neck and hung on a fence near the barn where it hang [sic] until the next year. During the next hunting season the rancher was in the saloon in Norwood and he told the saloon owner about the deer with an unusual set of "horns" he had killed the year before. The saloon owner asked the rancher to bring the antlers into town to put in his saloon window to attract hunters. This the rancher did and shortly after this the antlers were discovered and purchased by Mr. Paschall.*

The antlers were later sold to Dr. Vernon D. Holleman who had them officially scored by a B&C Official Measurer. The entry score put the deer at the top of the list, which warranted that the buck be sent to the Carnegie Museum where a panel of judges for the 12th Big Game Competition tallied a final score of 306-2/8 points. It currently ranks as the third-largest non-typical from Wyoming and is tied with Joseph A. Garcia's non-typical for 13th place overall. The greatest spread measures 38-5/8 inches and the rack includes 86-4/8 inches of abnormal points.

VINTAGE PHOTOS

JULIE TRIPP | B&C DIRECTOR OF PUBLICATIONS

One of the greatest assets of the Boone and Crockett Club is its archives of thousands of photographs of hunters from all eras and their trophy big game animals. Researchers who peruse the vast expanse of our record-entry files dating back to the Club's first competition held in 1947 always come away with a grin, amazed at the treasures they discover.

These images run the gamut from vintage photographs that offer a glimpse of the conditions these hunting pioneers experienced in the field to snapshots of old-school trophy mounts exhibiting the best taxidermy techniques of their day. Scouring through these treasured files, discovering photographic gems is indeed a highlight of any publishing project I work on for the Club. A designer's paradise!

Not all these vintage photos have been in our archives for decades. Some come to us generations later, when family members discover an heirloom is indeed a record trophy. That's how we ended up with the image of this hunting party (shown opposite), which includes Bill Walgren and his non-typical mule deer shot in 1932 but not entered in the Club's records program until 2006. The trophy buck is currently owned by Walgren's great-nephew Ryan Burke, who inherited it from Bill. The buck has 19 scorable points, 48-6/8 inches of non-typical points, and a greatest spread of 37 inches. Details abound in this vintage photograph. Each time I look at it I find some new curiosity I didn't see before—like the impressive ammo belt worn by the gentleman in the middle or the striped railroad overalls the hunter on the far left is sporting. Take another look and see what you missed the first time around.

Ryan Burke inherited his great-uncle's non-typical mule deer, which has a final B&C score of 258-4/8 points. The buck was taken in Beaver County, Utah, in 1932 by Bill Walgren.

Another "new" vintage photograph just ended up on my desk earlier in 2013. Max Rasmussen, now 93 years old, is still in possession of his trophy Utah non-typical taken while hunting with his cousins near Vernal, Utah, in 1950. In correspondence from Max, he notes, "The joy of reliving and retelling the story of that hunt over the years and keeping the memories of family and friends is what has helped me to stay young and still hunting." Max and his incredible mule deer are slated to be recognized at the Club's 28th Big Game Awards Banquet with a First Award for the top non-typical mule deer entered between 2010-2012. Along with his vintage field photograph, Max included a modern-day snapshot of himself and the buck along with sons Scott and Gale. This family is keeping our hunting heritage alive!

The images included in this book are vintage. The Club has skillfully ushered in a new era with the advancement and availability of photographic equipment. Today, our expectations consist of presenting a blood-free trophy and hunter in an uncluttered, natural environment. These guidelines were born out of respect for the animal and its habitat. I can't help but wonder, though, decades from now when the next person digs through our archives; will these new photographs offer the same history lesson as their predecessors?

FIRST PLACE

OPPOSITE: Max Rasmussen waited patiently for years, fantasizing about the mammoth bucks that lived on Diamond Mountain. Finally, in 1950, with his blue Chevy loaded to the brim with hunting gear, cousins, and dogs, he headed into the mountains for the hunt that would finally end with the monster buck of his dreams. He finally had the buck scored by a B&C Official Measurer 62 years later. Max and his award-winning buck—which has a final B&C score of 260-3/8 points—are front and center in this modern-day photo with his sons Scott and Gale.

ABOVE: Montanan Milton Z. Hunt displays his rifle in the rack of an impressive non-typical mule deer he harvested on a Washington County, Utah, hunt in October 1940. This deer was originally entered in the Club's records program before the new scoring system was in effect, so complete measurements are not available. Records indicate that the Club reached out to Milton several times to have the mule deer scored with the current scoring system, but to no avail. According to the original score chart, the buck had a 45-inch spread and 41 total points.

OPPOSITE: This brute was harvested in Unaweep Canyon near Grand Junction, Colorado, during the 1954 season by Ernest Mancuso. Notes on the original score chart indicate the buck weighed 317 pounds. In 1955, Mancuso sent the trophy to the American Museum of Natural History in New York City for the Club's seventh competition, which was held the following year. The buck was given a 3rd Place Award in the typical mule deer category with a final score of 201 points.

ABOVE: The original score charts for these Wyoming mule deer confirm they were owned by Lyman Brown of Evanston. All three bucks were scored in 1947 by R.E. Briggs. With an impressive spread of 44-3/8 inches, the mule deer on the left was killed by George Calvert in October 1940. By far the most outstanding feature of this deer is its 8-inch circumferences at the bases. It's not known the year the center mule deer was harvested, but the chart notes it was taken by Ben Chapin in Lincoln County and has a longest main beam of 29 inches. The deer on the right was taken during the fall of 1939 by Willis Barns. Its spread measures 33-1/2 inches and 19 scorable points. None of these deer were measured under the new scoring system.

Meat PROCES
SLAUGHT

D E E R

MAIN BEAM MEASUREMENT
FOR WHITE TAIL

MAIN BEAM MEA
FOR MULE AND

Method of Measuring

All measurements **must** be made with a flexible steel tape.

A. Length of outside curve: Measured along the main beam from the b

OPPOSITE: This classic typical mule deer sits atop another classic—a 1941 Oldsmobile Coupe. The buck was killed by Ben Ellwanger, Sr., in his home state of Washington in 1947. The original score chart shows the buck was a 5x5 with 25-inch main beams.

ABOVE: E.C. Treinen shot this clean 5x5 on October 26, 1946, near the North Platte River in Wyoming. The buck has a greatest spread of 32 inches and a B&C score of 180-4/8 points. A relative, Frank Treinen, had the buck measured in December of 1955 and promptly entered it into the Club's seventh competition.

RIGHT: This photograph doesn't do Bill Davis's non-typical mule deer justice! Davis shot the buck in Madison County, Montana, in October 1960. Three years later, B&C legend Dr. Philip L. Wright officially measured the buck at the University of Montana—where Wright taught ornithology and mammology for decades—scoring the buck at 226-1/8 points.

OPPOSITE: This Canadian buck was shot on November 1, 1929, by Jonas H. Webber, 10 miles north of La Glace, Alberta. Remarks on the chart note that it has a greatest spread of 32-1/2 inches and a broken point on the left antler. The buck wasn't measured with the Club's new scoring system, so no final B&C score exists.

ABOVE: Lieutenant Colonel Forrest F. Parham shot this extraordinary non-typical mule deer 14 miles northwest of Paonia, Colorado, on October 25, 1961. In January 1962, the buck was officially measured by Mr. Jonas, Jr., who calculated a final score of 253 points. Key measurements include 52-2/8 inches of abnormal points along with a greatest spread of 41-3/8 inches. The deer has 11 points on each beam. Parham indicated in a letter that accompanied the score chart that he was stationed in Colorado Springs at the time of the hunt.

MAIN BEA
FOR

UREMENT
LACKTAIL

A Le
o

B Ci
th

C Ci

D Gre
ho

Points

Remark
fro ... normal for this species. ... any characteristics which depart

Please provide photographs showing front view and ...

Horns-a-Plenty

Ernest Fait, W1104 Joseph, stands at the side of the newly mounted head of a big mule deer last hunting season on the

OPPOSITE: Long-time B&C measurer and Honorary Life Member Donald S. Hopkins scored this non-typical mule deer shot by Ernest Fait on November 29, 1960. The buck still ranks as the seventh largest in its category from Washington. Fait was hunting near LeClerc Creek when he harvested the buck. It has 69-4/8 inches of abnormal points and a greatest spread of 34-2/8 points. A photo of Fait and his impressive mule deer appeared in the local paper on April 22, 1961, with the headline "Horns-a-Plenty."

ABOVE: Roy C. Boyce's deer was initially entered into the Club's records program as a Columbia blacktail deer until it was later determined to be a mule deer, based on the location the deer was taken in relation to the Club's boundary for the Columbia blacktail category. The buck scores 160-5/8 points.

DEER

MAIN BEAM MEASUREMENT FOR WHITE TAIL

MAIN BEAM MEASUREM FOR MULE AND BLACK

Method of Measuring

All measurements **must** be made with a flexible steel tape.

A Length of outside curve: Measured along the main beam from the base of the burr to the tip of the most distant point on the main beam.

B Greatest spread: Measured between parallels and at right angles to th center line of the skull.

C Circumference: Measured midway between the basal snag and the firs

OPPOSITE: This incredible mule deer was shot on October 20, 1939, roughly 26 miles north of Vernal, Utah, in the Ashley National Forest. The hunter, Glen A. Lambert, measured the buck on March 3, 1947. Key measurements include a 43-inch spread and 28-inch main beams. The buck was not officially scored with the Club's new system, which went into effect in 1950.

ABOVE: Nebraska hunter Jerome Mischke shot this impressive mule deer in Albany County, Wyoming, during the 1948 season. Upon receiving the pamphlet of award winners from the Club's 1949 competition, Jerome penned a letter to B&C inquiring about the lack of a second- or third-prize winner. Included with his letter was the above photograph of the mule deer he entered. His letter states, "Only on the advice of my sportsmen friends am I sending it so you may see what you overlooked and what most of us consider the nicest head and horns we have seen." The early competitions of the Club were far more subjective, which is one of reasons the new scoring system was implemented in 1950. Unfortunately, Jerome's mule deer was never scored with the new system, so we'll never know how it would have stacked up.

ABOVE AND OPPOSITE: Both of these Washington mule deer were shot by Frank L. Vennum. The first, above, has a 29-5/8-inch spread and was harvested in October 1947. Records indicate the buck was destroyed by a fire in 1950 and therefore never scored under the Club's new scoring system. The second buck, shown opposite, was taken the following year near Meacham, Oregon.

LEFT: Local hunter Jay R. Anderson shot this typical mule deer in Utah's Summit County near Crandall Canyon in 1949. The buck has a final score of 190-1/8 points.

DEER

MEASUREMENT
HITE TAIL

MAIN BEAM MEASUR
FOR MULE AND BLAC

Method of Measuring

with a flexible steel tape.

OPPOSITE: Ross O'Neil shot this buck during the 1947 season at the head of Big Red Creek, Utah. The deer has a greatest spread of 40 inches, with main beams both measuring near 30 inches or more. It has 17 scorable points.

ABOVE: Texas hunter B.E. Brooks shot this mule deer near Gunnison, Colorado, in October 1954. Brooks originally sent in a hand-typed score chart along with the top-left Polaroid. After reviewing the measurements, the Club provided him with a score chart shortly thereafter and the buck was officially scored at 171-2/8 B&C with 13 scorable points. Brooks provided a photograph of the mounted trophy with the second chart.

OPPOSITE: Bernard O. Domries killed this excellent Colorado mule deer near Rangley. The buck was rescored at 192 points by B&C Official Measurer Elgin T. Gates in 1960 at the request of the Club in order to verify the measurements. In a letter to the Club, Bernard notes that he was most impressed with Elgin's "very critical but fair judge of my head."

ABOVE: This photograph shows the results of a successful hunt near Monticello, Utah, with several does hanging along with this impressive buck. R.G. Felski shot this mule deer, scoring 194-7/8 points, in October 1961.

LEFT: A 1962 hunting trip to Gunnison County, Colorado, proved successful with the harvest of this fine typical mule deer shot by Thomas M. Hanley. Key measurements for the deer include a greatest spread of 32-3/8 inches and main beams of 26 and 24-7/8 inches. Its final score is 187-7/8 points.

IMPLEMENTS

DEC . 59 . Phone

DOMRIES F

RROWING MACHINES
AND BLOCKERS
RROWS
RIDGERS
IELDS
TRAILERS

Boone and Croc
Records of North
Big Game Committe
5 Tudor City Place
New York 17, New York

Dear Mrs. Fitz:

I must congratul
Crocket Club on a very fine cho
T. Gates as one of your official
enjoyed meeting him as a person
critical but fair judge of my he
point of a phone call to you to
deduction of two points which I h
part of the Burr. I inked in the
points on the Burr and they shoul
photos sent in earlier.

I sincerely hope th
kill my chance in the 1959 contest

Yours sincere

Bernard

BD/hk

Bernard Domrie

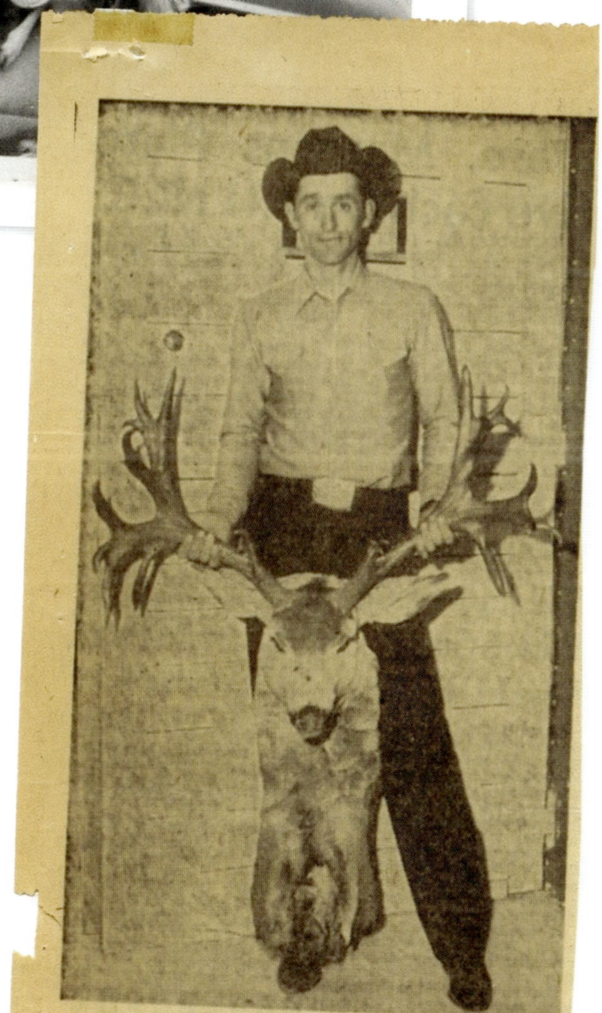

THEY KEEP GETTING BIGGER — Top (so far reported) in antler spread and hog-dressed weight deer taken so far this season appears to be the one shot by Richard Doud, Midland, shown above with the head of a 260-pound (hog-dressed) Mule deer which has a

OPPOSITE: This interesting mule deer was harvested near Hinton, Alberta, by H.R. Woodley in November 1960. The buck has a greatest spread of 38-3/8 inches and was scored as a 6x6. The score chart indicates a 4-inch abnormal point on the right antler, and a 5-1/2-inch abnormal point on the left, along with a main beam that dips downward. The final score on the buck is 192-4/8 points.

ABOVE: In 1988, John E. McCleary entered this impressive typical mule deer shot by James Odell McCleary decades earlier (October 1951). The buck has a final score of 199-6/8 points. Along with the standard, modern-day photos of the antlers that accompany trophy entries, John included this fantastic vintage photograph showing the hunter and his companions with their take for the trip.

RIGHT: ***They keep getting bigger!*** Richard Doud's non-typical mule deer has a final score of 206-2/8, with 19 scorable points. The buck was shot near Bad River in Jackson County, South Dakota, in 1954.

hat I have measured ... City N.Y.C. State ...
) A.M.N.H.
ese measurements and data are, to the best of my knowledge and belief,
with the instructions given.

Signature: T. Donald Carr...

INSTRUCTIONS

ements must be made with a flexible steel tape to the nearest one-eight
easurements cannot be taken for at least sixty days after the animal wa
ait photographs.

oint and tip of main beam.

ACKNOWLEDGEMENTS

... for scoring North American big game trophies was ori...

OPPOSITE: This award-winning mule deer was displayed at the Club's 1950 competition held at the American Museum of Natural History in New York City. Lyle K. Leedle shot the buck in 1940 in Okanogan County, Washington. A final score of 188-7/8 points earned the typical mule deer the 1st Prize.

ABOVE: Harry Irland killed this massive mule deer in 1919 near Columbia Creek in Elko County, Nevada. It was scored and entered under the old scoring system in 1947. Mrs. Irland had the buck measured under the new system in 1958, which netted a final score of 200-7/8 points.

RIGHT: Nebraska isn't necessarily considered a producer of big mule deer. However, Paul E. Pritts killed this impressive buck scoring 185-7/8 points in Custer County during the 1958 season. Accompanying the chart was a letter dated January 13, 1964, from Lloyd P. Vance, chief of Nebraska's Game Division. He notes, "Take of deer in Nebraska has grown at a phenomenal rate. In 1963, 10,586 deer were taken by 15,412 permit holders for permit success rate of 68.7 percent."

OPPOSITE: C. Ray Garverich shot this unique non-typical mule deer on November 4, 1945, in Treasure County, Montana. The buck was not measured under the new scoring system, but the original chart notes 26 scorable points and a greatest spread of 37 inches.

ABOVE: With a greatest spread of 41-1/2 inches and 20 points, this Nevada mule deer is an incredible trophy. Shot in 1946 by Clifford Williams, the buck wasn't measured with the new system, so we'll never know what the final B&C score would be.

LEFT: This New Mexico mule deer was shot by H.G. Bruno in October 1957. The buck has a final score of 179-6/8 points with a greatest spread of 28 inches.

OPPOSITE: Roger M. Allred killed this typical mule deer during the 1958 season with his .30-06 pushing 150-grain bullets. The buck wasn't officially measured and entered into the Club's records program until 1985. After all the calculations were tallied, the deer's final B&C score was 201-1/8 points.

ABOVE: This impressive non-typical mule deer has a final score of 273-5/8 points with 31 points and a greatest spread of 42-4/8 inches. Harold B. Rollins was shooting a .270 Winchester with a 130-grain bullet. Notes in the file indicate that Harold was hunting in Lost Creek drainage in Morgan County, Utah, in 1944 when he killed the buck. Mode of transportation is listed as a team of horses and a wagon.

RIGHT: Donald G. Heidtman's typical mule deer received a 1st Place Award at the Club's eighth competition with a final score of 195-1/8 points. Donald shot the deer in Elko County, Nevada, in October 1954.

AN ERA OF GOLD

BEFORE, DURING, AND AFTER THE "GOOD OLD DAYS"

GUY EASTMAN | EASTMAN'S HUNTING JOURNAL

The soft golden rays of sunlight were just beginning to peek over the snow-capped mountain tops of the Rubies when Joey sprung to life in the passenger seat of the Willys Jeep. His dad Jack let out a chuckle as the Jeep slid to a stop; the kid had managed to nod off yet again on one of the ruttiest roads in all of Elko County.

"Is it a big buck, Dad?" Joey squeaked with the highest of hopes.

"Not sure, son..." Jack snatched the beat-up old Panzer tank commander binoculars from the floorboard of the rig.

"Nope, just a buck with four does and a 3x4—not big enough for us Joe," Jack said half-heartedly.

"Ah shucks. Are you sure?"

The chains began to dig back into the frozen earth and move the Jeep northbound again. Like most 10-year-old boys, Joey was excited to spend a week with Dad and the guys. His two uncles, Billy and Don, had already headed south. Joey and his dad also decided to head south this morning to the top of a long hogback ridge sprinkled with juniper and cedars far in the frigid distance. After three long days, Joey was starting to get a bit bored with the same routine every day—eat dinner, evening card game, a short night of sleep, coffee, and out hunting first thing in the morning. Repeat process.

The late 1950s ushered in the beginning of the Golden Age of Mule Deer hunting. Big bucks like this one began to be more common than ever before.

MIKE EASTMAN

The now-distant thought of a huge buck nestled underneath a juniper tree was slipping further and further from reality as the hunt began to slowly wear on and on. Maybe this week-long trip with the guys was more like his mom had explained it over the years after all—just an excuse.

For Joey's dad, the yearly hunt was something much more. It was in his blood and had been since before he was Joey's age. Things were tough back then. The dust bowl had prompted a family move to the West Coast to find work in the farm country of the San Joaquin Valley west of Bakersfield. Jack and his brothers hunted deer more for survival than anything. Feeding a family in the 1930s was a tough job, and a good deer hunter was a true asset to the family. Jack killed his first deer at the age of 7; buck hunting was his destiny.

Finally awake for the day, Joey broke the silence, "Why do you and your brothers like to hunt deer so much, Dad?" It had been four long days, and Jack thought Joey would never ask.

Jack used the opportunity to explain to Joey the family's hunting heritage and the hunting lessons that he had been waiting 10 long years to pass down to his son. He began with the Grapes of Wrath-like story of the family moving west to find work. He and his brothers had learned the art of buck hunting from their dad and his buddies on the farm where they all worked long, hard hours to keep the family barely fed. Back in those days, deer hunting was far beyond a recreational endeavor; it was all-out survival. With deer few and far between, times were tough for everyone, including the wildlife.

Then came the Second World War. Jack and his brothers traveled overseas for the war. Jack had enlisted at age 17—five brothers in all, all sent different directions, all giving everything they had to the war effort, some in the Pacific and some in Europe. But their hearts and souls were still committed to the hills of western California and to the deer hunting they longed to return. Two of the brothers would never return home; three would make it through that hell on earth.

Life was much different when the brothers returned to California. Things were much better. The economy was booming, and suddenly the family was caught up in the newly created California middle class. Most of Jack's buddies had joined the local motorcycle club or moved even further west to enjoy the surfing lifestyle on the coast and a college education. Not Jack and his brothers—they chose to head back to the hills to hunt bucks, if there were any left.

By the mid-1950s, Jack and his brothers had branched out to hunting bucks in nearby Nevada and Arizona. They even headed to Colorado once in search of big deer from a tip given to them by the local gunsmith. Deer hunting had grown into more than a way to feed the family; the brothers had become part of the beginning of something big.

Hunting big mule deer bucks had become a passion for Jack and his two brothers. The handwritten letters back and forth during the war fueled a longing to go home and spend one more night in the backcountry chasing a big mule deer buck. That longing blossomed into a full-blown passion for mule deer.

While feeding the family was a nice byproduct of the newly refined sport, the true passion lay in the racks the bucks carried. Even though "you can't eat the horns," and they really didn't have much use, it became a joke with mom and the neighbor ladies. The meat, liver and heart were for the family; horns were for dad and his buddies to talk about over a cigar and a cold can of beer in the garage.

Jack and his brothers were not alone; the greatest generation had produced something unique. These veterans would come back from the war and become what most of us consider the greatest hunting generation. Jack's generation would continue to build America and its industrial core. One of these industries would become what we know today as the hunting and shooting industry. Along with that, they would have the opportunity of all opportunities: to live through the greatest mule deer hunting in modern history. A generation that would, for the most part, see over 80 percent of the top-50 mule deer hit the ground.

These veterans and their families would become the fathers of modern mule deer hunting. This mule deer era would last for the next 20 years, and even more importantly, this newfound passion would span the generation gap as hunting traditions were passed down from one generation to the next. Little Joey would become the first son of the second generation of modern mule deer hunters.

Just as Jack had finished transferring the passion of mule deer buck hunting to Joey, he pressed the brake on the Jeep ever so steadily. The machine slowly ground to a stop as Jack shut the engine down without the popping of the muffler and the clanging of the chains against the hard frozen ground.

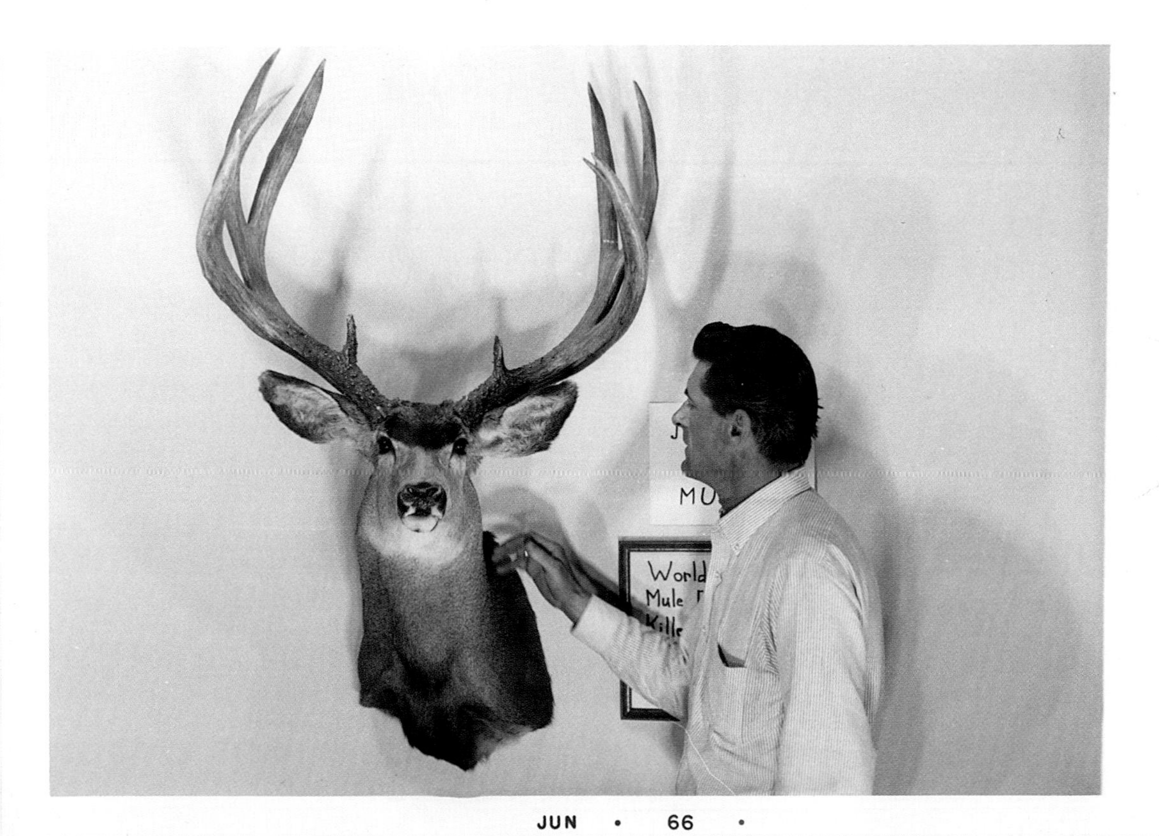

The late Gordon Eastman admiring the Hoback Buck, which was the World's Record at the time, circa 1965. It was the legend of this magnificent buck that lured the Eastman family to the mule deer-rich region of western Wyoming in the late 1950s.
EASTMAN FAMILY ARCHIVES

The silence was almost deafening—Joey's ears almost hurt.

"Now it's time to do some walking, son," Jack whispered as he took one final puff from his smoke.

Central Nevada can be a tough place at the end of November, particularly for a 10-year-old boy from the Central Valley. But Joey did his best to keep up as his dad hiked up the remainder of the ridge.

Jack eased out to the end of the ridge as quietly as possible and signaled to Joey to keep quiet and to walk inside his footprints. That would help keep the noise in the snow to a minimum.

"This is your grandfather's favorite lookout for big bucks," Jack whispered to Joey.

"Uh-huh," Joey said softly.

W. C. LAWRENCE

JACKSON HOLE MUSEUM

JACKSON, WYOMING

Moran, Wyoming.
April 17, 1964.

Mrs. Grancel Fitz, Secretary
Boone and Crockett Club
5 Tudor City Palce
New York, N. Y.

X

Dear Mrs. Fitz:

We just returned from the Southwest and find your letter waiting for us, I wish I had known sooner about you wanting some information on the World's record mule deer. Will send along this information even though I know I am too late.

This dder was killed for the meat about 1925 in the Hoback Canyon south of Jackson, Wyoming. The antlers were left and some ranch hand brought them into Jackson, for many years the antlers hung in the old Mike Meek's Saloon. After the saloon closed the antlers were stored and finally showed up at the Handicraft Shop in Jackson where Lewis E. Ray a taxidermistt saw them and purchased the head, he sent it to Boone and Crockett for measurements where it was discovered it was a World's Record Head. W. C. Lawrence of the Jackson Hole Museum purchased the head from Lewis Ray and it is now on exhibit in the Museum.

Kindest regards,

Sincerely

W. C. Lawrence

JACKSON HOLE MUSEUM | TENTH COMPETITION

CERTIFICATE OF MERIT | NEW WORLD'S RECORD

Lewis E. Ray, owner of Ray's Taxidermy in Jackson, Wyoming, sent this mule deer mount—which he purchased from a handicraft shop—to the Club's tenth competition. The deer was recognized with a Certificate of Merit and certified as a new World's Record. Ray sold the trophy to the W.C. Lawrence of the Jackson Hole Museum where the trophy still resides to this day. The buck has a final score of 217 points and was killed in 1925. Since it was declared a World's Records in 1959, two other deer have superceded it as World's Record. It still ranks as the Number 3 typical mule deer in the Club's Records Program.

Just then, like it was on cue, the head of a deer popped up between two cedar trees 180 yards below Joey on the backside of the ridge.

"Damn it," Jack cursed. "They heard us, son."

The doe focused ever so intently on the two as they did their best to freeze. And freeze they did—the temperature was in the single digits! Joey was starting to feel the sting of the cold Nevada north wind.

Just about when Jack figured Joey could not take the cold wind any longer, the doe finally became restless. She took one step forward and revealed something that would change the two buck hunters forever!

Behind the doe stood not just a buck, but the buck of all bucks—a true giant of all giants. He was too wide for Jack to even realistically take a stab at judging his width; too many points to count, and his horns were even heavier than the heaviest of heavy deer. The shine alone from the sun off the buck's horns almost blinded Jack, putting him into such a deep trance that he almost forgot about his rifle.

"Get him Dad!"

Jack snapped back to consciousness at Joey's abrupt, inappropriate, and downright novice outburst. Dropped out of his trance, Jack slowly raised the beat-up .30-30 to his shoulder. This was no ordinary gun. She had been through hell and three generations to boot—no prize for a museum, but a sweet, straight-shooter for sure. As Jack touched off the round, the noise and percussion almost knocked Joey to his knees.

Jack knew what the crack-thump noise meant. Joey had no idea.

As the buck took two bounces out of sight, Joey couldn't help himself, "You missed him, Dad!"

By the late 1960s the pioneers of modern mule deer hunting were forging into very remote country like the Wyoming Range of western Wyoming in search of big mule deer bucks.
EASTMAN FAMILY ARCHIVES

An icy river crossing on Wyoming's Snake River produces another big Wyoming typical buck for early mule deer hunters in the late 1950s.

MIKE EASTMAN

The look on Jack's face told a different story. "Naw, he's done for sure, son," Jack proclaimed with a slight smirk.

Jack and his son spent the next 30 minutes tracking blood in the fresh, crisp snow. Weaving through the junipers for what seemed like a mile, Jack could finally tell life was starting to slip away from the old monarch. His footing was starting to falter, and his front left shoulder was beginning to stiffen, making his leg drag a bit in the snow. Even though the blood trail was all but gone, this buck was on his last legs—he just didn't know it yet. After two more twists and turns through the junipers Jack picked up the color of deer hide peeking between two big, gnarly cedar trees.

"Are we ever gonna find this buck, Dad?" Joey finally asked.

After a long breath to regain his composure, Jack calmly said, "Go check behind those two big cedar trees, son." Joey did just that.

As Joey rounded the corner of the shadows of those two cedar trees, his life would change forever! The big buck lay in a pile of snow, hair, blood and horn!

"Holy hell, dad, he's a big 'un," Joey screeched.

"Watch your mouth, son!" Jack struck back by pure reflex, but Joey was right. This was the buck of all bucks, the biggest buck Jack had ever laid eyes on—with hooves still attached, anyway.

Joey couldn't help himself, and he ran over to his dad's buck to try to pick the head of the behemoth from the frozen turf and snow. It was way too heavy for the youngster to handle, and Joey slipped and fell down under the sheer weight of the head of the old Roman-nosed monarch. Flat on his back and nose-to-nose with the buck, Joey had gotten fresh blood on his new red plaid Woolrich coat Mom bought him for his birthday. But no one seemed to worry about a little dirt and blood stain in a moment like this.

For the first time in his life, the pungent smell of a rutting, cedar buck flooded Joey's nostrils as he thrashed around to regain his footing. Just as Dad's big rough hand grabbed a fistful of wool and lifted Joey to his feet, the clouds parted and the bright, full-morning sun lit up the countryside. It was almost like a divine entity had turned the light on in celebration of both a successful hunt and a father who had passed on to his son an honest life—a life in the outdoors. Little did Joey know he would spend the rest of his life chasing that pungent rut smell to relive that day.

Jack and Joey's hunt would mark the beginning of the true golden age of mule deer hunting. The next two decades would produce some of the biggest mule deer bucks ever recorded and lots of them. More than one in four of the total records book bucks would be taken during this short, next 20-year period, and those are just the bucks we know to exist. Unfortunately, many of these massive deer would fall to obscurity in the basement of a house, the roof of a shed, or loft of a barn. No one really knows how many big deer really were killed during those years, but as more of them are recovered and recorded each year, we continue to put the pieces together of the true golden days of our mule deer hunting heritage.

The Boone and Crockett Club continues to record the antler measurements of these huge bucks, recognizing the buck first and the hunter second, as it should be. This first generation of buck hunters didn't do it for the recognition. A very modest group, they hunted for the excitement and adventure, not the notoriety. They did it for the passion. These guys were some of the toughest, most skilled, hard-core hunters the country had ever seen—many of the best deer hunters no one ever heard of; names of men who would have fallen completely into obscurity but for a records book and a family big buck story.

For the next 20-some years, Jack's family and thousands more would head to some of the most remote places in the Lower 48 in pur-

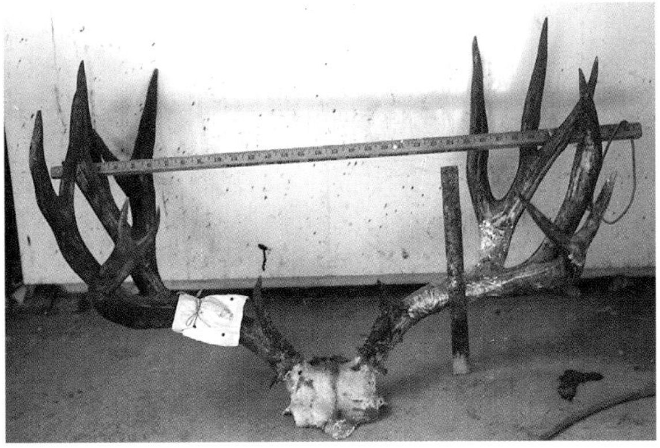

Good examples of the type of bucks that could be found at any taxidermist studio or meat locker during the Golden Age of Mule Deer hunting, many of these fine trophies have been lost to time and obscurity.

EASTMAN FAMILY ARCHIVES

suit of some of the best mule deer hunting our continent probably has ever seen. Hunters in hot spots like Flagstaff, Arizona; Jackson, Wyoming; Cedar City, Utah; Elko, Nevada; Soda Springs, Idaho; and Montrose, Colorado, would put on the ground some of the biggest mule deer ever to be seen by modern man.

These buck hunters, their families and friends would quietly lay the foundation for a mule deer hunting culture like the country had never seen before. Many of these early pioneering buck hunters would never know each other and would not have cared to anyway. With very little magazine coverage and no hunting television shows, the boom in mule deer hunting would go completely unnoticed by most American hunters. This modest, silent fraternity of big buck hunters would kill more big bucks than ever before and most of them surprisingly thought the golden era of mule deer hunting would never end. With over-the-counter buck tags available in almost every state and massive tracts of public and private acres at their disposal, who would have ever thought there could be an end? Not Jack, nor Joey for that matter.

No one really knows what caused the mule deer explosion in the late 1950s, but I believe it was a number of very unique and rare factors that would combine to create the best mule deer habitat conditions our country has ever seen. To start with, a world war that put most of the able-bodied American males on another continent thousands of miles away for nearly five long years would drop hunting pressure to historic lows. Add to that some extreme and controversial predator control measures that included trapping, shooting, and very scorched-earth poisoning methods that removed predation from the population control equation almost entirely.

To those factors add the fact that with the men all overseas fighting a war, the government and landowners put into effect some very aggressive slash-and-burn agricultural methods that would create some of the best wildlife habi-

Gordon Eastman poses with his Wyoming buck killed in the late 1950s in Jackson Hole, Wyoming.

MIKE EASTMAN

Mike Eastman and Bryon Wilson pose with two huge Wyoming non-typical bucks killed in 1972. By the early 1970s the Mule Deer Golden Age had hit its peak.

MIKE EASTMAN

tat the West had ever seen. And to top it all off, add a long run of very mild weather conditions but average snowfall and you have the makings of a wildlife phenomenon that may never be duplicated again.

I believe this historic mule deer hunting period took place somewhere between 1957 and 1976. It was during this short-lived 20-year run that more than 900 records-class deer would be taken by hunters in the West. These figures eclipse just 322 records-book deer that were recorded during the 20 years prior. It was during this time period that my family would relocate from Omak, Washington, to the valley of Jackson Hole, Wyoming, where the mule deer hunting was much, much better. As a first generation hunter, my grandfather Gordon Eastman would live out this era of gold, hunting the hills of western Wyoming for some of the biggest bucks he had ever laid eyes on. It would be here that he would pass along the skills, techniques and passions of mule deer hunting to his boys and eventually, down to me.

The long ride back to California with the buck on the roof of the Jeep would be interrupted with a brief but lucrative stop in the little desert boom town of Las Vegas. There they received a miraculous $1,000 windfall for first place in the annual big buck contest at one of the local casinos.

On a local system well short of the comprehensive scoring system of the Boone and Crockett Club, Jack's behemoth posted an impressive 65 points—a width of 38 inches and 27 points that you could hang a wedding ring on. With the prize money in hand, Jack would move the family north and use the funds for a down payment on a small ranch in the north end of Santa Clara County, a spot that would later be renamed Silicon Valley.

Jack and his family would continue hunting big mule deer fanatically for the next 20 years. With deer being treated like vermin by game agencies, ranchers and country folk, how could this ever end?

"We always thought, how on earth could we ever kill all of those deer," Jack said to the local paper years later, "even with three buck tags, we thought it would never...could never end."

But it did. Soon after Doug Burris, Jr., pulled the trigger on what would be the World's Record typical mule deer buck near Dolores, Colorado, in the fall of 1972, the tide began to swing the other way. The next five to ten years would see the mule deer herds and populations begin to slide into a tailspin.

The family ranch would eventually turn into a large cattle operation spanning thousands of acres of fertile California countryside. After Jack's passing, the family sold the ranch to a developer who built over a thousand homes for real estate-craving techies.

Joe and his family eventually relocated to Wyoming where they reside today, comfortably, in the heart of mule deer country. The family still hunts as hard as ever, mostly for truly massive big bucks they may never find again. But the thought of the mule deer golden era being well behind them does not deter them from heading to the hills each fall in search of that one-in-a-million buck—a buck that might hold a candle to Grampa Jack's Nevada giant.

Most of the first generation of mule deer hunters has all but moved on now, but for the rest of us, we are waiting for the next golden era of mule deer hunting. In the meantime, the hills are welcoming the third, fourth, and even fifth generation of hardcore mule deer hunters, all looking for that once-in-a-lifetime buck. The records, stories, and folklore of the first era of mule deer gold still live on today, fuel for the fiery mule deer passion that many of us have contracted from our grandfathers and great-grandfathers. Our ancestors hunted mule deer in a time when no one thought it would ever end, when deer could be seen by the thousands and big bucks were nothing all that special, but certainly special enough to keep them coming back for more, year after year after year—an era of gold.

DNA OF A MULE DEER HUNTER

RYAN HATFIELD | WESTERN HUNTER & ELK HUNTER MAGAZINES

As the title *A Mule Deer Retrospective* implies, this book was created for those hunters with a strong passion for both mule deer and mule deer hunting history. For me, it's hard to decide which I like more—massive, deep-forked mulies or the hunters back in the old days who pursued them. I'm equally as drawn to the eye candy of a big non-typical mule deer rack as I am to an old-time hunting photo of someone in an old red velvet crusher and blue jeans holding a vintage .30-30 and wearing horn-rimmed glasses. Perhaps an old Willys jeep or a Tote Gote motorcycle somewhere within the frame might complete the perfect ensemble.

The hunters of that era were truly hardy by comparison to today's hunters. Most never had a pack, unless it was an old Forest Service pack board, and few even had a way to pack water. Most times, they simply strapped an old fixed-blade knife to their belt, put a candy bar in their shirt pocket, laced up the old work boots, and set out after meat and adventure.

There were no boot dryers for their non-insulated leather boots; only campfires or woodstoves. There were no ballistic turrets; back then it was open sights or at best, a simple 4x scope. There weren't any trail cameras either; and honestly, the entire thought of "scouting" in any form was largely nonexistent.

For those who like gadgets and technology, you might say hunting is better today. Hunting purists might argue just the opposite. I'm not saying it was better or worse back then, but there's no doubt it was much different.

As someone who has spent a large amount of time researching mule deer hunting history for both work and hobby, for me, the passion goes far beyond just big antlers and vintage photos. The hunters of that era had a real charm to them. I've interviewed literally thousands of them over the years, and almost without exception, they were/are a genuinely happy lot, with great charisma and social skills. Almost all of them experienced the Great Depression, lived through World War II, and epitomized all that was truly special about the Greatest Generation. Mostly unassuming and always with a welcoming smile, they were truly a special bunch.

For the author, the challenge of backpack hunting for mulies on public land up in the high country is as good as life gets.

BORN THAT WAY

From an early age—long before I was able to hunt—I was somehow instinctually drawn

specifically to mule deer. Something about their solitary nature, choice of habitat, and ever-unique headgear drew me in like a moth to a flame. No one forced it on me and I really can't explain it, but it was there, and it was strong in me.

I'd like to think that my own hunting-life experiences mirror what many hardcore mule deer hunters in the West have lived. I came from simple roots, growing up in a small hunting town in the mountains of central Idaho. Mule deer were a common staple of our hunting efforts. It quickly became a major part of who I am; my identity.

Perhaps where my heritage might be a bit more unique than most, though, are the generations of my family that led me to be a diehard buck hunter, with dreams and aspirations of taking a trophy like the ones being celebrated within these pages.

When I was younger, I thought I was pioneering my own path. However, the older I got and the more I learned—both about hunting and my own family—the more I realized that path had been laid down over many generations. I was simply retracing many family hunting trails, with the same eager mind and relentless pursuit as my family before me.

But when did it start, and where do I fit into it? Was it 1869? Or 1922? Or 1967? Or 1984? Is it living and hunting in the present, or about those who came before me? Or those who will hopefully come after? Is it about me? Or is it simply an honor to have been a part of the process—to have been able to take part in something as special as hunting for mule deer in rugged backcountry places? Back when I was a kid, these questions never existed, but as I think about my place in it, I think it's all of the above.

The author's great-great grandpa, Harry Purnel (far left), holds a small mule deer buck following a successful hunting trip with friends in 1927.

SEVEN GENERATIONS OF MULE DEER HUNTERS

My family first settled in central Idaho in 1869 when my great-great-great-great-grandfather Marvin Kilborn moved from the promised land of western Oregon to some mostly unsettled ground in a mountain valley in Idaho. I can't help but wonder what he witnessed through his own eyes—the last of the Indians and plowing virgin soil. Did he ever see a grizzly before they were eradicated? Did he ever see a truly giant mule deer in an era when mature bucks were all over those mountains?

Another branch of my family settled in the same area in 1916. Harry and Rosa Purnel and their large young family made it there by pushing a Model T up and over some of the extreme travelways of the time to get there. He died long before I was born, but I have a photo of him and several other men on a deer hunt near my hometown in 1927. He's holding a yearling buck, and several other deer are shown as well—a truly successful hunt in an era when not a lot of mule deer were to be found due to heavy subsistence hunting.

I look at that photo with all my local expertise and years of knowledge of exploring that same country and try to pick apart where they might have been hunting. I can't help but wonder if I've hiked the same ridge where he downed that little meat buck.

Yet another branch of my family—and perhaps the lineage where the "hunting gene" is the strongest—is the Daniels family. My great-grandpa Lewis Daniels was a strong and well-respected man. He was a leader; a tough man who did many things reflective of that gritty era of the Great Depression. At one point, as the first federally appointed game warden in eastern Idaho, he was paid to patrol the Idaho-Wyoming line on snowshoes, apprehending elk poachers in efforts to let the elk population grow.

In 1922, he and some like-minded friends of adventurous spirit went on an expedition into the Middle Fork of the Salmon River, later known as the Idaho Primitive Area, and finally as the Frank Church Wilderness. While on that hunt, he killed a giant mule deer (a 28-point buck according to his own writing on the photo). They also had over-the-counter tags and took mountain goats (yes, you could just buy a mountain goat tag and go hunting back then). I'd give just about anything to see that big buck rack and to know what happened to it, but as was the way of that era of hunters, it slipped away, likely gone forever. Antlers and horns were simply a novelty.

The Daniels side of my family, from Lewis all the way down to me, were all true explorers, with a strong desire to see the next basin or breathtaking view. Perhaps the most prominent was my great-uncle Henry "Hank" Daniels. Lewis's son Hank was a hunting and exploring addict. Any spare moment might find him exploring a new jeep trail, working a job that would land him in the mountains, or chasing anything from big ol' bucks to waterfowl.

Hank had a keen wit and adventurous spirit for hunting and was fortunate to live in the golden era of mule deer hunting in Idaho—the 1950s through the 1970s. Hank's ability to zero in on a big buck was legendary among the locals. He paid attention like few in that era did. He had amazing intuition about the instincts of big mule deer, what made them tick, and how to work it to his advantage. He also set out on occasion specifically to find and kill a big buck, which was not nearly as common then as it is today.

As such, it's with a really sweet irony that a favorite story he would tell was hooking up with my great-grandfather Albert Kilborn simply because Albert had one of the first four-wheel-drive jeeps to be found anywhere in the region. It didn't take Hank long to see the value of such a setup for hunting late-season bucks in the rut—a time when deep snows often discouraged other hunters.

From my mid-teen years—roughly the same time the mule deer hunting gene really began to express itself intently—I was drawn to Hank. Hank had a way of drawing people to him anyway. A charismatic man with everything but a serious answer, he always had a way of commanding the room. He was also a natural at most everything he tried. He built his own house, was an accomplished and self-taught wildlife artist, a woodworker, and plenty of other things; but the quality that caught hold of me the most was his hunting prowess and ability to tell a story.

Back in the day, Hank was a big buck magnet. He and his M1 Garand.30-06 with the quick-loading 8 shot clips were a lethal combination. He and his partners were so good, in fact, that they took several B&C-class mule deer—as many or more truly giant bucks as anyone I know.

In 1966, Hank and his hunting partner, Ed Martin, drove out in mid-November to a likely hunting spot and found two sets of tracks in the snow. Both were huge bucks, and each man followed a different set. Hank wasn't able to take the buck he was after, but Ed found the mother lode. At the other end of that set of tracks was a 279-5/8 B&C non-typical giant—a thick-necked, roman-nosed monster with Coke-can-thick bases and 39 points. It was nearly 40 inches wide and had massive points radiating in nearly every direction. A true pioneer of his era, Hank even got the buck on film—perhaps the biggest buck ever filmed in that era.

One year later, in 1967, Hank was at it again. He and his brother-in-law, my great-uncle Ferd Muller, along with another friend, Harold Whitaker, were hunting a transition zone where mule deer rut in that area. Spaced about 50 yards apart, the men were pushing a draw when a heavy, deep-forked non-typical jumped up. Ferd fired quickly and knocked the buck down, but had only stunned it by hitting it in the antler. Hank followed up by killing the buck. It was a massive, big-framed buck that would later be scored at 238 3/8 by B&C's Director of Big Game Records, Jack Reneau.

In 1975, Hank was at it again. He had his 11-year-old son James with him. Still too young to pack a rifle, James was there to watch and learn—and learn he did, from one of the best. There were several men in the hunting party, and they were spaced somewhat equally apart in some lower foothills country, making a deer drive through the sagebrush.

Hank possessed an uncanny big-buck savvy, and his instincts told him that if there was a big buck there, it would likely hunker down until the marching line of hunters had passed and then sneak out on their back trail. On nothing more than that hunch, Hank pulled up and waited, long past when everyone else had gone. As James's young mind grew impatient and he seemed more interested in throwing rocks, Hank kept his steely gaze where it needed to be. Sometime later, a buck appeared like a ghost, head low to the ground as it wound its way through the sage, doing exactly as Hank had pictured it.

When the fireworks had ended and the dust settled, Hank had another monster mule deer on the ground. This jaw-dropper had ultra-heavy bases, with so many points they were nearly impossible to count. When it was officially scored at 249-2/8 B&C, it was determined the buck had 43 scoreable points—the most ever recorded on any deer in Idaho history.

Hank, who was also a meat cutter and familiar with the finer observations of a carcass, noted that this old warrior had been through the wringer in his day. The buck had a healed-over bullet wound across the top of his rump, another through his neck (signified by white dots on each side of his neck), and at some point, the deer had also taken a load of buckshot in the face. There's no doubting when looking at the photo of that deer, with the big roman nose and scar on his neck, that this was a true grizzled veteran and fine trophy.

Sadly for me, Hank's big buck hunting days were over by the time I was old enough to hunt. He had long since figured out that cow elk tasted a whole heck of a lot better than rut-

Shots Net 35 Points

ED MARTIN OF BOISE got five points for every one of the seven shots that he fired at a buck. The antlers of the deer killed in the Council area had 17 points on one side and 18 on the other.

Hunter Bags Trophy After Tough Chase

The first two shots only slowed down the 35-point buck that Ed Martin of Boise saw moving 150 yards away.

Martin found a trail of blood and followed it for half a mile before the buck came in view again. Martin fired five more times before the buck tumbled for good.

Five of the seven shots had hit their mark. One shot, possibly the first he had fired, had broken a front leg.

Although the buck was gaunt, it weighed 240 pounds when it was field dressed. The buck had no incisors and the molars were worn down until they were hardlly visible.

From the description of the teeth, Levi Mohler, game research coordinator at the Idaho Fish and Game Department, estimated that the buck probably was 10-plus years old.

"When their teeth go bad, they are not long for this world," Mohler said as he doubted that the buck would have lasted through the winter.

Martin had the meat smoked. He said it turned out good. He took the antlers to E. Kliess Brown, information director at the Idaho Fish and Game Department, to have them measured for entry in the Boone and Crockett Club's trophy listings.

Brown said that preliminary measurements indicated the antlers would score 274 points for 20th place in the all-time records of the club for non-typical antlers.

The antlers had 17 points on one side and 18 on the other. There are only four other deer entered in the record books for non-typical mule deer that had more points. The Number One deer had 43, another had 40 and two had 36.

After he concluded his measurements, Brown said that the rack could "very well rank in top place for the biennium" in Boone and Crockett records which are published every two years.

BOONE AND CROCKETT ... 4400 Forbes Ave. Pittsburgh

NON-TYPICAL MULE DEER

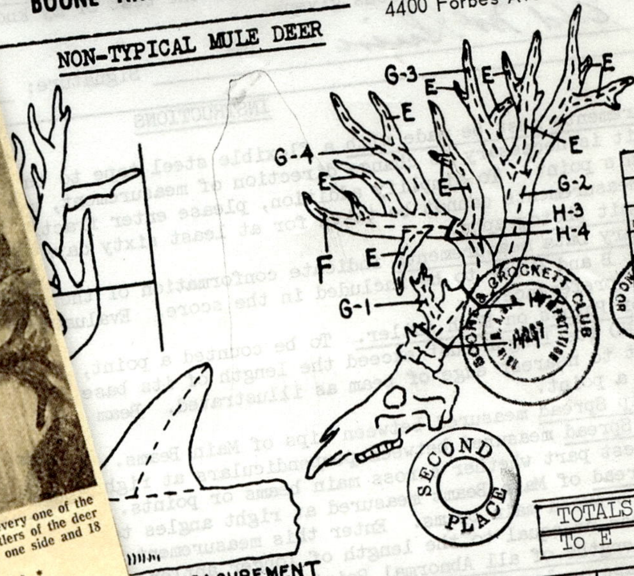

ABNORMAL Points Line E

R	L
8 3/8	2 1/8
4 6/8	8 6/8
	3
	3
	2
2 5/8	2 1/8
5 3/8	2 5/8
2 4/8	11 3/8
4 7/8	2 1/8
2 3/8	6 2/8
4 1/8	1 1/8
TOTALS 59	45 4/8
To E	104 4/8

Supplementary Data R.	L.	Column 1 Spread Credit	Column 2 Right Antler	Column 3 Left Antler	Column 4 Difference
18	17				
30 3/8					
39					
		22 5/8			2 1/8
104 4/8			21 7/8	22 5/8	6/8
			4 1/8	3 4/8	5/8
			14 4/8	14 1/8	3/8
			10 3/8	9 6/8	5/8
			8 6/8	6 2/8	2 4/8
			6 3/8	6 2/8	1/8
			5 3/8	5 2/8	1/8
			5 1/8	4 6/8	3/8
			5 1/8	4 4/8	5/8
104 4/8		22 5/8	81 5/8	77	6 1/8 14

H-1. Between Bu... Circumference ... H-2. Between Fi... Place. Circumferen... H-3. Between Main Beam and Third Point. Circumference at Smallest Place H-4. Between Second and Fourth Points

RH interview 8-6-02

TOTALS	
Column 1	22 5/8
Column 2	81 5/8
Column 3	77
Total	181 2/8
SUBTRACT Column 4	6 1/8 ~~14~~
Result	175 1/8 ~~167 2/8~~
Add Line E Total	104 4/8
FINAL SCORE	279 5/8 ~~271 6/8~~

Exact locality where killed: Adams Co., ID ~~Cuprum,~~ Idaho (Lick Creek)

Date killed 11/11/66 By whom killed Ed Martin

Present owner Ed Martin, Idaho Surveying & Rating Bureau

Address Boise, Idaho 83702

Guide's Name and Address None

Remarks: (Mention any abnormalit...

331738

SENT TO Mr Ed Martin

STREET AND NO.

P. O., STATE, AND ZIP CODE

PITTSBURGH, PA. MAY 13 1968

EXTRA SERVICES FOR ADDITIONAL FEES Return Receipt: Shows to whom and date delivered 10¢ fee; Shows to whom, date, and where delivered 35¢ fee; Deliver to Addressee only 50¢ fee (See other...

NO INSURANCE COVERAGE PROVIDED— NOT FOR INTERNATIONAL MAIL

ED MARTIN | THIRTEENTH COMPETITION
SECOND PLACE

Ed Martin's giant Idaho non-typical, taken on a hunt with the author's great-uncle, Henry "Hank" Daniels in 1966, is the largest mule deer ever taken by a hunter in that area. Ed's big buck caused quite a stir and was featured in the big Boise newspaper, the *Idaho Statesman*. Ed's buck was invited to the Club's thirteenth competition in 1968, which was held in Pittsburgh, Pennsylvania, at the Carnegie Museum. He received a Second Place Award with a final score of 271-6/8 points. The remarks on the original score chart note:

> *This deer still had some velvet. Weighed 240 lbs., hog dressed. Was a "gummer," but very good meat.*

Decades later, the Club decided that deducting inside spread that exceeded the longer main beam from the final score in addition to not counting any excessive spread over the longer main beam in tabulations was double penalizing the trophy. This was changed to allow the recording of an inside spread up to the length of the longer main beam with no deduction taken if measures greater. This resulted in a new score for Ed's mule deer at 279-5/8 points. He received a letter from B&C in 1990 with the updated score.

Abnormal Points	
Right Antler	Left Antler
1 4/8	1 4/8
1 4/8	2 1/8
1 2/8	2 6/8
1 7/8	1 4/8
3 3/8	4 4/8
5 7/8	3 3/8
3 6/8	3
4 1/8	2 4/8
1 3/8	6 3/8
2	2 1/8
Subtotals 42 0	49 6/8
Total to E 91 6/8	

SEE OTHER SIDE FOR INSTRUCTIONS

				Column 1 Spread Credit	Column 2 Right Antler	Column 3 Left Antler	Column 4 Difference
No. Points on Right Antler	21	No. Points on Left Antler	22				
Tip to Tip Spread	16 1/8	C. Greatest Spread	31 7/8				
Inside Spread of Main Beams	21 4/8	(Credit May Equal But Not Exceed Longer Antler)		21 4/8			
Total of Lengths of Abnormal Points			91 6/8				
Length of Main Beam					26 3/8	26 5/8	3/…
G-1. Length of First Point, If Present					3 2/8	3 4/8	4/…
G-2. Length of Second Point					18	13 6/8	4…
G-3. Length of Third Point, If Present					4 7/8	—	4…
G-4. Length of Fourth Point, If Present					3 3/8	3 1/8	
H-1. Circumference at Smallest Place Between Burr and First Point					6 4/8	6 4/8	
H-2. Circumference at Smallest Place Between First and Second Points					6 1/8	5 4/8	
H-3. Circumference at Smallest Place Between Main Beam and Third Point					4 6/8	4 4/8	
H-4. Circumference at Smallest Place Between Second and Fourth Points					5 1/8	5 2/8	
TOTALS				21 4/8	78 4/8	69 0	1…

B&C BIG GAME AWARDS 23 1995-1997

Adams Co., Idaho (15)

ADD	Column 1	21 4/8
	Column 2	78 4/8
	Column 3	69 0
	Subtotal	169 0
SUBTRACT Column 4		11 4/8
	Subtotal	157 4/8

Exact Locality Where Killed: * Unit 22 near Council, Adams Co.

By Whom Killed: ~~Charles~~ (Henry) Danie…

Date Killed: 10-20-75

Present Owner: * Ray Cross Raymond (OK)

Owner's Address:

Guide's Name and Address:

Remarks: (Mention Any Abnormalities or Unique Qualities)

… Hatfield

ting mule deer, so he had little interest in resurrecting that part of his hunting legacy, even as I was chomping at the bit for it. I had to settle for tagging along on his cow hunts, still eager to spend time with him and still hanging on his every word. He was a special man who lived and hunted in a special era, and I'll always be envious of that.

A DOMINO EFFECT CHANGES EVERYTHING

In some ways, even though it wasn't direct or intentional, Hank had a huge impact on many things that happened in my life. In the early 1990s, Hank sold those two big mule deer to an antler collector. He needed money for some home improvements and since the antlers were more novelty than treasure to him, he let them go for the money he needed. I was devastated.

However, that simple act set in motion a domino effect for me. It got me thinking about those big bucks and all the history that went with them, so I interviewed him and wrote down his stories, more for myself than anything. After I had them documented, it led me to think about Howard Paradis, Clarke Childers, Ed Martin, Roy Eastlick, and many others around my hometown who had taken big bucks back in the old days and whose names were listed in the Boone and Crockett records books that I had practically memorized by that point in my life. Those men were all in their 60s or 70s by then, and all that history was in danger of slipping away.

It ultimately led me to write a book called *Idaho's Greatest Mule Deer*, a 400-page hardcover book that preserved a huge amount of history in stories and photos of many of the biggest mule deer ever taken in my home state. To this day, it remains one of the things in my life that I'm most proud of. Many of the hunters who were featured in that book are gone now, but to have been able to talk with each of them and hear those remarkable stories from their own mouths was truly special, and I'm grateful for the experience.

ABOVE: Hank Daniels poses with two of his most outstanding trophy mule deer. In his hands is his massive 1967 prize, which scores 238-3/8 B&C. At his feet is his big buck taken in 1975. This buck, which scores 249-2/8 B&C, has 43 scoreable points—the most of any deer in Idaho history.

OPPOSITE: Hank's 43-point buck, complete with roman nose, thick neck, and assorted scars, was taken with an M1 Garand shooting a 180-grain Speer bullet in low sagebrush foothills from about 100 yards.

The author's dad, Rusty Hatfield (right), surveys the scene following a successful hunt for a big buck circa 1969.

Those dominoes continued when the writing of that book led me to be offered a job as Boone and Crockett Club's Assistant Director of Big Game Records, working with and for Jack Reneau.

That move also led me to my wife, children, and ultimately, my current career as editor of *Western Hunter* and *Elk Hunter* magazines—one of today's voices for big game hunting in the West. For me, it's the chance to be a true steward of the hunt; to protect it and present it in a respectful way and hopefully help steer it in a better direction. All this because of my love for mule deer and a simple act of a hero of mine selling his mule deer antlers—a hunter's "butterfly flapping its wings", if you will. On a side note, which I will say with a smile, those two big non-typicals that Uncle Hank sold now reside on my wall, where I consider it an honor to be their caretaker.

FOLLOWING FAMILIAR FOOTSTEPS WHILE CHASING MY OWN DREAMS

When I think back to all these hunts in my family over so many decades—nearly all in the exact same country—it makes me think of many things. How many hundreds of miles have I hiked and canyons have I glassed that my own family before me also hunted? What did they see that was the same and what was different?

It's also interesting to see how each generation in my family seems to mirror some of the common themes of the day. With my great-grandpa Lewis Daniels, it was the old .30-40 Krag and some high lace-up boots, exploring his home state. With his son, my great-uncle Hank, it was the M1 Garand leftover from WWII and an occasional leaning toward specifically hunting for big bucks. My dad hunted with the standard Remington .30-06 and had the advantage of four-wheel drives and more modern equipment. Now it trickles down to me—a hardcore backpack hunter with a .300 Win Mag; a hunter who applies for tags in multiple states with hopes of hunting big mulies in historic destination areas such as the Gunnison Basin of Colorado, the high basins of western Wyoming, and the famed mule deer grounds of Utah, in addition to my home state of Idaho.

In some ways, I feel like an island; as though this love for hunting big, solitary mule deer all started and ended with just what I've done and known as a hunter. Yet there is proof, in things I've seen and other things I'll never see or know, that my family laid that foundation long before I ever existed. It's a dizzying, yet intriguing thought—one that crosses my mind more often as I get older.

When I first started hunting mule deer, all I had was "the itch" and the good fortune of close proximity to good hunting. I spent incalculable hours and days hiking along hoping to find a big buck—a trophy mule deer like one would see in Outdoor Life back then. I'd never seen a buck like that, but I knew they must exist, because they were there in photos and on my own family's walls. I plastered my bedroom wall with big buck photos as the internal fire to find such a trophy built intensely inside of me.

From an eager, yet ignorant teen to the man I've become today, I'm somewhat proud to say that fire hasn't waned. To the contrary, it's as intense as ever. As is often the progression of a hunter, I've gotten older and wiser. I'm now a legitimate predator threat to even the savviest of big mule deer. I'm at that stage where my overall knowledge and physical ability are still strong, and my ability to strategize and decipher information is great. Yet I also live in an information age and competitive era where it becomes more and more difficult to fasten a tag to such a grand prize.

Perhaps my best trait, though, is my hunter's resolve—the ability to see each day as a fresh, clean slate where that big mule deer I seek so desperately could be right in front of me. It's the ability to wash away day after day after day of defeat; to wake up each morning at a ridiculous hour and put my body in treacherous terrain and circumstance; to suffer greatly both

LEFT: Taken in 2010 on an Idaho backcountry backpack hunt, this fine typical buck is about as good a trophy as a hunter can expect in a general-season hunting unit.

OPPOSITE: A classic Wyoming trophy mulie taken on a high country backpack hunt in exceptionally rugged terrain in 2012. This type of hunt, which tests the mettle of even the best hunter, is the type of hunt the author prefers. This hunt was featured on the TV show, *The Western Hunter*.

physically and emotionally, time and time again, with the dream that today might be that day; the day I find "the one." However, perhaps defining the success of the hunt that way is ultimately a disservice to the hunt itself. I've actually been fairly fortunate. I've taken a fine collection of big mule deer in my time.

In 2008, I was fortunate enough to take a fine 30-inch, very mature buck on the Rocky Mountain Front in Montana. The Front is a grand and historic mule deer area full of giant rock reefs and grizzlies.

The next year I took my largest buck to date—a 34-inch, 200-class monster buck in the famed high country of western Wyoming, not all that far from where the Wyoming state record typical (the Hoback Buck) was taken. Truth be told, I probably didn't deserve that buck. He simply walked out in the open and I shot him. I'd like to think it was a gift for all my efforts and suffering over the years and for bucks I perhaps did deserve that simply got away.

Even this past year, I took another fine buck in Wyoming on a grueling backpack hunt in steep country at 10,000 feet. That hunt tested my resolve physically, but the end result was a fantastic dark-antlered typical that just missed B&C. There are other fine deer as well—too many to list here—that occupy special places on my wall and in my mind.

Ultimately, the question arises though. What if? What if I never accomplish my dream of taking a B&C mule deer like Hank did? Will I have failed? Will the disappointment sting after my body gives out and I'm left with nothing but photo albums of past hunts? Resoundingly and emphatically, I must say, "No!"

Why? Because to have hunted mule deer at all is to have truly lived. To think of each day that tested my mettle, or to think of each view I witnessed, or every memory I made along the way with friends and family is priceless. Hunting mule deer—for a true hardcore public land mule deer hunter like me—is about a special journey. It's a journey laced with views of high mountain basins, the smells of sage and pine sap, the feeling of extreme cold and burning legs, of lungs begging for air, and a lifetime of sweat equity. Taking a big buck is truly nothing more than the icing on an already perfect cake.

WOMEN AND WESTERN DEER

WAYNE VAN ZWOLL | B&C PROFESSIONAL MEMBER

Adventure has drawn women to wilderness since covered wagons crossed deer trails. Augusta Higgins Farnham arrived in Denver with her husband during the summer of 1860 atop a wagonload of whisky barrels behind six oxen. They traveled on to Canon City, then Salt Lake City where, she said, there were only three other Gentile women.

Conformity was not Augusta's style. Her marriage ended in divorce, a rare event back then. She joined her brother, Thomas Higgins, seeking land in northwestern Colorado. At Lily Park, a couple days' ride west of Craig, they met Allen Grant (A.G.) Wallihan. Sometime later, A.G. and Augusta may have become snowbound in a remote cabin. Details have dimmed, but evidently to protect their honor, the two wed in the spring of 1885, traveling to Rawlins, Wyoming for the ceremony.

Photographs show Augusta a stocky woman, distinctive for her shoulder-length "sausage curls." The frontier didn't pamper women, but Mrs. Wallihan took care with her appearance, even when shooting game. Posing with a couple of fine mule deer bucks she downed with a single bullet from her Remington-Hepburn rifle, she looked ready for a carriage ride to church. She had by some accounts a vitriolic tongue and was determined to carve her own path. But Augusta Wallihan never renounced her feminine side.

Standing over one of her many trophy mule deer, subsistence-and-sport huntress Augusta "Gusty" Wallihan appears every inch the frontier matron with her dressy bonnet, prairie-pattern cartridge belt, floral-embroidered gauntlets, hunting knife, and Remington-Hepburn rifle—circa 1895.

IMAGE COURTESY MUSEUM OF NORTHWEST COLORADO, 02-79-11

Such contradictions must have puzzled the men of her time, even her husband, 22 years younger than Augusta. But the union endured. A.G. was consumed by photography in an era when photographs in untamed places were notoriously difficult. After they settled in Lay, 20 miles west of Craig, he took up as town postmaster–though was apparently loath to do physical chores. Augusta may well have tended the milk cow and other resident livestock, and maintained the local weather station. She accounted for much of the venison taken from their sizable property and surrounding federal lands.

Augusta's skill with the rifle brought her an invitation to the 1895 Sportsman's Expo at Madison Square Garden—a remarkable offer, given the gender assumptions of the day. She attended.

Despite her affinity for the hunt, Augusta Wallihan shared with A.G. concern that grew to outrage over the decimation of western wildlife by market hunters. She vented her disapproval in letters to various periodicals. Meanwhile, she and her husband took every chance to photograph wildlife. Both hardened to the trail, they spent long days afield with burdensome box cameras. The glass negative of each precious shot was developed at night under a ruby lamp.

Legend has it Augusta's first camera came by way of a traveler who accepted in trade a pair of gloves she'd fashioned from buckskin.

Depending on whose account you read, Augusta Wallihan fueled–even ensured–her husband's success as a photographer. Indisputably, both contributed a great deal to the photo records of the post-Civil War West, and to growing public awareness of sharp declines in game herds. Wallihan images drew such acclaim that Augusta and A.G. were invited to the Paris World Exposition of 1900. They exhibited again in 1904 at the St. Louis World's Fair.

Augusta Wallihan's 86 years spanned the Mexican War and World War I. She saw the Rockies as they were before settlement and hunted mule deer where no white sportsman had hunted before. She saw the early results of her push for wildlife conservation in legislation signed by Theodore Roosevelt. With rifle and camera, she was, for her time, the quintessential outdoors woman.

Nearly a century after Mrs. Wallihan's death, women remain a small subset of big game hunters worldwide. But they're an important part of that group–more so, in fact, than the numbers suggest. Both their participation and success in hunting mule deer have grown recently.

A quick perusal of Boone and Crockett records shows a couple of women's names near the top of the typical mule deer chart. Myra Smith shot a truly outstanding buck; with a score of 210, it ranks 25th overall. Katie Norman's entry, taping 206, places 73rd in the crowded top tier of the best mule deer ever shot. B&C's non-typical list puts Catherine Keene's tremendous 285-inch deer in 45th place.

These bucks were shot in 2006, 1990 and 2004, respectively. The non-typical deer killed by Alice O'Brien seems an anomaly. This 277-inch giant dates to 1949, when very few women entered deer in the records books. Even this small sample suggests more women are shooting big mule deer now than in the past–and by extension, more women are hunting!

Such a trend should please all hunters, as women's views on hunting carry more weight in public discourse than those of men–especially among people who don't hunt.

Long ago, while guiding hunters in fine mule deer country, I was asked by a female client, "Why don't more women come here?" My ready answer was the hunt's cost, deterring women and men alike! "What about summer? You don't have to hunt to fall in love with this country. Host a camp. Offer shooting and archery, horseback riding and fly fishing...." She agreed to bring a contingent of women while I gathered gear and instructors and set the week's agenda. That adventure proved a success and became an annual event. A women-only hunting safari followed in Namibia for kudu, gemsbok, and other big game.

That was nine summers ago. Every woman who's taken these trips has returned with a fresh and enthusiastic view of hunting–even those who'd not before considered killing game.

"I'll just photograph animals. I don't think I could shoot one." Such reticence shows a laudable concern for life. A hunt that delivers exhilaration at a kill properly brings remorse as well.

Alas, you cannot understand hunting unless you hunt; nor can you know hunters as conservationists until you've earned a kill. People unwilling to become predators can watch video

clips showing predation, but such clinical exposure falls short of experience. "You don't have to fire," I reply. "But neither a hunt nor that decision makes any sense until you've game in your sights."

Every woman on these trips has taken big game. "Life-changing!" say some. It is so because their lives had little in common with that of Augusta Wallihan, who prospered close to the land and understood the raw cycles that shape the natural world. An upbringing in artificial environs blurs the line between conservation and preservation. It can produce distorted views of wild places, creatures and rhythms. As hunters, women reconnect with the wild. More importantly, they return able to articulate that relationship to families and friends, colleagues and constituents.

One woman, with no shooting experience, came afield so she could "talk hunting" with her son. That October, she shared in his first successful deer hunt. She may never take up a rifle herself, but she's an advocate for hunters.

Seemingly attired for church instead of the field, Gusty Wallihan poses in commemoration of her remarkable shooting feat. She invariably hunted with her .40-70 Remington-Hepburn single-shot rifle, an arm that required composed shooting under any circumstances. Circa 1893.

IMAGE COURTESY MUSEUM OF NORTHWEST COLORADO, 02-79-12.

Not long ago I lay prone, tasting the hot dust and squinting into my binocular as a huntress took careful aim. "Good shot!" I gushed the obvious as the animal, struck perfectly, collapsed. Teri picked the hot hull from her .300 and smiled graciously. "Thanks. It was closer than my last mule deer."

A century earlier, some guy probably heard the same from Augusta Wallihan.

ELEANOR O'CONNOR

Eleanor, age 23 when this photo was taken (left), and Jack O'Connor, then age 29, moved from Alpine, Texas, to Flagstaff, Arizona, the summer of 1931. In October they hunted deer on the Kaibab National Forest from a U.S. Forest Service-managed deer camp. Eleanor shot this big mule deer—her very first deer—as it trotted through the junipers at about 125 yards. Her rifle was a model 30-S Remington in the now-obsolete .25 Remington caliber. Jack's deer was a fork-horn. In the midst of the depression, both deer were valued for their meat. Note the iron sights; scopes were not yet in common use.

This photo shows Eleanor at age 56 in October of 1964 with a mule deer that field-dressed 182 pounds, taken in the breaks of the Joseph Plains in Idaho. When this buck jumped up below them, both Eleanor and Jack shot at the same time. Both Eleanor's 7x57mm bullet and Jack's .270 bullet hit the deer in the lungs.

PHOTOS COURTESY ELDON "BUCK" BUCKNER

1911

SOPHIE N. GOLDEN

1928

BABE HANSEN

1946

CORINNE FIELDS

1956

MARGUERITE HILL

1955

VIRGINIA S. HUTH

1954

FRANCES BECHER

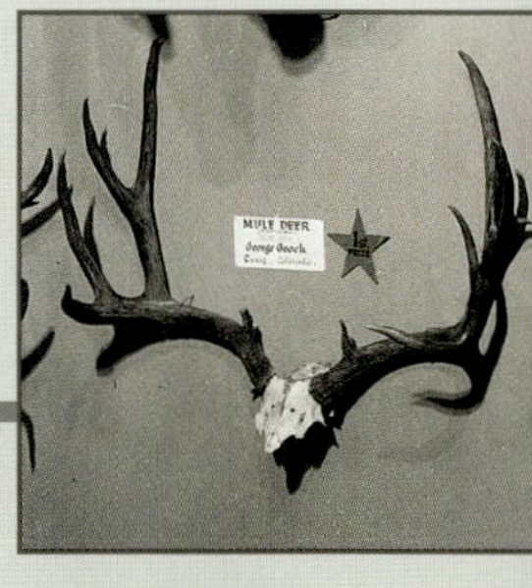

1951

LUCILLE GOOCH

1956

DOROTHY MAE DIBLER

1957

ORA McGURN

1957

PEGGY KEEN

WOMEN AND DEER HUNTING

TROPHY BUCKS THROUGH THE YEARS

1948

KATE HAMILTON

1948

EDNA SANDERS RYTTING

LADY NIMROD—Alice O'Brien, 5515 Cottage, used just one bullet from a .32 Winchester to drop this big buck 20 miles south of Bly midway in the now-past season. The horn spread measured 39½ inches, with 13 points on one side, 11 on the other.

1949

ALICE C. O'BRIEN

1949

JoREVA BEANE WELLBORN

1949

MARY LOU DODD

1950

NANCY McCRAE

1950

MRS. MILROY POWELL

1958

BERNICE PETERSEN

1961

LAVONNE BUCEY BREDEHOFT

1963

CELIA GARCIA

1971

PHYLLIS O. CROOKSTON

HUNTRESS
SOPHIE N. GOLDEN

I killed this deer the 15th day of Sept 1911. My rifle was made to order in Springfield Mass, in 1894 The barrel is 32 inches long.
I want Gary to have this picture, rifle, and deer head when I am gone

SOPHIE N. GOLDEN

NON-TYPICAL MULE DEER | 218-5/8 POINTS

Colorado resident Sophie N. Golden shot this impressive non-typical buck on September 15, 1911. She was hunting near Dallas Divide in Ouray County, Colorado, shooting a 170-grain bullet through her custom .32-40 Winchester rifle that was made in Springfield, Massachusetts, in 1894. The rifle had a 32-inch barrel.

A handwritten note included with the trophy entry states: *I want Gary to have this picture, rifle, and deer head when I'm gone.*

Our records do not indicate exactly who Gary was or whether he is a relative of the current trophy owner Aaron Galloway, who entered the deer in the Club's records program in 2004.

HARRIET "BABE" HANSEN

NON-TYPICAL MULE DEER | 305-3/8 POINTS

Harriet "Babe" Hansen and her husband Henry opened the Sawtooth Lodge in Grandjean, Idaho, in 1927. Hansen Lake in that vicinity is her namesake. Back then she was known as a packer, and by all accounts she must have been pretty tough.

In the fall of 1928, she was packing in some elk hunters. They hadn't gone far that day when the party came across this big buck. They didn't have time to mess with him, so they let him go. On the way back out from dropping off the hunters, she found the buck again and decided he was plenty big enough to take.

The non-typical mule deer was officially measured by longtime scorer L. Victor Clark (pictured above) in 1997 for then-owner of the buck, Don Schaufler. With a final B&C score of 305-3/8 points, the buck still ranks as the No. 3 non-typical mule deer in Idaho. The trophy was sold to Cabela's in 2001.

ADDITIONAL INFORMATION PROVIDED BY RYAN HATFIELD, *IDAHO'S GREATEST MULE DEER.*

OFFICIAL SCORING SYSTEM FOR NORTH AMERICAN BIG GAME TROPHIES

Records of North American Big Game

BOONE AND CROCKETT CLUB

Old Milwaukee Depot
250 Station Drive
Missoula, MT 59801

MONT

Minimum Score: Awards 225 All-time 240

NON-TYPICAL MULE DEER

RECEIVED CK22665 B1150.00 AUG 20 1997 6 OF 46 8-19-97 MA BOONE & CROCKETT CLUB

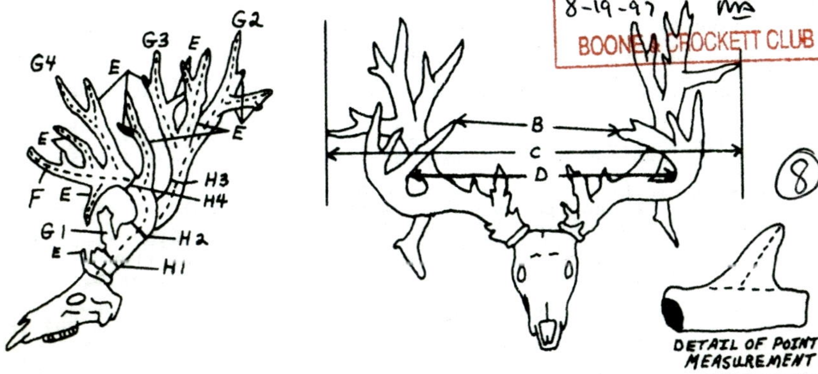

Abnormal Points	
Right Antler	Left Antler
1 0/8	4 1/8
2 2/8	1 6/8
9 2/8	3 5/8
5 4/8	11 7/8
13 0/8	5 4/8
5 2/8	3 6/8
8 3/8	5 2/8
11 3/8	10 4/8
	1 4/8
	4 4/8
	2 2/8
	6 4/8
Subtotals 56 0/8	58 1/8
Total to E 114 1/8	

(8) (13)

SEE OTHER SIDE FOR INSTRUCTIONS				Column 1	Column 2	Column 3	Column 4
A. No. Points on Right Antler	13	No. Points on Left Antler	17	Spread Credit	Right Antler	Left Antler	Difference
B. Tip to Tip Spread	21 0/8	C. Greatest Spread	33 0/8				
D. Inside Spread of Main Beams	22 2/8	(Credit May Equal But Not Exceed Longer Antler)		22 2/8			
E. Total of Lengths of Abnormal Points			114 1/8				
F. Length of Main Beam					25 1/8	26 4/8	1 3/8
G-1. Length of First Point, If Present					3 1/8	2 7/8	2/8
G-2. Length of Second Point					19 2/8	18 1/8	1 1/8
G-3. Length of Third Point, If Present					7 1/8	7 1/8	0/8
G-4. Length of Fourth Point, If Present					12 2/8	12 3/8	1/8
H-1. Circumference at Smallest Place Between Burr and First Point					4 6/8	4 5/8	1/8
H-2. Circumference at Smallest Place Between First and Second Points					4 7/8	4 7/8	0/8
H-3. Circumference at Smallest Place Between Main Beam and Third Point					6 1/8	4 5/8	1 4/8
H-4. Circumference at Smallest Place Between Second and Fourth Points					4 7/8	4 7/8	0/8
Boise Co. TOTALS		Idaho (15)		22 2/8	87 4/8	86 0/8	4 4/8

B&C BIG GAME AWARDS 23 1995 1997

ADD	Column 1	22 2/8	Exact Locality Where Killed: (GRAND JEAN) IDAHO
	Column 2	87 4/8	Date Killed: 1928 By Whom Killed: BABE HANSEN
	Column 3	86 0/8	Present Owner: Cabela's, Inc. (Deceased)
Subtotal		195 6/8	Owner's Address: One Cabela Drive, Sydney, NE 69160
SUBTRACT Column 4		4 4/8	Guide's Name and Address: NONE
Subtotal		191 2/8	Remarks: (Mention Any Abnormalities or ... 2002
Add Line E Total		114 1/8	SEVERAL CHOICES FOR G-3, I LEFT them
FINAL SCORE		305 3/8	MARKED WITH TAPE (meas 3/3/97) C OMO

...rds of North American Big Game

BOONE AND CROCKETT CLUB

Alexandria, Virginia 22314

...mum Score: 240

NON-TYPICAL MULE DEER

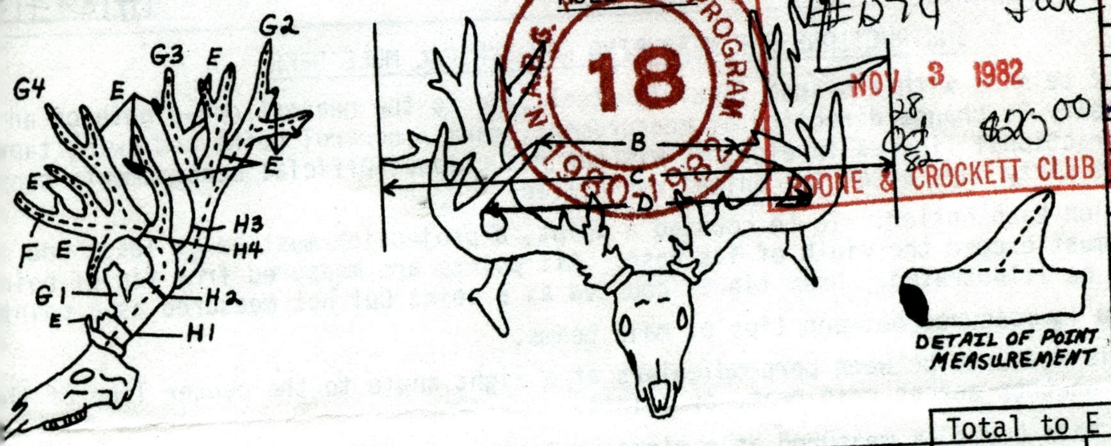

N.A.B.G. AWARDS PROGRAM 18 1980-1982

RECEIVED #D74 JWR NOV 3 1982 $20.00 BOONE & CROCKETT CLUB

Abnormal Points	
Right	Left
11 —	1 5/8
6 6/8	5 6/8
2 3/8	6 —
7 —	
5 4/8	
Total to E 17 7/8	13 3/8

SEE OTHER SIDE FOR INSTRUCTIONS			Column 1 Spread Credit	Column 2 Right Antler	Column 3 Left Antler	Column 4 Difference
Number of Points on Each Antler	R. 10	L. 8				
Tip to Tip Spread		25 5/8				
Greatest Spread		35 —				
Inside Spread of Main Beams	28 1/8	Credit may equal but not exceed length of longer antler	26 4/8			~~1 3/8~~
E Spread exceeds longer antler, enter difference						
. Total of Lengths of Abnormal Points		31 2/8				
. Length of Main Beams				26 2/8	26 4/8	4/8
-1. Length of First Point, if present				3 2/8	2 6/8	4/8
-2. Length of Second Point				16 4/8	18 1/8	1 5/8
-3. Length of Third Point, if present				14 —	14 4/8	4/8
-4. Length of Fourth Point, if present				14 —	12 5/8	1 3/8
H-1. Circumference at Smallest Place Between Burr and First Point				5 4/8	5 5/8	1/8
H-2. Circumference at Smallest Place Between First and Second Points				5 —	5 —	—
H-3. Circumference at Smallest Place Between Main Beam and Third Point				4 4/8	4 6/8	2/8
H-4. Circumference at Smallest Place Between Second and Fourth Points				4 7/8	4 7/8	—
TOTALS		31 2/8	26 4/8	93 7/8	95 —	4 7/8 ~~6 2/8~~

Klamath Co., Oreg.

ADD	Column 1	26 4/8	Exact locality where killed Williamson River O...
	Column 2	93 7/8	Date killed 1946 By whom killed Corinne Fields
	Column 3	95 —	Present Owner Corinne Fields
	TOTAL	215 5/8	Address
SUBTRACT	Column 4	4 7/8 ~~6 2/8~~	Guide's Name and Address None
210 6/8	Result	~~209 3/8~~	Remarks: (Mention any abnormalities or unique qualities)
Add	Line E Total	31 2/8	
FINAL SCORE		~~240 5/8~~ 242	B— MAIL M— H044

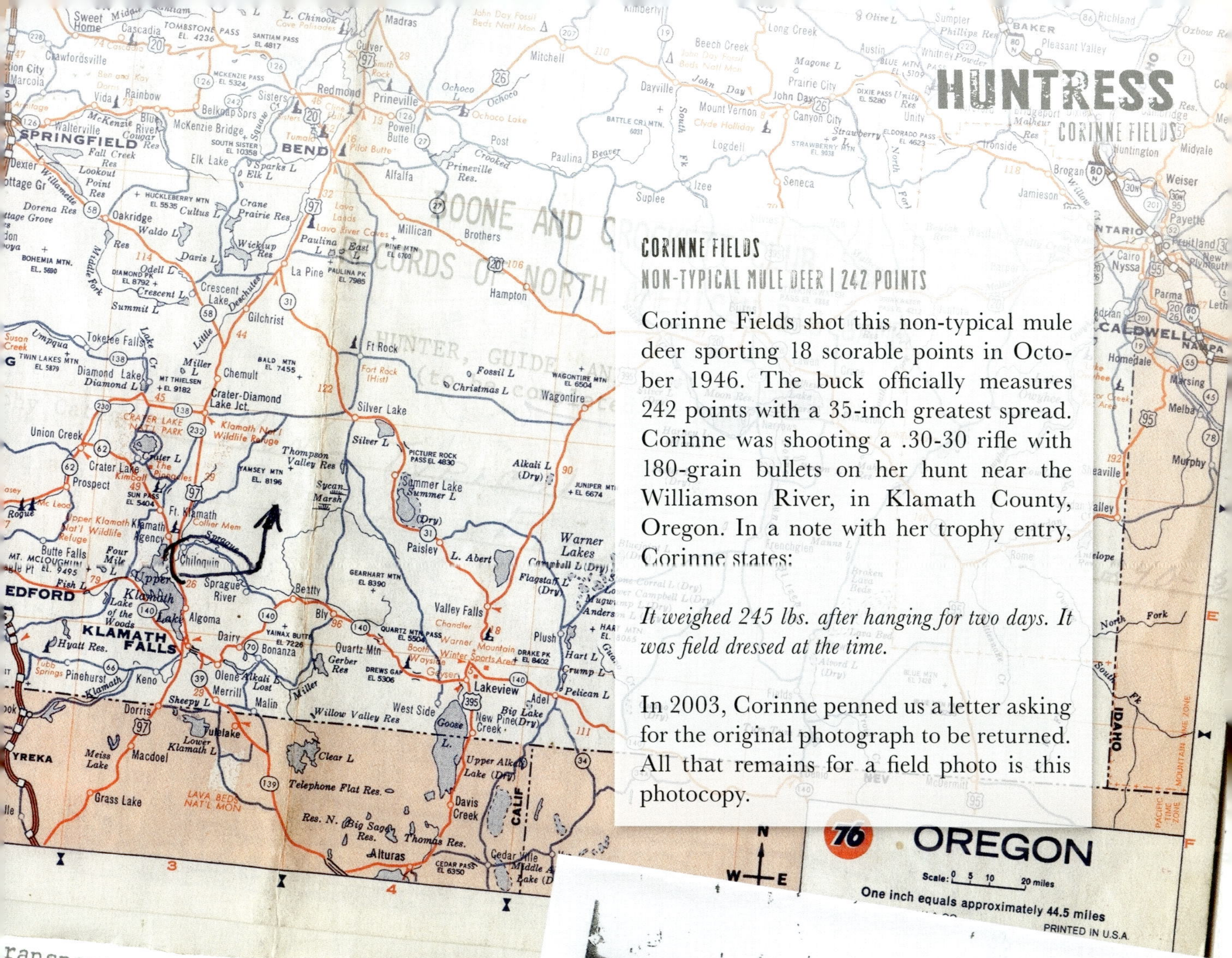

CORINNE FIELDS

NON-TYPICAL MULE DEER | 242 POINTS

Corinne Fields shot this non-typical mule deer sporting 18 scorable points in October 1946. The buck officially measures 242 points with a 35-inch greatest spread. Corinne was shooting a .30-30 rifle with 180-grain bullets on her hunt near the Williamson River, in Klamath County, Oregon. In a note with her trophy entry, Corinne states:

It weighed 245 lbs. after hanging for two days. It was field dressed at the time.

In 2003, Corinne penned us a letter asking for the original photograph to be returned. All that remains for a field photo is this photocopy.

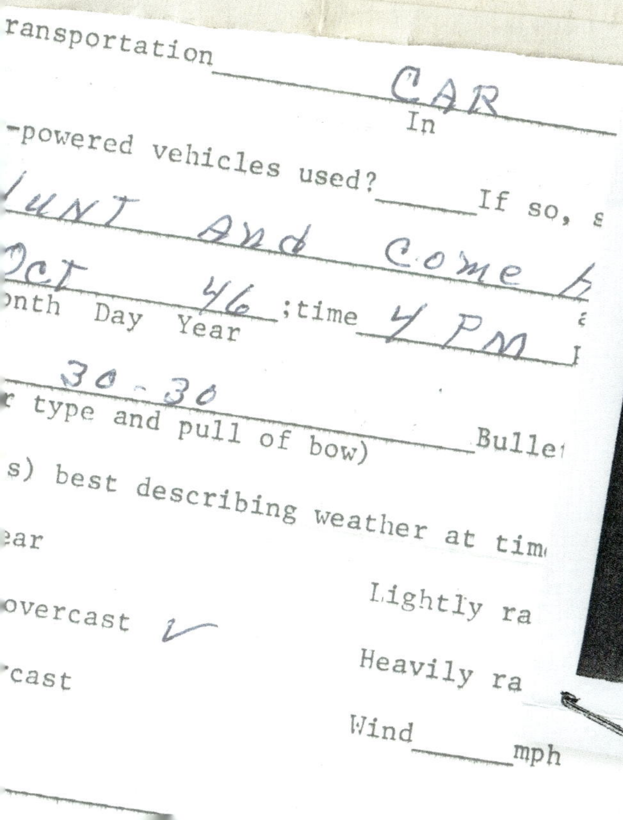
ransportation CAR
In
-powered vehicles used? If so, s
lunt and come
Oct 46 ;time 4 PM
onth Day Year
30-30
r type and pull of bow) Bulle
s) best describing weather at tim
ear
overcast ✓ Lightly ra
cast Heavily ra
Wind mph

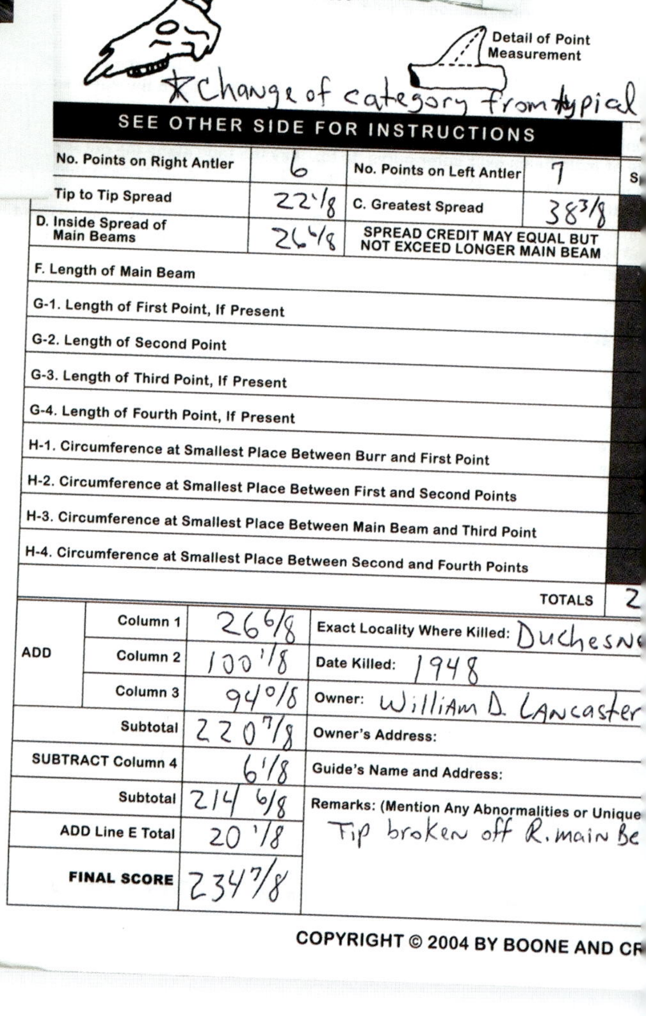

SEE OTHER SIDE FOR INSTRUCTIONS

No. Points on Right Antler	6	No. Points on Left Antler	7
Tip to Tip Spread	22 1/8	C. Greatest Spread	38 3/8
D. Inside Spread of Main Beams	26 4/8	SPREAD CREDIT MAY EQUAL BUT NOT EXCEED LONGER MAIN BEAM	

F. Length of Main Beam
G-1. Length of First Point, If Present
G-2. Length of Second Point
G-3. Length of Third Point, If Present
G-4. Length of Fourth Point, If Present
H-1. Circumference at Smallest Place Between Burr and First Point
H-2. Circumference at Smallest Place Between First and Second Points
H-3. Circumference at Smallest Place Between Main Beam and Third Point
H-4. Circumference at Smallest Place Between Second and Fourth Points
TOTALS 2

ADD Column 1	26 6/8	Exact Locality Where Killed:	Duchesn
Column 2	100 1/8	Date Killed:	1948
Column 3	94 0/8	Owner:	William D. Lancaster
Subtotal	220 7/8	Owner's Address:	
SUBTRACT Column 4	6 1/8	Guide's Name and Address:	
Subtotal	214 6/8	Remarks: (Mention Any Abnormalities or Unique	
ADD Line E Total	20 1/8	Tip broken off R. main Be	
FINAL SCORE	234 7/8		

KATE HAMILTON

NON-TYPICAL MULE DEER | 234-7/8 POINTS

This non-typical mule deer was harvested by Kate Hamilton in 1948 in Utah's Duchesne County. The buck was entered in the Club's 21st Big Game Awards Program in 1990 by Raymond R. Cross in the typical category with a score of 194-5/8 points. The trophy was sold to William D. Lancaster in 2006. At his request, the buck was recategorized as a non-typical mule deer with a new final score of 234-7/8 points. Unfortunately, our records do not have any field photographs of Kate with her trophy buck. The entry materials indicate that she was deceased at the time the deer was entered—42 years after she shot the buck.

21st AW

st AWARDS

250 Station Drive
Missoula, MT 59801
(406) 542-1888

CLUB®
N BIG GAME TROPHIES

ER

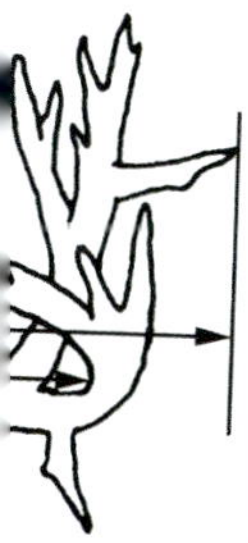

Abnormal Points	
Right Antler	Left Antler
2 0/8	13 0/8
	5 1/8
SUBTOTALS	
E. TOTAL	20 1/8

COLUMN 2	COLUMN 3	COLUMN 4
Right Antler	Left Antler	Difference
28 3/8	28 3/8	—
2 4/8	2 4/8	—
18 1/8	16 5/8	1 4/8
14 1/8	13 0/8	1 1/8
15 4/8	12 4/8	3 0/8
5 5/8	5 5/8	—
5 3/8	5 3/8	—
4 7/8	4 6/8	1/8
5 5/8	5 2/8	3/8
100 1/8	94 0/8	6 1/8

MT
ate Hamilton
Telephone #:

OM I.D. Number B032

LUB®

OFFICIAL SCORING SYSTEM FOR NORTH AMERICAN BIG GAME TROPHIES

Records of North American Big Game

BOONE AND CROCKETT CLUB

P.O. Box 5
Dumfries, VA 220

Minimum Score:	Awards	All-time
	185	195
	120	130
	100	108

TYPICAL MULE AND BLACKTAIL DEER

Kind of Deer *Mule*

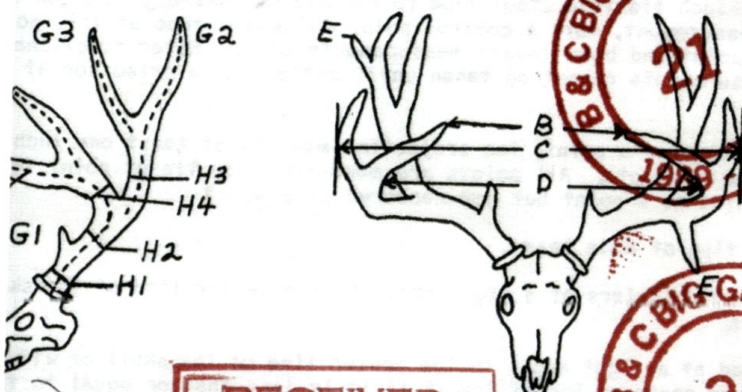

B & C BIG GAME AWARDS 21 1989-1991

B & C BIG GAME AWARDS 21 1989-1991

RECEIVED
$125.00 12/19/90
FEB 12 1991
CK# 4696
BOONE & CROCKETT CLUB

Abnormal Points	
Right Antler	Left Antler
2 0/8	13 0/8
	5 1/8
E. Total of Lengths of Abnormal Points	20 1/8

SEE OTHER SIDE FOR INSTRUCTIONS				Column 1	Column 2	Column 3	Column 4
No. Points on Right Antler	6	No. Points on Left Antler	7	Spread Credit	Right Antler	Left Antler	Difference
Tip to Tip Spread	22 1/8	C. Greatest Spread	38 3/8				
Inside Spread of Main Beams	26 6/8	(Credit May Equal But Not Exceed Longer Antler)		26 6/8			
Length of Main Beam					28 3/8	28 3/8	—
Length of First Point, If Present					2 4/8	2 4/8	—
Length of Second Point					18 1/8	16 5/8	1 4/8
Length of Third Point, If Present					14 1/8	13 0/8	1 1/8
Length of Fourth Point, If Present					15 4/8	12 4/8	3 0/8
Circumference at Smallest Place Between Burr and First Point					5 5/8	5 5/8	—
Circumference at Smallest Place Between First and Second Points					5 3/8	5 3/8	—
Circumference at Smallest Place Between Main Beam and Third Point					4 7/8	4 6/8	1/8
Circumference at Smallest Place Between Second and Fourth Points					5 5/8	5 2/8	3/8
TOTALS				26 6/8	100 1/8	94 0/8	6 1/8

Total of Columns 1, 2, and 3	220 7/8	Exact Locality Where Killed:	Duchesne County, Utah
Subtract Column 4	6 1/8	Date Killed: 1948 R	By Whom Killed: Kate Hamilton (deceased)
Subtotal	214 6/8	Present Owner:	Ray Cross (mond R)
Add Line E Total of Lengths of Abn. Points	20 1/8	Guide Name and Address:	NONE
FINAL SCORE	194 5/8	Remarks:	Tip broken off R. main beam

— — /m-/— / B032

2nd

1948

Boone and Crockett Club

RECORDS OF NORTH AMERICAN BIG GAME
AND
NORTH AMERICAN BIG GAME COMPETITION

IN CARE OF
AMERICAN MUSEUM OF NATURAL HISTORY
CENTRAL PARK WEST AT 79TH STREET
NEW YORK 24, N. Y.

COMMITTEE

HAROLD E. ANTHONY, CHAIRMAN
R. R. M. CARPENTER
ALFRED ELY
KARL T. FREDERICK
A. C. GILBERT

UNDER THE AUSPICES OF THE NATIONAL MUSEUM OF HEADS AND HORNS OF THE NEW YORK ZOOLOGICAL SOCIETY

DEER

SPECIES .... Mule ....

MEASUREMENTS	RIGHT	LEFT
Length of outside curve **A**	26.50	26.00
Greatest spread **B** 38.75		
Circumference of main beam **C**	4.50	4.50
Number of points on antler	9	8
Circumference of burr **D**	7.	7.

Exact locality where killed Pequop Mtn's Elko County, Nev

Date killed ... Nov. 4, 1948

By whom killed ... Edna Sanders Rytting

Owner ... Western SPORTSMAN 530 Idaho St.

Address ... ELKO, NEVADA

Present location of trophy ... Western SPORTSMAN 530 Idaho St. ELKO, NEVADA

Remarks: Deer Weighted 300 lbs. Cleaned

... Horns grow straight off main Branch

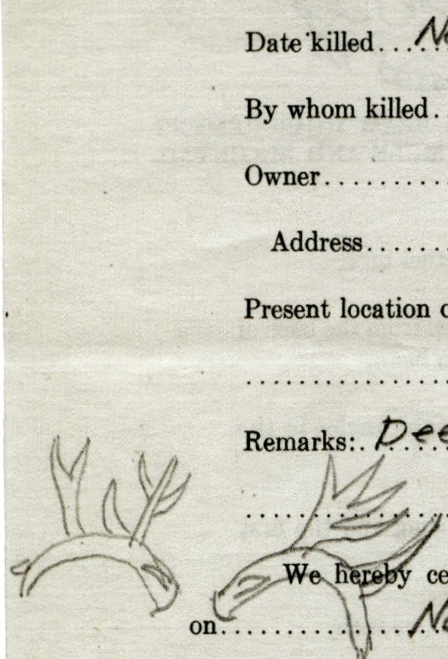

We hereby certify that we have measured the above described trophy on ... Nov. 8 ... 1948, and that these measurements are correct and made in accordance with the directions overleaf.

By Ralph L. Druehl

D E E R

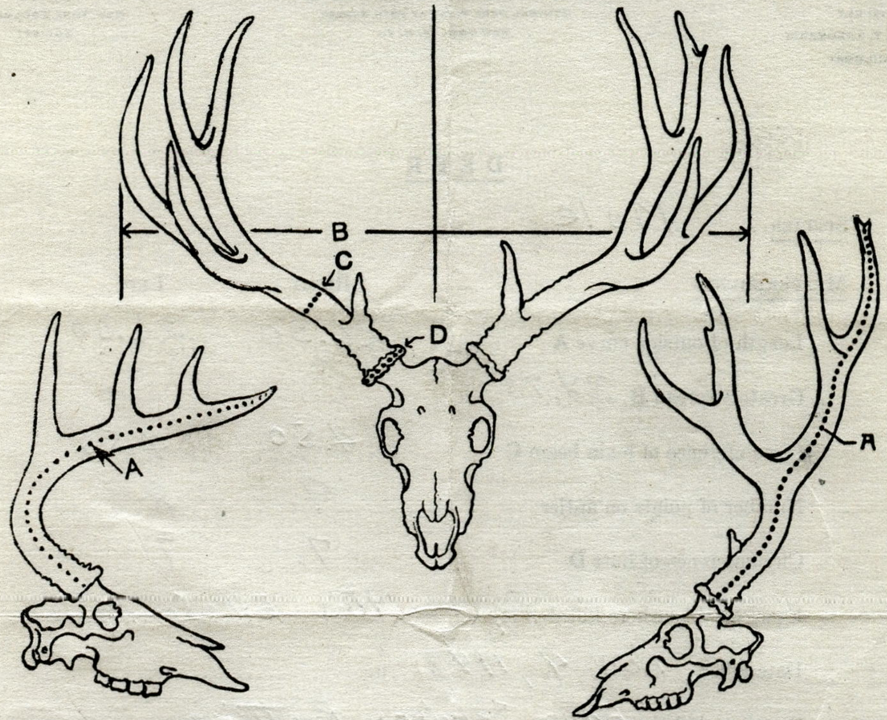

MAIN BEAM MEASUREMENT
FOR WHITE TAIL

MAIN BEAM MEASUREMENT
FOR MULE AND BLACKTAIL

Method of Measuring

All measurements **must** be made with a flexible steel tape.

A Length of outside curve: Measured along the main beam from the base of the burr to the tip of the most distant point on the main beam.

B Greatest spread: Measured between parallels and at right angles to the center line of the skull.

C Circumference: Measured midway between the basal snag and the first fork.

Points: No point shall be counted unless it extends at least one inch.

D Circumference of burr.

Remarks: State whether the trophy has any characteristics which depart from the normal for this species.

EDNA SANDERS RYTTING

MULE DEER | 26-1/2-INCH MAIN BEAM

No photographs accompanied this mule deer entry received by the Club in 1948, which was before our new scoring system was implemented. Note the drawing and remarks on the chart.

LADY NIMROD—Alice O'Brien, 5515 Cottage, used just one bullet from a .32 Wi to drop this big buck 20 miles south of Bly midway in the now-past season. The hor measured 39½ inches, with 13 points on one side, 11 on the other.

ransportation FORD ½T PICKUP In SAME Out

or-powered vehicles used?

pose

kill OCT Month

of weapon 32 WIN.

of bullet ?

of bow if bow and arrow used

ximate distance from trophy

SUBTR

ALICE C. O'BRIEN

NON-TYPICAL MULE DEER | 277-1/8 POINTS

David O'Brien inherited this fine trophy from his grandmother, Alice O'Brien. The buck went unmeasured and unrecognized as one of the top mule deer ever taken in Oregon for 24 years until it was officially scored in March 1973 by L.M. Mathisen. The buck's final score is 277-1/8 points. It still ranks as the No. 5 non-typical mule deer in Oregon. Following is an excerpt from the November 1973 edition of *Oregon Outdoors*:

> *On October 11th, Alice O'Brien, a lady deer hunter from Klamath Falls, dropped a big buck with one shot from a .32 Winchester. A few days later a picture of the gal and her fine buck appeared in the local newspaper. The antler spread was reported to be 39-1/2 inches, with 13 points on one side, 11 points on the other, and the site of the kill was listed as being 20 miles south of Bly in eastern Klamath County....*

The buck has since changed hands, first to antler collector Don Schaufler in the 1980s and most recently to Cabela's where it is currently on display in their Kansas City store.

JoREVA [BEANE] WELLBORN
TYPICAL MULE DEER | 194-7/8 POINTS

JoReva Beane Wellborn was about 200 yards out when she pulled the trigger on her .257 Roberts and brought down this typical mule deer during the 1949 season. She was hunting in the Book Cliffs area, 10 miles north of Grand Junction in Mesa County, Colorado. The buck, with 10 points on the right antler and 7 on the left, has a final B&C score of 194-7/8 points. The greatest spread measures over 31 inches. JoReva waited over 50 years before finally having it measured.

OFFICIAL SCORING SYSTEM FOR NORTH AMERICAN BIG GAME TROPHIES

Records of North American Big Game

BOONE AND CROCKETT CLUB®

250 Station Drive
Missoula, MT 59801
(406) 542-1888

Minimum Score:	Awards	All-time
mule	180	190
Columbia	125	135
Sitka	100	108

TYPICAL
MULE DEER AND BLACKTAIL DEER

Kind of Deer: Mule Typ

RECEIVED
CK 4995 25-
JAN 1 8 2000
1-9-00 WN
BOONE & CROCKETT CLUB

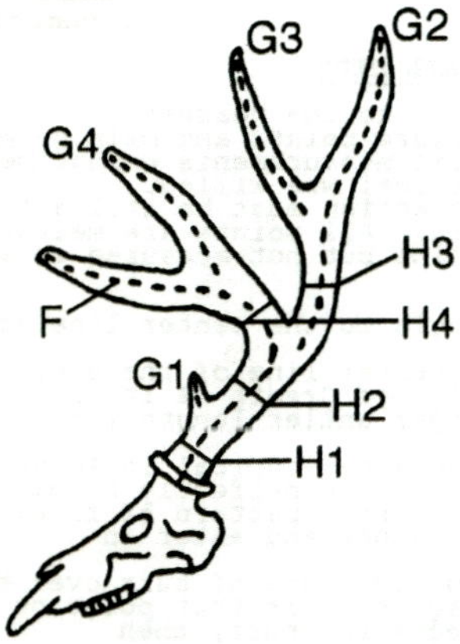

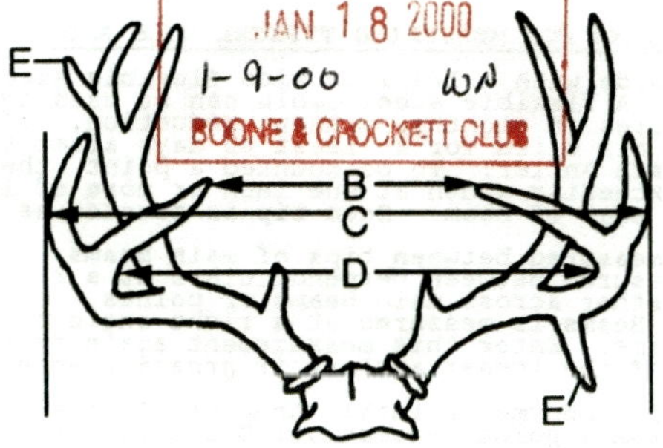

Abnormal Points	
Right Antler	Left Antler
1 4/8	1 7/8
1 1/8	1 0/8
1 1/8	
1 4/8	
3 7/8	
Subtotals 9 1/8	2 7/8
Total to E 12 0/8	

(5) (2)

SEE OTHER SIDE FOR INSTRUCTIONS				Column 1	Column 2	Column 3	Column 4
A. No. Points on Right Antler	10	No. Points on Left Antler	7	Spread Credit	Right Antler	Left Antler	Difference
B. Tip to Tip Spread	19 0/8	C. Greatest Spread	31 1/8				
D. Inside Spread of Main Beams	23 5/8	(Credit May Equal But Not Exceed Longer Antler)		23 5/8			
E. Total of Lengths of Abnormal Points							12 0/8
F. Length of Main Beam					24 7/8	25 6/8	~~1 7/8~~ 7/8
G-1. Length of First Point, If Present					3 5/8	3 5/8	0 0/8
G-2. Length of Second Point					19 0/8	17 0/8	2 0/8
G-3. Length of Third Point, If Present					14 4/8	15 1/8	0 5/8
G-4. Length of Fourth Point, If Present					12 5/8	12 1/8	0 4/8
H-1. Circumference at Smallest Place Between Burr and First Point					5 4/8	5 1/8	0 3/8
H-2. Circumference at Smallest Place Between First and Second Points					5 2/8	5 1/8	0 1/8
H-3. Circumference at Smallest Place Between Main Beam and Third Point					4 3/8	4 5/8	0 2/8
H-4. Circumference at Smallest Place Between Second and Fourth Points					5 0/8	4 7/8	0 1/8
Mesa Co., CO				TOTALS 23 5/8	94 6/8	93 3/8	~~17 7/8~~ 16-7/8

B&C BIG GAME AWARDS 24 1998 2000 · 19-0/8

ADD			
Column 1	23 5/8	Exact Locality Where Killed:	Mesa Co. Colorado Book Cliffs
Column 2	94 6/8	Date Killed: 10/15/49	Hunter: JoReva Wellborn
Column 3	93 3/8	Owner: Same	Telephone #:
Subtotal	211 6/8	Owner's Address:	
SUBTRACT Column 4	~~17 7/8~~	Guide's Name and Address: None	
FINAL SCORE	~~193 7/8~~ 194-7/8	Remarks: (Mention Any Abnormalities or Unique Qualities) This Trophy was Taken 50 years Ago.	K002

Competition

MULE and BLACKTAIL DEER   KIND OF DEER Mule

Boone and Crockett Club

Records of North American Big Game
and
North American Big Game Competition
in care of
American Museum of Natural History
Central Park West at 79th Street
New York 24, N.Y.

Committee

Harold E. Anthony, Chairman
William K. Carpenter
Alfred Ely
Karl T. Frederick
A. C. Gilbert
Catherine Sayers, Secretary

Under the Auspices
of
The National Museum
of Heads and Horns
of the
New York Zoological
Society

D E E R

Species .... MULE

Measurements

	Right	Left
Length on outside curve A	25	26
Greatest spread B .. 37 1/4		
Circumference of main beam C	5 1/2	5 1/4
Number of points on antler	8	9
Circumference of burr D	7 1/2	7 5/8

Exact locality where killed .. Ft. Robinson, Nebraska

Date killed .... December 22, 1949

By whom killed .. Mary Lou Dodd

Address ...... Crawford, Nebraska

Owner ...... Mary Lou Dodd

Address ...... Crawford, Nebraska

Remarks .. Points mostly flat, and three ..... broken off.

Measured by [signature], Deputy Conservation Officer

Owner's signature .. Mary Lou Dodd

Dodd 9/50

72 1/2 Column 3		
161 3/4 TOTAL	197 3/4	Address
SUBTRACT Column 4	23	Guide's Name and Address
25 FINAL SCORE	173 1/4	Remarks: (Mention any abnormalities) Freak side points - 3 broken off

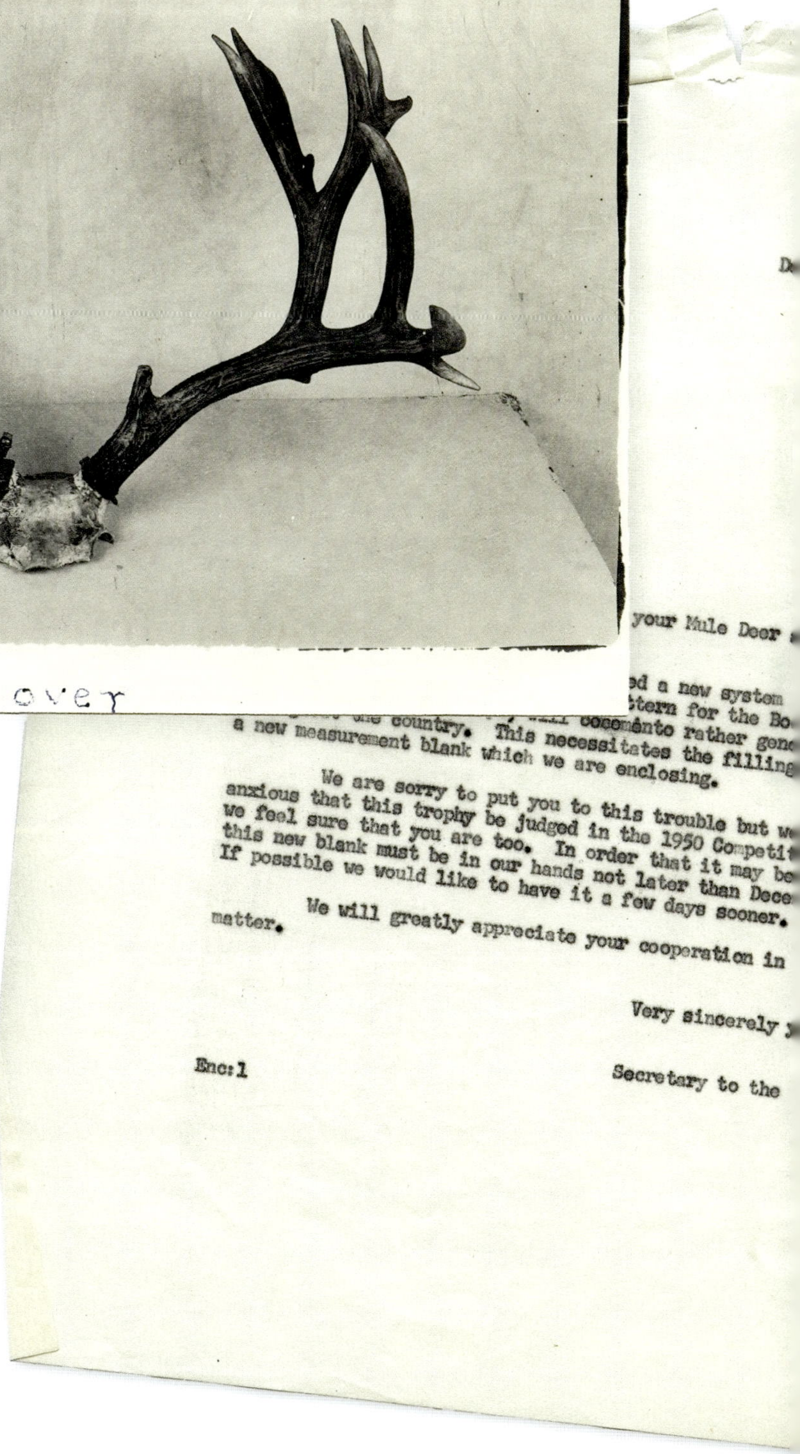
your Mule Deer

ed a new system
ttern for the Bo
the country. This necessitates the filling
a new measurement blank which we are enclosing.

We are sorry to put you to this trouble but w
anxious that this trophy be judged in the 1950 Competi
we feel sure that you are too. In order that it may be
this new blank must be in our hands not later than Dece
If possible we would like to have it a few days sooner.

We will greatly appreciate your cooperation in
matter.

Very sincerely

Enc: 1

Secretary to the

MARY LOU DODD

NON-TYPICAL MULE DEER | 26-INCH MAIN BEAM

This unique mule deer was taken by Mary Lou Dodd about four miles west of Fort Robinson, Nebraska, in 1949. The chart notes that points are mostly flat and three were broken off. This entry arrived at Boone and Crockett Club before the new scoring system was in place. A letter to Mary Lou on December 1, 1950, formally asked her to submit the measurements necessary to receive an official B&C score. An error was made on the new chart giving the buck a spread credit of 63-1/4 inches. However, with the correct credit spread of 25 inches, the final score dropped to 136-6/8 points.

Records of North American Big Game

RECEIVED 2508 40.00
MAY 2 2004
BOONE & CROCKETT CLUB

BOONE AND CROC
OFFICIAL SCORING SYSTEM FOR NORTH

NON-TYPI
MULE DEER AND BL

MINIMUM SCORES	AWARDS	ALL-TIME
mule deer	215	240
Columbia blacktail	155	155
Sitka blacktail	118	118

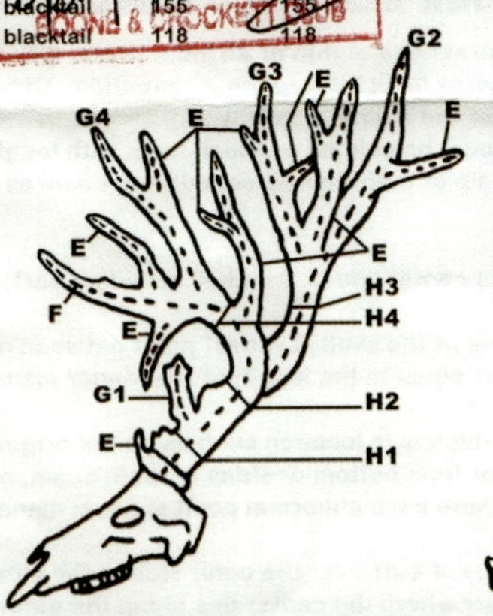

Detail of Point Measurement

	4 2/8	0
	4 4/8	0
	6 5/8	0
	0	0
SUBTOTALS	24 4/8	26 4/8
E. TOTAL	51 2/8	

SEE OTHER SIDE FOR INSTRUCTIONS				COLUMN 1	COLUMN 2	COLUMN 3	COLUMN 4
A. No. Points on Right Antler	13	No. Points on Left Antler	10	Spread Credit	Right Antler	Left Antler	Difference
B. Tip to Tip Spread	19 0/8	C. Greatest Spread	28 0/8				
D. Inside Spread of Main Beams	22 4/8	SPREAD CREDIT MAY EQUAL BUT NOT EXCEED LONGER MAIN BEAM		22 4/8			
F. Length of Main Beam					26 7/8	26 4/8	3/8
G-1. Length of First Point, If Present					4 0/8	4 4/8	4/8
G-2. Length of Second Point					13 4/8	13 4/8	2/8
G-3. Length of Third Point, If Present					12 2/8	10 3/8	1 7/8
G-4. Length of Fourth Point, If Present					14 0/8	13 4/8	4/8
H-1. Circumference at Smallest Place Between Burr and First Point					5 0/8	5 0/8	0
H-2. Circumference at Smallest Place Between First and Second Points					4 4/8	4 4/8	0
H-3. Circumference at Smallest Place Between Main Beam and Third Point					3 4/8	3 2/8	2/8
H-4. Circumference at Smallest Place Between Second and Fourth Points					4 2/8	4 5/8	3/8
Wallowa Co, OR			TOTALS	22 4/8	87 7/8	86 2/8	4 3/8

B&C BIG GAME AWARDS 26 2004 - 2006

ADD	Column 1	22 4/8	Exact Locality Where Killed:	PAWATKA RIDGE, WALLOWA COUNTY, OR
	Column 2	87 7/8	Date Killed: 1950	Hunter: NANCY McCRAE
	Column 3	86 2/8	Owner: NORMAN McCRAE	Telephone #:
Subtotal		196 5/8	Owner's Address:	
SUBTRACT Column 4		4 3/8	Guide's Name and Address: NONE	
Subtotal		192 2/8	Remarks: (Mention Any Abnormalities or Unique Qualities)	
ADD Line E Total		51 2/8		
FINAL SCORE		243 4/8		OM I.D. Number M 1 3 8

NANCY McCRAE
NON-TYPICAL MULE DEER | 243-4/8 POINTS

Norman M. McCrae entered his mother's non-typical mule deer in the Club's records program in 2006, 56 years after she shot the buck on Powatka Ridge in Oregon's Wallowa County. Nancy's buck has 23 scorable points with a total of 51-2/8 non-typical inches, and a greatest spread of 28 inches.

BOONE AND CROCKETT CLUB

Mrs. Grancel ...
5 Tudor City Place, NYC 17, NY.

NON-TYPICAL MULE DEER

SECOND PLACE — Medal

SIXTH N.A.B.G. COMPETITION 1953 — 2

BOONE AND CROCKETT OFFICIAL CLUB

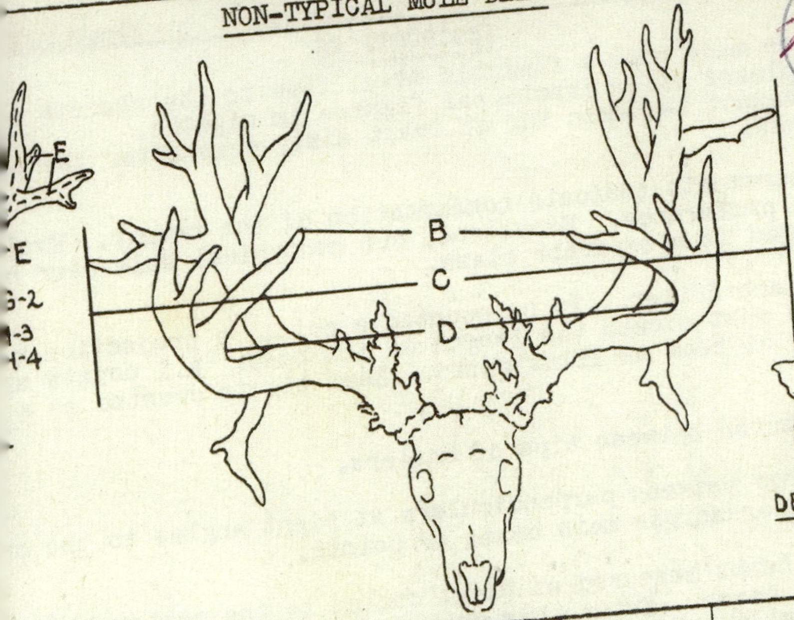

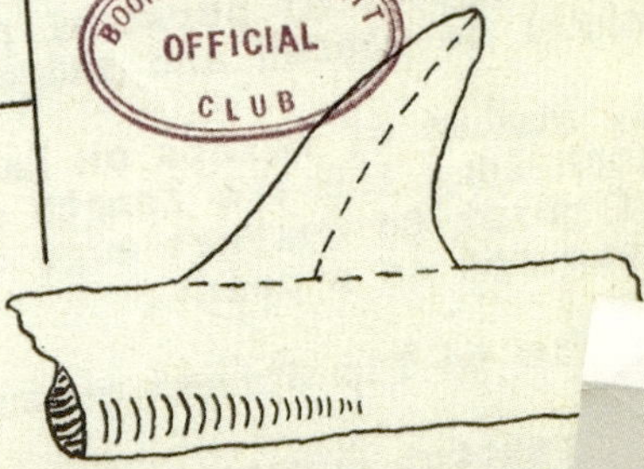

DETAIL OF POINT MEASURE...

... FOR INSTRUCTIONS	Supplementary Data R.	Supplementary Data L.	Column 1 Spread Credit	Column 2 Right Antler	Column 3 Left Antler	Colu... Diff...
	12	14				
...on Each Antler	12 7/8					
	33 6/8					
Spread credit may equal but not exceed length of longer antler			20 5/8			
5/8 ... of Main Beams exceeds longer ...nter difference						
... of all Abnormal Points	50 2/8					
...eam				25 4/8	25 1/8	
...st Point, if present				2 6/8	5	
...ond Point				12 7/8	16	
...rd Point, if present				9 6/8	9	
...rth Point, if present				12	10 7/8	
... at Smallest Place ... and First Point				5 1/8	5	
...e at Smallest Place ...t and Second Points				5	5	
...e at Samllest Place ... Beam and Third Point				4 2/8	4 4/...	
...e at Smallest Place ...nd and Fourth Points				4 6/8	5	
	50 2/8		20 5/8	82	85 4...	

1	20 5/8	Exact locality where killed Kaibab Forest, South ...
2	82	Date killed 11-2-50 By whom killed Mrs. Mi...
3	85 4/8	Present owner ~~Mrs. Milroy Powell~~
	188 1/8	Address
4	8 2/8	Guide's Name and Address Delvin Hamblin, Kanab, ...
	179 7/8	Remarks: (Mention any abnormalities)
1	50 2/8	

JOANN POWELL

NON-TYPICAL MULE DEER | 230-1/8 POINTS

Delvin Hamblin of Kanab, Utah, guided Joann Powell to her award-winning non-typical mule deer scoring 230-1/8 points. The buck was recognized at the Club's sixth competition with a 2nd Place Award in 1953. The buck's score—verified at the American Museum of Natural History by legendary scorers Donald S. Hopkins and Grancel Fitz—featured 26 scorable points and over 50 inches of abnormal points. The Powells were hunting in the famed Kaibab National Forest of Arizona in 1950. Joann's husband Milroy with the help of her father Dan Auld also shot an impressive non-typical on that hunt, which scored 279-6/8 points (see page 256).

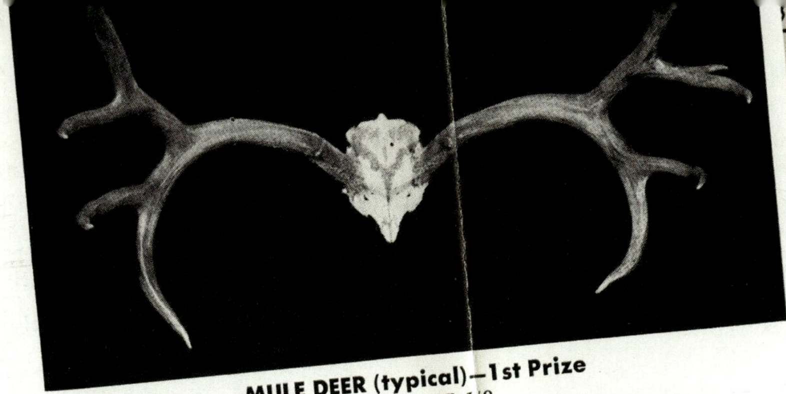

MULE DEER (typical)—1st Prize

Score—197-1/8

Length—(R) 26-6/8 (L) 26-5/8
Inside Spread—28
Circumference Between Burr and First Point—(R) 5-2/8 (L) 5-2/8
Points—(R) 6 (L) 6

Locality—Craig, Colo.—1951
Hunter—Lucille Gooch
Guide—None
Owner—George Gooch

WHITETAIL DEER (non-typical)—1st Prize

Score—166-6/8 : 31-6/8—198-4/8

Length—(R) 24-2/8 (L) 23-1/8
Inside Spread—18
Circumference Between Burr and First Point—(R) 5-2/8 (L) 5-4/8
Points—(R) 13 (L) 12

Locality—Cow Creek, Wyo.—1951
Hunter—Mrs. Thelma Martens
Guide—None
Owner—Mrs. Thelma Martens

1951 JUDGES Milford Baker, Chairman
Grancel Fitz • Donald S. Hopkins • George H. Lesser • Ernst

...IG GAME TROPHIES 1 / 1951

% Am. Museum of Natural History
Central Park West at 79th Street
New York 24, New York

KIND OF DEER Mule – Typ.
MULE DEER
(typical)

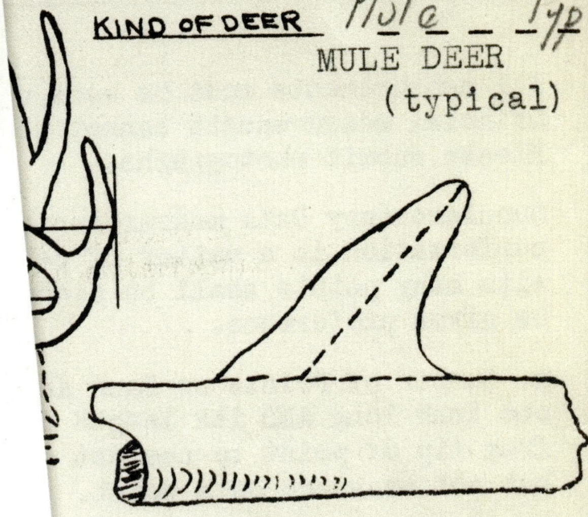

DETAIL OF POINT MEASUREMENT

	Column 1	Column 2 Right Antler	Column 3 Left Antler	Column 4 Difference
				~~1 3/8~~
				2 5/8
		26 6/8	26 5/8	1/8
		2 2/8	2 5/8	3/8
		19	20	1
		9 4/8	10 5/8	1 1/8
		12 4/8	11	1 4/8
		5 2/8	5 2/8	–
...lace ...n First and Second Points		4 5/8	4 6/8	1/8
...ference at Smallest Place ...n Main Beam and Third Point,		4 1/8	4 1/8	–
...ference at Smallest Place ...n Second and Fourth Points		5	4 6/8	2/8
	26 6/8	89	89 6/8	7 1/8 ~~3 3/8~~

Moffat Co., Colo.

...umn 1 26 6/8 Exact locality where killed Near Craig on ~~xxxxx~~ ranch
...lumn 2 89 Date killed Oct. 30, 1951 By whom killed Lucille Gooch
... 89 6/8 Present owner George Gooch Geo Gooch

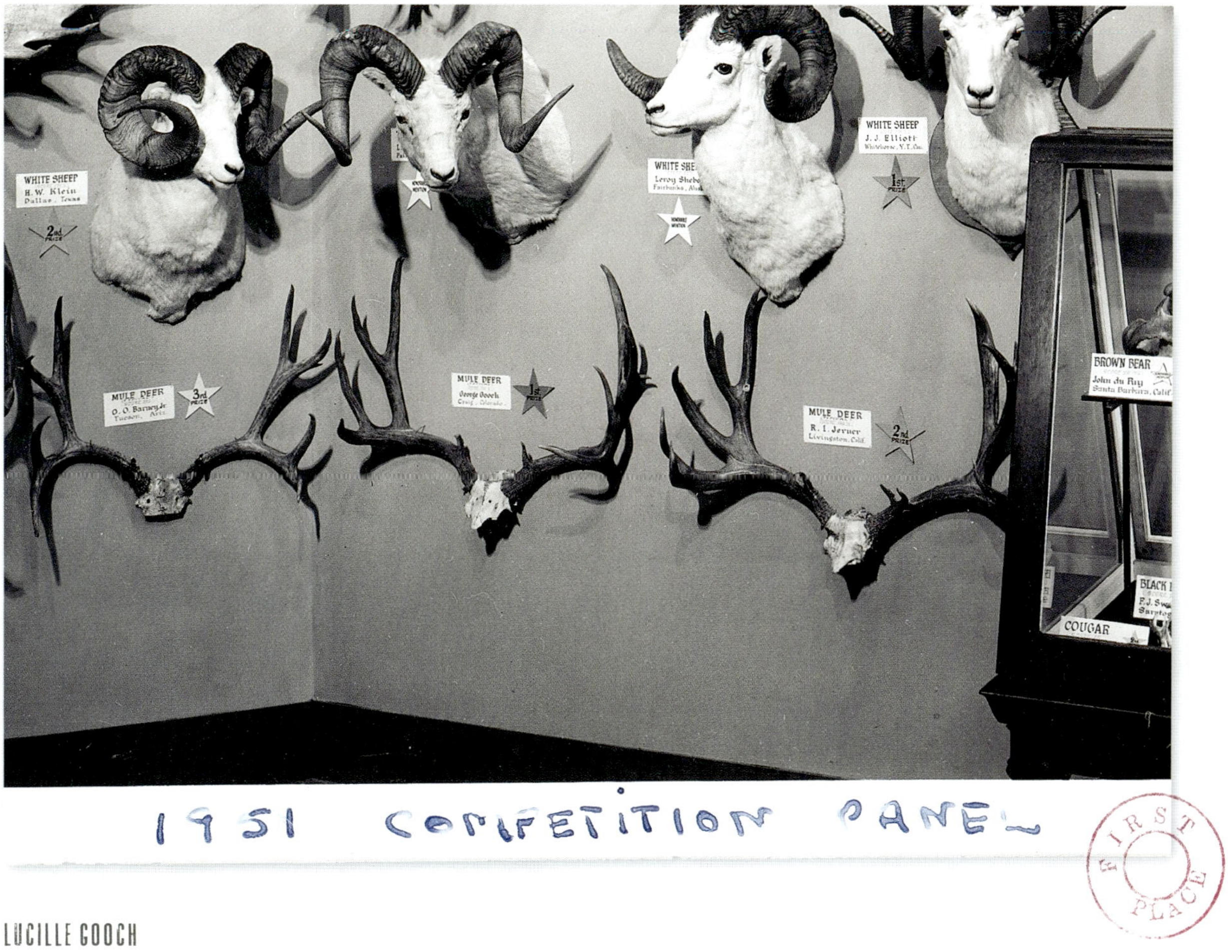

LUCILLE GOOCH

TYPICAL MULE DEER | 198-3/8 POINTS

Lucille Gooch's typical mule deer, scoring 198-3/8 points, received the 1st Place Award at the fifth competition held at the American Museum of Natural History. She shot the buck near Craig, in Moffat County, Colorado, on October 30, 1951. The buck was entered by George Gooch, presumably her husband. Each antler had a small abnormal point, for a total of 2-5/8 inches of deductions on the otherwise clean 5x5 mule deer.

Records of North American Big Game

Jerry Schwaderer
Dolores CO 25th
TROPHY: E4 186-6/8
KDAT:
KLOC:

BOONE AND CROCKETT CLUB

OFFICIAL SCORING SYSTEM FOR NORTH AMERICAN BIG GAME TROPHIES

B&C BIG GAME AWARDS 25 2001 2003

MINIMUM SCORES	AWARDS	ALL-TIME
mule deer	180	190
Columbia blacktail	125	135
Sitka blacktail	100	108

TYPICAL MULE DEER AND BLACKTAIL DEER

KIND OF DEER (check one)
- [x] mule deer
- [ ] Columbia blacktail
- [ ] Sitka blacktail

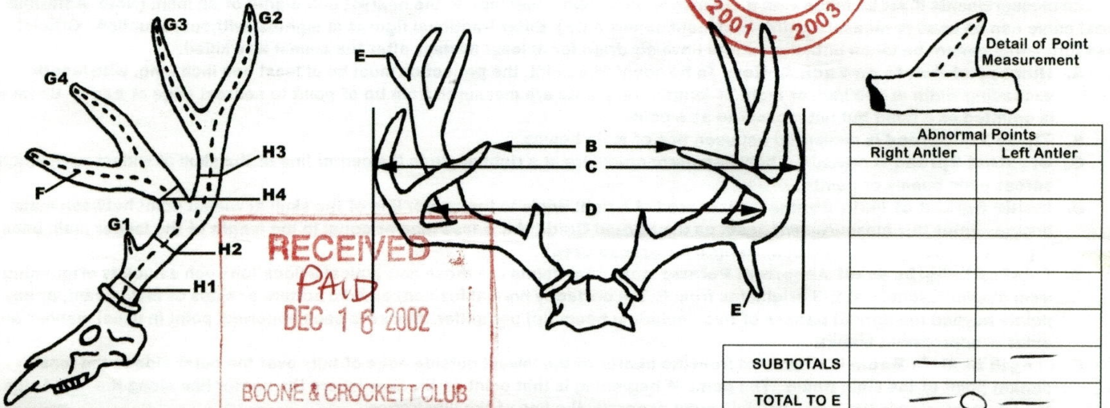

RECEIVED PAID DEC 1 6 2002 BOONE & CROCKETT CLUB

Abnormal Points Right Antler	Left Antler
SUBTOTALS	—
TOTAL TO E	—0—

SEE OTHER SIDE FOR INSTRUCTIONS				COLUMN 1	COLUMN 2	COLUMN 3	COLUMN 4
A. No. Points on Right Antler	5	No. Points on Left Antler	5	Spread Credit	Right Antler	Left Antler	Difference
B. Tip to Tip Spread	25 3/8	C. Greatest Spread	31 2/8				
D. Inside Spread of Main Beams	27 7/8	SPREAD CREDIT MAY EQUAL BUT NOT EXCEED LONGER MAIN BEAM		27-			
E. Total of Lengths of Abnormal Points							—
F. Length of Main Beam					25 3/8	27-	1 5/8
G-1. Length of First Point, If Present					4 7/8	2 7/8	2-
G-2. Length of Second Point					16-	14 6/8	1 2/8
G-3. Length of Third Point, If Present					11 3/8	12 2/8	7/8
G-4. Length of Fourth Point, If Present					7 7/8	9 3/8	1 4/8
H-1. Circumference at Smallest Place Between Burr and First Point					5 1/8	5 1/8	—
H-2. Circumference at Smallest Place Between First and Second Points					4 5/8	4 6/8	1/8
H-3. Circumference at Smallest Place Between Main Beam and Third Point					4 2/8	4 2/8	—
H-4. Circumference at Smallest Place Between Second and Fourth Points					3 5/8	4-	3/8
Dolores Co., CO			TOTALS	27-	83 1/8	84 3/8	7 6/8

ADD	Column 1	27-	Exact Locality Where Killed: DOLORES COUNTY
	Column 2	83 1/8	Date Killed: 10-54 Hunter: Frances Becher Jr
	Column 3	84 3/8	Owner: Jerry Schwaderer Telephone #:
	Subtotal	194 4/8	Owner's Address:
SUBTRACT Column 4		7 4/8	Guide's Name and Address: N/A
FINAL SCORE		186 6/8	Remarks: (Mention Any Abnormalities or Unique Qualities) L061

FRANCES BECHER

TYPICAL MULE DEER | 186-6/8 POINTS

Between the two of them, Frances Becher and her husband James have four mule deer entries in the Club's Big Game Records Program—three for James and one for Frances. Her buck, with an official B&C score of 186-6/8 points, was shot in 1954 in Dolores County, Colorado. She was hunting near Dry Canyon on a snowy October day when she killed the buck from 75 yards with her .250-3000 Savage. All four of the Becher's trophy mule deer are now owned by Jerry Schwaderer.

VIRGINIA S. HUTH

NON-TYPICAL MULE DEER | 212-1/8 POINTS

Virginia Huth and her husband Alvin traveled from San Antonio, Texas, to hunt Arizona's North Kaibab in the fall of 1955. They were joined on their hunt by their friend Clair Pearson, who had worked as a professional guide in the area years earlier, but joined the Huths as a hunting companion. A letter to Betty Fitz at the Club's office notes:

> *...if it had not been for Mr. Pearson's outstanding, remarkable tracking ability, she would never have found her deer. For these reasons we feel that Mr. Pearson deserves credit for his great help to my wife [with] her kill. We believe he should be listed as guide, but want it understood that his help was not upon any professional-hire basis.*

This unique deer has 24 scorable points, with nearly 45 inches of abnormal points adding into the final B&C score of 212-1/8.

Mrs. Grancel Fitz, Sec
5 Tudor City Place, NY

MULE and BLACKTAIL DEER

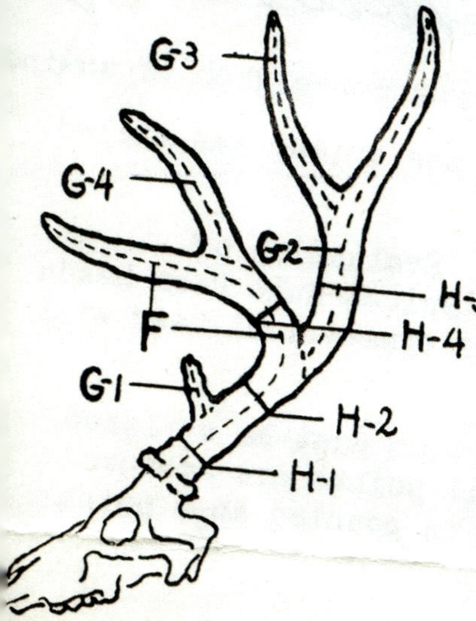

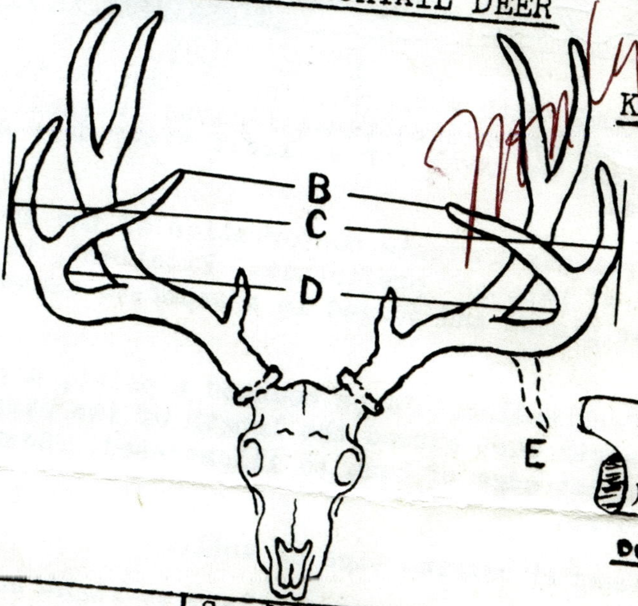

KIND OF DEER

EIGHTH N.A.B.G. COMPETITION 1957

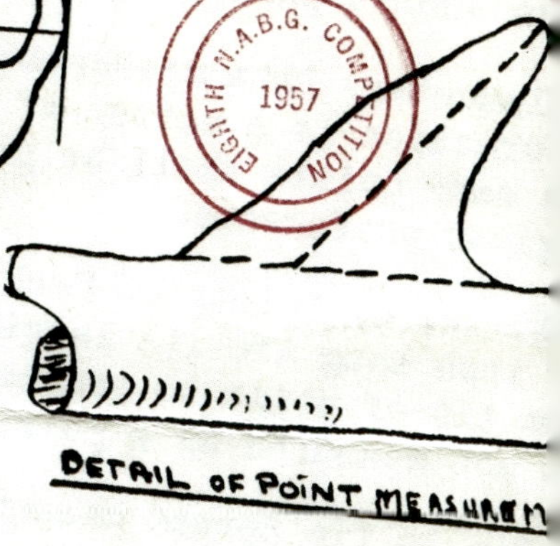

SEE OTHER SIDE FOR INSTRUCTIONS	Supplementary Data R.	L.	Column 1 Spread Credit	Column 2 Right Antler	Column 3 Left Antler	Colu[mn 4] Differ[ence]
umber of Points on Each Antler	14	10				
p to Tip Spread	22					
eatest Spread	32 4/8					
side Spread MAIN BEAMS 23 2/8 — Spread credit may equal but not exceed length of longer antler						
ead of Main Beams exceeds longer … difference			23			
all Abnormal Points (44 7/8)						2/8
oint, if present				19	23	4
Point				8	8 6/8	6/8
oint, if present				12 2/8	11	1 2/8
Point, if present				7	8	1
Smallest Place First Point				3 6/8	6	2 2/8
Smallest Place d Second Points				8 6/8	7 2/8	1 4/8
Smallest Place um and Third Point.				6 2/8	7 1/8	7/8
Smallest Place and Fourth Points				8 2/8	5 6/8	2 4/8
				4 2/8	4 6/8	4/8
	44 7/8		23	77 4/8	81 5/8	14 7/8

23	
7 4/8	Exact locality where killed Kiabab North Arizona
1 5/8	Date killed Nov. 20, 1955 By whom killed Virginia S. Huth
182 1/8	Present owner Virginia S. Huth
14 7/8	Address
167 2/8	Guide's Name and Address Clair Pearson, Fredonia, Arizona
44 7/8	Remarks: (Mention any abnormalities)
212 1/8	See photo attached.

MARGUERITE HILL
TYPICAL MULE DEER
200-5/8 POINTS

This outstanding typical mule deer from Chaffee County, Colorado, was shot by Marguerite Hill in October 1956 and entered in the Club's 11th Big Game Competition in 1963 with a score of 197-7/8 points. Fast-forward to the 1980s; in a letter to the Club from Alan Butts, the deer's current owner, he describes his encounter with Marguerite:

> *Upon first meeting the Hills I inquired if Marguerite had killed a B&C typical mule deer in the 1950s. She beamed and assured me that she had and asked how I knew that. I told her that I had a copy of Colorado's Biggest Bucks and Bulls and had read her name. Only a full-blown antler nut like [me] would remember that. In the late 80s I went to measure an elk rack for George [Hill] to determine if it was a possible B&C contender... During that visit I asked Marguerite if she still had her mule deer rack. She retrieved it from the basement! Even in its weathered faded glory I knew what I was looking at.*

Marguerite's son inherited the buck when she passed on and gave it to a neighbor who had been watching his parent's property. Alan Butts finally acquired the rack in 2012. By that time, the original score chart had been misplaced and thought lost forever so Marguerite's mule deer was rescored by special instruction from the Club's headquarters with a final score of 200-5/8 points. Research for this book unearthed the old chart from the 1960s, which is shown at right.

IG GAME TROPHIES

Address Correspondence to
Mrs. Grancel Fitz, Secret
5 Tudor City Place, NYC

KIND OF DEER *Mule*

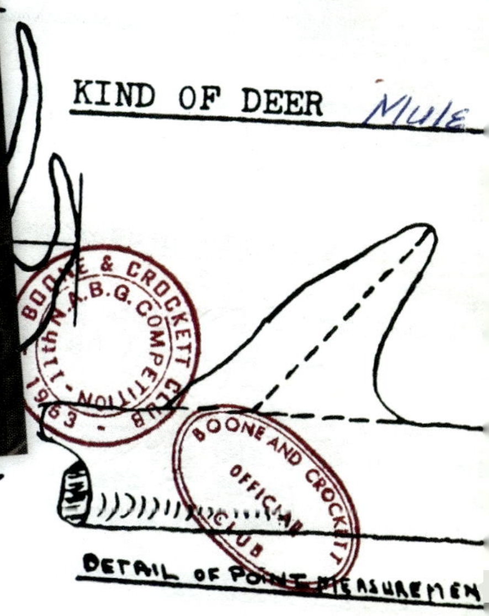

Supplementary Data		Column 1	Column 2	Column 3	Column
.	L. 8	Spread Credit	Right Antler	Left Antler	Differen
25 4/8					
29					
but not antler		26 2/8			
					4 3/8
			27 7/8	27	7/8
			2 7/8	3 2/8	3/8
			16 6/8	19 1/8	2 3/8
			9 5/8	11 4/8	1 7/8
			13 7/8	13 5/8	2/8
			5 2/8	5	2/8
			4 5/8	4 5/8	~~0/8~~ 0
Between Main Beam and ... Circumference at Smallest Place Between Second and Fourth Points			3 7/8	4 1/8	2/8
			4 5/8	4 5/8	
OTALS		26 2/8	89 3/8	92 7/8	~~11 4/8~~

Column 1	26 2/8	Exact locality where killed *Pony Cub CREEK, Chaffee Co*
Column 2	89 3/8	Date killed *Oct 56* By whom killed *Marguerite Hill*
Column 3	92 7/8	Present owner *Marguerite Hill*
TOTAL	208 4/8	Address
T Column 4	~~10 11 2/8~~	Guide's Name and Address *NONE*
AL SCORE	~~197 2/8~~	Remarks: (Mention any abnormalities)

SCORI

H-3
-4

FOR INSTRUC

Each Antler

			Antler	Difference
	39 3/4			
" Spread credit may equal but not exceed length of longer antler	~~29 1/2~~ 30 1/8			~~12 7/8~~ 12 2/8
f Main Beams exceeds longer er difference				None
of all Abnormal Points		26 ~~3/4~~ 6/8	24 ~~1/2~~ 4/8	2 2/8
am		2	2 1/8	1/8
Point, if present		20 ~~1/2~~ 4/8	20 ~~3/4~~ 6/8	~~2/8~~ 2/8 5/8
d Point		9 ~~1/4~~ 2/8	11 ~~3/8~~ 2/8	2
l Point, if present		7 3/8	12 1/8	4 6/8
th Point, if present				—
at Smallest Place nd First Point		5	5	—
at Smallest Place and Second Points		4 ~~1/4~~ 2/8	4 ~~1/4~~ 2/8	—
at Smallest Place Beam and Third Point.		4	4	—
at Smallest Place d and Fourth Points		3 7/8	4 ~~1/4~~ 2/8	3/8
	~~26~~ 29 1/8	8 ~~3~~ 3	88 2/8	~~22 3/8~~ 19 7/8

29 4/8	Exact locality where killed Desert Clair - North Mountain Area Colo
82 6/8	Date killed 11/23/56 By whom killed Dorothy Mae Dibler
88 4/8	Present owner Dorothy Mae Dibler
200 4/8	Address Norwood - Colorado.
2 2/8	Guide's Name and Address None
	...arks: (Mention any abnormalities)

. Doro
01 Box
wood,

. Mrs.

that t
heck c

sed i
ere f
hart

see
cord
ight
6, j
on
own;
but
it f
tha

ar
t b
eve
ing

DOROTHY MAE DIBLER

TYPICAL MULE DEER | 176 POINTS

Correspondence between Dorothy Mae and Betty Fitz, B&C secretary, indicates that the score for Dorothy Mae's trophy mule deer was not calculated properly, resulting in a lower score in the Club's 1958 book than Dorothy Mae anticipated. In a return letter from Betty, she states:

> *We can see how you were disappointed when you saw the record[s] book, but any trophy that makes the book is a mighty fine one. My own mule deer, killed in 1956, just missed the book by a few units. The penalty on the excessive spread is what brought your score down; this same thing wrecked a wapiti for my husband [Grancel Fitz]. But it is a beautiful trophy to own, and even though it is at the bottom of the list, we'd rather have it than a lot we've seen that score higher.*

Dorothy Mae's trophy has a final score of 176 points and was shot on November 23, 1956, near Norwood, Colorado. The excessive spread penalty that Betty references in her letter was done away with decades later, resulting in new scores for hundreds of mule deer trophies.

P. O. Box No.
Norwood, Colorado

ber 15, 1

Mrs. Gran
Boone and
5 Tudor C
New Y

iled to
Boone an
belonging
your 1958

illiams
book as
r the

t reply,
ope for

urs

bler
. Box No. 25
wood, Colorado

Jan. 14, 1959

Mae Dibler
25

er:

hristmas rush is over I've had time
ur Mule deer trophy.

copy of our chart. The figures in
es in error and when we corrected
final score was 176.

you were disappointed when you saw
k, but any trophy that makes the book
ne one. My own mule deer trophy, killed
missed the book by a few units. The
excessive spread is what brought your
s same thing wrecked a wapiti for my
is a beautiful trophy to own and even
the bottom of the list, we'd rather
lot we've seen that scores higher.

her questions, don't hesitate to write.
o speedy in replying, but you'll hear
lly. (We have no staff and the competitions
rapidly, don't know what we are going

ORA McGURN

TYPICAL MULE DEER | 203-2/8 POINTS

Ora McGurn was hunting in Crook County, Wyoming, in 1957 when she shot this impressive mule deer. Her daughter Frances Shepherd inherited her mother's mule deer and discovered the buck was a trophy when she went to have it mounted on a plaque. The antlers were officially measured in 1973 with a final score of 203-2/8 points. A note from her daughter says: *My mother hunted by horseback, and she was also a guide during hunting season. She loved to hunt and was an outdoors lady.*

The trophy changed owners several times over the years. After Frances inherited the deer, she transferred ownership to her stepson, George L. Cooper, shown above. In 1993, George sold the trophy rack to Bob R. Butler, the current owner.

OFFICIAL SCORING SYSTEM FOR NORTH AMERICAN BIG GAME TROPHIES

RECORDS OF NORTH AMERICAN BIG GAME COMMITTEE

BOONE AND CROCKETT CLUB

Boone and Crockett Club
Records of North American Big Game Committee
c/o Carnegie Museum
4400 Forbes Ave. Pittsburgh, Pa. 15213

MULE and BLACKTAIL DEER

MINIMUM SCORE
TYPICAL MULE DEER 185

KIND OF DEER

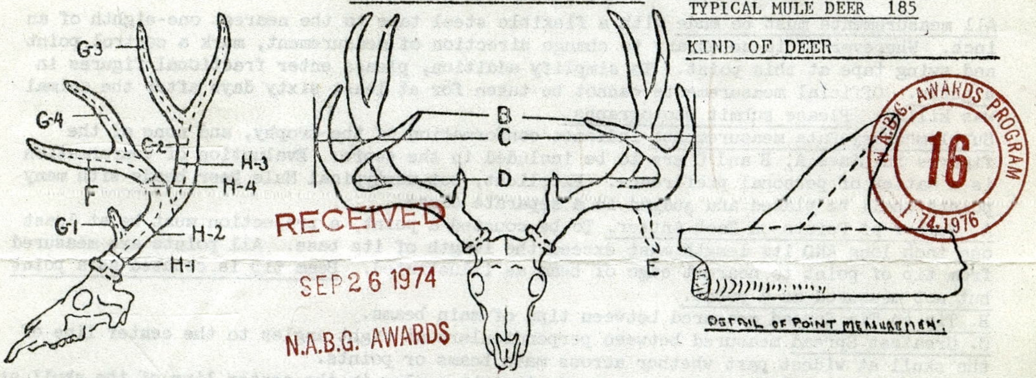

SEE OTHER SIDE FOR INSTRUCTIONS	Supplementary Data R.	Supplementary Data L.	Column 1 Spread Credit	Column 2 Right Antler	Column 3 Left Antler	Column 4 Difference
A. Number of Points on Each Antler	6	7				
B. Tip to Tip Spread	21 2/8					
C. Greatest Spread	33 1/8					
D. Inside Spread of MAIN BEAMS 24 6/8 — Spread credit may equal but not exceed length of longer antler			24 6/8			
IF Inside Spread of Main Beams exceeds longer antler length, enter difference						—
E. Total of Lengths of all Abnormal Points						3 6/8
F. Length of Main Beam				25 3/8	25 7/8	4/8
G-1. Length of First Point, if present				2 4/8	2 2/8	2/8
G-2. Length of Second Point				20 2/8	19 4/8	6/8
G-3. Length of Third Point, if present				13 2/8	14 4/8	1 2/8
G-4. Length of Fourth Point, if present				12 6/8	14 2/8	1 4/8
H-1. Circumference at Smallest Place Between Burr and First Point				4 6/8	4 5/8	1/8
H-2. Circumference at Smallest Place Between First and Second Points				4 7/8	4 7/8	—
H-3. Circumference at Smallest Place Between Main Beam and Third Point				4	4 2/8	2/8
H-4. Circumference at Smallest Place Between Second and Fourth Points				4 4/8	5	4/8
TOTALS Crook Co., Wyo. 5 ART			24 6/8	92 2/8	95 1/8	8 7/8

ADD	Column 1	24 6/8	Exact locality where killed Oshoto, Wyo.
	Column 2	92 2/8	Date killed 1967 Oct 1957 By whom killed Ora McGurn
	Column 3	95 1/8	Present owner ~~Frances Shephard~~ ~~George L. Cooper~~ Bob R. Butler
	TOTAL	212 1/8	Address
SUBTRACT	Column 4	8 7/8	Guide's Name and Address see attached
FINAL SCORE		203 2/8	Remarks: (Mention any abnormalities) 273

George L Cooper transferred ownership to Bob R. Butler. (See Attached)

G-3

FEB • 56

10	6
7	
2	
7	4
2	4
3	3
1	1

53/8   36 2/8

[illegible]AIL OF POINT MEASUREMENT

			[illegible] 2	Column 3	Column 4
			[illegible]	Left Antler	Difference
[illegible]					—
Inside Sp[illegible]					
[illegible]ler length, enter di[illegible]			22 3/8	25	2
[illegible]al of Lengths of all Abnormal Points			2	2 2/8	
[illegible]ngth of Main Beam			17	14 7/8	2
Length of First Point, if present			10 7/8	10 4/8	6/8
Length of Second Point			8 4/8	8 2/8	
Length of Third Point, if present			6 6/8	6 1/8	
Length of Fourth Point, if present			6 5/8	6	
Circumference at Smallest Place Between Burr and First Point			5 7/8	5 6/8	
Circumference at Smallest Place Between First and Second Points			5 2/8	5 6/8	
Circumference at Samllest Place Between Main Beam and Third Point					
Circumference at Smallest Place Between Second and Fourth Points					
TOTALS	89 4/8	23 2/8	85.2	84.1	8

Column 1	23.2	Exact locality where killed Sublett, Idaho
Column 2	85.2	Date killed 10/31/51 By whom killed Mrs Jack Ke[illegible]
Column 3	84.1	Present owner Mr. & Mrs. Jack Keen
Total	192.5	Address Burley, Ida[illegible]
[illegible]TRACT Column 4	8.7	Guide's Name and Address None
Result	183.6	Remarks: (Mention any abnormalities)
[illegible]d Line E Total	89.4	At Museum

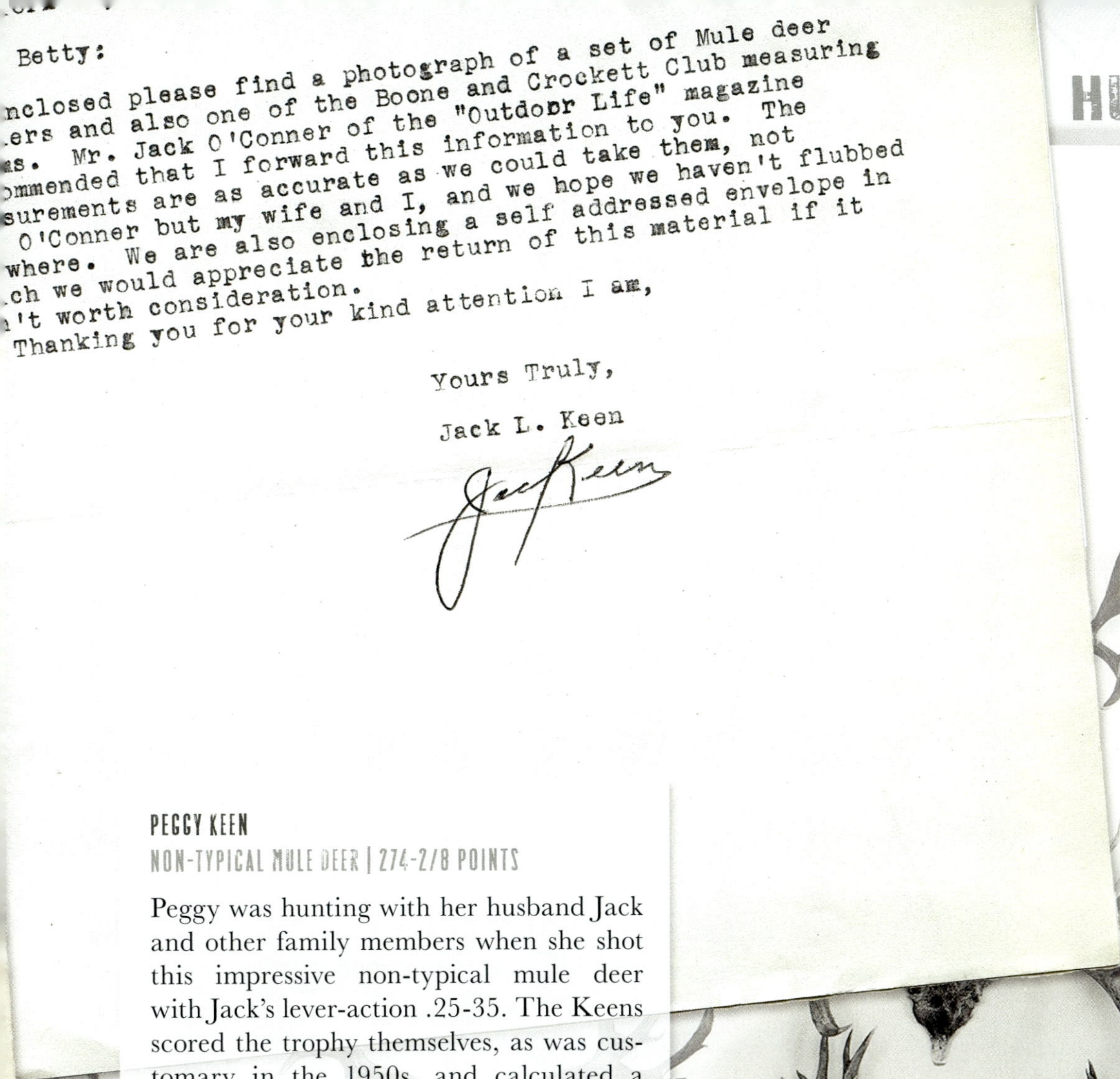

Betty:

nclosed please find a photograph of a set of Mule deer
.ers and also one of the Boone and Crockett Club measuring
ms. Mr. Jack O'Conner of the "Outdoor Life" magazine
ommended that I forward this information to you. The
surements are as accurate as we could take them, not
O'Conner but my wife and I, and we hope we haven't flubbed
where. We are also enclosing a self addressed envelope in
.ch we would appreciate the return of this material if it
't worth consideration.
Thanking you for your kind attention I am,

Yours Truly,

Jack L. Keen

Jack Keen

PEGGY KEEN

NON-TYPICAL MULE DEER | 274-2/8 POINTS

Peggy was hunting with her husband Jack and other family members when she shot this impressive non-typical mule deer with Jack's lever-action .25-35. The Keens scored the trophy themselves, as was customary in the 1950s, and calculated a score of 302-1/8 points. The Club requested they send the antlers to the eighth competition, where it was remeasured by a panel of judges. The buck has a greatest spread of 36-1/8 inches, as well as 26 scorable points, resulting in a final score of 274-2/8 points. Peggy's mule deer received a 2nd Place Award and is shown on display at right. A remark on the bottom of the original score chart states: *Abnormal horns resemble pieces of twisted driftwood.*

The Keens were hunting near Sublette, Idaho, on opening day of the 1957 season.

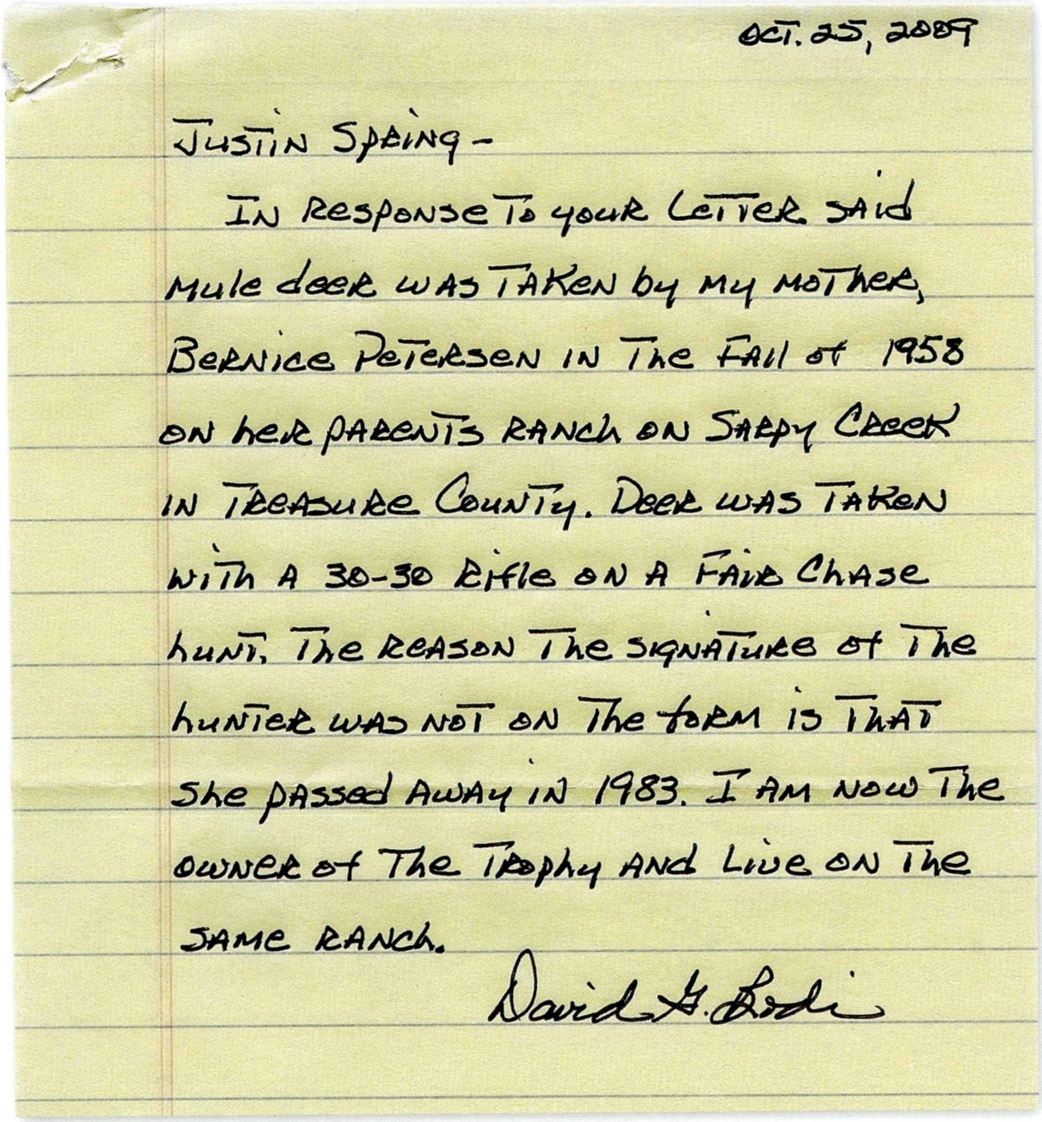

Oct. 25, 2009

Justin Spring -

In response to your letter said mule deer was taken by my mother, Bernice Petersen in the fall of 1958 on her parents ranch on Sarpy Creek in Treasure County. Deer was taken with a 30-30 rifle on a fair chase hunt. The reason the signature of the hunter was not on the form is that she passed away in 1983. I am now the owner of the trophy and live on the same ranch.

David G. Bodi

BERNICE PETERSEN

NON-TYPICAL MULE DEER | 226-1/8 POINTS

David G. Bodi had his mother's unique mule deer trophy measured in 2009, 51 years after she harvested the buck on the family ranch in Treasure County, Montana. The buck has 18 points and a greatest spread of 32-7/8 inches. The final score on Bernice's non-typical mule deer is 226-1/8 points.

As the note from David states, the mule deer:...*was taken by my mother, Bernice Petersen in the fall of 1958 on her parents' ranch on Sarpy Creek in Treasure County. Deer was taken with a .30-30 rifle on a fair-chase hunt.*

...typical mule deer
Date of Kill: 1/1/1958
Kill Location: Treasure Co., MT

CLU... N BI... ...ER

KIND OF DEER (...

☒ mule deer
☐ Columbia black...
☐ Sitka blacktail

Abnormal Points	
Right Antler	Left A...
7 2/8	2 2/...
1 4/8	3 0/...
8 6/8	2 7/...
1 4/8	1 2/...
SUBTOTALS 19 0/8	9 3...
E. TOTAL 28 3/8	

Detail of Point Measurement

PAID
BOONE & CROCKETT CLUB

B & C BIG GAME AWARDS 27 2007 - 2009

SEE OTHER SIDE FOR INSTRUCTIONS

				COLUMN 1	COLUMN 2	COLUMN 3	COLUMN 4
...No. Points on Right Antler	9	No. Points on Left Antler	9	Spread Credit	Right Antler	Left Antler	Difference
...ip to Tip Spread	31 5/8	C. Greatest Spread	32 7/8				
...nside Spread of Main Beams	30 0/8	SPREAD CREDIT MAY EQUAL BUT NOT EXCEED LONGER MAIN BEAM		26 4/8			
...ength of Main Beam					26 4/8	24 4/8	2 0/8
Length of First Point, If Present					7 0/8	7 1/8	1/8
Length of Second Point					16 5/8	16 1/8	4/8
Length of Third Point, If Present					13 2/8	10 4/8	2 6/...
...ength of Fourth Point, If Present					8 1/8	9 7/8	1 6/8
...ircumference at Smallest Place Between Burr and First Point					5 6/8	5 4/8	2/...
...ircumference at Smallest Place Between First and Second Points					5 0/8	4 7/8	1/8
...ircumference at Smallest Place Between Main Beam and Third Point					4 4/8	4 0/8	4/8
...ircumference at Smallest Place Between Second and Fourth Points					5 1/8	5 0/8	0
			TOTALS	26 4/8	91 6/8	87 4/8	8 0/8

Column 1	26 4/8	Exact Locality Where Killed:	Sec.3 T.3N R.37E - Treasure County - MT.
Column 2	91 6/8	Date Killed: 1958	Hunter: Bernice Petersen
Column 3	87 4/8	Trophy Owner: David Bodi	
Subtotal	205 6/8	Trophy Owner's Address:	Telephone #:
...TRACT Column 4	8 0/8	Trophy Owner's E-mail:	Guide's Name:
Subtotal	197 6/8	Remarks: (Mention Any Abnormalities or Unique Qualities)	
ADD Line E Total	28 3/8	None	
FINAL SCORE	226 1/8		

205 6/8
28 3/8

LAVONNE BUCEY-BREDEHOEFT

NON-TYPICAL MULE DEER | 269 POINTS

Nearly 43 years after taking this outstanding non-typical mule deer at the age of 12, Lavonne Bucey-Bredehoeft finally had the buck measured. The deer has a final score of 269 points and received a 2nd Place Award at the Club' 25th Big Game Awards Program in 2004. Lavonne recounts part of the adventure:

Dad took me to the local coffee shop; I was the center of attention.... Dad proceeded to tell everyone about teaching me to shoot the Rock Island .30-06 with peep sights (the same rifle with which he took his first deer).

> *I took her to the targets beside the barn and told her the rifle would kick. I pushed her shoulder hard with the heel of my hand to simulate the kick. She took the shot, hit dead on and was nearly knocked off her feet. Her eyes got big, and before she could react, I asked her if she was hurt. She said, 'No' and I told her to do it again. She did. Each time she was kicked and each time she went back and did it again...*

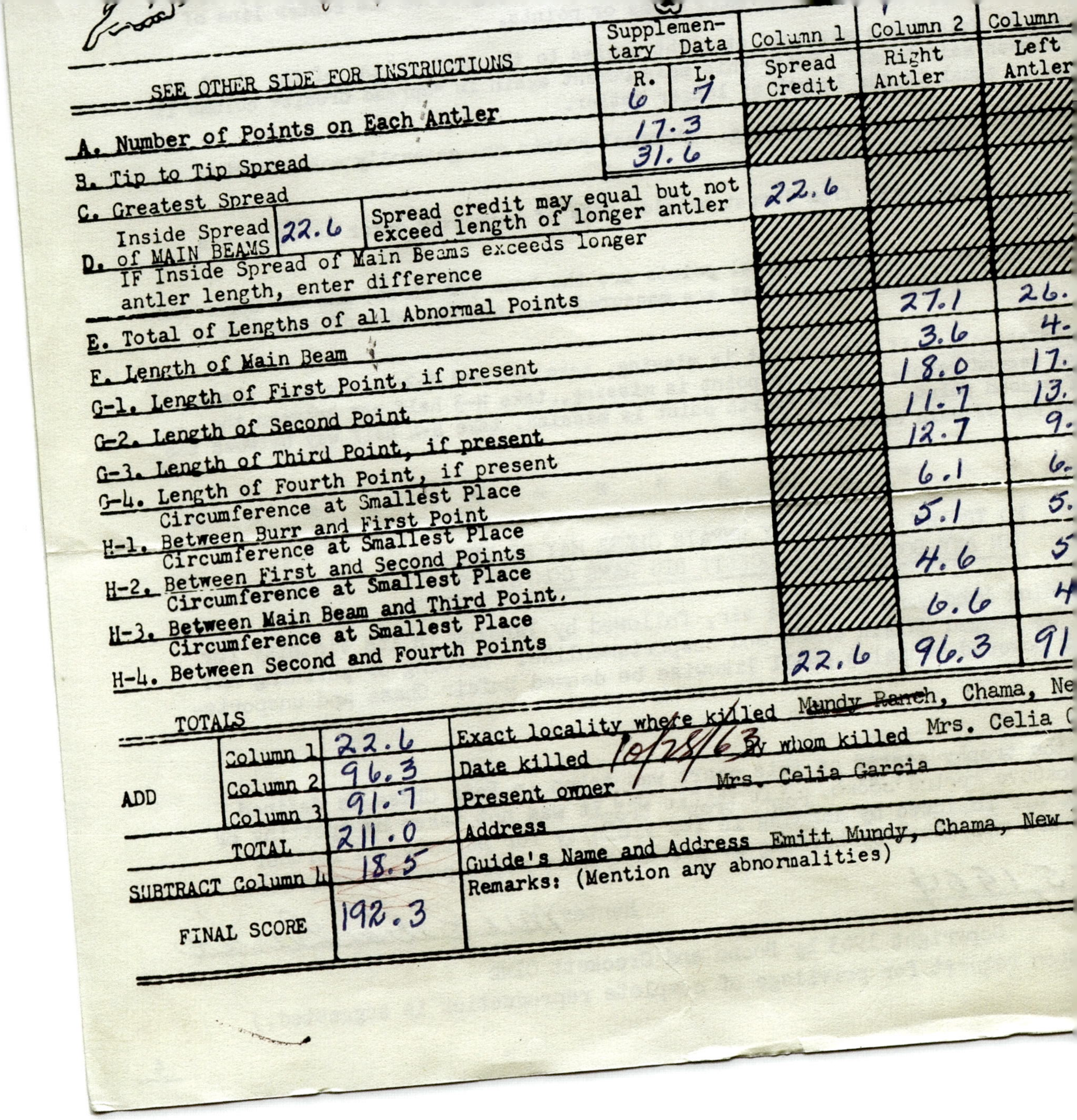

SEE OTHER SIDE FOR INSTRUCTIONS

	Supplementary Data R.	Supplementary Data L.	Column 1 Spread Credit	Column 2 Right Antler	Column 3 Left Antler
A. Number of Points on Each Antler	6	7			
B. Tip to Tip Spread	17.3				
C. Greatest Spread	31.6				
D. Inside Spread of MAIN BEAMS 22.6 — Spread credit may equal but not exceed length of longer antler			22.6		
IF Inside Spread of Main Beams exceeds longer antler length, enter difference					
E. Total of Lengths of all Abnormal Points					
F. Length of Main Beam				27.1	26.
G-1. Length of First Point, if present				3.6	4.
G-2. Length of Second Point				18.0	17.
G-3. Length of Third Point, if present				11.7	13.
G-4. Length of Fourth Point, if present				12.7	9.
H-1. Circumference at Smallest Place Between Burr and First Point				6.1	6.
H-2. Circumference at Smallest Place Between First and Second Points				5.1	5.
H-3. Circumference at Smallest Place Between Main Beam and Third Point.				4.6	5
H-4. Circumference at Smallest Place Between Second and Fourth Points				6.6	4
TOTALS			22.6	96.3	91

ADD	Column 1	22.6
	Column 2	96.3
	Column 3	91.7
	TOTAL	211.0
SUBTRACT Column 4		18.5
FINAL SCORE		192.3

Exact locality where killed ~~Mundy Ranch~~, Chama, Ne
Date killed 10/28/63 By whom killed Mrs. Celia (
Present owner Mrs. Celia Garcia
Address
Guide's Name and Address Emitt Mundy, Chama, New
Remarks: (Mention any abnormalities)

CELIA GARCIA

TYPICAL MULE DEER | 192-3/8 POINTS

Celia Garcia was hunting near Chama, New Mexico, with her husband Joseph, when they both shot records-book mule deer. Celia's typical buck—scoring 192-3/8 points—was shot on October 28, 1963, two days after her husband shot his non-typical. The Garcias had hired Emitt Mundy as their guide. The thick antlers on her buck measure over six inches each at the bases with its greatest spread measuring an impressive 31-6/8 inches. Joseph's non-typical buck has a final score of 306-2/8 points and received an award at the Club's 11th Big Game Competition. Flip to page 70 in the chapter on award-winning mule deer to learn more about Joseph's impressive non-typical.

umn 4
erence
0.0
8.1
1.1
0.4
0.6
1.3
3.6
0.1
0.0
1.0
1.7
18.5
co.

APR 18 1979
N.A.B.G. AWARDS

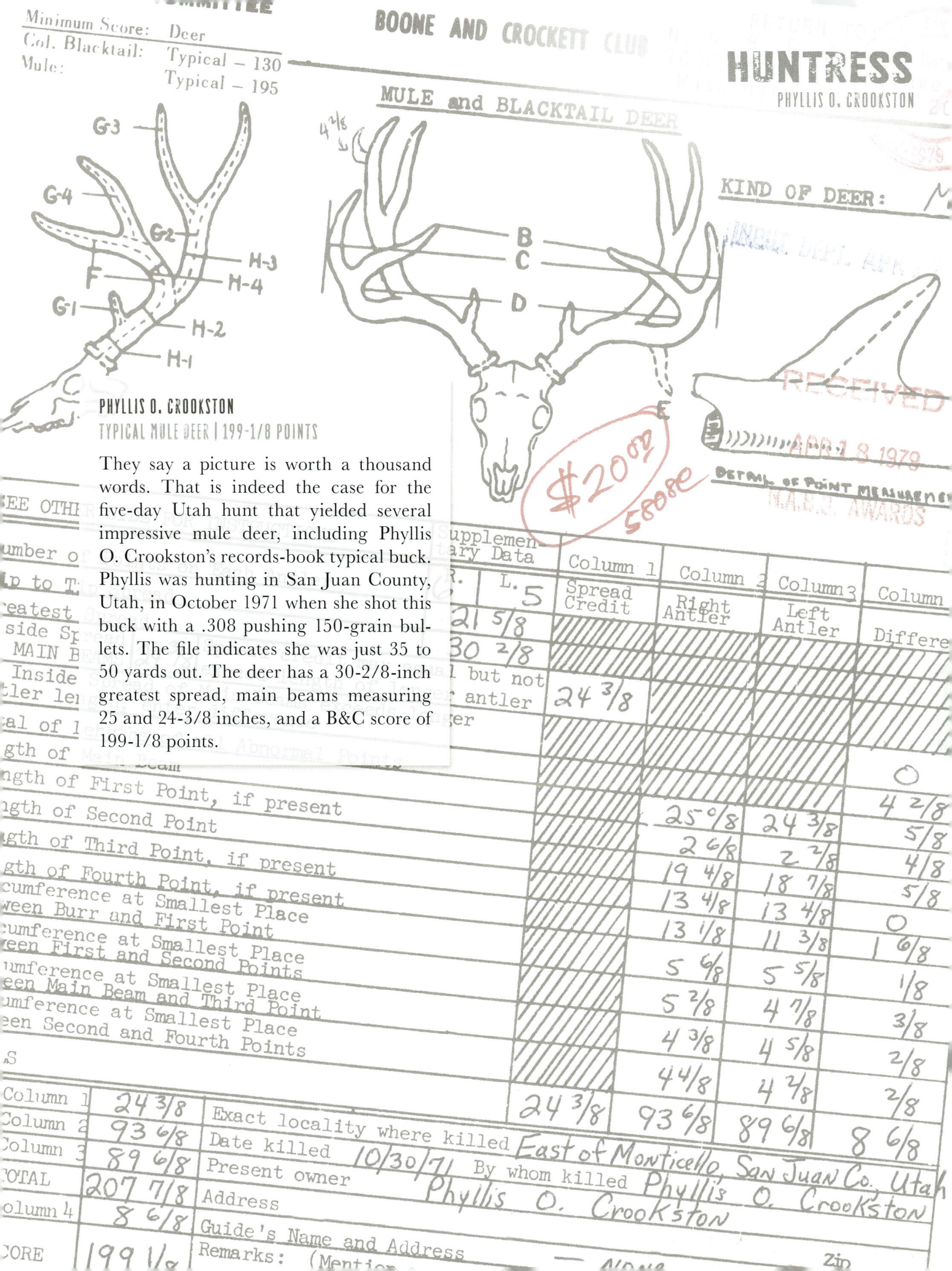

PHYLLIS O. CROOKSTON

TYPICAL MULE DEER | 199-1/8 POINTS

They say a picture is worth a thousand words. That is indeed the case for the five-day Utah hunt that yielded several impressive mule deer, including Phyllis O. Crookston's records-book typical buck. Phyllis was hunting in San Juan County, Utah, in October 1971 when she shot this buck with a .308 pushing 150-grain bullets. The file indicates she was just 35 to 50 yards out. The deer has a 30-2/8-inch greatest spread, main beams measuring 25 and 24-3/8 inches, and a B&C score of 199-1/8 points.

GOING FORWARD...

There are undoubtedly more women with trophy mule deer in the B&C records books than we've shown in this chapter with our in-depth look at several trophies from the early- to mid-1900s. Here are just four impressive modern-day trophies entered in the Club's Big Game Records Program in recent years—an indication that more women are shooting big mule deer now than ever before.

KATIE A. NORMAN
TYPICAL MULE DEER | 206-3/8 POINTS

Katie A. Norman was just 13 years old when she shot this amazing typical mule deer scoring 206-3/8 points. This photo was taken seven years later with the mounted trophy. She was hunting in Arizona's Coconino County during the 1990 season and made the shot with her .243 pushing 100-grain bullets. Her buck still ranks as the fifth-largest ever taken in that state and 75th overall. It is a 6x6, and its greatest spread measures over 33 inches.

CATHERINE E. KEENE
NON-TYPICAL MULE DEER | 285-4/8 POINTS

Catherine E. Keene was recognized at the Club's 26th Big Game Awards Program with a 1st Place Award for her impressive non-typical mule deer scoring 285-4/8 points. Catherine wrote about hunting in a story she submitted with her trophy entry:

> *I was exposed to hunting as a little girl... being carried on my mom's shoulders as my parents walked up a hill to get a deer my dad had just shot. I began carrying a gun and shooting my own game soon after I met my husband, who has become my own personal guide and hunting partner. I look forward every year [to] hunting season...*

Catherine's 6-year-old daughter was along on her hunt; hopefully she has fond memories of the experience she can pass on to future generations of young girls so they may become hunters as well.

MYRA S. SMITH
TYPICAL MULE DEER | 210-2/8 POINTS

Myra S. Smith's typical mule deer scoring 210-2/8 points ranks it as the largest mule deer ever recorded from Mexico and taken by a woman hunter. It also holds the 26th spot overall. She received a 1st Place Award at the Club's 26th Big Game Awards Program held in 2007. The buck is a classic 5x5 with no abnormal point deductions and an impressive greatest spread of over 38 inches.

In a story about the experience, she recounts how she got a glimpse of the buck the previous day:

> *I usually fall asleep when my head hits the pillow. This night, however, I lay there with my heart pounding while [my husband] Greg slept. Buck fever was getting the best of me.*

The next morning Myra shot the buck with her Browning A-Bolt .300 Winchester Short Mag with 150-grain, Nosler Ballistic Tip bullets.

KYLIE S. SONDERMANN
NON-TYPICAL MULE DEER | 218-4/8 POINTS

It was Kylie's third season hunting when she harvested this Nevada non-typical mule deer. She was 14 at the time and had set a goal to shoot a bigger mule deer each season. She's going to have a tough time topping this one, which has a final score of 218-4/8 points with 34-1/8 inches of non-typical points. Its greatest spread measures 35-6/8 inches. Kylie was one of the winners in the Club's first-ever youth essay contest. From that day on the mountain:

> *Everyone was yelling. My dad and JJ were running around like little kids. We ran up the hill to look at the buck. I knew right away this was not like any other buck I had ever seen. My dad told me that in all his years of hunting and guiding, he had never taken a deer this big. We sent pictures from the mountain to friends and family to let them know the good news. By the time we arrived home, there were several people waiting to see the deer. I think it's safe to say that I met my goal of getting a bigger mule deer than last year.*

KAIBAB PLATEAU
LAND OF THE GIANTS

JIM HEFFELFINGER | B&C PROFESSIONAL MEMBER

The Kaibab Plateau is known to most serious mule deer hunters as home to the most famous deer herd of all time. This plateau in northern Arizona sits between the Grand Canyon and the Utah border, covering about 1,100 square miles and ranging generally between 6,000-9,000 feet above sea level. Lower-elevation areas surrounding the plateau serve as important winter and transitional range for the deer herd. The plateau is covered with porous limestone, which accounts for the near total lack of surface water. There are no streams and very few ponds offering water sources for wildlife. The Kaibab Plateau is ecologically unique in the region, partially because it is isolated on three sides, with the Grand Canyon to the south, the lesser canyon of Kanab Creek to the west, and steep slopes and escarpments on the east. This isolation has resulted in bears, turkeys, wolves, and elk never occurring in large numbers, despite their abundance in other similar forests in the region.

Mule deer, however, were abundant and the plateau was well-known and well-hunted by Native Americans. The dry caves around the Grand Canyon contained small twig figures in the shape of deer that date back thousands of years—perhaps offerings to assure a successful hunt. The Paiute tribes were hunting deer on the Kaibab at the time of European settlement in the 1880s and traded deer hides with the Europeans and Navajos in the region. The plateau was even referred to as Buckskin Mountain in historical documents, but the name Kaibab was eventually adopted from the Native American language meaning "mountain lying down." The productive and isolated Kaibab deer herd has always fluctuated more or less independently from the deer populations in the surrounding areas.

By the 1850s, the first Mormon settlers found their way to the region and formed a small community and began grazing livestock on the surrounding ranges. These settlers relied on venison and deer leather to eke out a living in this remote corner of the Southwest. Even as the human population began to grow, the Kaibab always had quality deer due to its remote-

Deer in the Slide Tank squeeze-corral in the 1950s. They were then moved individually into the squeeze-chute where they were de-antlered, ear-tagged and loaded for shipping.

Kaibab mule deer being coaxed into a crate for transportation elsewhere, 1929-30.

PHOTO COURTESY MIKELE PAINTER/USFS

ness. Being so far from towns with lack of decent roads meant its isolation left no chance of humans exerting enough deer-harvest pressure to lower the age structure. However, the Kaibab gained its fame initially because of deer quantity and not quality.

THE DEER ERUPTION

Theodore Roosevelt developed a keen interest in the Kaibab Plateau because of several trips there to hunt mountain lions—he had a log cabin about a mile south of the current Ryan Station owned by the Arizona Game and Fish Department. In November 1906, President Roosevelt created the Grand Canyon National Game Preserve, encompassing the entire Kaibab Plateau and the Grand Canyon for the protection of game animals. Part of this protection came in the form of intensive and extensive control of any animal that might kill a deer. This predator-control program took place until 1931 and the reported tally included removal of 781

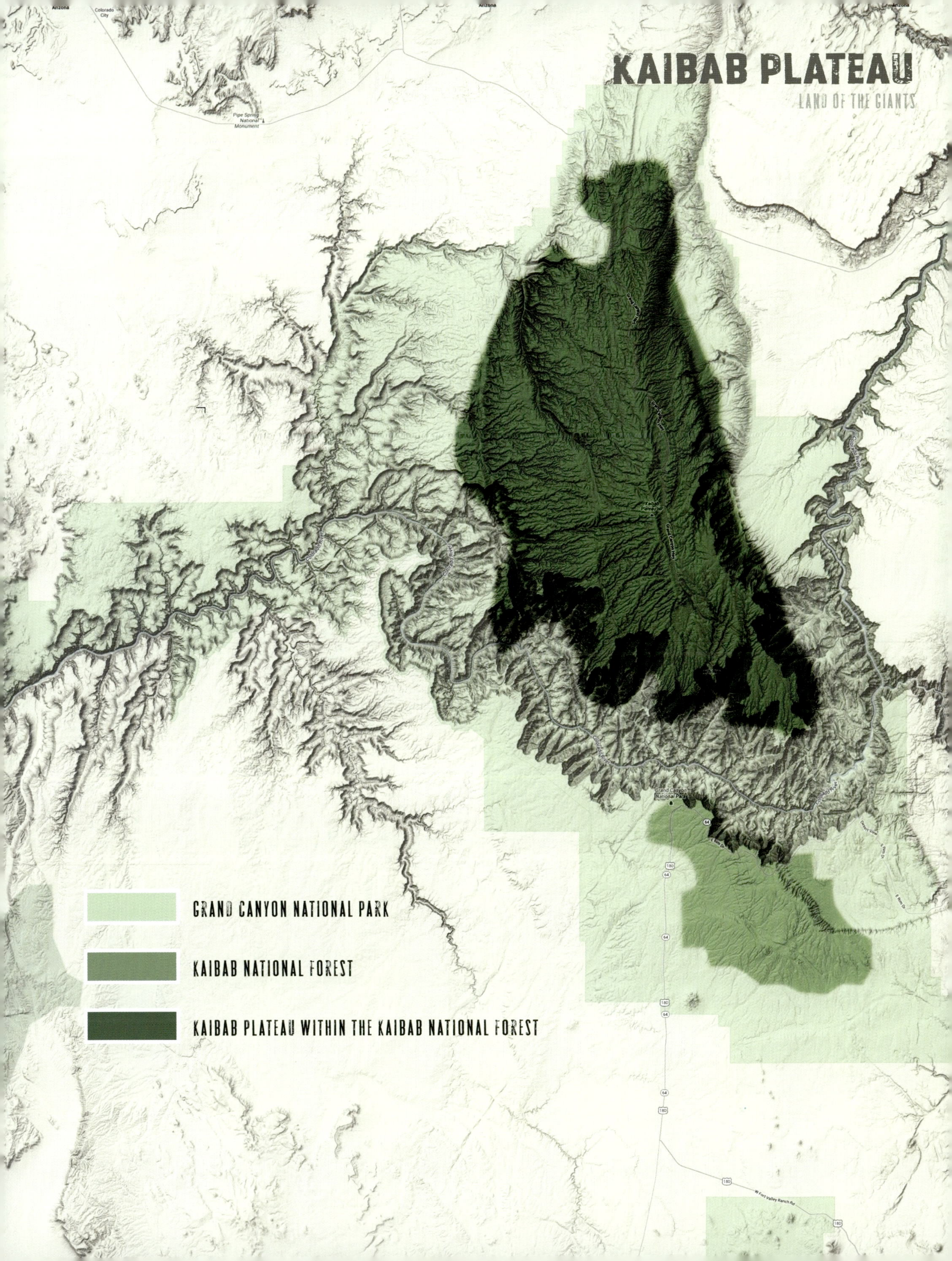
KAIBAB PLATEAU
LAND OF THE GIANTS
GRAND CANYON NATIONAL PARK
KAIBAB NATIONAL FOREST
KAIBAB PLATEAU WITHIN THE KAIBAB NATIONAL FOREST
Pipe Spring National Monument
Grand Canyon National Park
W Fort Valley Ranch Rd

mountain lions, 4,849 coyotes, 30 wolves, and 554 bobcats.

During this period of predator control, the deer population increased dramatically and peaked in 1924 before crashing to a level that was probably well-below the original population. The habitat was severely over-browsed, and the deer population simply collapsed under its own weight. It is this population eruption and crash that first brought the plateau to fame. The relationship was immediately drawn between lack of predators and deer overpopulation, and many used this as an example of what happens when you remove predators.

The Kaibab Plateau became the epicenter of the genesis of deer management knowledge for early biologists all over the country. What was later termed "The Terrible Lesson of the Kaibab Plateau" has been taught for decades, mostly incorrectly, to every university student majoring in wildlife management throughout the country. However, the interrelationships of ecosystems are rarely this simple; there were a number of other changes taking place during those years on the Kaibab.

By presidential proclamation, no deer hunting was allowed from 1906 to 1924. Although removing only bucks will not keep a deer population from growing, the establishment of the game preserve also stopped the harvest of female deer, which helps to keep a deer herd from over-populating the habitat. Fires were not suppressed like they are today, and this natural disturbance altered habitat in such a way that favored species like deer that thrive on the resultant habitats (brushy cover and browse with abundant weeds).

During this period, the amount of livestock grazing on the plateau was also greatly reduced. An early U.S. Forest Service (USFS) report from 1931 estimated there were 20,000 cattle and 200,000 sheep grazing the Kaibab Plateau and surrounding desert country in 1887-89. At the turn of the century, there were also several dairies and large numbers of horses on the same range. By 1924, grazing pressure had been reduced to about 4,000 cattle and 3,500 sheep. The earlier numbers were only rough estimates and doubtless exaggerations, but there is no doubt the intensity of grazing was reduced substantially during this period. The reduction of this intense grazing resulted in more forage available for deer, further aiding the build-up of the deer population.

By 1918, the vegetation was showing signs of damage from over-browsing by the burgeoning deer population. Inspections of winter range for several years thereafter spawned reports of a rapid deterioration of the range. Conditions worsened until Henry C. Wallace, secretary of agriculture, assembled a special investigative committee of experienced game biologists from around the country to report on the condition of the deer herd and its habitat. This committee entered the Grand Canyon National Game Preserve on August 16, 1924 and reported that "The conditions of forage throughout the preserve can only be characterized as deplorable; in fact they were the worst that any member of the committee had ever seen. When not only the leaves but the annual growth of trees, bushes, shrubs, and grass are so closely cropped that seeding is impossible, the condition of the range moves swiftly towards utter destruction." The final report issued by this committee contained several recommendations aimed not only at preserving the Kaibab deer herd in a healthy condition, but also at halting and restoring the range damage from over-browsing. They stated that, "The committee believes that as an immediate remedy for the present situation, no reduction of less than 50 percent of the existing deer herd would be effective. We, therefore, recommend that one-half of the existing herd be removed and that this removal be accomplished as quickly as possible."

Curiously, their first recommendation for accomplishing this was not hunting, but rather

by trapping deer and moving them to deer habitat elsewhere. This recommendation is understandable when placed in context; most other mule deer populations were at low levels elsewhere.

TRAPPING AND TRANSPLANTING

To those dealing with this issue at the time, it just made sense to capture deer from this over-abundant population and move them to areas where they were scarce. How best to do that had not yet been figured out since this was the very beginning of deer management in North America. The solution of live-capturing deer was a two-pronged approach. First, bucks, does and fawns would be trapped in large corral traps in fall and winter and transported directly to release areas. Secondly, fawns would be snatched from the field in June and July, raised with bottled milk on local dairy farms until

TOP: Kaibab mule deer in crates being loaded onto transport trucks, 1929-30. INSET: Building the deer crates.

PHOTOS COURTESY MIKELE PAINTER/USFS

weaned, and then shipped in October. Most efforts to restore low deer populations elsewhere were done with the grown animals captured in traps. The fawns from the fawn farms were mostly purchased by individuals for private and public parks and zoos. Likely some private individuals purchased deer to release in the wild on their ranch.

TRAPPING

Trapping began in 1926 with 125 deer captured, but 40 of those were released at the capture site or died during capture. Of the 85 remaining that were shipped from the Kaibab Plateau, 23 more died in transit. Once trapped, antlered bucks were roped and their antlers were sawed off with a miter-box saw to minimize injury to other deer in confinement. In 1927, only 37 deer were captured with 13 of those dying and three released at the capture site. Efforts the next year were a little more successful with 96 deer captured and 65 released. An additional trap was added in 1929 which allowed for the capture of 403 mule deer, of which 298 were released in new areas. In fall of 1931, 159 deer were captured, but many were released at the capture site because the market was satiated and demand for Kaibab deer was waning. High losses associated with the methods of capture and transport was a concern, and it was becoming obvious this method was not contributing to a real reduction in the deer population. By 1932 all translocations ceased because the hunting seasons were deemed effective for deer population reduction and there were measurable improvements in the deer habitat on the plateau.

Kaibab mule deer were translocated to Santa Rosa Island more than 80 years ago, where their descendants flourished for decades. Most were eradicated by the end of 2011 as part of the agreement when the island was purchased by the U.S. National Park Service.
PHOTO COURTESY GORDON LONG

Until 1928, those wanting Kaibab mule deer simply had to pay an established cooperative fund fee of $35 per deer crated and delivered to a railroad point in Marysvale, Utah. This money was then used to fund the capture efforts. After 1928, applicants paid only $5 to $7 per live deer, but they had to supply the transportation and prepare the transport trucks.

Many translocation destinations are unknown, but there are vague references to Oklahoma; Denver, Colorado; Beverly, Massachusetts; the National Zoological Park in Washington, D.C.; London, Ontario, Canada; Detroit, Michigan; and San Pedro, California. Long-time Kaibab researcher, Clay McCulloch reported that "at least 383 of them went outside of Arizona to 34 other states and Canada." We will never know the full extent to which Kaibab deer have been spread across the continent and beyond.

Some of the deer captured in 1930 were released on Santa Rosa Island off the coast of California. Santa Rosa Island is 85 square miles and one of the Channel Islands northwest of Los Angeles. Records show that 30 Kaibab mule deer were released there by the Vail family who owned the entire island. That small nucleus grew to as many as 4,000-6,000 Kaibab mule deer inhabiting the island with no other additions to the gene pool. Thus, this island contained only descendants of those 30 Kaibab deer released more than 80 years ago.

This island was at the center of controversy after the Vail & Vickers Company, who owned the island since 1901, sold it to the federal government for $30 million in 1986. The island is

now part of the Channel Islands National Park. One of the stipulations of the original sale was that all non-indigenous (Kaibab) mule deer had to be removed by the end of 2011. They were largely successful and the National Park Service is currently monitoring the last 6-10 deer which have been fitted with radio-collars in the hopes that any other deer on the island will join them and be removed.

FAWN FARMS

While direct trapping of deer was occurring, another effort was underway to remove deer from the plateau. Applications for deer were accepted by the forest service, and men were hired to ride in likely fawning areas to capture fawns on the plateau. The fawns were then brought to one of four old dairy farms on the mountain and hand-reared, but many fawns died soon after capture. The remaining were weaned and released into larger pastures until they were shipped to many places inside and out of Arizona. In 1926, 178 fawns were caught, but only 68 were ever shipped. The next year, 24 local residents in Fredonia, Arizona, and Kanab, Utah, were authorized to capture and care for fawns using specifications provided by the forest service. That year (1927), 355 fawns were captured by authorized residents, but again, only 110 were shipped alive from the railroad point at Marysvale, Utah.

In 1928 the fawn-rearing involved 34 local participants that caught 403 fawns, but delivered less than 38 percent of those for shipment. Raisers were paid $27 for every fawn delivered alive on October 1. By 1931 the deer herd had been reduced through hunting, and fawn captures were discontinued.

THE FAMOUS DEER DRIVE OF 1924

With continued concerns over the in-

creasing deer population, at least one person was thinking outside the box. George McCormick, a Flagstaff resident, stepped forward and convinced then-Governor George Hunt that he could use a long line of people on foot and horseback to drive 5,000 to 8,000 mule deer off the plateau, across the Colorado River, and up the south rim of the Grand Canyon. Governor Hunt agreed to pay $2.50 for each deer successfully driven in that manner. Famous author Zane Grey offered $5,000 for exclusive movie rights of the whole affair. With tongue-in-cheek, Flagstaff residents promised to raise an addition $1,000 if he could drive 1,000 deer through the streets of Flagstaff! A group of 125 enthusiastic drivers pushed through the deer habitat in a large driveline; the deer were driven from the men, but not in any consistent direction. The drive was abandoned when it was evident there were many more deer behind than in front of

LEFT: Fawns were held in large, fenced enclosures until weaned, before being placed in crates and translocated off the plateau. ABOVE: The two children of Mrs. Annie Judd of Kanab, Utah, with two Kaibab fawns in 1930.

PHOTOS COURTESY MIKELE PAINTER/USFS

the drivers. The now-famous Kaibab deer drive was a predictable failure, with no deer driven across the Colorado River and into Coconino County to the south. In the words of Jack Fuss, one of the participants, it was "the most crazy damn thing I ever heard of."

HUNTING

Almost immediately after the committee's final report in October 1924, the forest service announced it would open a hunt. Governor Hunt heard about the forest service's plans to open a hunt and was vehemently opposed to federal control of the deer herd. To maintain control of the situation, Governor Hunt sent the Coconino County Sheriff to arrest anyone leaving the Kaibab forest with a deer because the state of Arizona had not opened a deer hunt on the Kaibab. In five days, about 200 hunters each harvested deer before the arrest of three hunters on November 20 by the sheriff put an end to the hunting. A week later, an agreement was reached between the state of Arizona and the forest service allowing hunters to harvest up to three deer each for a $5 permit fee. Only 270 hunters were willing to participate, but they harvested 675 deer during the 17-day season.

After that hunt, and on the heels of that year's dry summer, an early snow in the fall of 1924 caused massive winter kill as weakened deer were forced onto poor winter range earlier than usual. Another cooperative agreement to hunt the second year was reached; however, the meager number of deer removed that fall was inadequate to protect the deer herd from itself.

Annual agreements between state and federal authorities allowed hunts to continue from 1925 to 1927, but the harvest was woefully inadequate to reduce the deer population sufficiently, and many deer died each winter. The road from the nearest sizeable city (Flagstaff, Arizona) to the Kaibab was 170 very primitive miles and took several days to complete. This remoteness, and the fact that the Colorado River had to be crossed by ferry, resulted in much less interest in deer hunting the Kaibab than there is today. Curiously, the intense predator removal efforts continued throughout all these attempts to drastically reduce the deer population and save the habitat from destruction. Perhaps they should have let the predators help them during that part of the Kaibab's history.

In 1928, a lawsuit reached the Supreme Court to settle once and for all the issue of who had jurisdiction over the Kaibab deer herd. The Supreme Court ruled that the forest service had the right to protect the range they were responsible for managing. That winter, the forest service authorized government shooters to remove deer, but the public outcry was so intense that this practice was discontinued the next year.

By most accounts, it appears that the Kaibab herd was reduced enough by 1934 to allow a recovery of the browse. With the help of several wet years in the late 1930s, deer body condition improved, and browse plants showed vigorous annual growth. Lessons learned on the Kaibab—both biological and political— set the stage for the further refinement of deer management throughout the West.

The Kaibab deer population continued to recover and increase through the 1940s, and by 1950, the deer population on the Kaibab Plateau was high enough once again to require a reduction in numbers to protect the winter range from overuse. Doe hunts during this period were again used to help control the deer population. With this period of abundance, deer trapping and translocation began again. In the fall of 1950, a large corral trap was also built to surround Slide Tank on the west side winter range. Over the next decade, about 300

Willis F. Nielson was hunting the Kaibab in November 1953 when he shot this non-typical buck. It has a final B&C score of 222-1/8 points and an impressive 40-inch greatest spread.

National Park Service rangers ear tag and age a deer for translocation to the Navajo Nation. Desert View Subdistrict, Grand Canyon National Park, December 20, 1961.

PHOTO BY ANDREW C. WOLFE

deer were trapped in large corral traps and translocated from the Kaibab, but this was not significant enough to aid in reducing the population there.

The number of hunting permits was increased as more and more damage was detected on the winter range browse, but the herd continued to grow. In the winter of 1954 the plateau experienced another deer die-off and the combination of the hunts and the die-off that year reduced the deer herd by about two-thirds. After that, range conditions improved and the body weights of deer started to increase again as the herd recovered. The herd grew once again through the late-1950s and into the 1960s before declining somewhat unexpectedly once again between 1966 and 1976.

TRANSITION FROM DEER CONTROL TO MANAGEMENT

After this last decline, research activity increased in the late 1970s to try to learn more about the herd and what made it fluctuate. Either because of, or in spite of, the research, the deer herd again increased through a very high period in the mid-1980s due to high precipitation, reduced cattle grazing, and buck-only hunting. This increase in the deer population forced the Arizona Game and Fish Department to split the hunts into an east side /west side hunt in 1983. The east side hunt was managed as a trophy hunt with fewer permits. Drier conditions returned through the 1990s and the first decade of this century and, predictably, the Kaibab deer herd has declined.

As the herd fluctuated, it remained a destination for those who wanted the adventure of a remote part of the Southwest where big bucks roamed. The human population increased in the Southwest and roads improved everywhere. Increasing timber harvest added logging roads to new areas of the Kaibab, and that allowed hunters access to a larger proportion of the deer herd. The increasing interest in hunting Buckskin Mountain was also fueled by outdoor writers who wrote about their exploits hunting giant mule deer on the Kaibab Plateau.

Originally, the Kaibab Plateau became famous for quantity, but with the development of a science-based and modern wildlife management profession, we can now do a better job of managing abundance and demographics (sex/age) of the deer population. No trophy deer management program is successful without actively keeping the population within the capacity of the habitat. Antlerless hunts were recognized in the 1920s as the most effective tool to managing the number of deer on the landscape. Any time we have a period of above-average precipitation on the Kaibab Plateau, female deer will have to be harvested to maintain the health of individual deer and the quality of the winter range habitat. History shows us that the deer population declines during periods of lower precipitation and higher deer and cattle numbers. We have little control over the precipitation, but we can still manage the size of the herd through female harvests to keep the population down to a level that the limited winter range shrubs can support the entire winter.

Because of the early interest in this deer herd, a check station was established on the plateau in 1924 to collect important information. This harvest-related data (age, spread, number of points, weight) provided critical data to monitor the success of both the hunters and the management program. This check station has been operated continuously since 1924, making it the longest string of continuous game management data anywhere in the country. This unprecedented dataset continues to help guide management.

Although the quantity of deer on the Kaibab is not the same as past years, the quality certainly rivals the Good Ol' Days in many respects. Hunt success for the Kaibab late seasons run 70-85 percent. Management guidelines currently call for the late trophy hunt to consist of 55-75 percent bucks 3 years old or older (the 2011 harvest was 88-100 percent). Since antler size generally peaks at 5-7 years of age, guidelines also state that 20-30 percent of the late-season harvest must be at least 5 years of age (the 2011 harvest was 31-75 percent 5 years old or older).

THE TRUE LESSON OF THE KAIBAB

The Terrible Lesson of the Kaibab Plateau that all budding wildlife biologist learned for decades was so overly-simplistic, it was of little value in advancing our understanding of deer populations and the relationships between predators and their prey. Some might even say it was damaging in that it told hunters (and young biologists) that simply removing predators resulted in a deer behind every bush.

Trophy management is not possible without keeping the deer herd under control with antlerless hunts.

PHOTO BY AUTHOR

HISTORICAL HARVEST KAIBAB PLATEAU

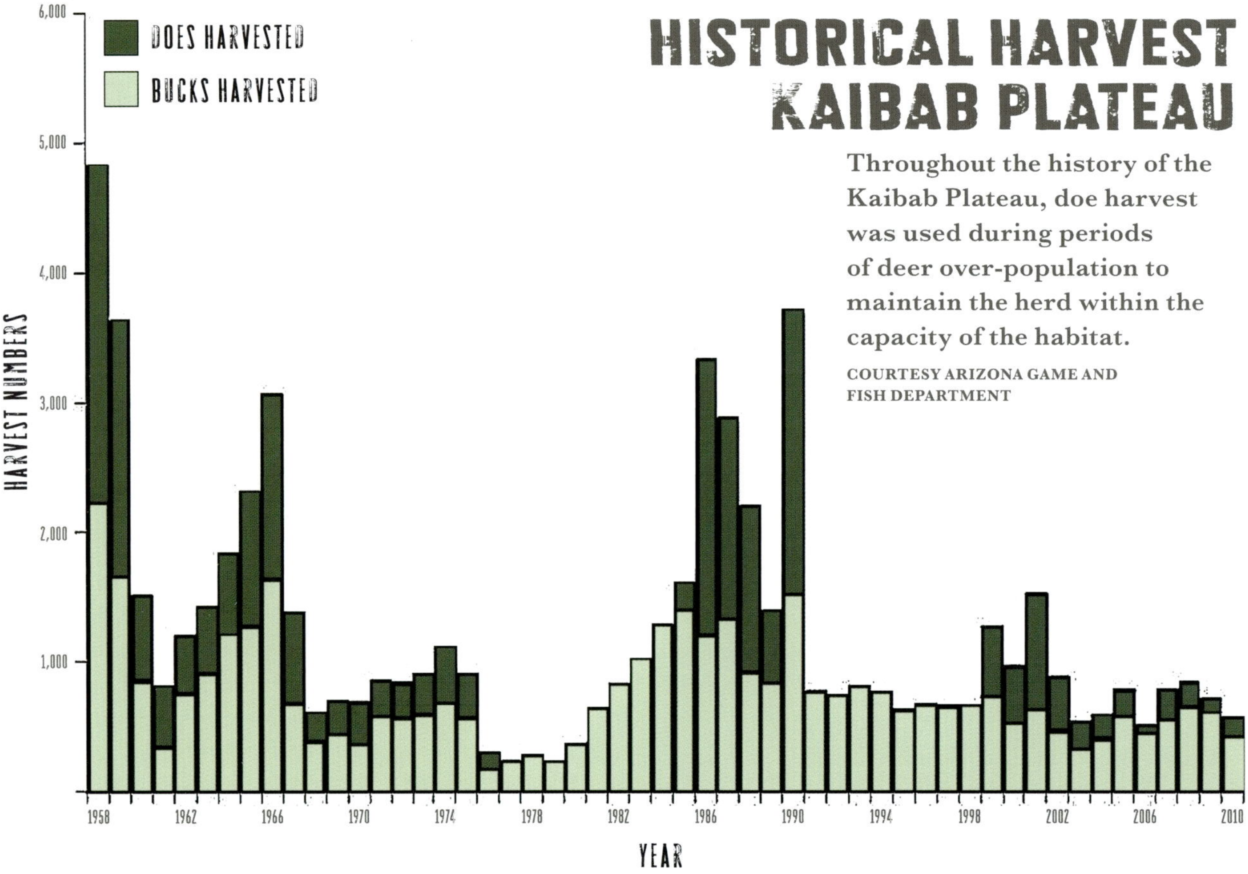

Throughout the history of the Kaibab Plateau, doe harvest was used during periods of deer over-population to maintain the herd within the capacity of the habitat.

COURTESY ARIZONA GAME AND FISH DEPARTMENT

Nature, and wildlife management, is not this simple. Because many factors were involved, it is difficult to assess how much each one contributed to the dramatic increase in deer numbers leading to the die-off. Given what we know about other deer population eruptions, it seems likely the combination of reduced predator densities, regulation against the harvest of does, increased precipitation, reduction of livestock grazing, and fire all contributed in a substantial way. Always searching for simple relationships, early biologists, administrators, and the public framed the predator control as the sole reason for the deer population explosion.

The account of the deer eruption itself was accompanied by exaggerated deer population estimates. This was not intentional; but rather, due to the limited knowledge and resources for deer population estimation at the time. The various estimates of Kaibab deer abundance throughout this period of population increase and crash are not based on any real data and represent mere guesses. Some of the population estimates were made by individuals who spent less than two weeks on the plateau. Although there is no doubt the deer population increased tremendously and then crashed, there is little value in repeating the actual numbers that are often used to describe this eruption of deer numbers.

This outstanding Kaibab mule deer was harvested in 2013 by Gilbert T. Adams III. It's too early for an official B&C score at the time of this printing, but all green measurements indicate a top-ranking buck.
PHOTO COURTESY GILBERT ADAMS III

What we did learn in a general, albeit graphic, way is that too many deer can damage the habitat and hamper the population's ability to bounce back from a die-off. After seeing the habitat damage that the Kaibab deer population eruption caused, Aldo Leopold wrote: "While a buck pulled down by wolves can be replaced in two or three years, a range pulled down by too many deer may fail of replacement in as many decades."

Deer over-population reduces the health of individual deer. Good nutrition is one of the foundations of producing trophy specimens. Not having adequate nutrition does not allow a buck to reach his full genetic potential for antler growth. Still, through the decades, the Kaibab Plateau kept producing some of the finest mule deer specimens in North America. Time has proven its reputation is well-justified as the Land of Giants.

The following pages are illustrated with the trophy entry files—including score charts and photographs—of mule deer harvested from the 1930s up through the 1950s. Many of these have since dropped out of the Club's records program due to the increase in minimum scores or the lack of sufficient measurements recorded when the new system was implemented in 1950.

18E40027
211

\# 317

OFFICIAL SCORING SYSTEM FOR NORTH AMERICAN BIG GAME TROPHIES

RECORDS OF NORTH AMERICAN BIG GAME COMMITTEE

BOONE AND CROCKETT CLUB

Boone and Crockett Club
205 South Patrick Street
Alexandria, VA. 22314

Minimum Score: Deer
Col. Blacktail: Typical – 130
Mule: Typical – 195

MULE and BLACKTAIL DEER

KIND OF DEER MULE

RECEIVED JUN 1981 BOONE & CROCKETT CLUB

N.B.G. AWARDS PROGRAM 18 1980-1982

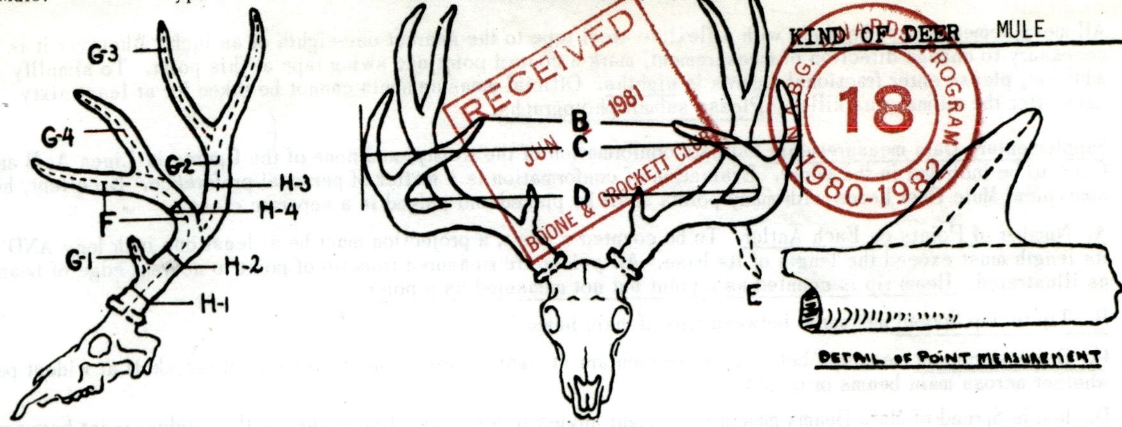

SEE OTHER SIDE FOR INSTRUCTIONS	Supplementary Data R.	L.	Column 1 Spread Credit	Column 2 Right Antler	Column 3 Left Antler	Column 4 Difference
A. Number of Points on Each Antler	7	6				
B. Tip to Tip Spread	18 5/8					
C. Greatest Spread	32 7/8					
D. Inside Spread of MAIN BEAMS 23 3/8 — Spread credit may equal but not exceed length of longer antler			23 3/8			
IF Inside Spread of Main Beams exceeds longer antler length, enter difference						
E. Total of Lengths of all Abnormal Points						7 3/8
F. Length of Main Beam				27 5/8	26 6/8	7/8
G-1. Length of First Point, if present				1 3/8	1 3/8	-----
G-2. Length of Second Point				20 7/8	19 7/8	1
G-3. Length of Third Point, if present				11 7/8	13 6/8	1 7/8
G-4. Length of Fourth Point, if present				11 3/8	11 7/8	4/8
H-1. Circumference at Smallest Place Between Burr and First Point				5 3/8	5 2/8	1/8
H-2. Circumference at Smallest Place Between First and Second Points				5	4 7/8	1/8
H-3. Circumference at Smallest Place Between Main Beam and Third Point				4 1/8	4 3/8	2/8
H-4. Circumference at Smallest Place Between Second and Fourth Points				4 4/8	4 4/8	-----
TOTALS			23 3/8	92 1/8	92 5/8	12 1/8

ADD	Column 1	23 3/8	Exact locality where killed Kaibab Forest, AZ
	Column 2	92 1/8	Date killed unknown P1930 By whom killed Graves Peeler
	Column 3	92 5/8	Present owner The John E Connor Museum
	TOTAL	208 1/8	Address Texas A&I Univ, Kingsville, Texas 78363
SUBTRACT	Column 4	12 1/8	Guide's Name and Address
FINAL SCORE		196	Remarks: (Mention any abnormalities) JOHNE.-C. I

M— Y003 03

GRAVES PEELER

PRIOR TO 1930

Historical records indicate that Graves Peeler was quite the unique Texan. He faced danger many times as a brand inspector for the Texas and Southwest Cattle Raisers Association, where he was instrumental in catching cattle thieves. He also is attributed with preserving the Longhorn breed when he put together a set of cattle that provided the genetic diversity to maintain and grow the breed. Graves was also a prolific trophy hunter—initially in Texas, and later in life, traveling as far north as Alaska to hunt on a fairly regular basis. The Kaibab buck shown here was taken by Graves prior to 1930 and is one of his five mule deer trophies listed in the Club's records program. Several of his entries were submitted by the John E. Conner Museum in 1981.

CHARLES F. SHIELD

1933

Little information remains on this vintage entry received by the Club in 1939. The buck was not remeasured with the new system, so no final score is available.

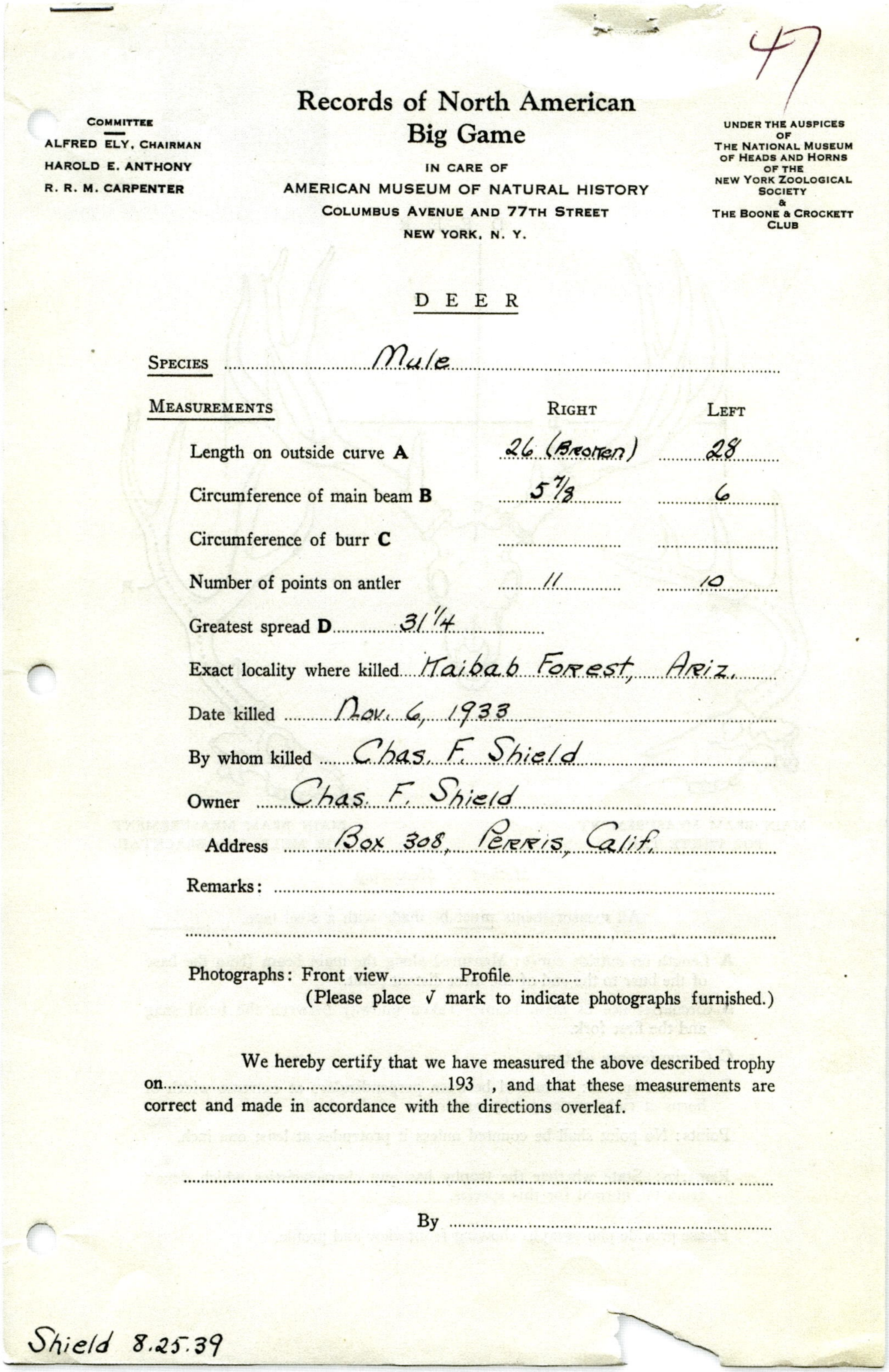

47

Records of North American Big Game

COMMITTEE
ALFRED ELY, CHAIRMAN
HAROLD E. ANTHONY
R. R. M. CARPENTER

IN CARE OF
AMERICAN MUSEUM OF NATURAL HISTORY
COLUMBUS AVENUE AND 77TH STREET
NEW YORK, N. Y.

UNDER THE AUSPICES OF THE NATIONAL MUSEUM OF HEADS AND HORNS OF THE NEW YORK ZOOLOGICAL SOCIETY & THE BOONE & CROCKETT CLUB

DEER

SPECIES Mule

MEASUREMENTS	RIGHT	LEFT
Length on outside curve A	26 (Broken)	28
Circumference of main beam B	5 7/8	6
Circumference of burr C		
Number of points on antler	11	10

Greatest spread D 31 1/4

Exact locality where killed Kaibab Forest, Ariz.

Date killed Nov. 6, 1933

By whom killed Chas. F. Shield

Owner Chas. F. Shield

Address Box 308, Perris, Calif.

Remarks:

Photographs: Front view .... Profile ....
(Please place √ mark to indicate photographs furnished.)

We hereby certify that we have measured the above described trophy on ....193 , and that these measurements are correct and made in accordance with the directions overleaf.

By ....

Shield 8.25.39

4th

OFFICIAL SCORING SYSTEM FOR NORTH AMERICAN BIG GAME TROPHIES

Records of North American Big Game and North American Big Game Competition

BOONE AND CROCKETT CLUB

% Am. Museum of Natural History
Central Park West at 79th Street
New York 24, New York

MULE and BLACKTAIL DEER

KIND OF DEER MULE

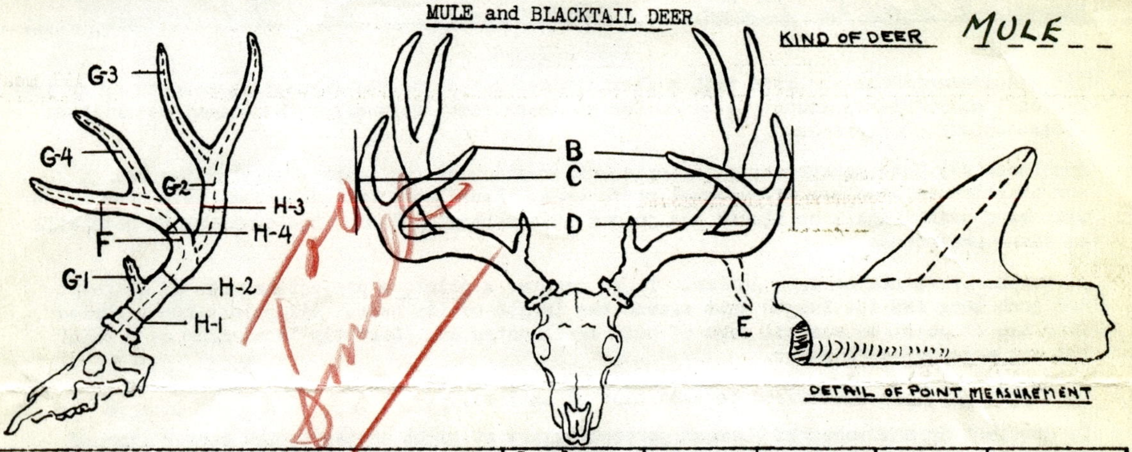

SEE OTHER SIDE FOR INSTRUCTIONS	Supplementary Data R.	Supplementary Data L.	Column 1 Spread Credit	Column 2 Right Antler	Column 3 Left Antler	Column 4 Difference
A. Number of Points on Each Antler	4	6				
B. Tip to Tip Spread	21 3/4"					
C. Greatest Spread	30 1/4"					
D. Inside Spread of MAIN BEAMS 21 3/4 — Spread credit may equal but not exceed length of longer antler			21 3/4			
IF Inside Spread of Main Beams exceeds longer antler length, enter difference						
E. Total of Lengths of all Abnormal Points						
F. Length of Main Beam				22 1/4	22 3/4	2/4
G-1. Length of First Point, if present				2 1/4	3 1/8	7/8
G-2. Length of Second Point				18 3/8	19 3/4	1 3/8
G-3. Length of Third Point, if present				8 7/8	8 1/2	3/8
G-4. Length of Fourth Point, if present				none	6	6
H-1. Circumference at Smallest Place Between Burr and First Point				4 3/4	4 3/4	0
H-2. Circumference at Smallest Place Between First and Second Points				4 1/8	4 1/4	1/8
H-3. Circumference at Smallest Place Between Main Beam and Third Point				4 1/8	4 1/8	0
H-4. Circumference at Smallest Place Between Second and Fourth Points				3 1/8	3 1/8	0
TOTALS			21 3/4	67 7/8	76 3/8	9 2/8

ADD	Column 1	21 3/4	Exact locality where killed KAIBAB NAT'L FOREST
	Column 2	67 7/8	Date killed 1935 By whom killed JOHN HARNESS
	Column 3	76 3/8	Present owner JOHN HARNESS
	TOTAL	166	Address CALIF.
SUBTRACT Column 4		9 2/8	Guide's Name and Address
FINAL SCORE OK		156 6/8	Remarks: (Mention any abnormalities) 8th Head - P. 448 - 1939 Records

Ack. 10/24/50

R.M.

A book of the Boo[...]

KAIBAB DEER - 1930S

JOHN HARNESS

1935

This buck was taken in the Kaibab National Forest in 1935 by John Harness. The initial measurements show a longest main beam of 31-1/2 inches as it was listed in the 1939 edition of *Records of North American Big Game*. In 1950, John received notification to submit complete measurements for the new scoring system. Unfortunately, the buck failed to meet the minimum score of 165 points, making it ineligible, and no photo exists. Six years later, John was joined by two other family members on a Kaibab hunt that resulted in three spectacular deer being harvested.

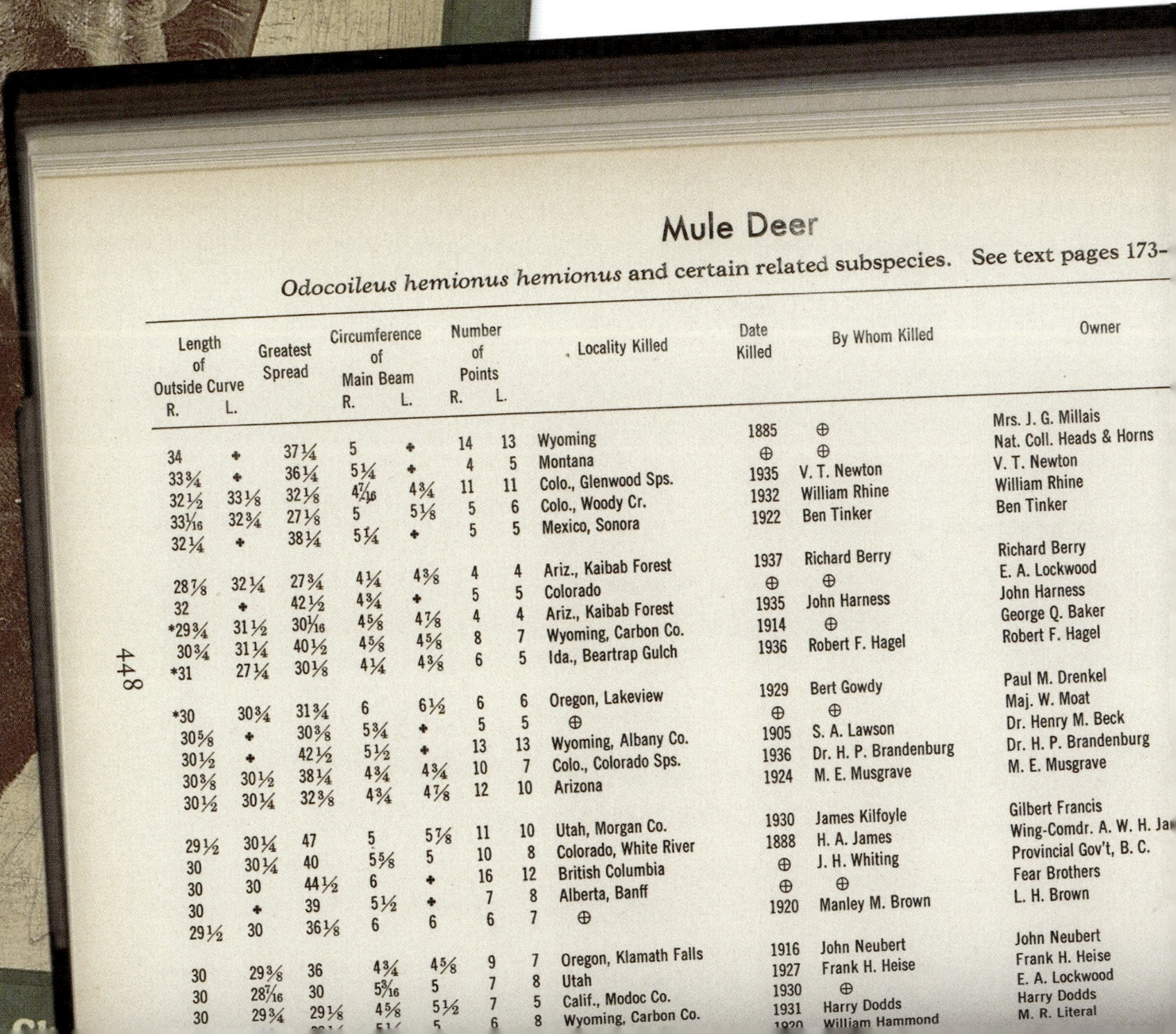

Mule Deer

Odocoileus hemionus hemionus and certain related subspecies. See text pages 173–

448

Length of Outside Curve R.	Length of Outside Curve L.	Greatest Spread	Circumference of Main Beam R.	Circumference of Main Beam L.	Number of Points R.	Number of Points L.	Locality Killed	Date Killed	By Whom Killed	Owner
34	✤	37¼	5	✤	14	13	Wyoming	1885	⊕	Mrs. J. G. Millais
33¾	✤	36¼	5¼	✤	4	5	Montana	⊕	⊕	Nat. Coll. Heads & Horns
32½	33⅛	32⅛	4 7/16	4¾	11	11	Colo., Glenwood Sps.	1935	V. T. Newton	V. T. Newton
33 1/16	32¾	27⅛	5	5⅛	5	6	Colo., Woody Cr.	1932	William Rhine	William Rhine
32¼	✤	38¼	5¼	✤	5	5	Mexico, Sonora	1922	Ben Tinker	Ben Tinker
28⅞	32¼	27¾	4¼	4⅜	4	4	Ariz., Kaibab Forest	1937	Richard Berry	Richard Berry
32	✤	42½	4¾	✤	5	5	Colorado	⊕	⊕	E. A. Lockwood
*29¾	31½	30 1/16	4⅝	4⅞	4	4	Ariz., Kaibab Forest	1935	John Harness	John Harness
30¾	31¼	40½	4⅝	4⅝	8	7	Wyoming, Carbon Co.	1914	⊕	George Q. Baker
*31	27¼	30⅛	4¼	4⅜	6	5	Ida., Beartrap Gulch	1936	Robert F. Hagel	Robert F. Hagel
*30	30¾	31¾	6	6½	6	6	Oregon, Lakeview	1929	Bert Gowdy	Paul M. Drenkel
30⅝	✤	30⅜	5¾	✤	5	5	⊕	⊕	⊕	Maj. W. Moat
30½	✤	42½	5½	✤	13	13	Wyoming, Albany Co.	1905	S. A. Lawson	Dr. Henry M. Beck
30⅜	30½	38¼	4¾	4¾	10	7	Colo., Colorado Sps.	1936	Dr. H. P. Brandenburg	Dr. H. P. Brandenburg
30½	30¼	32⅜	4¾	4⅞	12	10	Arizona	1924	M. E. Musgrave	M. E. Musgrave
29½	30¼	47	5	5⅞	11	10	Utah, Morgan Co.	1930	James Kilfoyle	Gilbert Francis
30	30¼	40	5⅝	5	10	8	Colorado, White River	1888	H. A. James	Wing-Comdr. A. W. H. Ja
30	30	44½	6	✤	16	12	British Columbia	⊕	J. H. Whiting	Provincial Gov't, B. C.
30	✤	39	5½	✤	7	8	Alberta, Banff	⊕	⊕	Fear Brothers
29½	30	36⅛	6	6	6	7	⊕	1920	Manley M. Brown	L. H. Brown
30	29⅜	36	4¾	4⅝	9	7	Oregon, Klamath Falls	1916	John Neubert	John Neubert
30	28 7/16	30	5 3/16	5	7	8	Utah	1927	Frank H. Heise	Frank H. Heise
30	29¾	29⅛	4⅝	5½	7	5	Calif., Modoc Co.	1930	⊕	E. A. Lockwood
[illegible]	[illegible]	[illegible]	[illegible]	5	6	8	Wyoming, Carbon Co.	1931	Harry Dodds	Harry Dodds
[illegible]	[illegible]	[illegible]	[illegible]	[illegible]	[illegible]	[illegible]	[illegible]	1920	William Hammond	M. R. Literal

1948 Comp.
Mms. accepted
Ju

Boone and Crockett Club

RECORDS OF NORTH AMERICAN BIG GAME
AND
NORTH AMERICAN BIG GAME COMPETITION
IN CARE OF
AMERICAN MUSEUM OF NATURAL HISTORY
CENTRAL PARK WEST AT 79TH STREET
NEW YORK 24, N. Y.

E

, CHAIRMAN

UNDER THE AUSPI
OF
THE NATIONAL MU
OF HEADS AND H
OF THE
NEW YORK ZOOL
SOCIETY

DEER

CS Odocoileus hemionus

UREMENTS	RIGHT	LEFT
ength of outside curve A	30"	29 1/2"
Greatest spread B 32 1/8		
Circumference of main beam C	5"	4 3/4"
Number of points on antler	5	7
Circumference of burr D	7"	7"

Exact locality where killed Big Saddle Camp, Kaibab Natl. Forest, Arizona

Date killed Oct or Nov. 1938

By whom killed Bob Mitchell

Owner "

Address

Present location of trophy same.

Remarks: Head unmounted.

We hereby certify that we have measured the above described trophy November 5 194 8, and that these measurements are rrect and made in accordance with the directions overleaf.

x John Mazzoni

By Seth B. Benson – Curator of Mammals
Museum Technician

ED AND SWORN TO BEFORE ME
N MAZZONI
NOV 4 1948

G-1. Length o
G-2. Length o
G-3. Length o
G-4. Length o
Circumfe
H-1. Between
Circumfe
H-2. Between
Circumfe
H-3. Between
Circumfer
H-4. Between S

TOTALS

DD	Column
	Column
	Column

TOTAL

BTRACT Column

KAIBAB DEER - 1930S

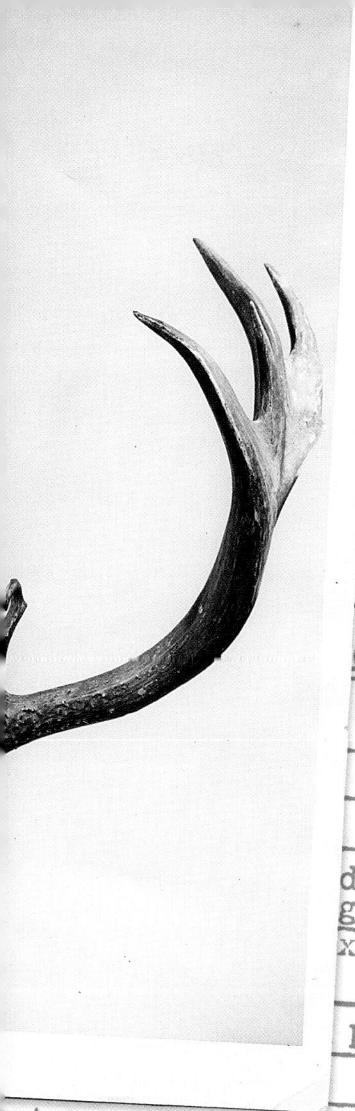

BOB MITCHELL

1938

Bob Mitchell originally entered this Kaibab mule deer for the second competition in 1948, when it was recognized with an honorable mention. Bob had the buck remeasured once the new scoring system debuted. The final score came in at 173-3/8 points and was listed in the Club's records until the minimum score was raised to 175 points in 1961. Along with a greatest spread of 31-7/8 inches, the buck also had two non-typical points on its left antler.

OFFICIAL SCORING SYSTEM

ds of North American
ame and North American
ame Competition

BOONE AND CROCKETT CLUB

% Am. Museum of Natural History
Central Park West at 79th Street
New York 24, New York

MULE and BLACKTAIL DEER

KIND OF DEER *MULE DEER*

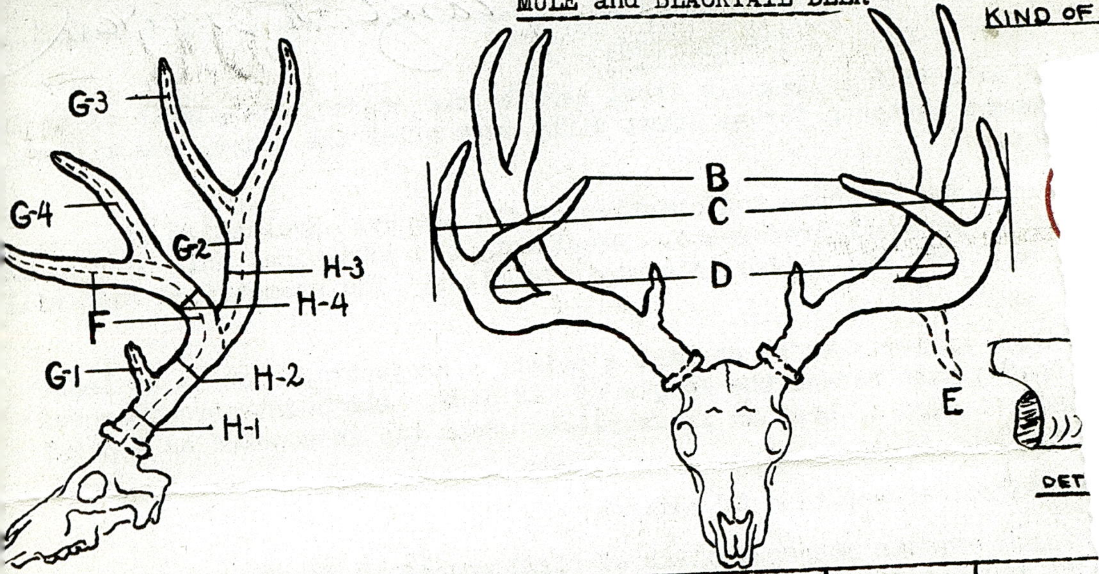

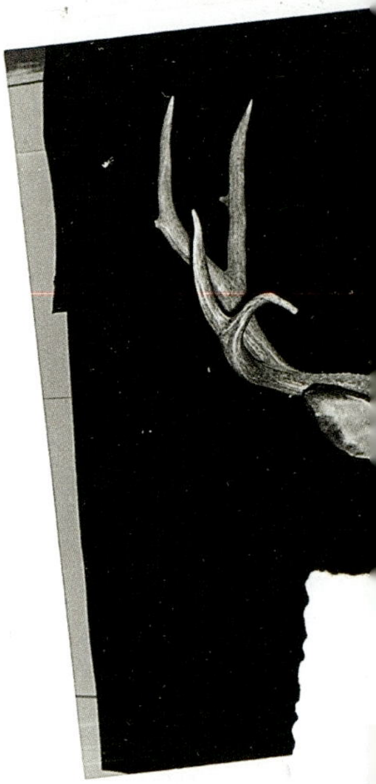

SEE OTHER SIDE FOR INSTRUCTIONS	Supplementary Data R.	Supplementary Data L.	Column 1 Spread Credit	Column Right Antler	
Number of Points on Each Antler	*5*	*5*			
Tip to Tip Spread	*24 5/8*				
Greatest Spread	*36 —*				
Inside Spread of MAIN BEAMS *27 6/8* — Spread credit may equal but not exceed length of longer antler			*27 6/8*		
IF Inside Spread of Main Beams exceeds longer antler length, enter difference					
Total of Lengths of all Abnormal Points				*25 7/8*	*29 5/8*
Length of Main Beam				*1 7/8*	*1 6/8*
1. Length of First Point, if present				*21 2/8*	*20 1/8*
2. Length of Second Point				*14 2/8*	*12 6/8*
3. Length of Third Point, if present				*8*	*9 4/8*
4. Length of Fourth Point, if present				*5 4/8*	*5 2/8*
Circumference at Smallest Place -1. Between Burr and First Point				*5 1/8*	*5 1/8*
Circumference at Smallest Place -2. Between First and Second Points				*4 4/8*	*4 4/8*
Circumference at Smallest Place -3. Between Main Beam and Third Point.				*4 4/8*	*5 —*
Circumference at Smallest Place -4. Between Second and Fourth Points					
TOTALS			*27 6/8*	*90 7/8*	*93 5/8*

ADD	Column 1	*27 6/8*	Exact locality where killed *KAIBAB FOREST, A*
	Column 2	*90 7/8*	Date killed *1939* By whom killed *HERB G*
	Column 3	*93 5/8*	Present owner *HERB GRAHAM deceased*
	TOTAL	*212 2/8*	Address
SUBTRACT Column 4		*8 6/8*	Guide's Name and Address *(NONE)*
			Remarks: (Mention any abnormalities) *trophy at relatives — Mrs. W. J. Graham*
FINAL SCORE		*203 4/8*	

HERB GRAHAM

1939

This award-winning Kaibab deer was shot by Herb Graham during the 1939 season and entered in the Club's seventh competition in 1955. The buck—scoring 203-4/8 points—has a greatest spread of 36 inches and no abnormal points. However, the main beams are uniquely formed and seem to flatten out and taper downward at the end.

AND CR... CLUB

Dec. 21, 1955

...RESS CORRESPON...
... GRANCEL FITZ, S...
5 TUDOR CITY PL...
...EW YORK 17, NEW...

...m our records that the fine Mule Deer (typica...
American Big Game Competition is one of the...
... For this reason it is necessary to have...
...ct it, measure it officially and compare it...
... class. The trophy will then be hung in a...
... Museum of Natural History, which...

...your trophy
...est at 79th
...eads and horns
...s of the owner;
...e items will
...aution will
...one and Crockett
... trophies either
... the entries will
...ce.

...ill appreciate
...ce it in the
... Museum is

... and thank you
...ican Big Game

...rs,

...B. ...

Chairman

SBW:H

Since your trophy has been officially scored, you do not need to send it to New York unless you want it exhibited. If you do not send it

PHILIP K. COFFEEN

1939

William A. Coffeen entered Philip's Kaibab non-typical in the Club's records program in 1991. With a score of 294-1/8 points, the buck still ranks as the third-largest non-typical from that area and 31st overall. This outstanding buck also has a net-typical frame of 207-7/8 points. It has 20 non-typical points that measure 86-2/8 inches. Information provided by the owner of the trophy indicates that Philip was hunting by horseback and carrying a .270 rifle when he shot the buck in October 1939.

OFFICIAL SCORING SYSTEM FOR NORTH AMERICAN BIG GAME TROPHIES

Records of North American Big Game — BOONE AND CROCKETT CLUB — 241 South Fraley Boulevard, Dumfries, Virginia 22026

Minimum Score: 240

NON-TYPICAL MULE DEER

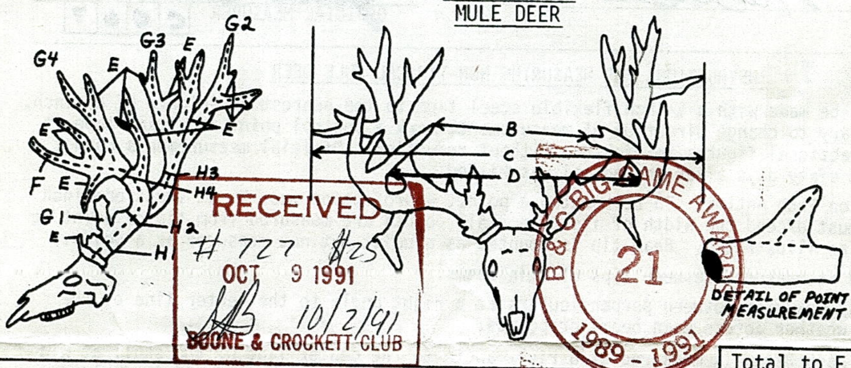

35 5/8 50 3/8

Abnormal Points	
Right	Left
1 6	7 1
2 -	1 2
6 2	8 5
2 4	5 2
8 2	3 1
3 1	6 2
6 6	2 5
3 5	10 7
1 3	1 5
	1 7
	2
Total to E	86 2/8

SEE OTHER SIDE FOR INSTRUCTIONS		Column 1	Column 2	Column 3	Column 4
A. Number of Points on Each Antler	R. 14 L. 16	Spread Credit	Right Antler	Left Antler	Difference
B. Tip to Tip Spread	18 -				
C. Greatest Spread	36 -				
D. Inside Spread of Main Beams 24 3	Credit may equal but not exceed length of longer antler	24 3			
IF Spread exceeds longer antler, enter difference					
E. Total of Lengths of Abnormal Points	86 2/8				
F. Length of Main Beams			27 1	26 1	1 -
G-1. Length of First Point, if present			2 7	3 7	1 -
G-2. Length of Second Point			15 4	16 -	4/8
G-3. Length of Third Point, if present			12 2	13 4	1 2/8
G-4. Length of Fourth Point, if present			13 -	12 -	1 -
H-1. Circumference at Smallest Place Between Burr and First Point			5 7	5 6	1/8
H-2. Circumference at Smallest Place Between First and Second Points			5 6	5 7	1/8
H-3. Circumference at Smallest Place Between Main Beam and Third Point			5 6	6 2	4/8
H-4. Circumference at Smallest Place Between Second and Fourth Points			5 6	6 2	4/8
TOTALS Coconino Co., Ariz. (3)	86 2/8	24 3/8	93 7/8	95 5/8	6 -

ADD	Column 1	24 3/8	Exact locality where killed KAIBAB NATIONAL FOREST, AZ
	Column 2	93 7/8	Date killed 1939 By whom killed P.K. Coffeen
	Column 3	95 5/8	Present Owner W. A. Coffeen
	TOTAL	213 7/8	Address Thatcher, AZ 855
SUBTRACT	Column 4	6 -	
	Result	207 7/8	Guide's Name and Address
Add Line E Total		86 3/8	Remarks: (Mention any abnormalities or unique qualities) 20 ABNORMAL POINTS - 9 ABNORMAL ON RIGHT, 11 ABNORMAL ON LEFT
FINAL SCORE		294 1/8	

OFFICIAL SCORING SYSTEM FOR NORTH AMERICAN BIG GAME TR

Records of North American
Big Game Committee

BOONE AND CROCKETT CLUB

Addres
Mrs. G
5 Tudo

List of abnormal points

Right		Left
1-	2 6/8	1 6/8
2-	3 6/8	2 5/8
3-	7 1/8	5 7/8
4-	7 3/8	3 6/8
5-	7 6/8	2 6/8
6-	5 5/8	5 6/8
7-	8 2/8	9 5/8
8-	2 5/8	1 5/8
	45 2/8	33 6/8

Total = 79.0

NON-TYPICAL MULE DEER

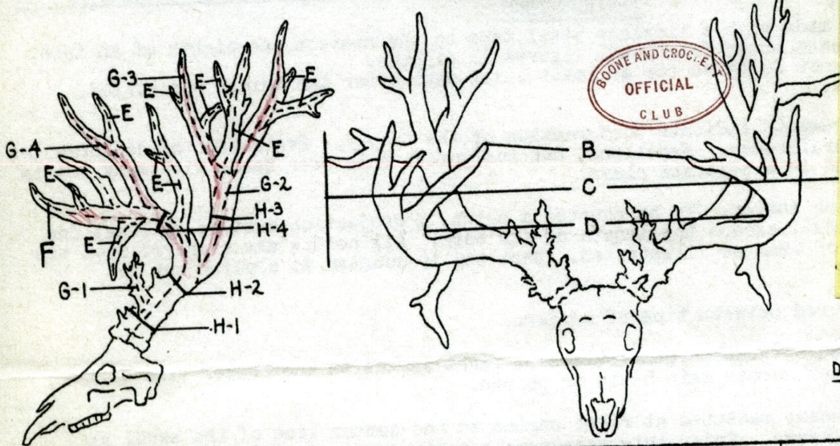

DETAIL OF POINT MEASUREMENT

SEE OTHER SIDE FOR INSTRUCTIONS	Supplementary Data R. 12	L. 12	Column 1 Spread Credit	Column 2 Right Antler	Column 3 Left Antler	Column 4 Difference
A. Number of Points on Each Antler						
B. Tip to Tip Spread	19					
C. Greatest Spread	33 4/8					
D. Inside Spread of MAIN BEAMS 25 4/8 — Spread credit may equal but not exceed length of longer antler			25 4/8			
IF Inside Spread of Main Beams exceeds longer antler length, enter difference						—
E. Total of Lengths of all Abnormal Points	79					
F. Length of Main Beam				26 3/8	27 5/8	1 2/8
G-1. Length of First Point, if present				NONE	NONE	—
G-2. Length of Second Point				13 2/8	11 4/8	1 6/8
G-3. Length of Third Point, if present				10 6/8	11 6/8	1 -
G-4. Length of Fourth Point, if present				11 4/8	12 -	4/8
H-1. Circumference at Smallest Place Between Burr and First Point				5 [illegible]	5 [illegible]	—
H-2. Circumference at Smallest Place Between First and Second Points				5 -	5 -	—
H-3. Circumference at Samllest Place Between Main Beam and Third Point				4 4/8	4 4/8	—
H-4. Circumference at Smallest Place Between Second and Fourth Points				4 5/8	4 7/8	2/8
TOTALS	79		25 4/8	81 [illegible]	82 2/8	4 6/8

ADD	Column 1	25 4/8	Exact locality where killed NORTH KAIBAB, ARIZONA
	Column 2	81 [illegible]	Date killed 1940 By whom killed NOT KNOWN
	Column 3	82 2/8	Present owner BOB HOUSHOLDER
	Total	18[illegible] 6/8	Address
SUBTRACT Column 4		4 6/8	Guide's Name and Address
	Result	184 [illegible]	Remarks: (Mention any abnormalities)
Add Line E Total		79 -	- 8 "abnormal" (non-typ.) points on each antler -
FINAL SCORE		263 [illegible]	- no eye guards (G-1)

BOB HOUSHOLDER

1940

Bob Housholder entered this north Kaibab mule deer in 1955. Records indicate the hunter is unknown, but the date was around 1940. The buck has 24 scorable points, 20 of which were deemed non-typical and add up to 79 inches of total abnormal points. Interestingly, the unique rack does not have any eye-guards.

KAIBAB DEER - 1940S

MARLEN D. MURPHY

1941

Harvested in 1941 by an unknown hunter, this non-typical Kaibab mule deer was submitted to the Club's records program 50 years later by Marlen D. Murphy. The buck has 27 scorable points and a greatest spread over 43 inches.

BOONE AND CROC

RECORDS

NO ERICAN BIG GAME

has AN

ST NORT 9-1991

AME AWARD

Y OF 25 SEPTE BER 1991

Chairman, Records of North American Big Game Committee

Dumfri

All-time
240

NON-TYPICAL
MULE DEER

Abnormal Points Right Antler	Le[ft Antler]
12 2/8	1
2 4/8	2
1 3/8	3
5 6/8	8
4	4
2	7
	3
	3
	2 1/8
	8 6/8
	4 7/8

SEE OTHER SIDE FOR INSTRUCTIONS

E. Total of Lengths of Abnormal Points: 27 7/8 | 76 | 48

				Column 1	Column 2	Column 3	Column 4
No. Points on Right Antler	11	No. Points on Left Antler	16	Spread Credit	Right Antler	Left Antler	Differ[ence]
Tip to Tip Spread	23 6/8	C. Greatest Spread	43 1/8				
Inside Spread of Main Beams	29 4/8	(Credit May Equal But Not Exceed Longer Antler)		29 4/8			
Length of Main Beam					29	31 2/8	2 2/8
Length of First Point, If Present					2	2 7/8	7/8
Length of Second Point					17 1/8	18	7/8
Length of Third Point, If Present					10 3/8	7 6/8	2 5/8
Length of Fourth Point, If Present					12 7/8	13 1/8	2/8
Circumference at Smallest Place Between Burr and First Point					5 1/8	5 4/8	3/8
Circumference at Smallest Place Between First and Second Points					4 7/8	4 7/8	–
Circumference at Smallest Place Between Main Beam and Third Point					4 7/8	3 7/8	1
Circumference at Smallest Place Between Second and Fourth Points					4 6/8	5 1/8	3/8
TOTALS				29 4/8	91	92 3/8	8 5/8

[C]onino Co., Ariz.

Total of [Colum]ns 1, 2, and 3	212 7/8	Exact Locality Where Killed:	* Kaibab Plateau, S. of Fredonia, Arizon[a]		
[Subtr]act Column 4	- 8 5/8	Date Killed:	1941	By Whom Killed:	UNKNOWN
[To]tal	204 2/8	Present Owner:	MARLEN D. MURPHY		
[Add Line] E) Total of Lengths [of Abn]ormal Points	76	Guide Name and Address:	N/A		

VERNON WILSON
1941

This very impressive Kaibab mule deer has 43 scorable points totaling 105-1/8 inches of non-typical points that add to an amazing net-typical frame of 206-5/8 giving it a final score of 311-6/8 points. The buck was shot by Vernon Wilson in 1941, but not entered into the Club's records program until 1982 by the owner, the Heritage Gun Room in California. It was shipped to the Club for inclusion in the 18th Big Game Awards Program, and it was recognized with a Certificate of Merit. It's currently owned by Cabela's, Inc., and still ranks as the ninth-largest non-typical mule deer of all-time, as well as the second-largest from Arizona.

Cert Merit

corrected

OFFICIAL SCORING SYSTEM FOR NORTH AMERICAN BIG GAME TROPHIES

Records of North American Big Game

BOONE AND CROCKETT CLUB

205 South Patrick Street
Alexandria, Virginia 22314

Minimum Score: 240

NON-TYPICAL
MULE DEER

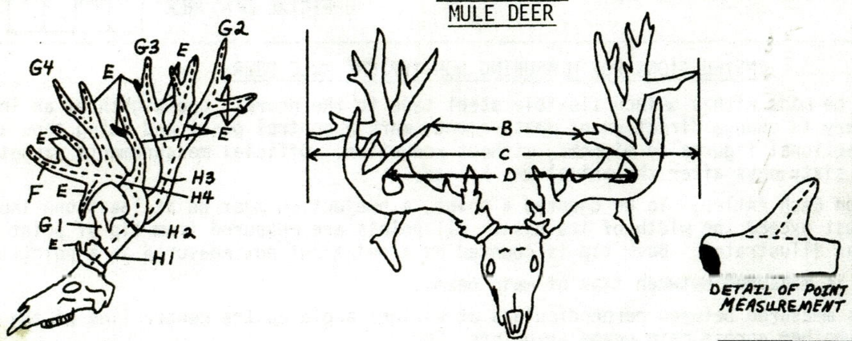

Abnormal Points			
Right		Left	
1 1	4 3	1 6	2
1 7	3 3	3	1 5
2	2 3	1 1	3 4
2 4	3 3	2 6	8 2
2 1	1 6	1 4	4
6 3	1 3	1 5	
1 3	4 3	2 2	
3 4		2 1	
5 5		1 3	
10 6		7 1	
	58-1	3 2	47
Total to E	105-1/8		

SEE OTHER SIDE FOR INSTRUCTIONS			Column 1	Column 2	Column 3	Column 4
A. Number of Points on Each Antler	R. 22	L. 21	Spread Credit	Right Antler	Left Antler	Difference
B. Tip to Tip Spread		20 7				
C. Greatest Spread		32 5/8				
D. Inside Spread of Main Beams	24 1/8	Credit may equal but not exceed length of longer antler	24 1/8			
IF Spread exceeds longer antler, enter difference						—
E. Total of Lengths of Abnormal Points		105-1/8				
F. Length of Main Beams				26 7/8	24 7/8	2
G-1. Length of First Point, if present				3 2/8	3 6/8	4/8
G-2. Length of Second Point				17 2/8	18 6/8	1-4/8
G-3. Length of Third Point, if present				12 3/8	11 4/8	7/8
G-4. Length of Fourth Point, if present				11 3/8	13 3/8	2
H-1. Circumference at Smallest Place Between Burr and First Point				6 1/8	6 5/8	4/8
H-2. Circumference at Smallest Place Between First and Second Points				6 1/8	5 4/8	3/8
H-3. Circumference at Smallest Place Between Main Beam and Third Point				6 3/8	5 4/8	1-2/8
H-4. Circumference at Smallest Place Between Second and Fourth Points				6	6 2/8	2/8
TOTALS		105-1/8	24-1/8	95-6/8	96	9-2/8

N.A.B.G. AWARDS PROGRAM 18 1980-1982

ADD	Column 1	24-1/8
	Column 2	95-6/8
	Column 3	96
	TOTAL	215-7/8
SUBTRACT Column 4		9-2/8
	Result	206-5/8
Add Line E Total		105-1/8
FINAL SCORE		311-6/8

Exact locality where killed

Date killed By whom killed

Present Owner ~~Heritage Gun Room~~ ~~Homer Saye~~

Address Cabela's, Inc. One Cabela Drive Sydney, NE 69160 ~~Don Schaufler~~

Guide's Name

Remarks: (Mention any abnormalities or unique qualities)

47 Cert

COMMITTEE
ALFRED ELY, CHAIRMAN
HAROLD E. ANTHONY
R. R. M. CARPENTER

Record of North American Big Game

IN CARE OF
AMERICAN MUSEUM OF NATURAL HISTORY
COLUMBUS AVENUE AND 77TH STREET
NEW YORK, N. Y.

UNDER THE AUSPICES OF THE NATIONAL COLLECTION OF HEADS AND HORNS OF THE NEW YORK ZOOLOGICAL SOCIETY & THE BOONE & CROCKETT CLUB

DEER

SPECIES: MULE DEER

MEASUREMENTS	RIGHT	LEFT
Length of outside curve A	21"	23"
Greatest spread B: 30"		
Circumference of main beam C	5"	
Number of points on antler	10 PTS	8
Circumference of burr D	4 3/4"	

Exact locality where killed: KAIBAB ARIZONA

Date killed: 11-13-41

By whom killed: Jim Harness

Owner: " "

Address: Winnba, Cal.

Present location of trophy: Burcharts taxidermy 2319 - 21 Ave S.F.

Remarks: This is John Harness's Son's head the 39½" spread was his fathers and the 39" spread his own.

We hereby certify that we have measured the above described trophy on .... 194 , and that these measurements are correct and made in accordance with the directions overleaf.

....

By ....

Mitchell, Bob 2/3/42

JIM HARNESS

1941

The Harness family harvested three impressive mule deer in 1941. The first buck, shot by Jim Harness on November 13, has a greatest spread of 30 inches and a longest main beam measuring 23 inches, according to the chart. Unfortunately, this buck was not remeasured with the Club's new and improved scoring system, so we don't know how it scores by today's standards.

1947 123d

Committee
Alfred Ely, Chairman
Harold E. Anthony
R. R. M. Carpenter

Record of North American Big Game

In care of
American Museum of Natural History
Columbus Avenue and 77th Street
New York, N. Y.

Under the auspices of The National Collection of Heads and Horns of the New York Zoological Society & The Boone & Crockett Club

DEER

Species .... MULE DEER

Measurements	Right	Left
Length of outside curve A	26½"	26"
Greatest spread B 39½		
Circumference of main beam C	6"	
Number of points on antler	12	12
Circumference of burr D	5⅞"	

Exact locality where killed .... KAIBAB FOREST ARIZONA

Date killed 11-14-41

By whom killed .... H. H. Harness

Owner .... H. H. Harness

Address .... P.O. Box 246 Dinuba, Cal

Present location of trophy .... at present in taxidermy shop in S. F. I will deliver same to

Remarks .... Mr Harness at Dinuba shortly

....

We hereby certify that we have measured the above described trophy on ....194 , and that these measurements are correct and made in accordance with the directions overleaf.

....

By ....

P.S. This head is now at the taxidermy studio of Ernst G. Burkhart 2319-21 1st Ave S.F.

Mitchell, Bob 2/3/42

H.H. HARNESS

1941

This buck was shot by H.H. Harness the day after Jim harvested his Kaibab mule deer. Taxidermist Ernst G. Burkhart is pictured with the trophy mount. H.H.'s buck had a greatest spread of 39-1/2 inches along with 24 scorable points.

47 Cert.

COMMITTEE
ALFRED ELY, CHAIRMAN
HAROLD E. ANTHONY
R. R. M. CARPENTER

Record of North American Big Game

IN CARE OF
AMERICAN MUSEUM OF NATURAL HISTORY
COLUMBUS AVENUE AND 77TH STREET
NEW YORK, N. Y.

UNDER THE AUSPICES OF THE NATIONAL COLLECTION OF HEADS AND HORNS OF THE NEW YORK ZOOLOGICAL SOCIETY & THE BOONE & CROCKETT CLUB

DEER

SPECIES: MULE

MEASUREMENTS	RIGHT	LEFT
Length of outside curve A	25"	24 1/8"
Greatest spread B 39"		
Circumference of main beam C	8 1/2"	
Number of points on antler	23	15
Circumference of burr D	8 1/2"	

Exact locality where killed: KAIBAB FOREST ARIZONA

Date killed: 11-15-41

By whom killed: John Harness

Owner: John Harness

Address: P.O. Box 246 Dinuba Cal.

Present location of trophy: Ernest G. Burkhart (taxidermist) 2319 - 21st Ave S.F.

Remarks: The forest service man in charge of the Kaibab camp informed Mr Harness this was a record head for the Kaibab and the heaviest antlers to ever come out of the KAIBAB

We hereby certify that we have measured the above described trophy on .... 194 , and that these measurements are correct and made in accordance with the directions overleaf.

Bob Mitchell

By 478-12 Ave, S.F.

Nitchell, Bob - 2/3/42

P.S. I have photos of this head also the others

JOHN HARNESS

1941

John Harness shot the largest of the three mule deer harvested by his family during a hunt to the Kaibab in November 1941. John's buck has 38 scorable points and a greatest spread of 39 inches. A handwritten note on the chart by Bob Mitchell states, *The forest service man in charge of the Kaibab camp informed Mr. Harness this was a record head for the Kaibab and the heaviest antlers to come out of the Kaibab.*

s This a Record-breaking Deer Spread

The yardstick is too short to measure the spread of this mule-deer rack from Arizona. It's 47⅞ inches, no less!

A MULE-DEER BUCK with a 47⅞-in. spread was killed not long ago in the Kaibab National Forest, Arizona. This figure exceeds by ⅜ in. the greatest spread of any muley head whose measurements appear in North American Game, the record book of big-game trophies; so the newcomer—with 11 points on one antler and 9 on the other—probably rates well toward the top of the list, which is graded according to length of outside curve.

However, the expert hunter that bagged this deer will never see his name in the records for he himself was shot dead within a mile of where he brought down his deer. That sudden end was justified, for this was no ordinary hunter, but a four-footed killer in the form of a 150-lb. mountain lion.

To go back a bit: Jack Butler, Jack Rice, and Ralph Steinhoff were hunting the north rim of the Grand Canyon with a pack of five dogs. The hounds picked up the big cat's trail and jumped him right after he had ... record kill,
treeing him about ... A
shot from a .30/3...
lion's career, and ...
hangs on the w...
along with the ...
giant buck.

The trio who ...
slayer are we...
throughout the ... hunter. Butler, one of the greatest mountain-lion trackers living today, has more than 500 of the felines to his credit. And many marines and ex-marines will remember Capt. Ralph Steinhoff as range officer at Camp Mathews, Calif., and later at Parris Island, S. C., where he helped train thousands of "boots" in the use of the Garand M-1 rifle.

Mountain lions are the Western stockmen's No. 1 public enemy, for they have an insatiable appetite for calves and colts. However, they also prey on deer—concentrating in early spring on does that are heavy with fawn, then switching to the fawns themselves as soon as they are dropped by does that haven't been molested. From late spring until early fall the cats kill whatever they can catch, but after the deer's rutting season the lions' diet consists almost exclusively ...ld bucks.

... the predators follow the ... and feed on ... at the

TS

standing b...
feet away...
balanced ...
I was p...
ing he sh...
count by...
coolly lo...
much ti...
no wish...
place.
while I...
slowly...
den mo...

KAIBAB DEER - 1940S

RALPH STEINHOFF

1942

This Kaibab mule deer was killed by a mountain lion in 1942, and the Club's records indicate that it was found by Jack Butler, Jack Rice, and Ralph Steinhoff shortly after they dispatched the lion. Ralph entered it in the Club's 1949 competition. The deer has a very impressive greatest spread measuring over 46 inches. A short newspaper article from October 1947 gives the full account of the hunt. An interesting note on the original score chart states, "This is a perfect specimen. There are no extra points sticking out on either side." Curious, considering the rack has thirteen non-typical points!

Even more curious is a copy of the deer skull photo shown below left that was sent to the Club in 2013 by one of our trophy owners, who owns the original photograph. On the back in handwritten text it says,

> *Kaibab, found by Earl Sorreal & Bob Vaughn in 1940 near Big Saddle. Killed by a lion. They were hunting lions for the A.G.F. They sold it 1 or 2 years later fore [sic] 200 dollars to a guy named Jack Rice from Calif. He died and they never found the head. The head is over 48" wide with very little cheaters, Earl said.*

We may never know the true story about this buck or its official score since it was never remeasured using the Club's new scoring system.

COLONEL H.W. MEISCH

1942

Colonel H.W. Meisch shot this unique non-typical mule deer while hunting the Kaibab National Forest in November 1942. The buck has 45 inches of abnormal points and a greatest spread of 31-6/8 inches. The Club did not receive the official score chart until 1966. The final tally is officially 248-4/8 points.

OFFICIAL SCORING SYSTEM FOR NORTH AMERICAN BIG GAME TROPHIES

RECORDS OF NORTH AMERICAN BIG GAME COMMITTEE

BOONE AND CROCKETT CLUB

Boone and Crockett Club
Records of North American Big Game Committee
c/o Carnegie Museum
4400 Forbes Ave. · Pittsburgh, Pa. 15213

NON-TYPICAL MULE DEER

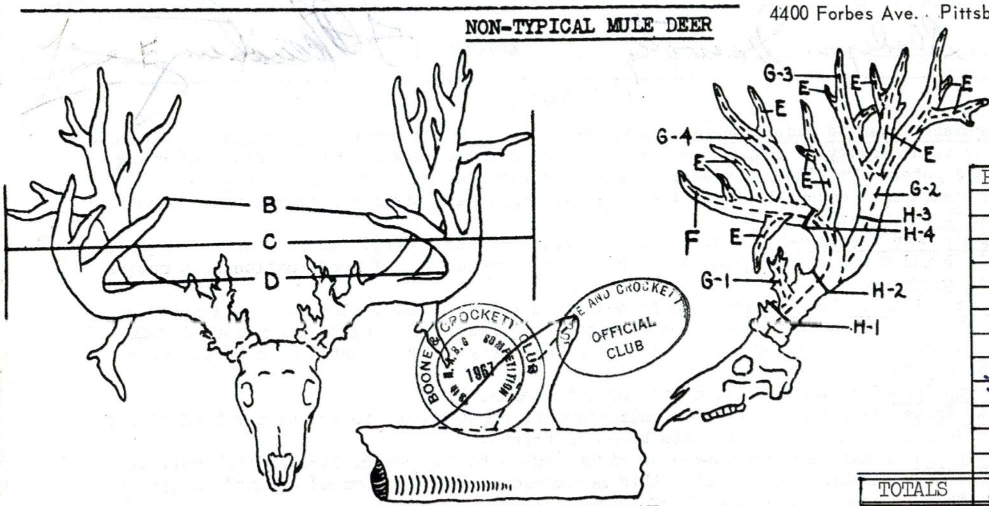

DETAIL OF POINT MEASUREMENT

ABNORMAL Points Line E	
R	L
1	1
2	1
5 .6	2 .4
4	4 .2
3 .4	2
6	1
3 .4	
7 .2	
TOTALS 33	12
To E 45	

SEE OTHER SIDE FOR INSTRUCTIONS	Supplementary Data R.	Supplementary Data L.	Column 1 Spread Credit	Column 2 Right Antler	Column 3 Left Antler	Column 4 Difference
A. Number of Points on Each Antler	13	11				
B. Tip to Tip Spread	27					
C. Greatest Spread	31 4/8					
D. Inside Spread of MAIN BEAMS 26 — Spread credit may equal but not exceed length of longer antler			25 4/8			
IF Inside Spread of Main Beams exceeds longer antler length, enter difference						~~4/8~~
E. Total of Lengths of all Abnormal Points	45					
F. Length of Main Beam				25 .4	25 .1	.3
G-1. Length of First Point, if present				3 .4	3	.4
G-2. Length of Second Point				17 .2	16	1 .2
G-3. Length of Third Point, if present				13	10	3 .0
G-4. Length of Fourth Point, if present				14	14 .1	.1
H-1. Circumference at Smallest Place Between Burr and First Point				5 .6	5 .5	.1
H-2. Circumference at Smallest Place Between First and Second Points				5 .4	5 .2	.2
H-3. Circumference at Smallest Place Between Main Beam and Third Point				5	4 .7	.1
H-4. Circumference at Smallest Place Between Second and Fourth Points				6	5 .1	.7
TOTALS	45		25 4/8	95 4/8	89 1/8	~~7 4/8~~ 6 5/8

Column 1	25 .4	Exact locality where killed **Kaibab Forest, Arizona**
Column 2	95 .4	Date killed **Nov. 1942** By whom killed **Col. H.W. Meisch**
Column 3	89 .1	Present owner **Col. H.W. Meisch**
Total	210 1/8	Address **Fort Sam Houston, Texas**
SUBTRACT Column 4	~~7 4/8~~ 6 5/8	Guide's Name and Address **none**
Result	203 4/8	Remarks: (Mention any abnormalities) OK NLC
Add Line E Total	45	RECD AUG 19 1966
FINAL SCORE	~~248~~ 248 4/8	

ack 8/30/66 mcm

WILLIAM L. MURPHY

1943

William L. Karam entered his late father-in-law's Kaibab buck in the Club's records program in 1970—nearly 30 years after William L. Murphy shot the deer on November 14, 1943. The non-typical mule deer was measured by Eldon L. "Buck" Buckner, current vice president of the Club's North American Big Game Records Committee. With a final score of 324-1/8 points, the buck still ranks as the fifth-largest non-typical in the Club's records program, as well as the Arizona state record. It has 33 scorable points, with a total of 115-2/8 inches of non-typical points. The greatest spread is recorded at an unbelievable 43-4/8 inches. As with most aesthetic giant non-typical mule deer, this one has an impressive typical frame of 208-7/8 points, as well.

ichael R. Karam
es, Arizona

Mr. Karam:

score of your Non-typic
were among those receiv
end their trophies in f
entrant was requested
ld or would not send in
eived such a card from y
s time in order to compl

Mr. Buckner mailed you
tter stating that he woul
turned to you if it were

ay we please hear from yo

hank you for your coopera

P

cc: Mr. Eldon "Buck" Buc

ARIZONA WILDLIFE FEDERATION
Box 1769 • Phoenix, Arizona 85001 • Phone 602-253-4903

Blue Ridge Ranger Station
Happy Jack, Arizona 86024
May 26, 1970

Records of North American Big Game Committee
Boone and Crockett Club
c/o Carnegie Museum
4400 Forbes Avenue
Pittsburgh, Pennsylvania 15213

Dear Sirs:

Enclosed please find photos, chart, check, etc. for Michael Kara
Non-Typical Mule Deer entry. This was not too difficult a head
measure, so my score is fairly accurate I feel. I'm sure the he
will go #2 in the records, unless a larger one has been entered
the '64 book was published. If the head is needed for measuring
the judges panel later on, please notify me as well as the owne
I told him I would arrange for someone to escort it back. The
will not ship it, as he is afraid something might happen to it.
there is an Arizona Measurer on the Panel this year, possibly h
see that the head arrived safely.

I would also like to correct an entry in the '64 edition of "Re
at the request of a hunter, Mr. D.B. Sanford. He is listed as
owner of a cougar trophy taken by Ted Ferguson in the Ruby Mts.
1961 with a score of 14 11/16. Mr. Sanford says he is not the
of the skull, he just sent it in for Ferguson. However, in vi
the new minimum of 15, I don't suppose it will make much diffe

I also have a request which I hope you can fulfill. As Senior
for the Trophy Book Committee of the AWF, I badly need a copy
score chart for Louis Dees' Desert Sheep taken in 1965 in the
in Arizona. The trophy scored 187 points and is the cur

BIG GAME COMMITTEE

BOONE AND CROCKETT CLUB

Records of North American Big Ga[me] ... GAME TROPHIES

Boone and Crockett C[lub]
c/o Carnegie Museum
4400 Forbes Ave. Pittsburgh,

...TYPICAL MULE DEER

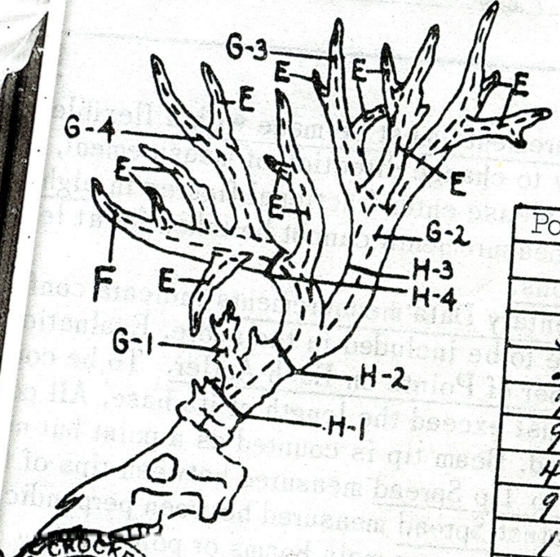

BOONE AND CROCKETT CLUB 14TH N.A.B.G. COMPETITION 1970

BOONE AND CROCKETT OFFICIAL CLUB

ABN[ORMAL] Points R
1 5/8
5.0
2.0
7 2/8
9 1/8
4 7/8
9 7/8
1 5/8
3 1/8
4 2/8
6 5/8
TOTALS 55 3/8
To E 115 ...

	Supplementary Data	Column 1 Spread Credit	Column 2 Right Antler	Column 3 Left Antler	Column 4 Difference
Tip Spread	17				
...t Spread	22⁰				
...Spread	43 4/8				
...BEAMS 32 7/8 — Spread credit may equal but not exceed length of longer antler		25 5/8			
...e Spread of Main Beams exceeds longer ...ength, enter difference					
... Lengths of all Abnormal Points	115 2/8				
... Main Beam			25 5/8	25 1/8	
...f First Point, if present			4 3/8	2 3/8	
...f Second Point			19⁰	16 7/8	
... Third Point, if present			13 5/8	14⁰	
... Fourth Point, if present			12⁰	12⁰	
...ence at Smallest Place ...urr and First Point			6 5/8	6 5/8	
...ence at Smallest Place ...rst and Second Points			5 4/8	5 6/8	
...nce at Smallest Place ...in Beam and Third Point			4 5/8	5⁰	
...ce at Smallest Place ...ond and Fourth Points			4 7/8	5⁰	
TOTALS	115 2/8	25 5/8	96 2/8	92 6/8	5 6/8 1 3/8

...1	25 5/8	Exact locality where killed: North Kaibab, Arizona
2	96 2/8	Date killed Nov 14 1943 (NO) By whom killed: William L. Murphy
3	92 6/8	Present owner: Michael R. Karam
	214 5/8	Address: Nogales, Arizona
	5 6/8 1 3⁰	Guide's Name and Address: NONE
	201 5/8	Remarks: (Mention any abnormalities) $56 ✓
	115 7/8	Right main be...

...rer

...ts.
...izona

...eded

THOMAS M. KNOWLES, JR.

1944

Thomas M. Knowles rode into the Big Saddle area of the Kaibab on horseback for his November 1944 mule deer hunt. On the third day of his hunt he shot this impressive non-typical—scoring 270-2/8 points—with a Winchester Model 54 .306 pushing a 180-grain bullet. Of note is the giant net-typical frame scoring 210-2/8 points!

OFFICIAL SCORING SYSTEM FOR NORTH AMERICAN BIG GAME TROPHIES

RECORDS OF NORTH AMERICAN BIG GAME COMMITTEE

BOONE AND CROCKETT CLUB

Boone and Crockett Club
Records of North American Big Game Committee
c/o Carnegie Museum
4400 Forbes Ave. Pittsburgh, Pa. 15213

NON-TYPICAL MULE DEER

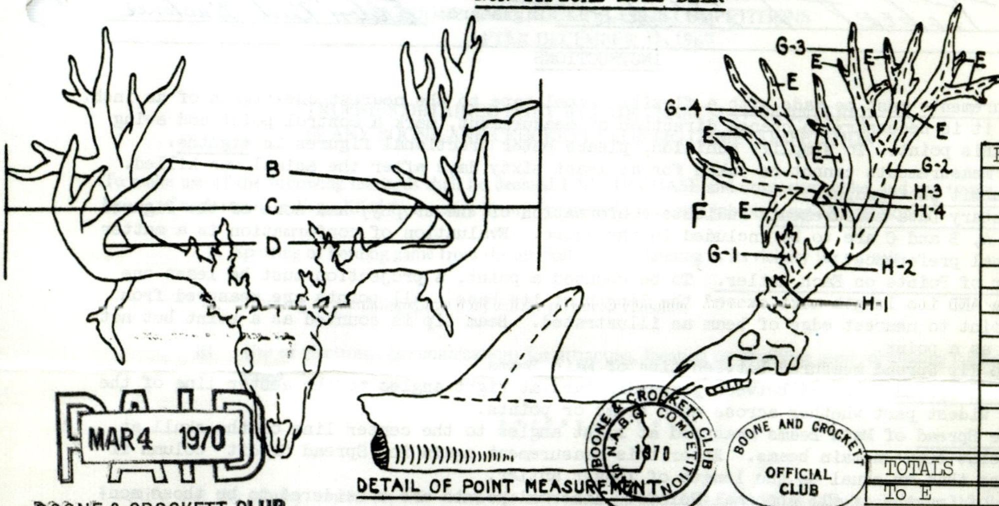

ABNORMAL Points Line E	
R	L
4 7/8	1^{0}
3 3/8	3 2/8
1 7/8	3
10 5/8	8 2/8
4 4/8	3 2/8
1	4 4/8
4 1/8	4 3/8
	2
TOTALS 30 3/8	29 5/8
To E	60^{0} ✓

~~BOONE & CROCKETT CLUB~~

SEE OTHER SIDE FOR INSTRUCTIONS	Supplementary Data R.	L.	Column 1 Spread Credit	Column 2 Right Antler	Column 3 Left Antler	Column 4 Difference
A. Number of Points on Each Antler	12	13				
B. Tip to Tip Spread	24 5/8					
C. Greatest Spread	42 3/8					
D. Inside Spread of MAIN BEAMS 28^{0} — Spread credit may equal but not exceed length of longer antler			28^{0}			
IF Inside Spread of Main Beams exceeds longer antler length, enter difference						—
E. Total of Lengths of all Abnormal Points	60^{0}					
F. Length of Main Beam				29 2/8	32 1/8	2 7/8 ✓
G-1. Length of First Point, if present				3 1/8	3^{0}	1/8 ✓
G-2. Length of Second Point				17 7/8	19 4/8	1 5/8 ✓
G-3. Length of Third Point, if present				9 4/8	14 2/8	4 6/8 ✓
G-4. Length of Fourth Point, if present				13 6/8	14 7/8	1 1/8 ✓
H-1. Circumference at Smallest Place Between Burr and First Point				4 6/8	4 6/8	—
H-2. Circumference at Smallest Place Between First and Second Points				4 5/8	4 5/8	—
H-3. Circumference at Smallest Place Between Main Beam and Third Point				3 7/8	4^{0}	1/8 ✓
H-4. Circumference at Smallest Place Between Second and Fourth Points				4 4/8	4 4/8	—
TOTALS	60^{0}		28^{0}	91 2/8	101 5/8	10 5/8

Column 1	28^{0}	Exact locality where killed Big Saddle North Kaibab, Arizona
Column 2	91 2/8	Date killed 11/10/1944 By whom killed Thomas M. Knoles, Jr.
Column 3	101 5/8	Present owner SAME
Total	220 7/8	Address
SUBTRACT Column 4	10 5/8	Guide's Name and Address NONE
Result	210 2/8	Remarks: (Mention any abnormalities)
Add Line E Total	60^{0}	North Kaibab tag no. 778
FINAL SCORE	270 2/8	

RECD MAR 4 1970

menaed 3/5/70

497

W.O. HART

1946

Unfortunately, no photographs of this fine trophy can be found in the Club's records archives. Texan W.O. Hart shot this Kaibab buck during the 1946 season. The chart indicates only one abnormal point deducting just one inch from the score of 198-2/8 inches. In 1990, the deer's score was adjusted to 198-4/8 points when the penalty for excessive spread was removed from the scoring system.

OFFICIAL SCORING SYSTEM FOR NORTH AMERICAN BIG GAME TROPHIES

Records of North American
Big Game Committee

BOONE AND CROCKETT CLUB

Address Correspondence to:
Mrs. Grancel Fitz, Secretary
5 Tudor City Place, NYC 17, NY.

MULE and BLACKTAIL DEER

KIND OF DEER Mule deer

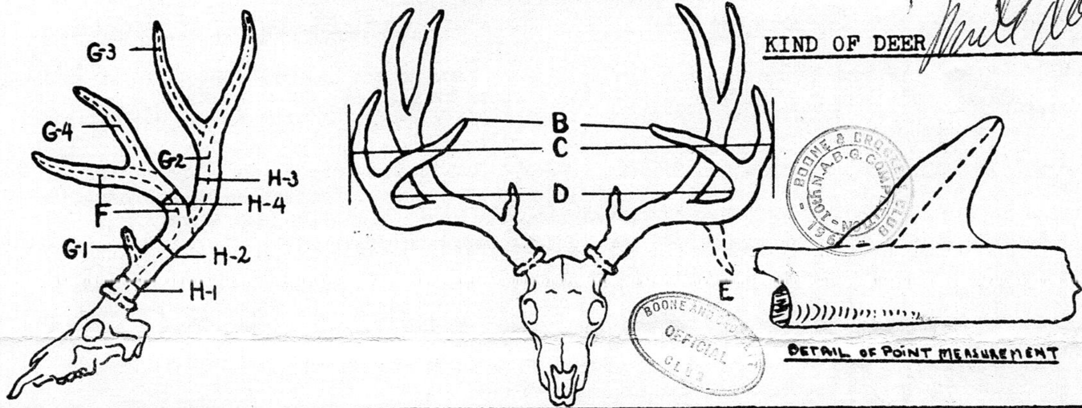

SEE OTHER SIDE FOR INSTRUCTIONS	Supplementary Data R.	Supplementary Data L.	Column 1 Spread Credit	Column 2 Right Antler	Column 3 Left Antler	Column 4 Difference
A. Number of Points on Each Antler	5	6				
B. Tip to Tip Spread	25 3/8					
C. Greatest Spread	31 3/8					
D. Inside Spread of MAIN BEAMS 28 2/8 — Spread credit may equal but not exceed length of longer antler			28			
IF Inside Spread of Main Beams exceeds longer antler length, enter difference						~~2/8~~
E. Total of Lengths of all Abnormal Points						
F. Length of Main Beam				28"	26 1/8	1 7/8
G-1. Length of First Point, if present				1	1 3/8	3/8
G-2. Length of Second Point				20 1/8	19 6/8	3/8
G-3. Length of Third Point, if present				11 1/8	11 3/8	2/8
G-4. Length of Fourth Point, if present				9 4/8	9 3/8	1/8
H-1. Circumference at Smallest Place Between Burr and First Point				5	5	
H-2. Circumference at Smallest Place Between First and Second Points				4 5/8	4 5/8	
H-3. Circumference at Smallest Place Between Main Beam and Third Point.				4 7/8	4 6/8	1/8
H-4. Circumference at Smallest Place Between Second and Fourth Points				4 1/8	4	1/8
TOTALS				88 3/8	86 3/8	4 3/8

ADD	Column 1	28	Exact locality where killed KAIBAB FOREST ARIZONA
	Column 2	88 3/8	Date killed 1946 By whom killed W.O HART
	Column 3	86 3/8	Present owner W.O HART
	TOTAL	202 6/8	Address
SUBTRACT Column 4		4 2/8 ~~4 4/8~~	Guide's Name and Address
FINAL SCORE		~~198 2/8~~ 198 4/8	Remarks: (Mention any abnormalities)

JAN 16 1952

18E50012
225

...ROPHIES #322

...TURN TO:

...and Crockett Club
...uth Patrick Street
...dria, VA. 22314

ABNORMAL

Points Line E R	L
8 4/8	5 4/8
4	3 3/8
2 4/8	5 7/8
3 1/8	2
2 5/8	4 1/8
2 1/8	1 1/8
1 7/8	2
2 2/8	1 4/8
1 7/8	2 5/8
3	
TOTALS 31 7/8	28 1/8
To E 60	

DETAIL OF POINT MEASUREMENT

SEE OTHER SIDE FOR INSTRUCTIONS	Supplementary Data R.	Supplementary Data L.	Column 1 Spread Credit	Column 2 Right Antler	Column 3 Left Antler	Column 4 Difference
A. Number of Points on Each Antler	15	14				
B. Tip to Tip Spread	25 6/8					
C. Greatest Spread	39					
D. Inside Spread of MAIN BEAMS 28 7/8 — Spread credit may equal but not exceed length of longer antler			28 7/8			
IF Inside Spread of Main Beams exceeds longer antler length, enter difference						---
E. Total of Lengths of all Abnormal Points	60					
F. Length of Main Beam				27 2/8	29	1 6/8
G-1. Length of First Point, if present				2 3/8	2 7/8	4/8
G-2. Length of Second Point				14 5/8	14 5/8	-----
G-3. Length of Third Point, if present				9 5/8	9 6/8	1/8
G-4. Length of Fourth Point, if present				9 2/8	8 7/8	~~5/8~~ 3/8
H-1. Circumference at Smallest Place Between Burr and First Point				5 5/8	5 5/8	-----
H-2. Circumference at Smallest Place Between First and Second Points				5 1/8	5 1/8	-----
H-3. Circumference at Smallest Place Between Main Beam and Third Point				5 6/8	6 4/8	~~5/8~~ 6/8
H-4. Circumference at Smallest Place Between Second and Fourth Points				5 1/8	5 1/8	-----
TOTALS	60		28 7/8	84 6/8	87 4/8	3 ~~5/8~~ 4/8

Column 1	28 7/8
Column 2	84 6/8
Column 3	87 4/8
Total	201 1/8
SUBTRACT Column 4	3 ~~5/8~~ 4/8
Result	197 ~~4/8~~ 5/8
Add Line E Total	60
FINAL SCORE	257 ~~4/8~~ 5/8

Exact locality where killed *Kaibab Forest, Arizona*

Date killed *1946* By whom killed *Graves Peeler*

Present owner *John E. Conner Museum*

Address *Texas A&I Univ., Kingsville, Texas 78363*

Guide's Name and Address

Remarks: (Mention any abnormalities)

— — M— Y003 03

GRAVES PEELER

1946

This 1946 Kaibab buck, shot by Graves Peeler, has 29 scorable points and a greatest spread of 39 inches. It is part of the John E. Connor Museum collection. Graves has five mule deer registered with the Boone and Crockett Club's records program. This is the first of Graves' two non-typicals, *both scoring 257-5/8 points.* An impressive achievement for sure.

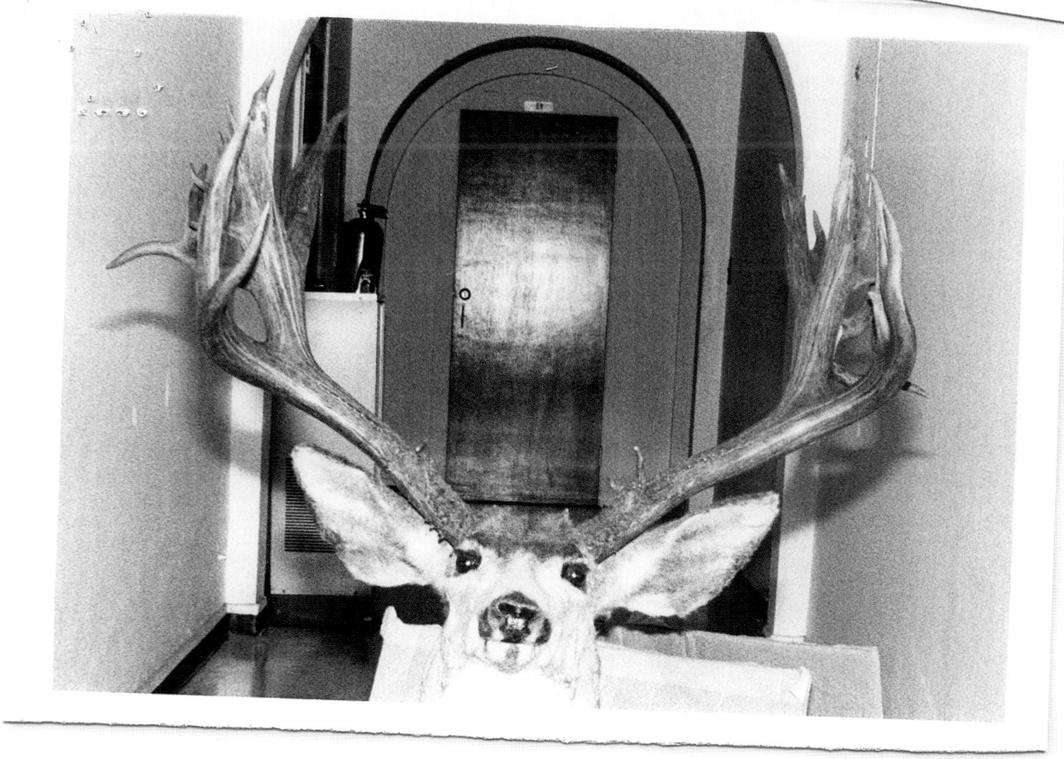

GRAVES PEELER
1947

One year after he shot another non-typical with the same score, Graves Peeler's 1947 Kaibab buck scored 257-5/8 points. This buck has 23 scorable points with a total of 54-2/8 abnormal inches adding into the final score. Of note is a greatest spread of 39-5/8 inches, as well as the net-typical frame of 203-3/8 points.

18E50011 224
#356

...ockett Club
...trick Street
VA. 22314

ABNORMAL Points Line E	
R	L
1 2/8	8
2 2/8	2 1/8
6 3/8	1 3/8
6 2/8	7 4/8
4 6/8	1
3 7/8	1 1/8
8 3/8	
...ALS 33 1/8	21 1/8

SEE OTHER SIDE FOR INSTRUCTIONS	Supplementary Data R.	Supplementary Data L.	Column 1 Spread Credit	Column 2 Right Antler	Column 3 Left Antler	Column 4 Difference
A. Number of Points on Each Antler	12	11				
B. Tip to Tip Spread	22 7/8					
C. Greatest Spread	39 5/8					
D. Inside Spread of MAIN BEAMS 25 1/8 — Spread credit may equal but not exceed length of longer antler			25 1/8			
IF Inside Spread of Main Beams exceeds longer antler length, enter difference						---
E. Total of Lengths of all Abnormal Points		54 2/8				
F. Length of Main Beam				25 7/8	26 5/8	6/8
G-1. Length of First Point, if present				2 3/8	3	5/8
G-2. Length of Second Point				16 5/8	17 2/8	5/8
G-3. Length of Third Point, if present				10 4/8	9 5/8	7/8
G-4. Length of Fourth Point, if present				13 1/8	13 7/8	6/8
H-1. Circumference at Smallest Place Between Burr and First Point				5 6/8	5 5/8	1/8
H-2. Circumference at Smallest Place Between First and Second Points				5 1/8	5 1/8	---
H-3. Circumference at Smallest Place Between Main Beam and Third Point				6 2/8	4 6/8	1 4/8
H-4. Circumference at Smallest Place Between Second and Fourth Points				6	7 7/8	1 7/8
TOTALS		54 2/8	25 1/8	91 5/8	93 6/8	7 1/8

Column 1	25 1/8	Exact locality where killed Kaibab Forest, Arizona
Column 2	91 5/8	Date killed 1947 By whom killed Graves Peeler Peeler
Column 3	93 6/8	Present owner The John E. Conner Museum
Total	210 4/8	Address Texas A & I Univ., Kingsville, Texas 78363
SUBTRACT Column 4	7 1/8	Guide's Name and Address
Result	203 3/8	Remarks: (Mention any abnormalities) one broken point right antler not measured
Add Line E Total	54 2/8	
FINAL SCORE	257 5/8	M—Y003 03

3RD2.

1949

Boone and Crockett Club
Records of North American Big Game
and
North American Big Game Competition
in care of
American Museum of Natural History
Central Park West at 79th Street
New York 24, N.Y.

Committee

Harold E. Anthony, Chairman
William K. Carpenter
Alfred Ely
Karl T. Frederick
A. C. Gilbert
Catherine Sayers, Secretary

Under the Auspices
of
The National Museum
of Heads and Horns
of the
New York Zoological
Society

DEER

Species ....Mule Deer....

Measurements	Right	Left
Length on outside curve A	25 13/16	25 7/8
Greatest spread B ..41 3/4"...		
Circumference of main beam C	5 1/8	4 3/4
Number of points on antler	12	10
Circumference of burr D	7 5/16	7 3/16

Exact locality where killed Fire trail on Timp. Pt. near Aspen Springs Kaibab Nat'l. For., Arizona

Date killed ...10/16/47...

By whom killed ....Joe Fisher....

Address ....Arizona

Owner ....Vic Blalack....

Address ...661 6th Ave. Yuma, Arizona

Remarks Long points extend out from both main beams making greatest spread unusual. End of main beams slightly palmated.

Measured by A. F. Halloran, Vic Blalack + Joe Fisher

Owner's signature V.E. Blalack

Halloran 3/31/49

JESS FISHER

1947

Jess Fisher was hunting off a fire trail near Aspen Springs in the Kaibab National Forest when he shot this mule deer on October 16, 1947. The buck was entered by Vic Blalock, who is listed as the owner of the deer. It has 22 scorable points and a note on the chart indicates "long points extend out from both main beams making greatest spread unusual. End of main beams slightly palmated."

The greatest spread is recorded at 41-3/4 inches. No photos exist in the Club's archives for this deer, nor was it ever remeasured with the new scoring system.

KAIBAB DEER - 1940S

JACK VERNER

1947

Jack Verner shot this extraordinary non-typical Kaibab buck in October 1947. With a final score of 262-4/8 points, the mule deer garnered an invite to the Club's sixth competition held in 1953 at the American Museum of Natural History. Unfortunately, it was not shipped to the museum and therefore, did not qualify for an award. The buck has 26 scorable points and a 41-2/8 inch greatest spread. The rack carries over 71 inches of abnormal points that add to the final score.

...rth American
...ommittee

BOONE AND CROCK...

NON-TYPICAL MULE DEER

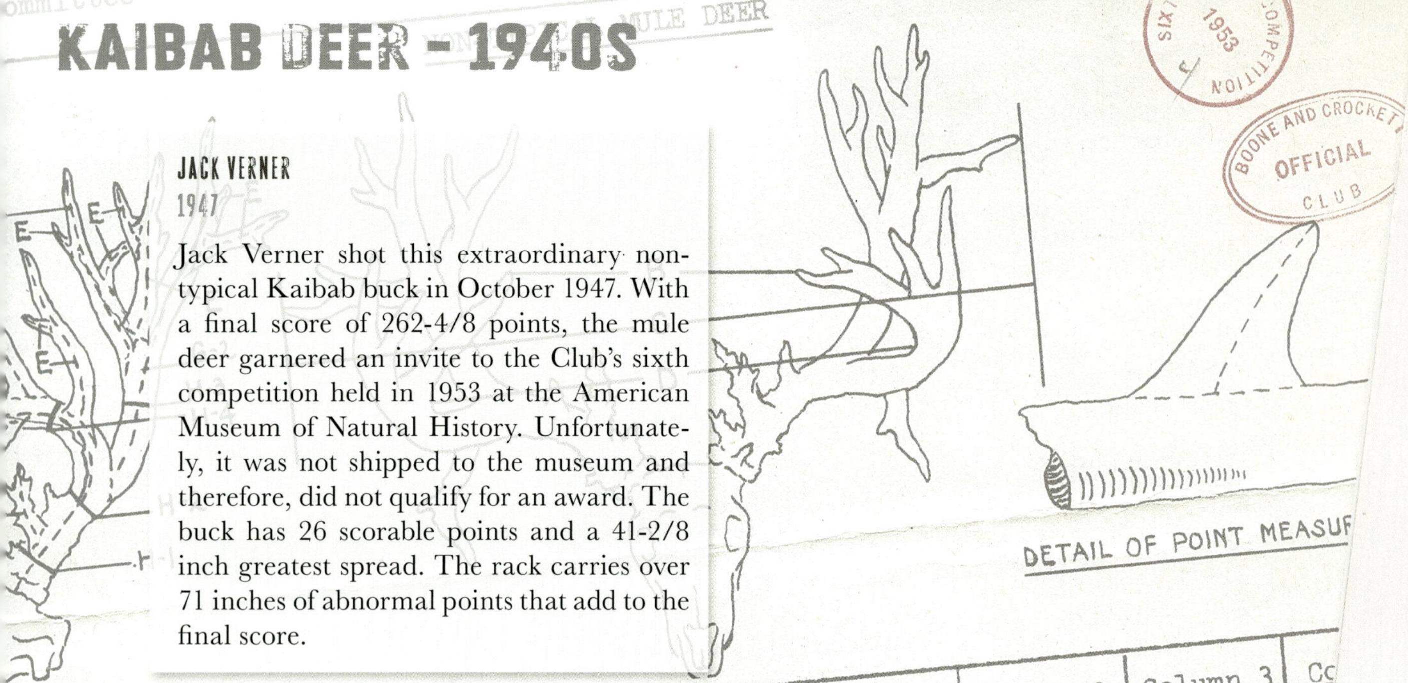

...E OTHER SIDE FOR INSTRUCTIONS	Supplementary Data R.	Supplementary Data L.	Column 1 Spread Credit	Column 2 Right Antler	Column 3 Left Antler	Co... Di...
...r of Points on Each Antler	14	12				
...o Tip Spread	23 5/8					
...est Spread	41 2/8					
...de Spread ...AIN BEAMS 28 — Spread credit may equal but not exceed length of longer antler			28			
...nside Spread of Main Beams exceeds longer ...er length, enter difference						
...l of Lengths of all Abnormal Points		71 4/8				
...th of Main Beam				28 3/8	29	
...ength of First Point, if present				2 1/8	2 1/8	
...ength of Second Point				14 3/8	14 7/8	.../8
...ength of Third Point, if present				7 7/8	7	4
...ength of Fourth Point, if present				8 3/8	12 5/8	
Circumference at Smallest Place Between Burr and First Point				5 4/8	5 4/8	
Circumference at Smallest Place Between First and Second Points				5 4/8	5 4/8	
Circumference at Samllest Place Between Main Beam and Third Point				4	4	
Circumference at Smallest Place Between Second and Fourth Points				7	6 4/8	
TOTALS		71 6/8	28	83	86 7/8	

TOTALS		
Column 1	28	Exact locality where killed KAIBAB NORTH, ARIZ...
Column 2	83	Date killed 1947 October By whom killed JACK VERNE...
Column 3	86 7/8	Present owner JACK VERNER
Total	197 7/8	Address Phoenix, Arizona
...TRACT Column 4	7 1/8	Guide's Name and Address NONE
		Remarks: (Mention any abnormalities)

be exercised against possib[illegible] Club nor the Committee can accept any responsibili[illegible] in transit or while in their possession. The return of the entries will be at the owner's expense for transportation and insurance.

A self-addressed postcard is enclosed and we will appreciate it if you will please fill in the data requested and place it in the mail. The deadline date for delivery of trophies to the Museum is January 31.

Congratulations to you upon such a fine trophy and thank you for your cooperation in connection with these North American Big Game Competitions.

Sincerely yours,

Samuel B. Webb

SBW:[illegible]

DEAN NAYLOR

1948

In 1948, World War II veteran Dean Naylor paid $5 for a permit so he could join his friend Jack Neal on a Kaibab mule deer hunt. Taxidermist C.H. Sievers saw the deer hanging in camp and offered Dean all he had with him—$5 and some elk skin gloves—for the deer. The buck has 20 scorable points and a final score of 270-3/8 points. Years later, the trophy was deceitfully entered under another name in the Club's program. An investigation ensued and Dean helped sort out the trophy entries. Photographs were painstakingly compared with the original entry, and several phone interviews were conducted. In the end, Dean's trophy remains in the book as the ninth-largest non-typical from the Kaibab—with the other entry deemed a fraud and rejected.

otographs and I am certain, without
three pictures are of the same deer
1948. The original picture is the
with his head, or chin, resting

...ICAL MULE DEER

BOONE AND CROCKETT OFFICI... B.G.

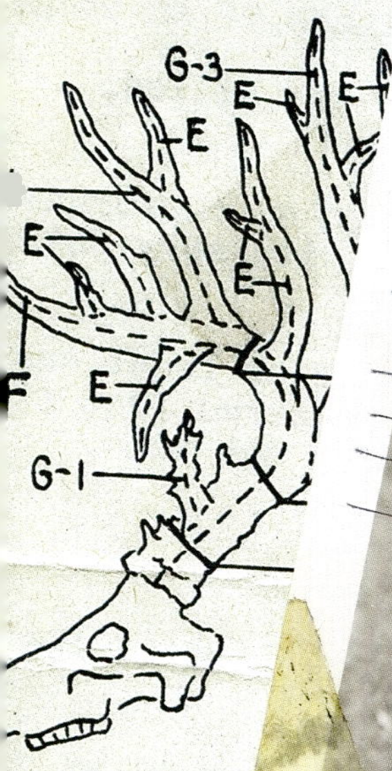

SEE OTHE...

...umber of Points on Each...

...p to Tip Spread

...eatest Spread

...side Spread of MAIN BEAMS | 27 4/8 | Spread credit may equal but not exceed length of longer antler | 39 3/... | ~~27 4/8~~ 25

...side Spread of Main Beams exceeds longer ...r length, enter difference

...of Lengths of all Abnormal Points | 69 3/8

... of Main Beam 2-3					
...th of First Point, if present			24	25	1
...h of Second Point			1 3/8	1 3/8	
...h of Third Point, if present			17 6/8	18 2/8	4/8
... of Fourth Point, if present			11 2/8	11 6/8	4/8
...ference at Smallest Place ...n Burr and First Point			12 4/8	12	4/8
...ference at Smallest Place ... First and Second Points 5-6			5 6/8	6	2/8
...erence at Samllest Place ... Main Beam and Third Point			5 4/8	5 4/8	–
...erence at Smallest Place ... Second and Fourth Points			4 4/8	4 4/8	–
			6	5 7/8	1/8
	69 3/8	~~27 4/8~~ 25	88 5/8	90 2/8	2 7/8

...mn 1	~~27 4/8~~ (25)
...mn 2	88 5/8
Column 3	90 2/8
Total	203 7/8 ~~206 3/8~~
Column 4	2 7/8 ~~5 3/8~~
Result	201 ~~201 0/8~~
E Total	69 3/8
SCORE	270 3/8 ~~272 3/8~~

Exact locality where killed Kaibab (North) Forest,

Date killed 10-7-48 By whom killed Dean Naylor

Present owner ~~C. H. Sievers~~ D. B. Hanford

Address Phoenix, Arizona

Guide's Name and Address

Remarks: (Mention any abnormalities)

B. F. re add and place in non typ.

KAIBAB DEER - 1940S

WILLIAM H. GEARE

1949

William H. Geare was hunting in the south Kaibab in 1949 when he shot his first deer—this impressive typical buck scoring 192-3/8 points. William didn't have the buck scored until 2005. The Official Measurer sent in a copy of the original photograph from 1949 with William and his deer draped across the front of his hunting partner's 1936 Chevrolet along with photographs of William holding the trophy when it was scored 56 years later. William shot the deer with a Winchester Model 94 in .30-30 from about 110 yards.

Jackson, WY
typical mule deer
Date of Kill:
Kill Location:

TT CLUB
RMATION SHEET
HUNTER)

Score: 19

(ZIP/POSTA
(ZIP/POSTA
(ZIP/POSTAL
NTRY)
/YEAR)
(YARDS)
YPE/ARROW WEIG
ng
ing
w on ground

This Kaibab non-typical was shot by David Bevly in October 1949 near Tater Canyon. The buck has 27 scorable points with a total of 81-6/8 inches of abnormal points adding to the final score of 260-4/8 points. The greatest spread tapes an impressive 41-5/8 inches.

E OTHER SIDE FOR INSTRUCTIONS	Supplementary Data R.	Supplementary Data L.	Column 1 Spread Credit	Column 2 Right Antler	Column 3 Left Antler	Column Differen
r of Points on Each Antler	13	14				
o Tip Spread	21 6/8					
est Spread	41 5/8					
e Spread IN BEAMS 26 6/8 — Spread credit may equal but not exceed length of longer antler			26 6/8			
nside Spread of Main Beams exceeds longer er length, enter difference						
l of Lengths of all Abnormal Points	81 6/8					
th of Main Beam				25 5/8	27	13/
ngth of First Point, if present				0	1 3/8	13/
ength of Second Point				15 3/8	15	2/
ength of Third Point, if present				10 3/8	11 4/8	11/
ength of Fourth Point, if present				12	3	9
ircumference at Smallest Place etween Burr and First Point				5 7/8	5 7/8	0
ircumference at Smallest Place etween First and Second Points				6	5 7/8	1/8
ircumference at Samllest Place etween Main Beam and Third Point				5 7/8	5 3/8	1/8
Circumference at Smallest Place Between Second and Fourth Points				6	5	1
TOTALS	81 6/8		26 6/8	86 3/8	80	14

Column 1	26 6/8	Exact locality where killed TATER CANYON - KAIBAB FOR
Column 2	86 3/8	By whom killed DAVID BE
Column 3	80	Date killed OCT. 1949
Total	193 1/8	Present owner DAVID BEVLY
TRACT Column 4	14 3/8	Address
Result	178 6/8	Guide's Name and Address
		Remarks: (Mention any abnormalities)

BERT ELLIS GEORGE

1949

This award-winning Kaibab buck was taken by Bert Ellis George on October 27, 1949. With a final score of 240-5/8 points, it received a third prize at the Club's fifth competition held in 1951 at the American Museum of Natural History in New York City. The buck has 23 scorable points with 43-7/8 inches of abnormal points counted in the final score.

OFFICIAL

OFFICIAL SCORING SYSTEM FOR NORTH AMERICAN BIG GAME TROPHIES 38 prize 1951

Records of North American
Big Game and North American
Big Game Competition

BOONE AND CROCKETT CLUB

% Am. Museum of Natural History
Central Park West at 79th Street
New York 24, New York

MULE and BLACKTAIL DEER

KIND OF DEER Mule deer
Nontypical

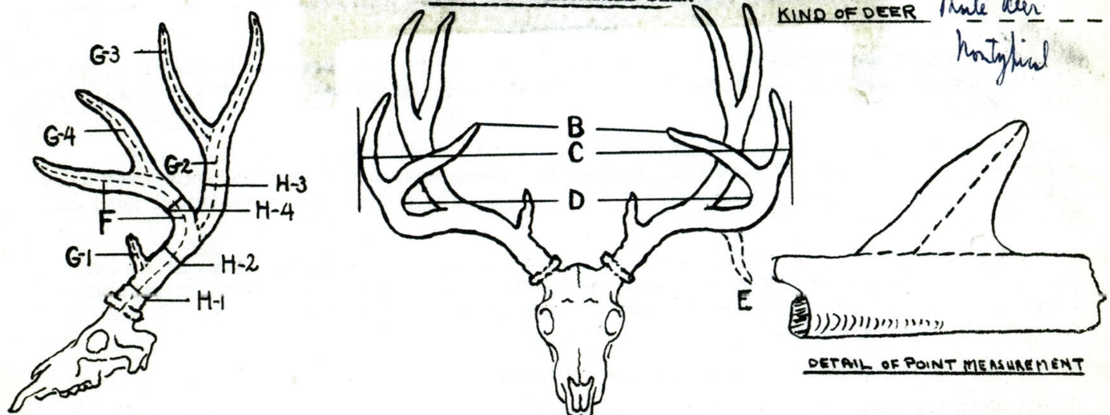

SEE OTHER SIDE FOR INSTRUCTIONS	Supplementary Data R.	Supplementary Data L.	Column 1 Spread Credit	Column 2 Right Antler	Column 3 Left Antler	Column 4 Difference
A. Number of Points on Each Antler 7-8	10	13				
B. Tip to Tip Spread	19	6/8				
C. Greatest Spread -4	32	7/8				
D. Inside Spread of MAIN BEAMS 23 2/8 — Spread credit may equal but not exceed length of longer antler			23 2/8			
IF Inside Spread of Main Beams exceeds longer antler length, enter difference						
E. Total of Lengths of all Abnormal Points						43 7/8
F. Length of Main Beam 2-3				26 4/8	27 6/8	1 2/8
G-1. Length of First Point, if present				3 6/8	3	6/8
G-2. Length of Second Point				17 2/8	17 1/8	1/8
G-3. Length of Third Point, if present				11 7/8	10 2/8	1 5/8
G-4. Length of Fourth Point, if present				12	9	3
H-1. Circumference at Smallest Place Between Burr and First Point 5-6				6	5 7/8	1/8
H-2. Circumference at Smallest Place Between First and Second Points				5 2/8	5 4/8	2/8
H-3. Circumference at Smallest Place Between Main Beam and Third Point.				5 2/8	5	2/8
H-4. Circumference at Smallest Place Between Second and Fourth Points				4 7/8	4 6/8	1/8
TOTALS			23 2/8	92 6/8	88 2/8	7 4/8

ADD	Column 1	23 2/8	Exact locality where killed	Kaibab Forest, Arizona 9
	Column 2	92 6/8	Date killed 10-27-49 10	By whom killed Bert Ellis George 11
	Column 3	88 2/8	Present owner B. E. George	Bert Ellis George 12
TOTAL		204 2/8	Address	
SUBTRACT Column 4		7 4/8	Guide's Name and Address	none
FINAL SCORE		196 6/8 43 7/8 240 5/8	Remarks: (Mention any abnormalities) 196 6/8 : 43 7/8 = 240 5/8	

EDITION RNABG 12

11

337

ition

MULE and BLACKTAIL DEER

KIND OF DEER _MULE_ _ _ _

OFFICIAL

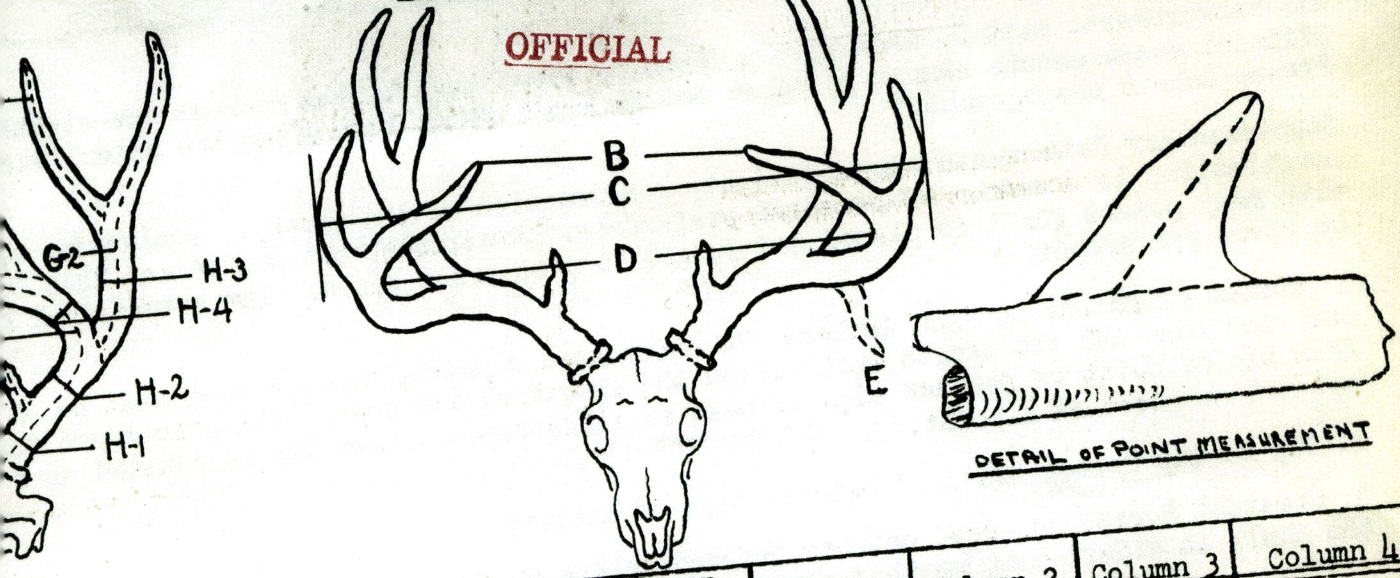

OTHER SIDE FOR INSTRUCTIONS	Supplementary Data R.	Supplementary Data L.	Column 1 Spread Credit	Column 2 Right Antler	Column 3 Left Antler	Column 4 Difference
of Points on Each Antler	5	6				
Tip Spread	23-2/8					
st Spread	30-4/8					
Spread 24-1/8 — Spread credit may equal but not exceed length of longer antler			24-1/8			
N BEAMS ide Spread of Main Beams exceeds longer length, enter difference						
of Lengths of all Abnormal Points				22-1/8	2	
n of Main Beam				1-1/8		
gth of First Point, if present				20-6/8	2	
gth of Second Point				13-6/8		
ngth of Third Point, if present				11-6/8		
ngth of Fourth Point, if present				4-6/8		
rcumference at Smallest Place tween Burr and First Point				4-6/8		
rcumference at Smallest Place etween First and Second Points				4-2/8		
ircumference at Smallest Place etween Main Beam and Third Point,				3-1/8		
ircumference at Smallest Place etween Second and Fourth Points						
			24-1/8	86-3/8		

OTALS			
Column 1	24-1/8	Exact locality where killed	Kaibab Forest
Column 2	86-3/8	Date killed 10/21/49	By whom killed
Column 3	80-1/8	Present owner	Tony Ganci
TOTAL	190-5/8	Address	
RACT Column 4	23-6/8	Guide's Name and Address	
		Remarks: (Mention any abnormalities)	
SCORE	167-1/8		

I certi
at (addr
and that
accordan

Witness:

All measu
Official
Please su

Supplement
conformati
with many
be given p

A. Number c
one inch lo
from tip of
but not mea

B. Tip to Ti

C. Greatest
the skull at

D. Inside Sp
widest point
it is less th

KAIBAB DEER - 1940S

TONY GANCI

1949

Tony Ganci had his Kaibab mule deer originally measured in early 1950 by taxidermist O.M. Corbett who recorded it with a longest main beam measuring 32-3/8 inches. It was later measured with the Club's new and improved scoring system at the fourth competition in 1950. The buck received an honorable mention with a final score of 167-1/8 points. Tony was preparing to make presentations to two different sportsmen's groups and corresponded with Betty Fitz in the Club's office regarding what constitutes an ideal head. You'll see her response at right.

of Heads and Horns
of the
New York Zoological
Society

Mr. Tony Ganci

Dear Mr. Ganci:

Receipt is acknowledged of your letter of M

Under separate cover I am sending you one of
chures which was circulated when we first began the co
While it is out of date in many respects it does give t
and regulations for the competitions and something of t
of the club. I am enclosing with it Pictorial Leaflets
1947, 1948, 1949 and 1950 Competitions. I am sorry tha
not be able to send these until next week when I receive
supply of 1950 Leaflets.

It is difficult for me to state what constitutes
ideal head in the eyes of the Judges. There are many fac
taken into consideration, such as, score, symmetry, weigh
(that is whether the trophy is a heavy or light one - actu
weight is not taken) and general appearance. The Judges s
an entire day judging and where trophies are very close in
they are measured and remeasured until the judges feel that
fair decision is reached.

I hope that the information I am sending you will b
sufficient for your purposes though I will be glad to answer
further questions if you have them.

hat I have measured the above trophy on Feb. 9 19 51
A.M.N.H. City N.Y. State N.Y.
se measurements and data are, to the best of my knowledge and belief, made in
ith the instructions given.

ED McGUIRE

Signature: T. DONALD CARTER

INSTRUCTIONS

nts must be made with a flexible steel tape to the nearest one-eighth of an i
urements cannot be taken for at least sixty days after the animal was killed.
photographs.

Data measur
s a matter
ts shall be
rence.

Evaluation of
typical Mule Deer heads
symmetrical head will

ints on Ea
ND its len
nt to near
d as a poi

tion must be at least
l points are measured
is counted as a point

read meas

ad measur
est part

of Main Beams measured at right angles to the center line of
een main beams. Enter th

GRAVES PEELER

1949

This is Graves Peeler's fourth records-book mule deer he shot in the Kaibab in the 1930s. This buck was taken with the aid of guide Clare Pierson of Fredonia, Arizona. A transcript from Graves notes that he shot this deer—weighing 275 when it was field dressed—plus another that didn't make the book, on the Buffalo Ranch on the Kaibab. This non-typical has a final score of 248-2/8 points with 57-3/8 inches of abnormal points adding to that score.

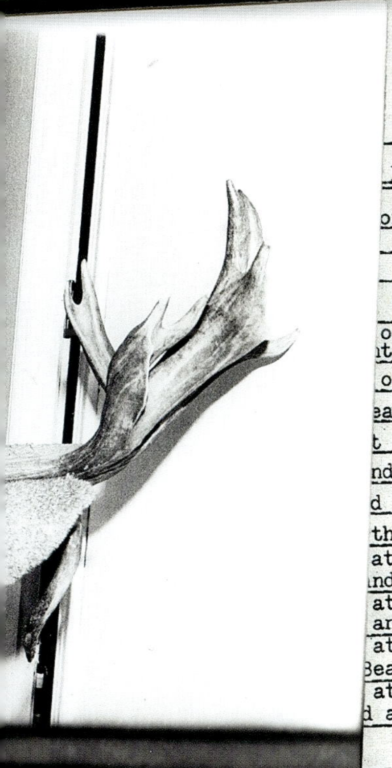

ORTH AMERICAN BIG GAME TROPHIES

ROCKETT CLUB

Address Correspondence to:
Mrs. Grancel Fitz, Secretary
5 Tudor City Place, NYC 17, NY.

BOONE AND CROCKETT OFFICIAL CLUB

MULE DEER

SEVENTH N.A.B.G. COMPETITION 1955

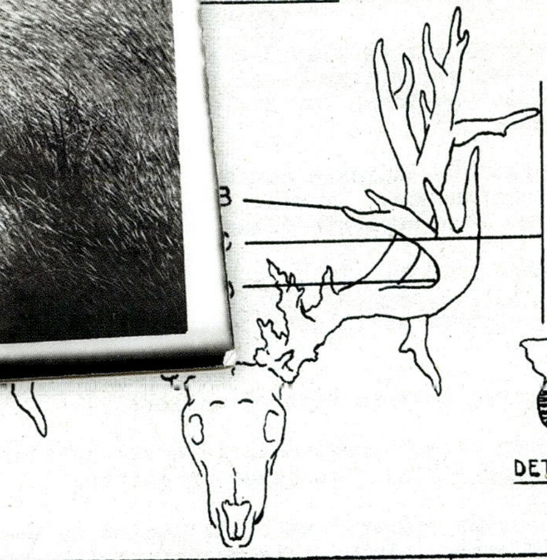

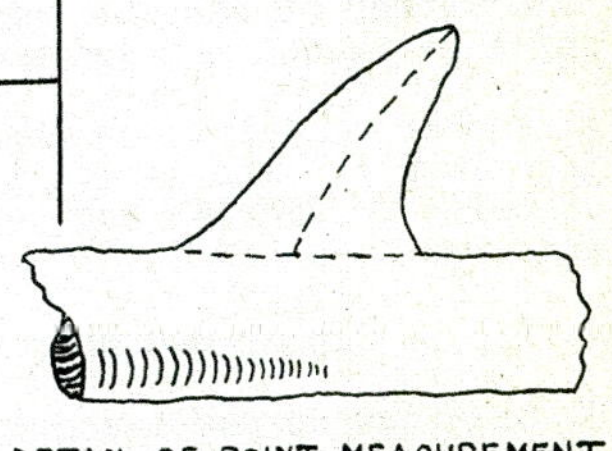

DETAIL OF POINT MEASUREMENT

FOR INSTRUCTIONS	Supplementary Data R.	L.	Column 1 Spread Credit	Column 2 Right Antler	Column 3 Left Antler	Column 4 Difference
on Each Antler	12	12				
		22 3/8				
		38 6/8				
7/ Spread credit may equal but not exceed length of longer antler			25 3/8			
of Main Beams exceeds longer ...ter difference						~~1 4/8~~
of all Abnormal Points		57 3/8				
...eam				25	25 3/8	3/8
...t Point, if present				3	3	--
...nd Point				11 7/8	13	1 1/8
...d Point, if present				11 4/8	7 6/8	3 6/8
...th Point, if present				13	11 2/8	1 6/8
at Smallest Place ...nd First Point				6 6/8	7	2/8
at Smallest Place and Second Points				6	6 1/8	1/8
at Samllest Place ...Beam and Third Point				4 7/8	4 7/8	----
at Smallest Place ...d and Fourth Points				6 2 8	6 7/8	5/8
		57 3/8	25 3/8	88 2/8	85 2/8	8 ~~9 4/8~~

ADD	Column 1	25 3/8	Exact locality where killed Kaibab Forest, Arizona
	Column 2	88 2/8	Date killed Nov 1911 By whom killed Graves Peeler
	Column 3	85 2/8	Present owner Graves Peeler
	Total	198 7/8	Address
SUBTRACT Column 4		8 ~~9 4/8~~	Guide's Name and Address Clare Pierson, Fredonia, Ariz.
190 7/8 Result		~~189 3/8~~	Remarks: (Mention any abnormalities)
Add Line E Total		57 3/8	
FINAL SCORE OK		248 2/8 ~~246 6/8~~	✓ cde 347

OFFICIAL SCORING SYSTEM FOR NORTH AMERICAN BIG GAME TROPHIES

Records of North American
Big Game Committee

BOONE AND CROCKETT CLUB

Address Correspondence to:
Mrs. Grancel Fitz, Secretary
5 Tudor City Place, NYC 17, NY.

NON-TYPICAL MULE DEER

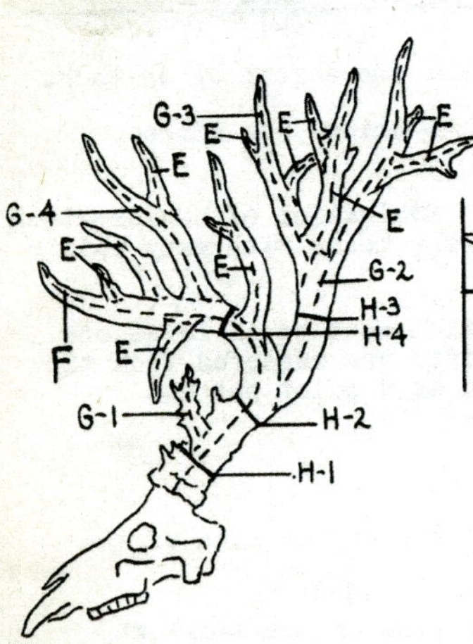

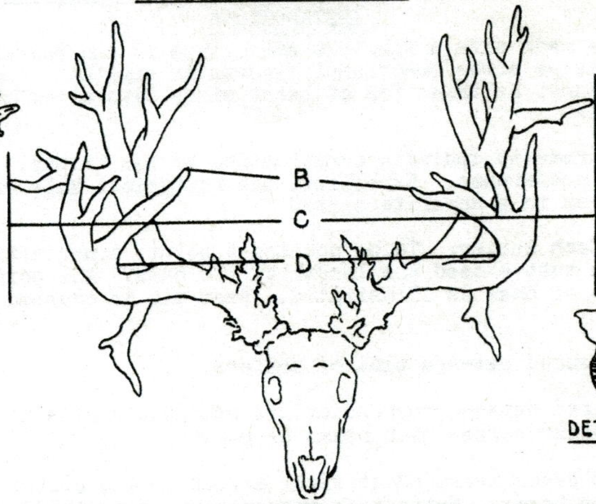

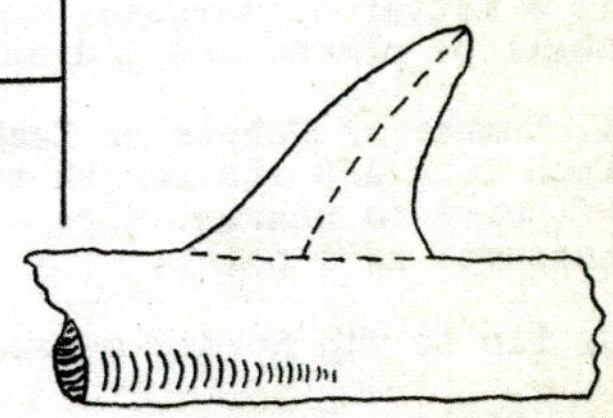

DETAIL OF POINT MEASUREMENT

SEE OTHER SIDE FOR INSTRUCTIONS	Supplementary Data R.	Supplementary Data L.	Column 1 Spread Credit	Column 2 Right Antler	Column 3 Left Antler	Column 4 Difference
A. Number of Points on Each Antler	15	13				
B. Tip to Tip Spread	26 2/8					
C. Greatest Spread	36					
D. Inside Spread of MAIN BEAMS 29 1/8 — Spread credit may equal but not exceed length of longer antler			28 7/8			
IF Inside Spread of Main Beams exceeds longer antler length, enter difference						~~2/8~~
E. Total of Lengths of all Abnormal Points	60 6/8					
F. Length of Main Beam				26 7/8	28 7/8	2
G-1. Length of First Point, if present				2 3/8	2 7/8	4/8
G-2. Length of Second Point				14 4/8	14 2/8	2/8
G-3. Length of Third Point, if present				9 1/8	8 1/8	1
G-4. Length of Fourth Point, if present				9	8 3/8	5/8
H-1. Circumference at Smallest Place Between Burr and First Point				5 3/8	5 5/8	2/8
H-2. Circumference at Smallest Place Between First and Second Points				5 1/8	5 1/8	----
H-3. Circumference at Samllest Place Between Main Beam and Third Point				5 7/8	6 3/8	4/8
H-4. Circumference at Smallest Place Between Second and Fourth Points				5 1/8	5 1/8	-----
TOTALS	60 6/8		28 7/8	83 3/8	84 6/8	5 1/8 ~~5 3/8~~

ADD	Column 1	28 7/8	Exact locality where killed Kaibab Forest, Ariz.
	Column 2	83 3/8	Date killed Prior 1951 By whom killed Graves Peeler
	Column 3	84 6/8	Present owner Graves Peeler
	Total	197	Address Christine, Texas
SUBTRACT Column 4		5 1/8 ~~5 3/8~~	Guide's Name and Address Clare Pierson, Fredonia, Ariz.
191 7/8 Result		~~191 5/8~~	Remarks: (Mention any abnormalities)
Add Line E Total		60 6/8	
FINAL SCORE		252 5/8 ~~252 3/8~~	

OK

clw 345

GRAVES PEELER

PRIOR TO 1951

This is Graves Peeler's fifth records-book mule deer he shot in the Kaibab. Unfortunately, photographic support for the trophy entry could not be located in the Club's records archives. This buck has 28 scorable points and lists Clare Pierson of Fredonia, Arizona as the guide. The chart shown at left shows the official measurements taken by Grancel Fitz, one of the developers of the Club's current scoring system. This buck has a final score of 252-5/8 points.

Jan. 12, 1955

Mr. Henderson Coquat
Milam Bldg.
San Antonio, Texas

Dear Henderson:

In checking my files I find that we had unofficial charts on Mr. Graves Peeler's non-typical mule deer. We made an effort to get these trophies officially scored before the 1952 book but were not able to do so. Mr. Peeler may be glad to know that each trophy scores ten to twelve points higher than om the original charts. Quite often we find that it is a benefit to the owner to have his trophy officially checked and this case proves it.

In checking the original charts, I note that the date killed was left blank. Can you get this information for me? One is a 24-point head; a 28-point head and an 18 point head. If they were killed in different years, identify the head by the number of points. On the chart there is a line "Present Owner". Do these trophies still belong to Mr. Peeler or will they be listed under your name?

Kind personal regards.

Yours sincerely,

OFFICIAL SCORING SYSTEM

rds of North American Game

imum Score:

BOONE AND CROCKETT CLUB®

NON-TYPICAL MULE DEER

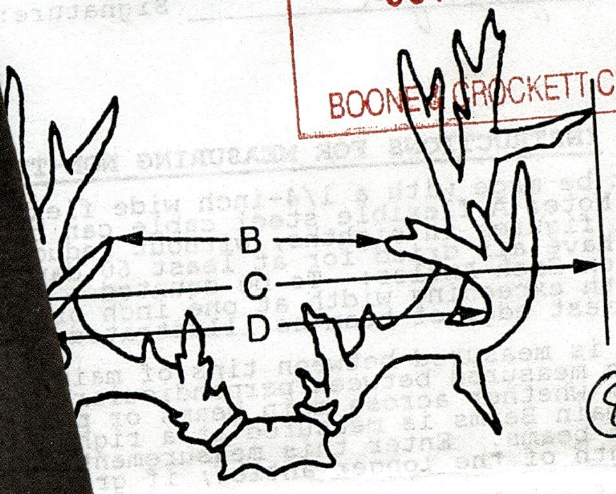

ail of Point
surement

JK 11th Comp.

	Abnormal Points
	Right Antler
	3
	9
	1
	1
	4
	1
	5 4/8
	5 5/8
Subtotals	32 6/8
E. Total	6

		Column 1	Column 2	Column 3
		Spread Credit	Right Antler	Left Antler
A. No. ... Rig...	11			
B. Tip ...	35 6/8			
D. Insi... Main...	25 6/8	(Credit May Equal But Not Exceed Longer Antler) 25 6/8	28 6/8	27
F. Length of Main Beam			4 2/8	3
G-1. Length of First Point, If Present			16 7/8	14
G-2. Length of Second Point			15 4/8	12
G-3. Length of Third Point, If Present			15 6/8	15
G-4. Length of Fourth Point, If Present			5 6/8	5
H-1. Circumference at Smallest Place Between Burr and First Point			5 4/8	5
H-2. Circumference at Smallest Place Between First and Second Points			6 2/8	6
H-3. Circumference at Smallest Place Between Main Beam and Third Point			6 4/8	6
H-4. Circumference at Smallest Place Between Second and Fourth Points				
TOTALS		25 6/8	105 1/8	98

ADD		Exact Locality Where Killed: Kaibab Nat'l Forest,
Column 1	25 6/8	Date Killed: Prior 1950 — Hunter: Picked-Up. Cliff Cox was previ...
Column 2	105 1/8	Telephone
Column 3	98 6/8	Owner: ~~Don Schaufler~~ Cabela's, Inc.
		Owner's Address: One Cabela Drive

KAIBAB DEER - 1940S

PICKED UP - CLIFF COX (OWNER)

PRIOR TO 1950

Cliff Cox entered this picked-up trophy from the Kaibab in the Club's 11th competition where it was awarded a Certificate of Merit with a score of 275-3/8 points. Thirty-four years later, B&C Official Measurer Eldon L. "Buck" Buckner saw the non-typical buck at antler collector Don Schaufler's home while scoring a different trophy. He noticed the original measurements had not accounted for the correct definition of a point resulting in some of the non-typical points not being calculated into the final score. He re-measured the mule deer and came up with a final score of 281-6/8 points. Amazingly, this giant non-typical also has an outstanding net-typical frame of 221-4/8 points! The buck is currently owned by Cabela's.

BOONE & CROCKETT CLU

1997

core Chart)

k-Up)

nd

by Schaufler's at Ennis to photo
has for the next edition of the
king at the Non-Typ head above,
Pick-Up, formerly owned by Cliff Cox,
originally measured by Dr. C.G. Clare
ed in the 1964 record book with a score
cked all the old records with the com-
correction changing the score to 274 3/8
looked at the head at Schaufler's,
Neither ... ive with what is listed in the book.
same. I decided to re-sco... , although the inside spread was the
closed chart is the result, with a score of 281 6/8. ... and see what I came up with. The en-
appears that some of the shorter non-typical points with broad bases that ... From what I see, it
did not qualify as points back in '63, do qualify now with the revised point
measurement system, ie, they qualify by the base being smaller at the length
at 1" from the tip of the point, even though the base at the main beam is
still slightly broader than the total length of the point, overall. I feel
this 281 6/8 is the accurate score for this head as it now stands, as I
went over it twice carefully. I suggest it be changed in the next edition
of the book.

he typical head is one that Don Schaufler bought from Garth Roberts, who
ound it as a lion kill several years ago in Utah. I measured it for Don,
nd am submitting it as a new pick-up entry.

you have any questions call me.

ncerely,

Eldon "Buck" Buckner

on "Buck" Buckner
cial Measu...

/8
2º
2 6/8
3/8
3/8
1/8
5/8
2/8
8 1/8
ona
owner
59729

MILROY POWELL & DAN AULD, JR.

1950

Milroy Powell and his father-in-law Dan Auld, Jr., shot this Kaibab buck on November 2, 1950. It was entered in the Club's seventh competition where it received a third prize with a score of 279-6/8 points. The non-typical buck has 28 scorable points with a total of 89-5/8 inches of abnormal points included. Milroy's wife, Joann, also shot an award-winning buck that day. Her trophy received a second prize in the previous competition. See page 157 for details on her Kaibab mule deer. Delvin Hamblin of Kanab, Utah, served as the guide for both hunts.

OFFICIAL SCORING SYSTEM FOR NORTH AMERICAN BIG GAME TROPHIES

Records of North American
Big Game Committee

BOONE AND CROCKETT CLUB

Address Correspondence to:
Mrs. Grancel Fitz, Secretary
5 Tudor City Place, NYC 17, NY.

NON-TYPICAL MULE DEER

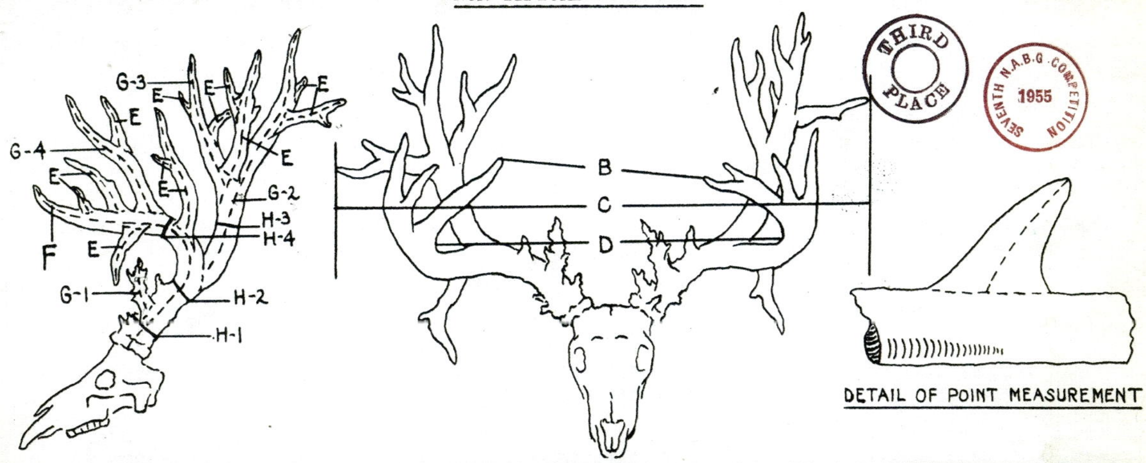

DETAIL OF POINT MEASUREMENT

SEE OTHER SIDE FOR INSTRUCTIONS	Supplementary Data R.	Supplementary Data L.	Column 1 Spread Credit	Column 2 Right Antler	Column 3 Left Antler	Column 4 Difference
A. Number of Points on Each Antler	18	10				
B. Tip to Tip Spread	7 3/8					
C. Greatest Spread	37 6/8					
D. Inside Spread of MAIN BEAMS 17 3/8 — Spread credit may equal but not exceed length of longer antler			17 3/8			
IF Inside Spread of Main Beams exceeds longer antler length, enter difference						
E. Total of Lengths of all Abnormal Points	89 5/8					
F. Length of Main Beam				26 6/8	24 2/8	~~3 6/8~~ 2 4/8
G-1. Length of First Point, if present				4 5/8	4 2/8	3/8
G-2. Length of Second Point				14 3/8	12 5/8	1 6/8
G-3. Length of Third Point, if present				10 7/8	12 3/8	(1 4/8) ~~1 6/8~~
G-4. Length of Fourth Point, if present				14 5/8	13	1 5/8
H-1. Circumference at Smallest Place Between Burr and First Point				6 4/8	5 4/8	1
H-2. Circumference at Smallest Place Between First and Second Points				5 6/8	5 2/8	4/8
H-3. Circumference at Samllest Place Between Main Beam and Third Point				5 3/8	7	1 5/8
H-4. Circumference at Smallest Place Between Second and Fourth Points				6 6/8	5 2/8	1 4/8
TOTALS	89 5/8		17 3/8	95 5/8	89 4/8	~~13 7/8~~ (12 3/8)

ADD	Column 1	17 3/8	Exact locality where killed Kaibab Forest, Ariz.
	Column 2	95 5/8	Date killed 11-2-1950 By whom killed Milroy Powell& Dan Auld, Jr.
	Column 3	89 4/8	Present owner MILROY POWELL.
(12 3/8)	Total	202 4/8	Address
SUBTRACT	Column 4	~~13 7/8~~	Guide's Name and Address Delvin Hamblin, Kanab, Utah
190 1/8	~~Result~~	~~188 5/8~~	Remarks: (Mention any abnormalities)
	Add Line E Total	89 5/8	at Museum 1955
	FINAL SCORE	~~278 2/8~~	(279 6/8) final score

339

OFFICIAL SCORING SYSTEM FOR NORTH AMERICAN BIG GAME TROPHIES 3d 1951

Records of North American Big Game and North American Big Game Competition

BOONE AND CROCKETT CLUB

% Am. Museum of Natural History
Central Park West at 79th Street
New York 24, New York

MULE and BLACKTAIL DEER

KIND OF DEER MULE DEER (Non-typical)

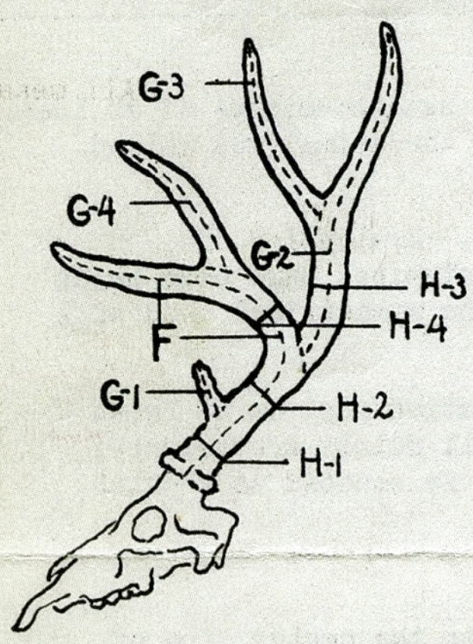

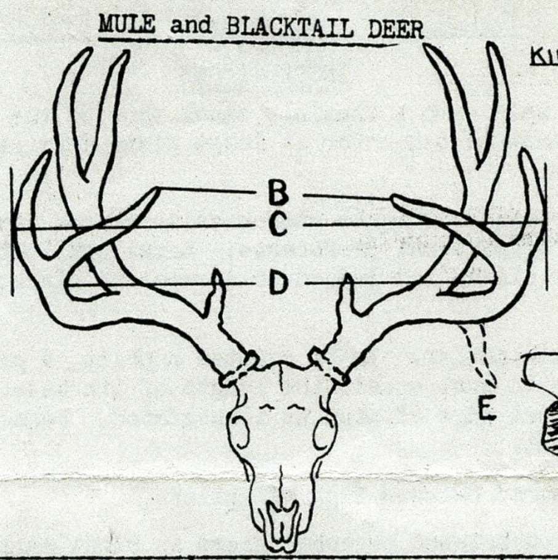

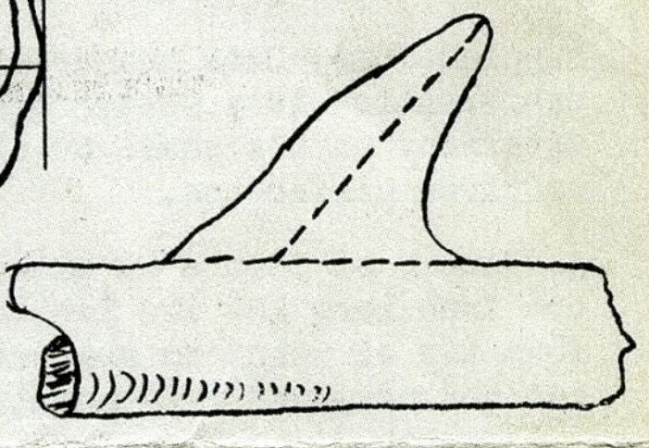

DETAIL OF POINT MEASUREMENT

SEE OTHER SIDE FOR INSTRUCTIONS	Supplementary Data R.	Supplementary Data L.	Column 1 Spread Credit	Column 2 Right Antler	Column 3 Left Antler	Column 4 Difference
A. Number of Points on Each Antler	8	10				
B. Tip to Tip Spread	23"					
C. Greatest Spread	34 5/8"					
D. Inside Spread of MAIN BEAMS 21 7/8 — Spread credit may equal but not exceed length of longer antler			21 7/8			
IF Inside Spread of Main Beams exceeds longer antler length, enter difference						
E. Total of Lengths of all Abnormal Points	11 1/8					11¼" 11 1/8
F. Length of Main Beam				24 3/4	23 3/8	1 3/8
G-1. Length of First Point, if present				5"	2 3/4	2¼
G-2. Length of Second Point				15 3/4	18½	2 3/4
G-3. Length of Third Point, if present				11½	13½	2"
G-4. Length of Fourth Point, if present				12½	3¼	9¼
H-1. Circumference at Smallest Place Between Burr and First Point				6½"	6 1/8	3/8"
H-2. Circumference at Smallest Place Between First and Second Points				6"	5 7/8	1/8"
H-3. Circumference at Smallest Place Between Main Beam and Third Point,				4 7/8	5 5/8	3/4
H-4. Circumference at Smallest Place Between Second and Fourth Points				5½	4 5/8	7/8
TOTALS	11 7/8		21 7/8	92 3/8	83 5/8	31

ADD	Column 1	21 7/8	Exact locality where killed North Kaibab National Forest, Ariz.
	Column 2	92 3/8	Date killed 10/8/50 By whom killed William H. Beers
	Column 3	83 5/8	Present owner William H. Beers
	TOTAL	197 7/8	Address
SUBTRACT Column 4		31	Guide's Name and Address None
OK FINAL SCORE		166 7/8	Remarks: (Mention any abnormalities) Exceptionally heavy beams with webb like formations between points. Well proportioned head with only one downward abnormal point.

(166 7/8)

Beers 1/22/50

3D EDITION ENABG 32

WILLIAM H. BEERS

1950

William H. Beers was hunting in the north Kaibab National Forest in October 1950 when he shot a typical mule deer. The remarks section of the score chart indicates *exceptionally heavy beams with webb [sic] like formations between points. Well proportioned head with only one downward abnormal point.* Unfortunately, no photographic record of the deer can be located in the files. However, a note attached to the score chart indicates the deer was considered for judging at the 1951 competition but the owner was not officially invited to bring the trophy to the competition.

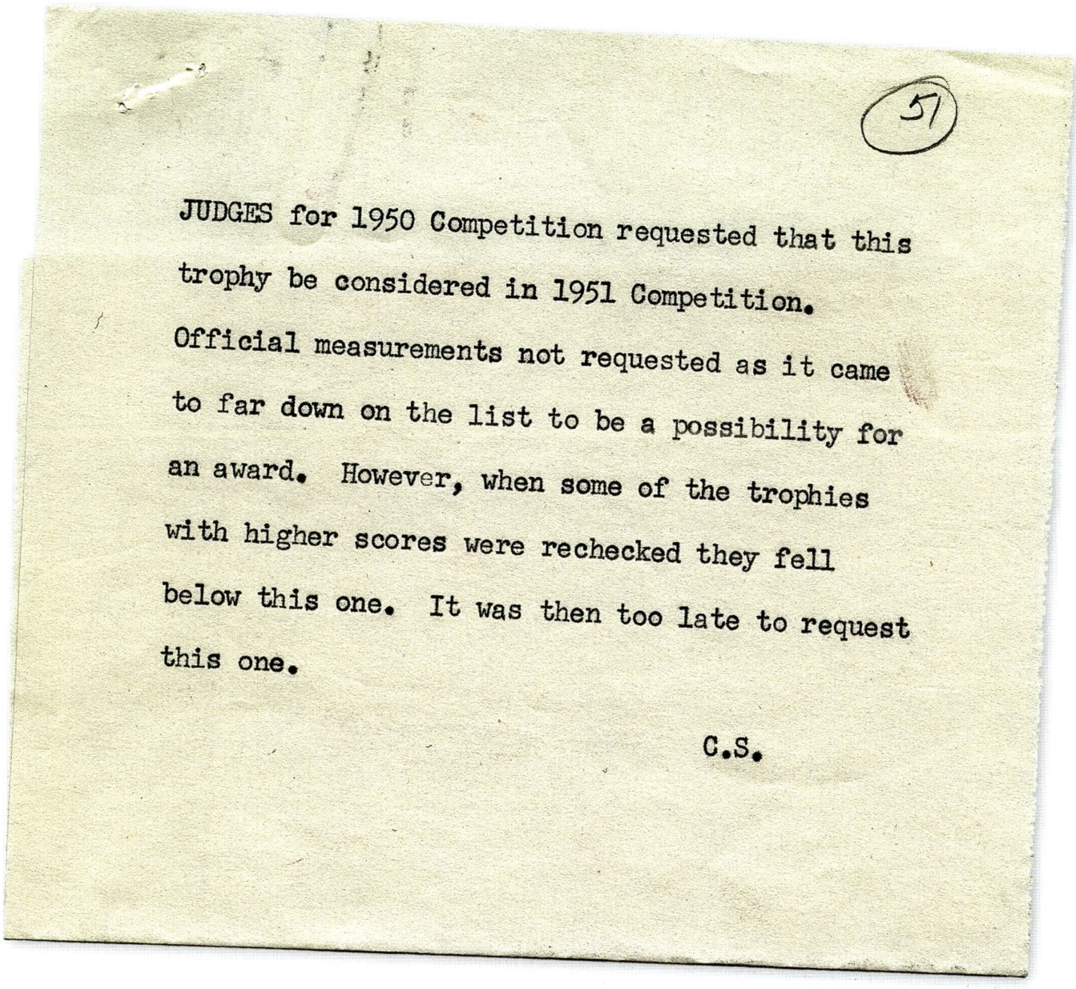

51

JUDGES for 1950 Competition requested that this trophy be considered in 1951 Competition. Official measurements not requested as it came to far down on the list to be a possibility for an award. However, when some of the trophies with higher scores were rechecked they fell below this one. It was then too late to request this one.

C.S.

MILROY POWELL

1952

Milroy Powell also entered this beautiful non-typical Kaibab buck in the Club's seventh competition along with the aforementioned deer he shot in 1950. The original chart has been misplaced, but the Club's database includes key measurements for the deer. It has 25 scorable points with 58-2/8 inches of abnormal points adding into the score. Additional information includes a greatest spread of 37 inches and main beam lengths both over 28 inches. The back of the photograph indicates the mule deer was killed in the Saddle Mountain area of the Kaibab. Floyd Burr is holding the antlers.

OFFICIAL SCORING SYSTEM FOR NORTH AMERICAN BIG GAME TROPHIES

Records of North American
Big Game Committee

BOONE AND CROCKETT CLUB

Address Correspondence to:
Mrs. Grancel Fitz, Secretary
5 Tudor City Place, NYC 17, NY.

BOONE AND CROCKETT OFFICIAL

SEVENTH N.A.B.G. COMPETITION 1955

NON-TYPICAL MULE DEER

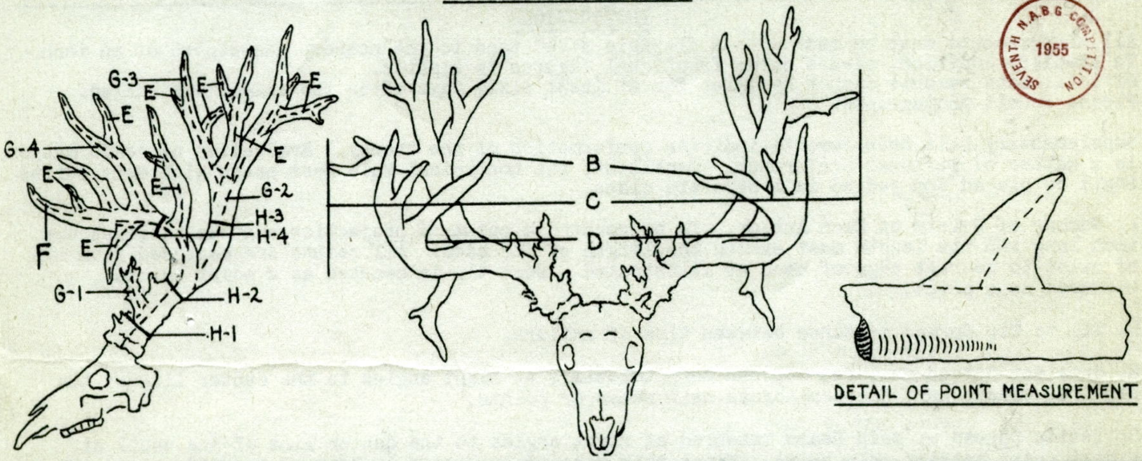

SEE OTHER SIDE FOR INSTRUCTIONS	Supplementary Data R.	Supplementary Data L.	Column 1 Spread Credit	Column 2 Right Antler	Column 3 Left Antler	Column 4 Difference
A. Number of Points on Each Antler	9	8				
B. Tip to Tip Spread	26 4/8					
C. Greatest Spread	38 1/8					
D. Inside Spread of MAIN BEAMS 28 4/8 — Spread credit may equal but not exceed length of longer antler			26 2/8			
IF Inside Spread of Main Beams exceeds longer antler length, enter difference						~~2 2/8~~
E. Total of Lengths of all Abnormal Points	38 4/8					
F. Length of Main Beam				24 4/8	26 2/8	1 6/8
G-1. Length of First Point, if present				1 5/8	—	1 5/8
G-2. Length of Second Point				17 5/8	16 4/8	1 1/8
G-3. Length of Third Point, if present				12 4/8	12 3/8	1/8
G-4. Length of Fourth Point, if present				13 3/8	14	5/8
H-1. Circumference at Smallest Place Between Burr and First Point				5 6/8	5 5/8	1/8
H-2. Circumference at Smallest Place Between First and Second Points				5 6/8	5 6/8	
H-3. Circumference at Samllest Place Between Main Beam and Third Point				5 6/8	5 6/8	—
H-4. Circumference at Smallest Place Between Second and Fourth Points				5 7/8	6 2/8	3/8
TOTALS	38 4/8		26 2/8	92 6/8	92 4/8	~~8~~ 5 6/8

ADD	Column 1	26 2/8	Exact locality where killed KAIBAB, Ariz
	Column 2	92 6/8	Date killed 1952 By whom killed RAY RAMSEY
	Column 3	92 4/8	Present owner RAY RAMSEY
	Total	211 4/8	Address
SUBTRACT	Column 4	~~8~~ 5 6/8	Guide's Name and Address None
205 6/8	Result	~~203 4/8~~	Remarks: (Mention any abnormalities)
Add Line E Total		38 4/8	
FINAL SCORE		~~215 4/8~~ ~~242~~ 244 2/8 OK	

350

ACK. BY CARD 1954

RAY RAMSEY

1952

This impressive mule deer, shot during the 1952 season in the Kaibab, is a 9x8 non-typical with a final score of 244-2/8 points. It has a greatest spread of 38-7/8 inches along with abnormal points totaling 38-4/8 inches. Even more impressive is the net-typical frame this deer carries at 205-6/8 points.

DALE SLOCUM

1953

Dale Slocum shot this north Kaibab mule deer in 1953. The score chart indicates he was guided by Leon Carlson. The buck has a final score of 226-4/8 points with more than 26 inches of abnormal points added into the score.

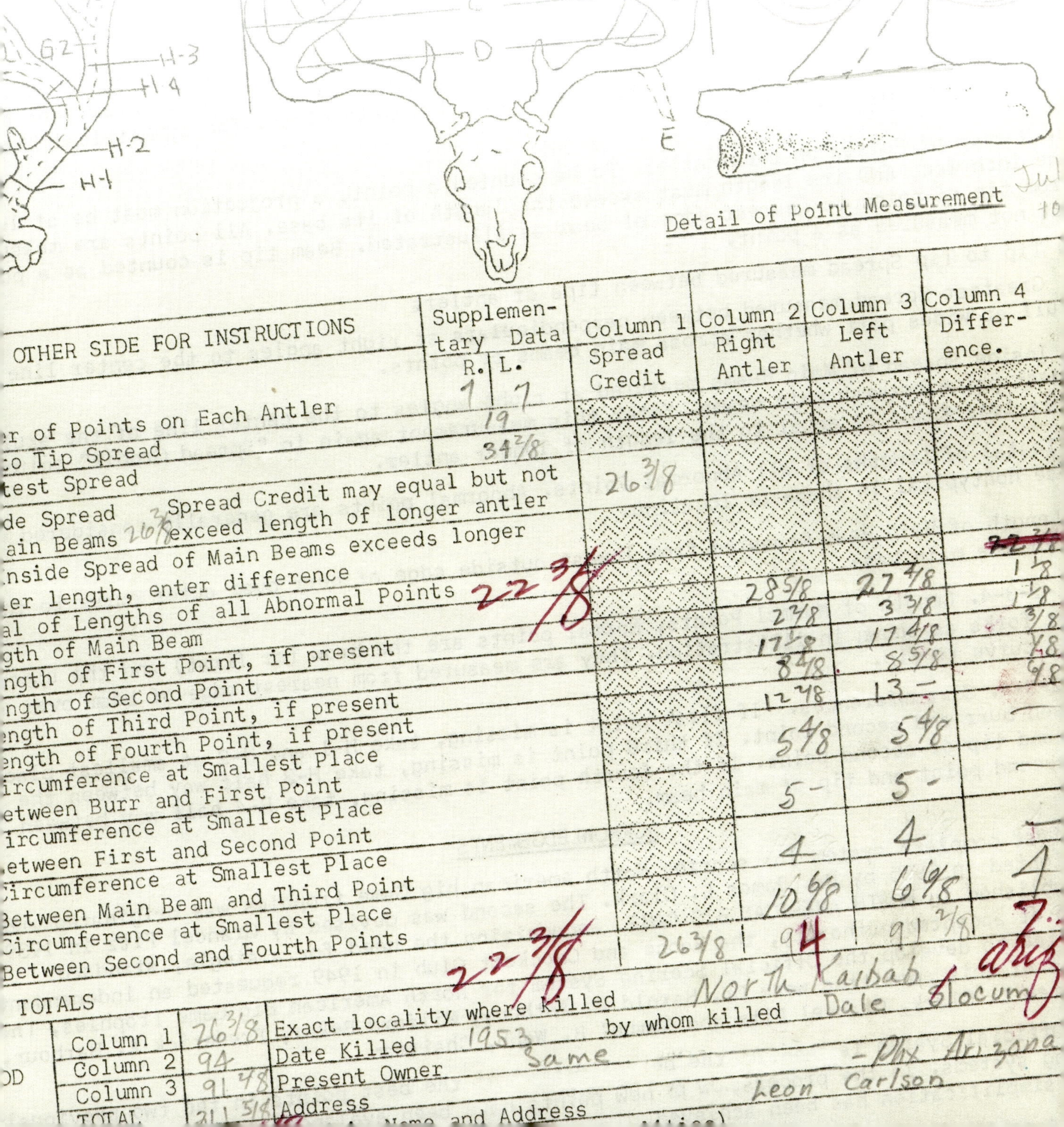

Detail of Point Measurement

OTHER SIDE FOR INSTRUCTIONS	Supplementary Data R.	Supplementary Data L.	Column 1 Spread Credit	Column 2 Right Antler	Column 3 Left Antler	Column 4 Difference.
...er of Points on Each Antler	7	7				
...o Tip Spread	19					
...test Spread	34 2/8					
...de Spread ...ain Beams 26 7/8 — Spread Credit may equal but not exceed length of longer antler			26 3/8			
...nside Spread of Main Beams exceeds longer ...er length, enter difference						~~22 2/8~~
...al of Lengths of all Abnormal Points	22 3/8					
...gth of Main Beam				28 5/8	27 4/8	1 1/8
...ngth of First Point, if present				2 2/8	3 3/8	1 1/8
...ngth of Second Point				17 [illegible]	17 4/8	3/8
...ngth of Third Point, if present				8 4/8	8 5/8	1/8
...ength of Fourth Point, if present				12 4/8	13 —	4/8
...ircumference at Smallest Place ...etween Burr and First Point				5 4/8	5 4/8	—
...ircumference at Smallest Place ...etween First and Second Point				5 -	5 -	—
...ircumference at Smallest Place ...etween Main Beam and Third Point				4	4	—
...ircumference at Smallest Place ...etween Second and Fourth Points				10 6/8	6 6/8	4
TOTALS	22 3/8		26 3/8	94	91 2/8	7

...DD		
Column 1	26 3/8	Exact locality where killed: North Kaibab
Column 2	94	Date Killed: 1953 — by whom killed: Dale Slocum
Column 3	91 4/8	Present Owner: Same
TOTAL	211 5/8	Address: Phx Arizona
		... Name and Address: Leon Carlson

C.H. SIEVERS

1953

Bob Housholder measured this typical mule deer—scoring 183-4/8 points—in 1957 for C.H. Sievers. The buck was harvested in the north Kaibab National Forest during the 1953 season. This classic 5x5 mule deer has a greatest spread of 30-6/8 inches and main beams both measuring more than 25 inches.

OFFICIAL SCORING SYSTEM FOR NORTH AMERICAN BIG GAME TROPHIES

Records of North American Big Game Committee

BOONE AND CROCKETT CLUB

Address Correspondence to:
Mrs. Grancel Fitz, Secretary
5 Tudor City Place, NYC, 17 N.Y.

MULE AND BLACKTAIL DEER

KIND OF DEER Mule

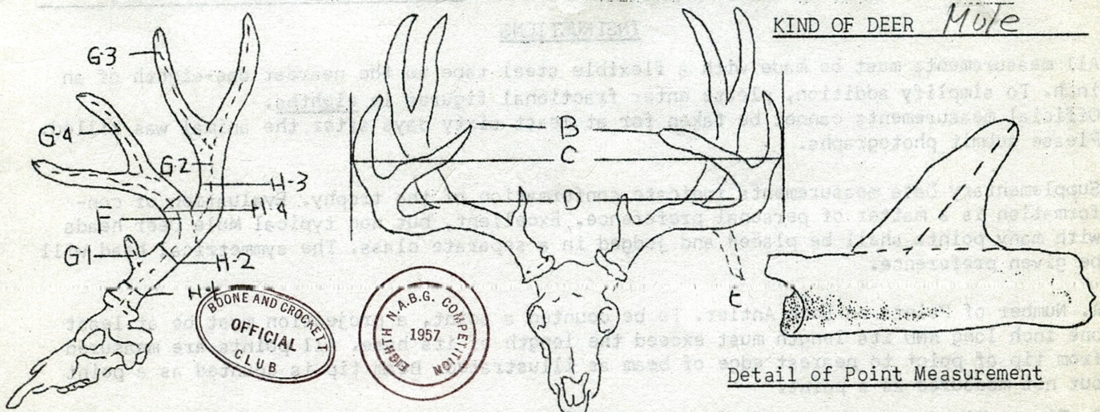

Detail of Point Measurement

SEE OTHER SIDE FOR INSTRUCTIONS	Supplementary Data R.	Supplementary Data L.	Column 1 Spread Credit	Column 2 Right Antler	Column 3 Left Antler	Column 4 Difference.
A. Number of Points on Each Antler	5	5				
B. Tip to Tip Spread	22 2/8					
C. Greatest Spread	30 6/8					
D. Inside Spread of Main Beams 26 2/8 — Spread Credit may equal but not exceed length of longer antler			25 7/8			
If Inside Spread of Main Beams exceeds longer antler length, enter difference						3/8
E. Total of Lengths of all Abnormal Points						—
F. Length of Main Beam				25 7/8	25 3/8	4/8
G-1 Length of First Point, if present				2	1 6/8	2/8
G-2 Length of Second Point				14 4/8	16 4/8	2 —
G-3 Length of Third Point, if present				10 —	10 7/8	7/8
G-4 Length of Fourth Point, if present				11 7/8	10 1/8	1 6/8
H-1 Circumference at Smallest Place Between Burr and First Point				5	5 2/8	2/8
H-2 Circumference at Smallest Place Between First and Second Point				4 2/8	4 4/8	2/8
H-3 Circumference at Smallest Place Between Main Beam and Third Point				3 6/8	4	2/8
H-4 Circumference at Smallest Place Between Second and Fourth Points				4 6/8	4 2/8	4/8
TOTALS			25 7/8	82 —	82 5/8	7

ADD	Column 1	25 7/8	Exact locality where killed ~~North~~ Kaibab ~~Forest~~ - Ariz
	Column 2	82	Date Killed 1953 by whom killed C.H. Sievers
	Column 3	82 5/8	Present Owner Same
	TOTAL	190 4/8	Address
SUBTRACT Column 4		7	Guide's Name and Address none
FINAL SCORE		183 4/8	Remarks: (Mention any abnormalities)

JAN 2 1957

1954

OFFICIAL SCORING SYSTEM FOR NORTH AMERICAN BIG GAME TROPHIES

Records of North American Big Game Committee

BOONE AND CROCKETT CLUB

Address Correspondence to:
Mrs. Grancel Fitz, Secretary
5 Tudor City Place, NYC 17, NY.

BOONE AND CROCKETT OFFICIAL CLUB

SEVENTH N.A.B.G. COMM. 1955

NON-TYPICAL MULE DEER

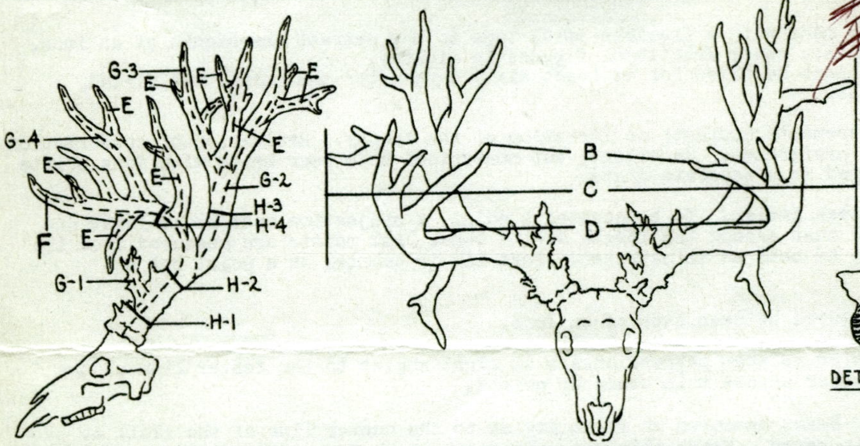

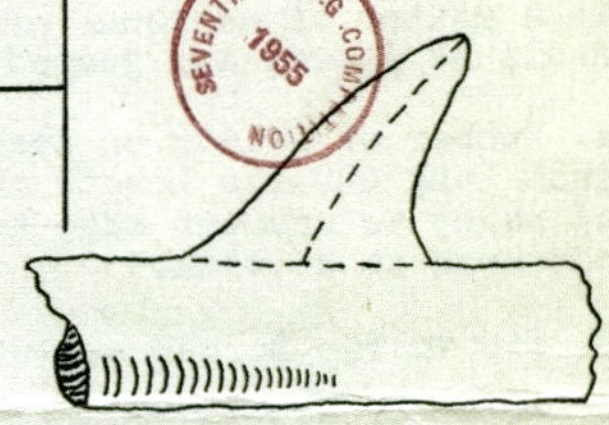

DETAIL OF POINT MEASUREMENT

SEE OTHER SIDE FOR INSTRUCTIONS	Supplementary Data R.	Supplementary Data L.	Column 1 Spread Credit	Column 2 Right Antler	Column 3 Left Antler	Column 4 Difference
A. Number of Points on Each Antler	11	11				
B. Tip to Tip Spread	27 2/4					
C. Greatest Spread	32 1/4					
D. Inside Spread of MAIN BEAMS 26 — Spread credit may equal but not exceed length of longer antler			26			
IF Inside Spread of Main Beams exceeds longer antler length, enter difference						
E. Total of Lengths of all Abnormal Points	56					
F. Length of Main Beam				24 3/4	26 3/4	~~2 2/4~~
G-1. Length of First Point, if present				4	4 1/4	1/4
G-2. Length of Second Point				18	16 3/4	1 1/4
G-3. Length of Third Point, if present				12	9 1/4	2 3/4
G-4. Length of Fourth Point, if present				8 1/4	10 3/4	2 2/4
H-1. Circumference at Smallest Place Between Burr and First Point				5	4 3/4	1/4
H-2. Circumference at Smallest Place Between First and Second Points				4 2/4	4 2/4	—
H-3. Circumference at Samllest Place Between Main Beam and Third Point				4 2/4	4 2/4	—
H-4. Circumference at Smallest Place Between Second and Fourth Points				4 2/4	4 2/4	—
TOTALS	56		26	85 1/4 (84 6/8)	86	~~8 3/4~~ 9

ADD	Column 1	26	Exact locality where killed Kaibab Forest Arizona
	Column 2	85 1/4	Date killed 14 Nov 1953 By whom killed C. M. Randal, Jr.
	Column 3	86	Present owner C. M. Randal, Jr.
	Total	~~142 2/4~~ 197 4/8	Address
SUBTRACT Column 4		~~8 3/4~~ 9	Guide's Name and Address None
	Result	188 3/4	Remarks: (Mention any abnormalities)
Add Line E Total		56	
FINAL SCORE		~~189 3/4~~ 244 4/8	

C.M. RANDAL

1953

Originally entered as a typical mule deer, this Kaibab buck was recalculated as a non-typical at 244-4/8 points. The buck, shot by C.M. Randal on November 14, 1953, has 22 scorable points with a total of 56 inches of abnormal points. Unfortunately, no photographic record exists at B&C headquarters.

OFFICIAL SCORING SYSTEM FOR NORTH AMERICAN BIG GAME TROPHIES

Records of North American
Big Game Committee

BOONE AND CROCKETT CLUB

Address Correspondence to:
Mrs. Grancel Fitz, Secretary
5 Tudor City Place, NYC 17, NY.

NON-TYPICAL MULE DEER

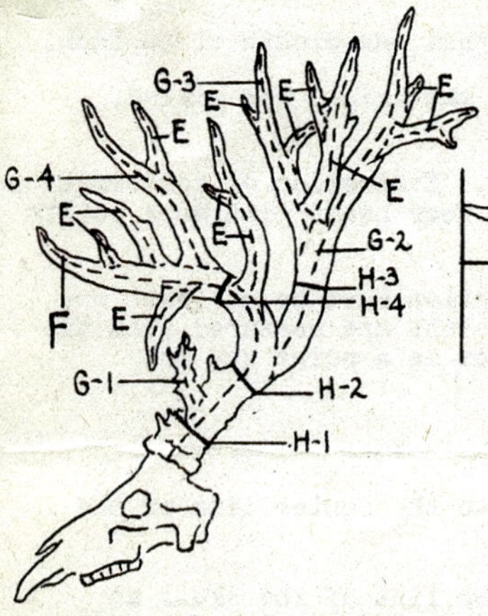

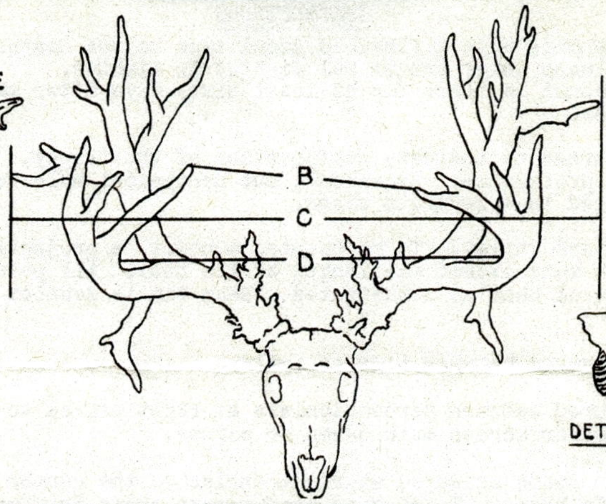

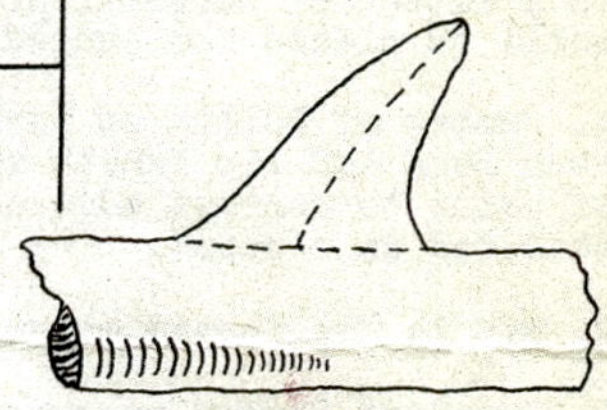

DETAIL OF POINT MEASUREMENT

SEE OTHER SIDE FOR INSTRUCTIONS	Supplementary Data		Column 1	Column 2	Column 3	Column 4
A. Number of Points on Each Antler	R. 10	L. 16	Spread Credit	Right Antler	Left Antler	Difference
B. Tip to Tip Spread	12-7					
C. Greatest Spread	41-2					
D. Inside Spread of MAIN BEAMS 23-4 — Spread credit may equal but not exceed length of longer antler			23-4			
IF Inside Spread of Main Beams exceeds longer antler length, enter difference						—
E. Total of Lengths of all Abnormal Points		62-3				
F. Length of Main Beam				26-3	26-6	— 3
G-1. Length of First Point, if present				4-0	3-3	— 5
G-2. Length of Second Point				15-7	17-7	2—
G-3. Length of Third Point, if present				8-6	10-0	1-2
G-4. Length of Fourth Point, if present				7-6	12-2	4-4
H-1. Circumference at Smallest Place Between Burr and First Point				5-4	5-2	— 2
H-2. Circumference at Smallest Place Between First and Second Points				5-0	4-6	— 2
H-3. Circumference at Samllest Place Between Main Beam and Third Point				4-7	4-4	— 3
H-4. Circumference at Smallest Place Between Second and Fourth Points				4-5	5-1	— 4
TOTALS		62-3	23-4	82-6	89-7	10-~~2~~ 8

ADD	Column 1	23-4	Exact locality where killed Kaibab, — Bone Gulch
	Column 2	82-6	Date killed 1953 By whom killed O.M. Corbett
	Column 3	89-7	Present owner O.M. Corbett
	Total	196-1	Address Calif.
SUBTRACT	Column 4	10-~~2~~ 8	Guide's Name and Address Knewell Bundy, Jack Church Outfitting, Kiabab
	Result	185-7	Remarks: (Mention any abnormalities) Because it is non-typical the measuring may not be quite absolute. Measuring some of the Abnormal points is a matter of judgement & could be a variable.
Add Line E Total		62-3	
FINAL SCORE		248-3/8	

OK

O.M. CORBETT

1953

Knewell Bundy of Jack Chaleh Outfitting led O.M. Corbett to an impressive non-typical mule deer near Bone Gulch in the Kaibab National Forest in 1953. No photo was included, but the chart indicates the buck had 10 points on the right antler and 16 on the left. The sixteen abnormal points add 62-3/8 inches to the final score of 248-3/8 B&C points. The measurer remarked there was some difficulty measuring the non-typical points. Also of note, the buck had an extraordinary greatest spread of 41-2/8 inches.

WILLIS F. NIELSON

1953

This Kaibab mule deer was shot by Willis F. Nielson during the 1953 season. The final score tapes in at 222-1/8 inches with 18 scorable points. The buck has an impressive greatest spread of 40 inches. The hunter is pictured holding the buck as he wheels it out on a deer cart.

OFFICIAL SCORING SYSTEM FOR NORTH AMERICAN BIG GAME TROPHIES

Records of North American
Big Game Committee

BOONE AND CROCKETT CLUB

Address Correspondence to:
Mrs. Grancel Fitz, Secretary
5 Tudor City Place, NYC 17, NY.

NON-TYPICAL MULE DEER

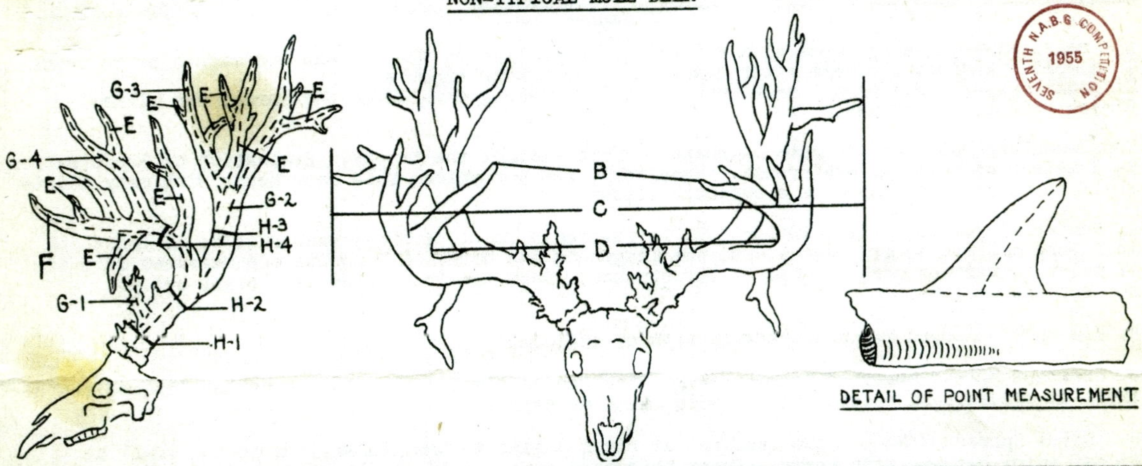

SEE OTHER SIDE FOR INSTRUCTIONS	Supplementary Data R.	Supplementary Data L.	Column 1 Spread Credit	Column 2 Right Antler	Column 3 Left Antler	Column 4 Difference
A. Number of Points on Each Antler	10	8				
B. Tip to Tip Spread	22 5/8					
C. Greatest Spread	40					
D. Inside Spread of MAIN BEAMS 25 6/8 — Spread credit may equal but not exceed length of longer antler			25 6/8			
IF Inside Spread of Main Beams exceeds longer antler length, enter difference						
E. Total of Lengths of all Abnormal Points		38 7/8				
F. Length of Main Beam				26 4/8	24 2/8	2 2/8
G-1. Length of First Point, if present				3	3	—
G-2. Length of Second Point				16 4/8	14 6/8	1 6/8
G-3. Length of Third Point, if present				8	9 1/8	1 7/8
G-4. Length of Fourth Point, if present				10 4/8	11 6/8	1 2/8
H-1. Circumference at Smallest Place Between Burr and First Point				5 2/8	5	2/8
H-2. Circumference at Smallest Place Between First and Second Points				4 4/8	4 4/8	—
H-3. Circumference at Samllest Place Between Main Beam and Third Point				4 2/8	4 2/8	—
H-4. Circumference at Smallest Place Between Second and Fourth Points				4 4/8	4 6/8	2/8
TOTALS		38 7/8	25 6/8	83	82 1/8	7 5/8

ADD			
ADD	Column 1	25 6/8	Exact locality where killed KAIBAB
	Column 2	83	Date killed 1953 By whom killed W.F. NIELSON
	Column 3	82 1/8	Present owner W.F NIELSON
	Total	190 7/8	Address
SUBTRACT	Column 4	7 5/8	Guide's Name and Address
	Result	183 2/8	Remarks: (Mention any abnormalities)
Add Line E Total		38 7/8	
FINAL SCORE		221 1/8	

OK

NOV 22 1954
ACK. BY CARD

OFFICIAL SCORING SYSTEM

f North American
me Committee

BOONE AND CROCKETT CLUB

Address Correspondence to:
Mrs. Grancel Fitz, Secretary
5 Tudor City Place, NYC 17, NY.

MULE and BLACKTAIL DEER

KIND OF DEER Mule

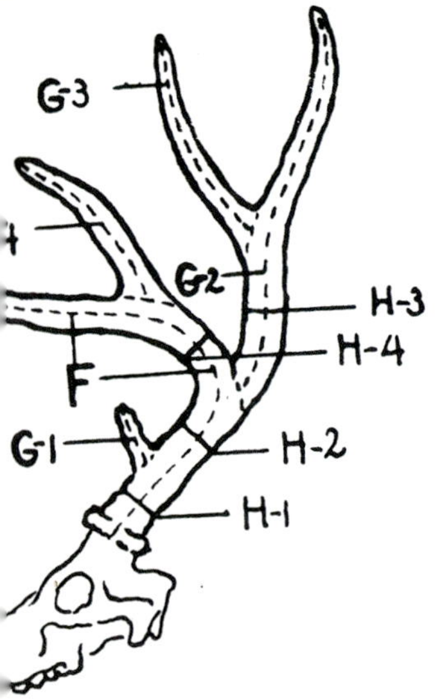

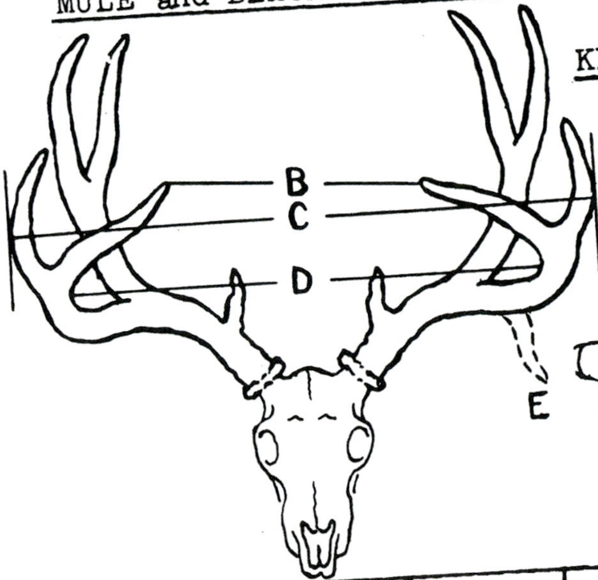

DETAIL OF POINT MEASUREMENT

SEE OTHER SIDE FOR INSTRUCTIONS	Supplementary Data R.	Supplementary Data L.	Column 1 Spread Credit	Column 2 Right Antler	Column 3 Left Antler	Column 4 Difference
mber of Points on Each Antler	7	7				
p to Tip Spread	21 4/8					
eatest Spread	33 3/8					
nside Spread OF MAIN BEAMS 26 5/8	Spread credit may equal but not exceed length of longer antler		25 7/8			
F Inside Spread of Main Beams exceeds longer ntler length, enter difference						6/8
otal of Lengths of all Abnormal Points						12
ength of Main Beam				25 7/8	25 5/8	2/8
Length of First Point, if present				3 6/8	3 5/8	1/8
Length of Second Point				20 1/8	19 7/8	2/8
Length of Third Point, if present				12 4/8	11 7/8	5/8
Length of Fourth Point, if present				10 3/8	11 5/8	1 2/8
Circumference at Smallest Place Between Burr and First Point				5 1/8	5 5/8	4/8
Circumference at Smallest Place Between First and Second Points				5 2/8	4 6/8	4/8
Circumference at Smallest Place Between Main Beam and Third Point				4 5/8	4 4/8	1/8
Circumference at Smallest Place Between Second and Fourth Points				4 3/8	4 4/8	1/8
TOTALS			25 7/8	92	92	16 4/8

Column 1	25 7/8
Column 2	92
Column 3	92
TOTAL	209 7/8
BTRACT Column 4	16 4/8
	193 3/8

Exact locality where killed Kaibab Forest, Ariz.

Date killed 11- 1953 By whom killed Thomas R. Wilson

Present owner THOMAS R. WILSON

Address

Guide's Name and Address Jack Tibus, Kanab, Utah

Remarks: (Mention any abnormalities)

THOMAS R. WILSON

1953

The original entry score for this Kaibab buck was 206-3/8 points, warranting an invite to the seventh competition held in 1956. Unfortunately, when the buck was sent to the museum for verification, the judges identified several non-typical points as well as symmetrical adjustments that were not made originally. The score dropped to 193-3/8 points, and no award was given. At that score, it is still an impressive buck, and one that hunter Thomas R. Wilson should be proud of! According to the chart, Thomas was guided on the November 1953 hunt by Jack Tibus of Kanab, Utah.

BOONE AND CROCKETT CLUB

RECORDS OF NORTH AMERICAN BIG GAME COMMITTEE

SAMUEL B. WEBB, CHAIRMAN 99 JOHN ST., N. Y.

MILFORD BAKER 285 MADISON AVE., N. Y.

FREDERICK K. BARBOUR 575 PARK AVE., N. Y.

ALFRED ELY 41 BROAD ST., N. Y.

ALFRED ... NEW H...

...DRESS CORRESP... ...S. GRANCEL FITZ 5 TUDOR CITY ... NEW YORK 17, N...

Mr. Thomas R. Wilson

Dear Sir:

Mule deer - typ... is one of the ...ssary to have ...nd compare it ... be hung in a ...story, which

...nd your trophy ...k West at 79th ...t heads and horns ...dress of the owner; These items will precaution will ... Boone and Crockett for trophies either ... of the entries will ...urance.

...we will appreciate ... place it in the ... the Museum is

...rophy and thank you ... American Big Game

... yours,

M FOR NORTH AMERIC

E AND CROCKETT CL

and BLACKTAIL

DETAIL OF POINT MEASUREMENT

SEE OTHER SIDE FOR INSTRUCTIONS	Supplementary Data R.	Supplementary Data L.	Column 1 Spread Credit	Column 2 Right Antler	Column 3 Left Antler	Column 4 Difference
A. Number of Points on Each Antler	5	6				
B. Tip to Tip Spread	20 1/8					
C. Greatest Spread	30 4/8					
D. Inside Spread of MAIN BEAMS 22 2/8 — Spread credit may equal but not exceed length of longer antler			22 2/8			
IF Inside Spread of Main Beams exceeds longer antler length, enter difference						
E. Total of Lengths of all Abnormal Points						3 1/8
F. Length of Main Beam				22 6/8	21	1 6/8
G-1. Length of First Point, if present				3 3/8	2 6/8	5/8
G-2. Length of Second Point				18 6/8	17 6/8	1 –
G-3. Length of Third Point, if present				13 –	11 2/8	1 6/8
G-4. Length of Fourth Point, if present				10 4/8	11 2/8	6/8
H-1. Circumference at Smallest Place Between Burr and First Point				5	5	–
H-2. Circumference at Smallest Place Between First and Second Points				4	4	–
H-3. Circumference at Smallest Place Between Main Beam and Third Point.				3 4/8	3 4/8	–
H-4. Circumference at Smallest Place Between Second and Fourth Points				3 4/8	3 2/8	2/8
TOTALS			22 2/8	84 3/8	79 6/8	9 2/8

ADD	Column 1	22 2/8	Exact locality where killed NORTH KAIBAB – ARIZONA
	Column 2	84 3/8	Date killed NOV. 1954 By whom killed BOB HOUSHOLDER
	Column 3	79 6/8	Present owner Same
	TOTAL	186 3/8	Address
SUBTRACT Column 4		9 2/8	Guide's Name and Address NONE
FINAL SCORE	OK	177 1/8	Remarks: (Mention any abnormalities) one abnormal point on left G2 (3 1/8")

BOB HOUSHOLDER

1954

This typical Kaibab mule deer was shot in November 1954 by Bob Housholder, who two years later founded the Grand Slam Club. The buck has a classic 5x5 rack with just one abnormal point deducting 3-1/8 inches from the final score of 177-1/8 points.

COMPETITION

ETT CLUB

1968 offered 100.00 Yes

7, 1958

ADDRESS CORRESPONDENC
MRS. GRANCEL FITZ, SECRE
5 TUDOR CITY PLACE
NEW YORK 17, NEW YOR

the fine Big Game Competition ~~is one of the~~ Typical Mule Dee ... For this reason it is necessary to have ... inspect it, measure it officially and compare it ... entries in its class. The trophy will then be hung in a ...mporary exhibit at the American Museum of Natural History, which will open shortly after the trophies have been judged.

We will greatly appreciate it if you will send your trophy to the American Museum of Natural History, Central Park West at 79th Street, New York 24, N. Y. The Committee requires that heads and horns sent to them be labeled with the name and complete address of the owner; be shipped and insured at the expense of the owner. These items will be given careful handling by the Committee and every precaution will be exercised against possible damage, but neither the Boone and Crockett Club nor the Committee can accept any responsibility for trophies either in transit or while in their possession. The return of the entries wil be at the owner's expense for transportation and insurance.

A self-addressed postcard is enclosed and we will appreciate it if you will please fill in the data requested and place it in the mail. The deadline date for delivery of trophies to the Museum is ~~January 31~~ Feb. 7, 1958.

Congratulations to you upon such a fine trophy and thank y for your cooperation in connection with these North American Big Game Competitions.

Sincerely yours,

Samuel B. W

Chairman

SBW:H

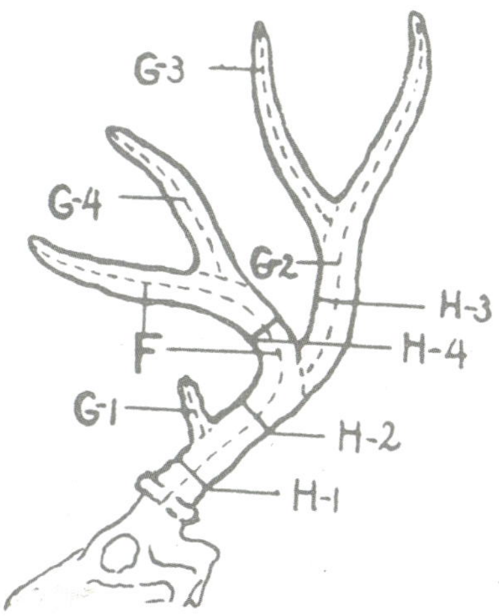

WILLIAM A. MCTYRE, JR.

1956

William A. McTyre, Jr., shot this typical Kaibab buck on November 10, 1956, on a self-guided hunt. The buck is a clean 5x5 with only 4-6/8 inches in symmetrical deductions, giving it a final score of 190-4/8 points. William received an invite to the eighth competition in January 1958. He sent in his trophy, which was recognized with an Honorable Mention.

JOHN N. WILLIAMS

1956

John N. Williams was hunting in the north Kaibab when he shot this typical mule deer in November 1956. The buck has a greatest spread of 32 inches and two abnormal points. The final score comes in at 178-4/8 points.

OFFICIAL SCORING SYSTEM FOR NORTH AMERICAN BIG GAME TROPHIES

Records of North American Big Game Committee

BOONE AND CROCKETT CLUB

Address Correspondence to:
Mrs. Grancel Fitz, Secretary
5 Tudor City Place, NYC, 17N.Y.

MULE AND BLACKTAIL DEER

KIND OF DEER Mule

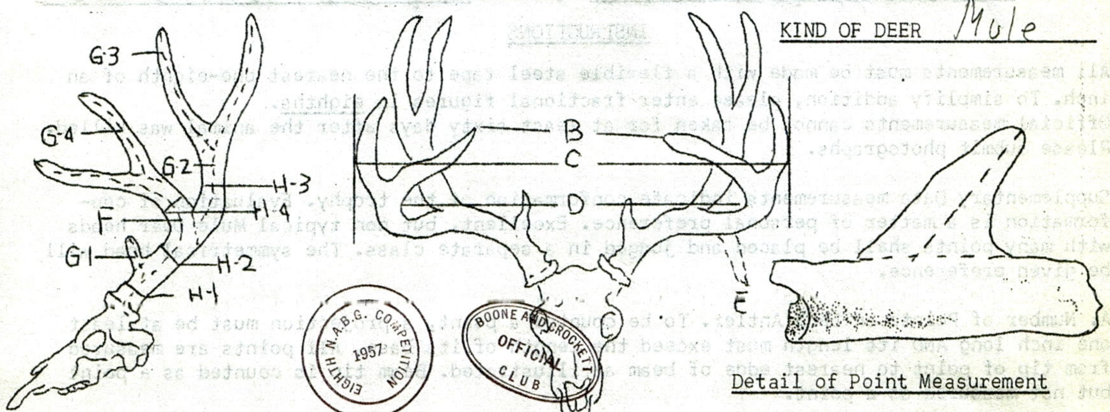

Detail of Point Measurement

SEE OTHER SIDE FOR INSTRUCTIONS	Supplementary Data R.	L.	Column 1 Spread Credit	Column 2 Right Antler	Column 3 Left Antler	Column 4 Difference.
A. Number of Points on Each Antler	7	5				
B. Tip to Tip Spread	25					
C. Greatest Spread	32					
D. Inside Spread of Main Beams 27 — Spread Credit may equal but not exceed length of longer antler			24 7/8			
If Inside Spread of Main Beams exceeds longer antler length, enter difference						2 1/8
E. Total of Lengths of all Abnormal Points						4 —
F. Length of Main Beam				24 2/8	24 7/8	5/8
G-1 Length of First Point, if present				1 4/8	1 1/8	3/8
G-2 Length of Second Point				18 2/8	19 6/8	1 4/8
G-3 Length of Third Point, if present				11 5/8	11 2/8	3/8
G-4 Length of Fourth Point, if present				7 2/8	8 2/8	1 —
Circumference at Smallest Place H-1 Between Burr and First Point				5	5 —	—
Circumference at Smallest Place H-2 Between First and Second Point				4 6/8	4 5/8	1/8
Circumference at Smallest Place H-3 Between Main Beam and Third Point				3 5/8	3 4/8	1/8
Circumference at Smallest Place H-4 Between Second and Fourth Points				4 2/8	4 —	2/8
TOTALS			24 7/8	80 4/8	83 5/8	10 4/8

ADD	Column 1	24 7/8	Exact locality where killed ~~North~~ Kaibab ~~Forest~~
	Column 2	80 4/8	Date Killed Nov. 1956 by whom killed John N. Williams
	Column 3	83 5/8	Present Owner Same
	TOTAL	189 —	Address
SUBTRACT	Column 4	10 4/8	Guide's Name and Address NONE
FINAL SCORE		178 4/8	Remarks: (Mention any abnormalities) none

OK

JAN 2 1957

JOHN N. WILLIAMS
1957

John N. Williams also had this Kaibab mule deer scored at the same time he had the buck he shot in the 1956 season taped. This buck was found in the north Kaibab and scores substantially better than the deer John shot. It's a classic 5x5 with a narrow rack and no abnormal points. The buck's final score is 189-7/8 points.

OFFICIAL SCORING SYSTEM FOR NORTH AMERICAN BIG GAME TROPHIES

Records of North American Big Game Committee

BOONE AND CROCKETT CLUB

Address Correspondence to:
Mrs. Grancel Fitz, Secretary
5 Tudor City Place, NYC,17N.Y.

MULE AND BLACKTAIL DEER

KIND OF DEER Mule

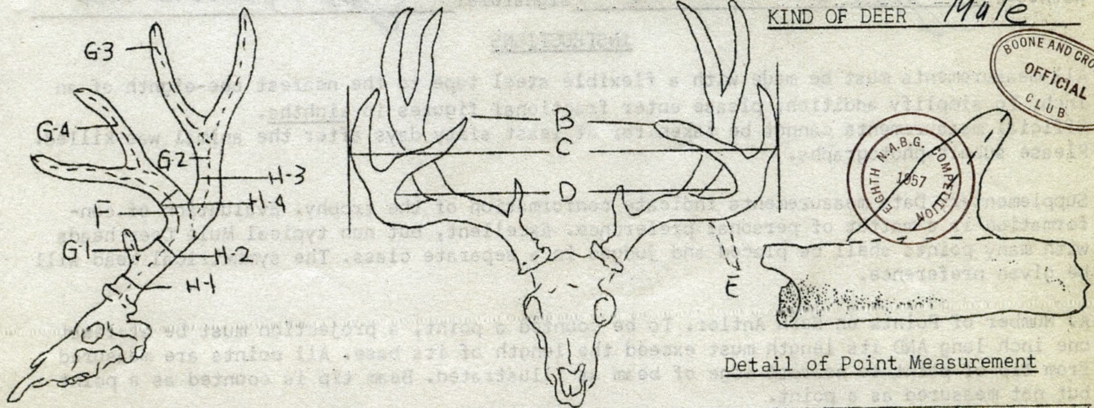

Detail of Point Measurement

SEE OTHER SIDE FOR INSTRUCTIONS	Supplementary Data R.	Supplementary Data L.	Column 1 Spread Credit	Column 2 Right Antler	Column 3 Left Antler	Column 4 Difference.
A. Number of Points on Each Antler	5	5				
B. Tip to Tip Spread	14 3/8					
C. Greatest Spread	24 4/8					
D. Inside Spread of Main Beams 19 3/8 — Spread Credit may equal but not exceed length of longer antler			19 3/8			
If Inside Spread of Main Beams exceeds longer antler length, enter difference						—
E. Total of Lengths of all Abnormal Points						—
F. Length of Main Beam				24	24 2/8	2/8
G-1 Length of First Point, if present				1 4/8	1 4/8	—
G-2 Length of Second Point				16 6/8	16 -	6/8
G-3 Length of Third Point, if present				13 -	11 4/8	1 4/8
G-4 Length of Fourth Point, if present				13 4/8	13 3/8	1/8
Circumference at Smallest Place H-1 Between Burr and First Point				5 2/8	5 2/8	—
Circumference at Smallest Place H-2 Between First and Second Point				5	5	—
Circumference at Smallest Place H-3 Between Main Beam and Third Point				4 4/8	4 4/8	—
Circumference at Smallest Place H-4 Between Second and Fourth Points				4 1/8	4 1/8	—
TOTALS			19 3/8	87 5/8	85 4/8	2 5/8

ADD	Column 1	19 3/8	Exact locality where killed ~~Picked up~~ - North Kaibab
	Column 2	87 5/8	Date ~~[illegible]~~ 1957 by whom killed unknown
	Column 3	85 4/8	Present Owner John N. Williams
	TOTAL	192 4/8	Address
SUBTRACT	Column 4	2 5/8	Guide's Name and Address
	FINAL SCORE	189 7/8	Remarks:(Mention any abnormalities)

JAN 2 1957

OFFICIAL SCORING SYSTEM FOR NORTH AMERICAN BIG GAME TROPHIES

Records of North American Big Game Committee

BOONE AND CROCKETT CLUB

Address Correspondence to:
Mrs. Grancel Fitz, Secretary
5 Tudor City Place, NYC 17, NY.

MULE and BLACKTAIL DEER

KIND OF DEER **Mule**

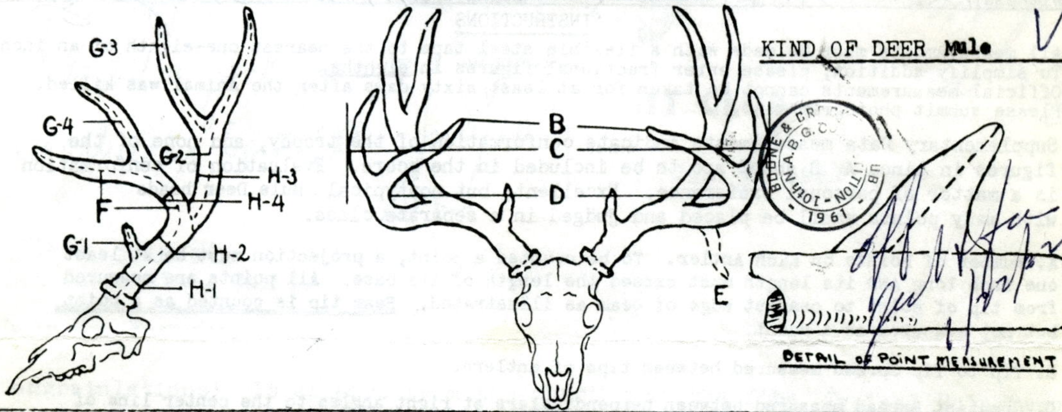

SEE OTHER SIDE FOR INSTRUCTIONS	Supplementary Data	Column 1	Column 2	Column 3	Column 4
A. Number of Points on Each Antler	R. 6 L. 6	Spread Credit	Right Antler	Left Antler	Difference
B. Tip to Tip Spread	23 6/8				
C. Greatest Spread	31				
D. Inside Spread of MAIN BEAMS 27 1/8 — Spread credit may equal but not exceed length of longer antler		26 6/8			
IF Inside Spread of Main Beams exceeds longer antler length, enter difference					~~3/8~~
E. Total of Lengths of all Abnormal Points					7 5/8
F. Length of Main Beam			26 2/8	26 6/8	4/8
G-1. Length of First Point, if present			4	2 6/8	1 2/8
G-2. Length of Second Point			18 6/8	20 7/8	2 1/8
G-3. Length of Third Point, if present			12 2/8	14 1/8	1 7/8
G-4. Length of Fourth Point, if present			12 2/8	12 2/8	0
Circumference at Smallest Place H-1. Between Burr and First Point			5 6/8	5 6/8	0
Circumference at Smallest Place H-2. Between First and Second Points			4 7/8	5	1/8
Circumference at Smallest Place H-3. Between Main Beam and Third Point			4 3/8	4 4/8	1/8
Circumference at Smallest Place H-4. Between Second and Fourth Points			4 6/8	4 6/8	0
TOTALS		26 6/8	~~93 2/8~~ 93 4/8	96 6/8	~~14~~ 13 5/8

ADD 93 2/8	Column 1	26 6/8	Exact locality where killed NORTH KAIBAB ARIZONA
	~~Column 2~~	~~93 6/8~~	Date killed NOV. 1957 By whom killed Monico Marquez
	Column 3	96 6/8	Present owner MonicoMarquez
216 6/8	TOTAL	~~216 2/8~~	Address
SUBTRACT	Column 4	~~14~~ 13 5/8	Guide's Name and Address None
FINAL SCORE		~~202 6/8~~ ~~203 2/8~~	Remarks: (Mention any abnormalities) 6 1/8 and 1 4/8 abnormal points

OK ~~202 6/8~~

203 1/8

JUL 28 1961

44

MONICO MARQUEZ

1957

This exceptional Kaibab mule deer was shot in November 1957 by Monico Marquez. The buck has a final B&C score of 203-1/8 and still ranks as the 13th-largest typical mule deer taken in Arizona. The buck has a greatest spread of 31 inches and two abnormal points totaling 7-5/8 inches in deductions.

ACKNOWLEDGEMENTS

A MULE DEER RETROSPECTIVE

A special thank you to all of the past chairmen of the Boone and Crockett Club's Records Committee for their hard work and dedication to the program:

Alfred Ely, Jr. *(deceased)*
Harold E. Anthony *(deceased)*
Samuel B. Webb *(deceased)*
Robert S. Waters *(deceased)*
Elmer M. Rusten *(deceased)*
Jack S. Parker *(deceased)*
Philip L. Wright *(deceased)*
Walter H. White *(deceased)*
C. Randall Byers *(deceased)*
Eldon L. "Buck" Buckner – Vice President
Richard T. Hale – Chairman

Snapshot of a mule deer taken in eastern Oregon in 1957 by R.G. Creager

Images and Memorabilia selected from the Boone and Crockett Club's Archives in Missoula, Montana, by:

Hanspeter Giger
Julie Tripp

Editorial Contributors:

Guy Eastman
Hanspeter Giger
Ryan Hatfield
Jim Heffelfinger
Miles Moretti
Julie Tripp
Wayne van Zwoll

Records Program Authorities:

Jack Reneau – Director of Big Game Records
Justin Spring – Assistant Director of Big Game Records

Design and Production:

Julie Tripp – Director of Publications

Additional Assistance:

Wendy Nickelson – Archive Filing Ace
Karlie Slayer – Designer
Abra Loran – Assistant Controller
Sandy Poston –Office Manager

Copy Editing:

Julie Cowan – WordCritter Creative

A Mule Deer Retrospective was designed on a MacBook Pro with Adobe Creative Cloud programs primarily using Baskerville and Roadkill typefaces. All photographs and ephemera are part of the Boone and Crockett Club's archives unless otherwise noted.

Printed in the USA by Sheridan Books, Inc.

Limited Editions bound by Roswell Book Bindery